Psychology Revivals

Love in the Machine Age

First published in 1930, the object of *Love in the Machine Age* was to popularize a modern and scientific view of behavior, and thereby help people to live happy and successful lives. The author traces in popular language for the time, the break-up of the patriarchal values held by most of society, and points out from the standpoint of modern psychiatric knowledge the inevitable effects upon sexual mores, personality adjustments and the growth of children. Topics covered include marriage, parenting, adolescence, with special emphasis paid to the "mating problems" of youth. Taking its lead from psychological theories prevalent at the time, today it can be read in its historical context.

This book is a re-issue originally published in 1930. The language used and views portrayed are a reflection of its era and no offence is meant by the Publishers to any reader by this re-publication.

Love in the Machine Age

A Psychological Study of the Transition from Patriarchal Society

Floyd Dell

Routledge
Taylor & Francis Group
LONDON AND NEW YORK

First published in 1930
by George Routledge & Sons Ltd

This edition first published in 2025 by Routledge
4 Park Square, Milton Park, Abingdon, Oxon, OX14 4RN

and by Routledge
605 Third Avenue, New York, NY 10017

Routledge is an imprint of the Taylor & Francis Group, an informa business

Publisher's Note
The publisher has gone to great lengths to ensure the quality of this reprint but points out that some imperfections in the original copies may be apparent.

A Library of Congress record exists under LCCN: 30010157

ISBN: 978-1-032-95191-1 (hbk)
ISBN: 978-1-003-58363-9 (ebk)
ISBN: 978-1-032-95195-9 (pbk)

Book DOI 10.4324/9781003583639

LOVE

IN THE MACHINE AGE

A PSYCHOLOGICAL STUDY OF THE TRANSITION FROM PATRIARCHAL SOCIETY

By

FLOYD DELL

LONDON
GEORGE ROUTLEDGE & SONS LTD.
1930

Made and Printed in Great Britain by
Percy Lund, Humphries & Co. Ltd.
3 Amen Corner, London, E.C.4
and at Bradford

CONTENTS

LOVE
IN THE MACHINE AGE

CHAPTER I

WHAT THIS BOOK IS ABOUT

The object of this book is to popularize a modern and scientific view of behavior, and thereby to help people to live happy and successful lives. The writer of this book is by profession a novelist; and since in recent years many practitioners of the art of fiction have pointedly renounced the wish to help people, to teach them anything—have, indeed, asserted that mankind is hopeless, civilization a failure, and human life necessarily a tragedy—and since, moreover, they have used the half-understood discoveries of modern psychological science to inculcate these aristocratic and patriarchal forms of pessimism—it is perhaps advisable to say at the outset that this book makes no pretences to this pseudo-modern aesthetic attitude. This book is written in the belief that knowledge can help human beings to achieve individual emotional happiness and to enjoy responsible social and economic relations to others, and that a novelist may properly take his share in the task of public education. An amateur in the educational field, lacking in the intellectual discipline afforded by scientific work, may perhaps be forgiven his technical shortcomings, and may perhaps be enabled by his literary and human studies and sympathies to present the scientific point of view in terms that have an educational value of their own.

This book, then, is ambitious in its scope; it aims to bring to intelligent readers the fruits of modern psychological discoveries in such a way as to be really useful to them—especially useful to them as parents in bringing up their children. But if such a book is to be useful, the reader must be persuaded that many of his views about love, the family, work, art, and education, are relics of patriarchal traditions that have no place in our modern world. So far as old-fashioned and conventional readers are concerned, they are used to being insulted in that fashion; and if they persist in reading such a book as this, it will be because they privately suspect that there may be some truth in the accusation, and because they really desire help in the task of understanding the young people with whom they have to deal. They may be at first bewildered, and then perhaps relieved, to find that, however this book outrages their incidental pieties and ideals, it squares with what they are accustomed to regard as their fundamental purposes. It remains to be seen whether such readers can accept the news that to accomplish these fundamental purposes they must throw overboard their traditional paraphernalia of ways and means, and adopt others which at first glance will seem to them to be conducive toward mere anarchy.

Quite different resistances will be put up by many readers who pride themselves upon being modern, broad-minded, and, in matters of sex, liberal or radical. It will not be easy for such readers to swallow the imputation that *their* favorite attitudes are also relics of an outworn time—musty-fusty compromises with life, timid and evasive and infantile. But they too must be prepared to learn something new, and to face the pain of discarding some of their most cherished notions. They may, if they prefer to hold fast to their familiar compromises, dismiss this work as reactionary and intolerant, a mere argument for conventional marriage—or as incredibly naive and romantic, a treatise on how to live happily ever after. Those phrases should sufficiently protect their endangered self-respect, and save them from the discomfort of discovering that they are not so modern as they would like to believe.

The natural appeal of this book would be to young people, who are not yet congealed into either 'conservative' or 'liberal' compromise-attitudes, but who make vast and eager demands upon life—except that such a book is necessarily dull, in comparison to life itself, from which the same lessons can be learned, more painfully no doubt, but much more excitingly.

The psychological, sociological, historical, and anthropological materials upon which this book is based are accessible to all, and in part familiar. But these materials are presented here in what is believed by the author to be a new way, which brings out sharply the revolutionary aspect of modern psychology. Science proceeds slowly and cautiously, and in this realm it is doubtless still at the beginning. Some of its generalizations, solidly established within the domain of present-day fact, require for simplicity and clearness of utterance an approach not only into the realms of sociology and economics but into those of history and prehistory. Upon these frontiers all but the most venturesome have halted. This book claims the privilege of an outsider, a poet's privilege, to cross those frontiers, and thus to say emphatically in historical and sociological terms what modern psychological science has thus far been content to hint at.

This book, then, undertakes to sharpen the outlines of modern psychological theory by restating it as far as possible in sociological and historical terms. This attempt is not in itself new. The early Freudian concepts which have revolutionized modern psychology have been eagerly seized upon by workers in the fields of education, social relief and correction, particularly in the United States, and have been found to be fruitful in their practical results. These workers have been obliged by their administrative tasks to correlate as far as possible the new psychological concepts with older sociological ones. That is because they are engaged in such tasks as the education of children, the administration of public and private aid to the economically disorganized and helpless, industrial psychiatry, court and institutional dealings with juvenile delinquents, prison administration, and the treatment of the insane—and engaged at the same time in beginning the gigantic task of reforming the methods by which these matters are handled, and in the necessary general education of the public in new principles and methods. All this has required a collaboration of modern-minded experts in every possible field of research and administration. It is from their pragmatic formulations, which are psychological in their foundations but sociological and historical in their superstructure, that the outlines of this present work are drawn. Practical necessity has forced these workers to formulate an implicit theory which unites history, sociology and psychology. The present essay seeks to make explicit that working theory.

There are many valuable books which state directly and in detail how children should be brought up, and what is wrong with the current ways of bringing them up. These books expound the causes and the proper treatment of every difficulty in child-training, from enuresis (bed-wetting) and anorexia (lack of appetite) to the final problems of adolescent adjustment to social realities. Many well-meaning but bewildered middle-class parents read these books, or receive similar instruction from psychiatrists, doctors, and teachers; and the extent to which they are able to carry these precepts into practice is, on the whole, the extent to which they have grasped the revolutionary social-historical concepts which underlie them—the extent to which they realize that *patriarchal training does not fit children for living in the modern world.* The extent to which they fail to put these precepts into practice, in spite of their best efforts, is, again, the extent to which these precepts are confused and negated in their minds by the patriarchal doctrines by which implicitly most of us still live. Such a book as the present one cannot fill the place of the expert scientific case-studies which help individuals to solve their specific problems of adjustment to love and work. It is intended rather to prepare their minds for such individual instruction as they may need—which, if this preparation is successful, should be more easily assimilated.

The aim of this book is to make people modern-minded, by explaining in sufficient detail exactly what are the differences between the psychological requirements of modern life and those of the patriarchal régime. It is believed by the writer that people want to know just that. But they are put off by vague generalities which teach them nothing, or by false prophecies which merely reassure and confirm them in their neurotic compromises.

Thus, for example, it is often said that the mechanization of our modern world is inevitably destroying romantic love and family life. This book will undertake to show that modern machinery and the modern economic system in general are destroying the last remnants of the *patriarchal* family, and with that destruction removing the ancient social uses and justifications of such patriarchal compromises with our biological instincts as are presented in the institutions of homosexuality, prostitution, arranged marriage, polite adultery, and sacred celibacy. It will be shown that by the destruction of the patriarchal family and its accompanying social-sexual institutions, *modern machinery has laid the basis for a more biologically normal family life than has existed throughout the whole of the historical period, or indeed in the whole life of mankind.* As for romantic love, it will be shown that modern life puts it back where it biologically belongs, as a part of the normal love pattern which leads through courtship and love-choice to mating and family life—instead of, as in the patriarchal era, leaving it outside, as an illusion to be pursued in homosexuality, prostitution-patronage, and polite adultery, serving thereby as a safety-valve to ensure the stability of the loveless arranged marriages characteristic of the patriarchal system. In brief, modernity re-establishes family life on the basis of romantic love. Only people trained to live modern lives can live them successfully in love and work. To train young people for adjustments to the patriarchal system is to train them for homosexuality, prostitution and prostitution-patronage, polite adultery, or sacred celibacy; and insofar as they cannot with social approval and inward satisfaction nowadays lead such careers, they are doomed to neurotic maladjustments to the actualities of life.

These statements imply a social and historical basis for modern neurotic maladjustments. They imply that modern neuroses occur because we are in a transition stage between our patriarchal past and our non-patriarchal future. Exactly how *ways of life which in the past were useful and socially acceptable mores have become mischievous and socially inacceptable neuroses* will be explained in this book. And that explanation rests upon a modern conception of psychic development. We find a natural and biologically-determined growth in emotion from the self-centered stage of infancy to the adult capacities for responsible social and sexual relationships. We find, however, that this emotional growth is controlled always by social education, which dictates how much development in love and usefulness shall be permitted to or required of the individual. And what we find historically is that the patriarchal period was one in which this emotional growth was halted, with regard to both love and work, in an infantile or childish stage—*that it was necessary, in order for the patriarchal system to exist, that nobody should ever grow up to complete adulthood.* If this seems an extravagance, or a mere paradox, the book is here to justify it; and its apparently extravagant or paradoxical character is one reason why so many pages are given to a discussion of the past. It is necessary that we should understand the nature of our break with the past, if we are to understand the precepts for happiness and success in modern life.

The present time appears to be the second great break with

tradition in our human life upon earth. The first—though here we are in shadowy and uncertain realms of prehistory with which this book does not deal—was the change from savage culture to patriarchal civilization, which occurred in the Mediterranean world in the dawn of the historical period. One of the features of prehistoric savage culture appears to have been a peculiar use of sexual relations for magical purposes. Nothing in archaic savage culture was more firmly established than the propriety of the religious sex-orgy. Women were taught that it was holy to submit themselves to sexual intercourse with the Horned God, or rather with his masked magician-priest, for the purpose of encouraging the procreation of food-animals. This archaic sexual witchcraft became abhorrent to patriarchal civilization—the Horned God became the Devil of medieval Europe, and his worship was exterminated as an obscene heresy. But many of the tolerated or approved sexual practices of the patriarchal regime—the relegation, for instance, of hordes of women to prostitution, and the treatment of 'bastard' children—are now coming to seem to us as cruel, indecent and silly as the orgies of savage devil-worship. We have made a second great break with tradition. We have outgrown these patriarchal sex-practices as the patriarchal régime outgrew sex-witchcraft.

We do not seek to exterminate outworn patriarchal sex-usages as heretical; that is not our modern way of doing things. We have learned the lesson of tolerance. We must be tolerant in order to understand, for it is only through understanding that we shall achieve our destiny. But unless we realize that our age has in truth made a break with the past, and that patriarchal sex-compromises have no place in our modern world, we are not truly modern minded.

The savage usages of sex as witchcraft arose out of food anxieties. The patriarchal sex-usages arose out of economic anxieties in general, and represented compromises of the property motive with the sexual instincts. As *magic* is the clue to savage distortions of sex, so is *property* the clue to patriarchal distortions of sex. And both distortions occur only through the halting of psycho-sexual development in an early stage. The savage use of sex as magic represents a halt at so very infantile a stage that when it occurs in modern life, as it does occasionally, it involves so complete a maladjustment to our civilized social scheme that it is classed as a psychosis, that is to say insanity. The patriarchal sex-usages, still normal in patriarchal countries, appear in the more fully mechanized and liberated parts of Western civilization as neuroses. It will be shown in some detail that (1) these patriarchal usages are the products of a psychic growth halted in a pre-adult stage, (2) that the patriarchal economic system required these usages and demanded this halting of psychic development, and (3) that our modern world requires increasingly a full development to adult psychic life and a corresponding set of adult practices in love. The same things will be shown more briefly as regards work.

This will involve a discussion in which such practices as prostitution-patronage and polite adultery, for example, will be shown as forms of timid compromise with the sexual instincts, and as being in modern life increasingly neurotic.

This will be followed by a detailed statement of the educational methods by which in the patriarchal regime children and young people were trained in permanently infantile attitudes. The chief of these patriarchal methods were compulsion, shame, and the permanent attachment of sexual emotions to the parents. It will be shown that these educational methods tend invariably to produce their patriarchal results in prolonged childishness, and hence neurotic maladjustment in a society which demands adult capacities. The different, non-patriarchal method of education, dispensing with the mechanisms of compulsion, shame and parental fixation—that is to say, a kind of child-training which will enable children to grow up to psychic adulthood and fit them for love and work in the modern world—will be outlined.

It will also be necessary to deal with certain current social ideals of one and another sort of sexual 'freedom', and show that they are not scientific prophecies, but ideological over-compensations against the emotional hurts of a transition era—and that when they are looked into carefully they are found to be simply the old patriarchal conventions and compromises and infantilities in a pseudo-modern disguise.

The requirements of modern adult life will by this time have been made plain. For the generality of mankind these requirements will be in the nature of a liberation; unpoisoned by patriarchal training, most people would prefer to choose their own work and their own mates, and would enjoy the responsibilities which these choices bring. Mankind, however, has always a vision wider than its immediate opportunities of life; and there is a social need for the imaginative enlargements of our human destiny which art and heroism can furnish. One of the most neglected tasks of modern psychology has been that of tracing the ways in which in general the socially inacceptable impulses of mankind can be made acceptable by sublimation in art and ritual; and in particular, the tracing of this process with respect to outworn mores. Some space has therefore been devoted to showing that maladjustment of impulse and opportunity may lead, not to neurotic unhappiness, but to new social adaptations. The most of mankind can be happy in a simple biological fashion; but no precepts for civilized happiness and success in life are complete which do not include those for art and heroism. The artist may break all social rules in fantasy, the hero may break them all in fact. Why they may do this—what is the practical difference between art and neurotic fantasy-making, between heroism and crime—will be discussed.

The way will then be clear for a consideration of the practical needs of modern adolescence, as a period when boys and girls are to be helped to grow up, rather than detained in an ambiguous childhood. In our transition era, an important part of the growing-up process will be what is currently called *'emancipation from the family'*. Coincident with that, the positive aspect of the same process, is *the achievement of heterosexuality,* or full capacity for love of the other sex. Learning some socially approved mode of *earning a living* is another part of this process, and one which may be considered as a part of achieving sexual adulthood. For both boys and girls this sexual-economic development is complicated by the partial entrance of women into the world of work outside the home, and by the resultant conflict between the demands of love and family life and those of outside work upon women. This love-and-work tangle, however, when discussed in the light of our modern conceptions of psychic development toward adulthood, can be understood very simply as a soluble problem of courtship and family life. And finally, as part of the same growing-up process, there is the task of *achieving a philosophy of life,* gaining a view of things, however implicit, which will serve to explain to boy and girl their place in the human scheme and reconcile them to their destiny of struggle. The successful achievement of all these things—emancipation from the parental family, full heterosexuality, economic capacity for co-operation with other adults, and a satisfying philosophy of life—constitute (along with physical growth) the standard of modern adulthood.

It will be noted that none of these things were demanded or permitted by the patriarchal régime; nor can an education based upon patriarchal principles help young people to achieve such adulthood.

Patriarchal education, with the best intentions, imprisons youth in the parental home. Its *property*-precepts about 'purity' or sex-fear, and its hostility to free courtship and love-choice, halt boys and girls in an infantile stage of development and doom them to inwardly compulsive careers of celibacy, or prostitution and prostitution-patronage, to marriages made tragic by sexual impotence and frigidity or the compromise-expedient of polite adultery. It hinders them from achieving the capacity for successful economic co-operation with others by limiting them to the patriarchal attitude of waiting for parental and quasi-parental favors. It bars them from finding their own philosophy of life by forcing upon them a traditional religion which contains no consolations for them, a traditional political formula which does not explain the workings of the world in which they have to live, and a traditional set of moral precepts to which nobody around them ever really conforms. Or, if unsuccessful in its negative effects, patriarchal education dooms these boys and girls to futile rebellions, to the prolonged waste of adult years in solving adolescent problems, and, if these remain unsolved, to the solaces of alcoholism and drug-taking, or even to the final confessions of inadequacy for adjustment to adult life in the infantile delusions of psychosis or the infantile revenge of suicide. The modern world needs modern education for its young people.

This, then, is the program of this book. It will be seen that it involves a discussion of love, marriage, children, education, work and economics in modern life, against a historical background. To build up this pyramid we now proceed, laying the historical groundwork. To encourage the reader to climb the pyramid, it is promised that the view from the top will be invigorating. To those to whom these views are but imperfectly known, the hope is extended that they will see their own lives and those of the younger generation in a new light; that dubious problems will be made simpler, and that they will be encouraged to deal with their tasks of adjustment in the belief that even in this confused transition age life offers the possibility of success and happiness to men and women of courage and understanding.

CHAPTER II

BIOLOGY VS. HISTORY

§ 1. The Simple Biological Pattern

The psychic development of the individual from infancy to maturity can be described roughly as proceeding through four stages. The first stage, that of helpless infancy, shows the individual's interests centering exclusively in himself, in his own bodily needs, functions and pleasures. The last stage shows him capable of enjoying responsible relations to society in general (work, and getting along with other people), and in particular to a mate and children (marriage and parenthood). This emotional capacity is psychological adulthood as biologically determined. To be real, it must have been reached in psychic development and not in mere physical fact. On the other hand, it can of course be reached in psychic development under circumstances which prevent its actual or direct accomplishment in physical fact. Thus it is not the fact of marriage or of parenthood that constitutes psychological adulthood, but the capacity for enjoyment of these responsible relationships.

Now between the early infantile state of complete dependence with its wholly self-centered interests, and the adult capacity for the enjoyment of responsible work and love, there is a great gulf to be bridged by the processes of emotional growth. We are enabled to see how great a gulf it is, through observation of those individuals in whom such emotional growth is prevented to an extreme degree. In them the infantile self-centered interests in their own bodily needs, functions and pleasures are manifested now on an adult plane of activity, but not in an adult way. Thus we may find them still cherishing the infantile excitements derived from the anus as a pleasure-zone, making them the center of their sexual lives through pederasty; we may also find childish cruelty become sadism, when conditioned by sex-experiences. We might thus—but here we shall not—run through the catalogue of the sexual perversions, which are simply infantile traits which have failed to be subordinated to the normal adult pattern of sexuality by the processes of psychic growth. Unmarriageability, or unsuitableness for normal marriage, is in general characteristic of the person who, growing up to physical adulthood, remains at a low infantile level of psychic development. Persons who are not grown up emotionally, who are still self-centered children themselves, cannot successfully bear parental responsibilities; and unless they are so fortunate as to be able to achieve a socially useful sublimation of their otherwise unsuitable tendencies through some kind of work, usually artistic, they are likely to have great difficulty in submitting to the adult discipline involved in co-operation with others. This applies more particularly to our modern world, for, as will be seen, the patriarchal régime sanctioned or sheltered a great deal of childishness in adults.

The normal psychic processes, which bridge this gulf between self-centered childish interests and the adult state, comprise two stages, of which the first extends from early infancy to puberty. There is in this period of childhood a play-life which leads on to adult work-interests, and a love-life within the family which prepares for later love-interests outside. The child learns to love others beside himself; and the original 'polymorphous' eroticism of childhood gives way, as puberty approaches, to a primacy of the genital zone, a gradual centering of interest in the opposite sex, and the adoption of a masculine rôle of aggression or a feminine rôle of quasi-passive encouragement. This development is dependent upon growth in physical and nervous (including brain) structure, and upon glandular changes. It is incomplete, however, at this stage. For a long time in this childhood period the love interests are still (normally) centered, to a considerable though decreasing extent in the self. And insofar as they flow out to others—parents and nurses, brothers and sisters, playmates, teachers—these love interests only lately and slowly come to involve any emotional preference for persons of the opposite sex. It is, indeed, in childhood that there is formed the emotional habit-basis for all those adult human relations in which erotic attractions are subordinated to the social purposes of work and play.

The immense glandular changes of puberty normally complete this process of psychic development. They enhance the attractions of the other sex by creating specific sexual tensions requiring the sexual act for their relief. These changes thus, in collaboration with other psychic influences, lead normally (that is, in the absence of cultural regulations to the contrary) through parade, flirtation, male rivalry and female encouragement (which latter may characteristically take the form of retreat)—through courtship, in short, to love-choice, sexual mating, parenthood, and family life. This appears to be the normal biological pattern, insofar as it can be distinguished from the results of social education, from the effects of which it is never in practice free. Psychologically it involves a centering of the deepest love-interests in persons of the other sex. This *hetero*sexuality, as it is called (from the Greek 'heteros', other, or different, or opposite,—but having the sense also of being a 'mate' in that difference, as the one sex is to the other), is one of the two essential qualities of biological adulthood. The other quality, the interest in and capacity for sustained efforts to gain food and shelter, comes with an increase in size and muscular strength and skill, and represents a narrowing and practical intensification of early scattered play-interests (the rest of the early play-interests being taken care of in adult social activities).

Now we have here a simple pattern of emotional development occurring as a result of biological growth from infancy to maturity. If it actually occurred as simply as that, life would be obvious and easy. It would contain no religion, art, crime or insanity. These are due to the strain upon human nature of social deviations from the biological pattern—they are the ways in which the discrepancies between biological impulses and social codes are patched up. These kinds of psychological patchwork can make human life hideous or beautiful; indeed they make it both. We are now, or so we believe, in an economic position which enables us to dispense with much of this patchwork, and we have learned enough to manage the remainder so as to produce more happiness and less misery.

It may, however, be asked at this point why we cannot go back to the simple biological pattern. We presumably cannot do so; but certainly we do not wish to do so. Our civilization is founded upon some of the discrepancies between simple biological impulses and social codes. When we consider what they are—they include fundamentally the incest-taboo and the deflection of a natural interest in anal matters which we apparently share with our remote canine relatives—it is fairly clear that we would not give up these civilized deviations from Nature, even if we could. It is not a question of becoming like savages or primitive folk; they already have created these taboos and built their culture upon them. If we went back to the life of the cave man of the Aurignacian period, a quarter of a million or more years ago, we should still apparently not have gone back far enough to avoid the discrepancies between nature and culture, of which the art of the cave-man presents us unmistakable evidences. We should have to go back millions of years beyond that. We cannot turn and live with the animals, because our germ-plasm has forgotten that way of life, has lost its neat and sufficient little set of inherited adaptations to environment. We must go ahead in our own human way.

We can, however, take advantage of the economic security afforded by modern machine production, and dispense with the special distortions and cripplings of our instincts made necessary by the poverty of patriarchal civilization. In fact, we are doing so. The next sections will show how and why patriarchal institutions were originally built up, and how and why they have been gradually overthrown.

§ 2. Patriarchal Economics

In order to approach this task simply, we shall be obliged to ignore the immense prehistoric background of the patriarchal family system, except for a few brief references. As we come upon the patriarchal system in the beginnings of European history, it is found unmistakably superimposed upon the ruins or remnants of an earlier clan organization of society, with matrilinear descent and considerable powers, both of a magical and of a social sort, pertaining to women. These quasi-matriarchal institutions (if we may for convenience call them that) leave their traces in legend, art, law, religion, and custom; they are retained to some extent in backward places, and among the lower classes, and they crop up again in later social structure—so that the patriarchal system is never purely patriarchal, but always some kind of compromise with earlier ways of life; and the social content of patriarchal institutions is thus often very different from its legal formulations. Women often have more freedom and power in practice than in legal theory. This is especially true of the Roman traditions, which represent the form in which the patriarchal system was passed on to Western civilization.

Moreover, because we cannot deal at length with the earlier quasi-matriarchal period, we shall have to treat as patriarchal many attitudes of mind which are inherited ultimately from prehistoric savagery. This will result, perhaps, in painting the patriarchal period in dark colors against a background which may be incorrectly imagined as being Paradisiacal in comparison.

The patriarchal family appears to have been a form evolved or adopted by nomadic shepherds, and to have taken on its more extreme forms in periods of tribal migration and war. It is an essentially military system, admirably adapted to the needs of a family on the march. It is equally well calculated to serve the purposes of alien conquerors ruling over a settled agricultural population. It is thus in early European history associated with ruling castes, and with the institutions of slavery, serfdom, landed property, and the military state. These in turn have influenced the conceptions and workings of the patriarchal family, the position of wives and children being often in legal theory—however modified by natural sentiments—akin to that of slaves, serfs, or cattle.

The economics of the patriarchal family were military economics. The family was a small ruling group set over a larger group of slaves or serfs, as once over its flocks and herds, both exploiting and taking care of the latter. Inwardly, the family was a kind of military commune. Every member had—within strategic limits—the right to the full protection and support of the whole body. Beyond these strategic limits, any member might be sacrificed for the family good. The father had generally the right to kill a child or sell him into slavery, and the legal position of the wife was usually the same as that of a child.

Even in the shattered form in which the patriarchal family

has descended into modern times, it has illustrated its military and communal virtues. It has afforded more economic security to its members—or to those not deliberately sacrificed for the common good—than the individualistic modern family does. The patriarchal family was better able to use for its own benefit the powers of prosperity, and better able to withstand—as a family—the ills of poverty. The neglectful treatment of the aged poor, which is one of the weaknesses and scandals of our transition era, could hardly occur under the patriarchal system. On the other hand, the military limitations upon family-member rights pressed hard upon women and children. Family security was attained—as will be shown—by a continual sacrifice of their interests. Patriarchal idealism justified these sacrifices, and what was complained of was merely that the sacrifices had often to be made uselessly at the whim of a tyrant who was himself wasting the family substance.

The methods of perpetuating family rule varied in early Europe. During the periods of conquest, the elder sons appear to have left the nest to carve out fortunes for themselves with the sword, and the paternal lands descended to the last-remaining, the youngest son—or sometimes, as in the fairy-tales which are relics of that period, to the youngest daughter, according to the quasi-matriarchal plan. In more settled times it became the eldest son who inherited. The family property could not be infinitely divided among sons and grandsons. It must remain as intact as possible.

Against the possibility of its remaining wholly intact there was the right of every daughter to a dowry. Each dowry cut off so much land, or so much treasure. That is why daughters were not favored, why so many of them in classic times were killed at birth, or in later times sent to nunneries. The expense of the dowries must be made up by fortunate marriages of the sons, which would restore their equivalent by the wife's dowry. That is why sons' marriages were regulated by the father, not left to love-choice.

There were several modes of patriarchal family organization. Several generations of male descendants of the patriarch, with their wives and children, might live in the same home, constituting what is called a 'great-family,' of which the headship was inherited by the eldest son. Or the sons, after their father's death, might live in different homes and maintain a 'joint-family' group. Or the collateral family bonds might become more informal, existing not so much as legalistic but rather as sentimentally sanctioned economic and social obligations, reinforced by family councils and gatherings and by an exact knowledge of all however remote family relationships. It is the last and loosest form in which the patriarchal family has been best known in Europe and America, though the first and strictest form is by no means unknown.

The patriarchal attitude toward social functions varied in detail with class, but in all classes it represented an adaptation to circumstances of the original attitude of the conquering family. In aristocratic theory there was only one kind of socially dignified effort, the defense of the State externally by military action and internally by political and religious rule. Aristocratic practice, however, in more settled and peaceful times, when all the land had been distributed, turned to the less heroic task of holding on to and getting an income from the family lands and from the political and religious positions which were the perquisites of the ruling-class families. In practice the families were paramount and the State their social instrument. Upon the eldest sons devolved the duty of keeping and passing on to their eldest sons the family lands, while the younger sons might 'serve the State' as they could and take their chances of any substantial rewards. The family estate was chargeable on behalf of the younger sons with the cost of an education befitting gentlemen and thus presumably fitting them to hold any ruling-class position; and sentimentally the family-head was under obligation to use all possible social influence to get them such positions. But when these resources had been exhausted, they needs must make their own way. If they could not make rich marriages for themselves, they might take minor positions in the army or navy, or drink themselves to death, or become colonists or adventurers. Since family estates were not infinitely divisible, the aristocracy's population problem was necessarily solved by disburdening the families of the later maintenance of their younger sons. And aristocratic male education had its function in reconciling young men to this state of affairs.

For this state of affairs involved the acceptance by young males of definite limitations upon the normal biological development of both their work and their love impulses. The temperamental bent of this or that son toward this or that activity could not be recklessly indulged; and still less could their impulses of love-choice be allowed freedom. The eldest son had to carry on the management of the family estate; and any other activities in which he might indulge had to fit in with that necessity. His career was laid out for him at birth; only death or a revolution could free him from it. He could not choose his work to suit himself, nor could he choose his wife to suit himself.

These limitations were not made effective without continuous training from childhood. They amounted to a blocking of the emotional path to adulthood. A man who is not free to choose his own work or his own wife is still to that significant extent a child. And this adult childishness was secured only by compensations. The blocked and stultified work and love impulses were released to socially irrelevant expression in other directions.

The creative impulses were kept on their early childish plane by a highly organized adult play-life; the egotistic impulses were cultivated in their most infantile form by a system of social opportunities for the exercise of personal power over others of lower station. No one who is permitted without social reproach to expend large amounts of adult energy in childish forms of play, and whose superiority to others is taken for granted, is likely to grow up psychologically to a point where a special work ambition becomes imperative.

The stultified love impulses were similarly drained off. The young male aristocrat was accustomed to the free expression of his sexual impulses with young women of the lower classes (as formerly with slave girls) upon the well-understood condition that these involved for him no social responsibilities, especially not those of parenthood. The family estate was not chargeable with the maintenance of illegitimate children. Permission for love without marriage thus made it possible for him to marry without love, to suit the family needs.

The daughters of the aristocracy had two approved social destinies—wifehood and the religious life. They were all in theory entitled to dowries; but if they were too numerous, some of them had to go to nunneries instead. It is true that when possible these brides of the deity were expected to bring a dowry, which they frequently did; but the heavenly bridegroom was less exacting than earthly bridegrooms in this matter. In such a heavenly marriage, women had opportunities for rulership, learning, artistic activities, and, in any event, work. They were cut off from mate-love and maternity. The others could achieve husbands and maternity, but were accustomed to dispense with the natural biological preliminary of being in love. A wifely devotion (resembling in many respects daughterly devotion) was regarded as sufficient and even preferable. Love-affairs after marriage with some other woman's husband were more or less permissible, at least upon Platonic but often upon realistic terms; but always upon condition that existing marital arrangements were not to be altered.

The middle class, getting its income from trade and manufacture or professional activities and not from land, aped these patriarchal formulas as far as possible. It treated its economic resources as though they suffered from the disability of land in not being infinitely divisible. These resources, like land, were accordingly handed down from father to son, in the patriarchal fashion. The earliest obstetrical forceps was thus kept a family secret for generations. Trades and crafts were family matters; and taking an apprentice was very much like adopting a child into the family. There was for a long time no free choice of work for the eldest son, in the middle class any more than in the aristocracy; he inherited the family 'mystery' (business, as we should say). No more was he permittted to marry to suit himself. There were, however, girls of a lower class, including prostitutes, with whom he could have irresponsible sexual relations. Nevertheless the power of the middle-class father over his sons was not absolute—since commercial and professional activities are not actually landed property, nor subject to its disabilities. The eldest son of a landed family could not very well go to another family if he did not like his own; but—strange and unnatural as the idea seemed at first in the patriarchal atmosphere—exactly that could happen with an eldest or any other son in the trades and professions. It was a discovery of the first importance, reluctantly made by the middle class, that the son did not have to follow his father's trade. The middle-class son could, however, be bribed to remain loyal to the family interests. Even so, the middle-class ideal of marriage ventured to include some elements of biologically normal courtship and marital love. The middle class might have taken its stand more whole-heartedly and quickly upon the side of biology, except that 'love' as celebrated in romantic fiction and poetry was the extra-marital diversion of the idle aristocracy, and as thus understood did not fit in with the middle-class ideal.

The middle class was destined to overthrow the aristocracy, and with it the whole patriarchal scheme. It was to destroy the absolute powers of the patriarchal State and of patriarchal religion. It was in more than one land to destroy the system of primogeniture. It was to displace the family as the economic unit, landed property as the center of economic life. It was to repudiate arranged marriage, establish love-choice, institute divorce, refuse its moral sanction to prostitution and polite adultery, and even undertake to secure paternal recognition and support for children born out of wedlock. But it was never, at least till the present, to understand quite the significance of all these actions. While destroying the patriarchal system, it was at the same time trying to preserve and maintain all sorts of aristocratic values and ideals. Among these, unfortunately, was the aristocratic system of education, formal and informal. So that the middle class has been and still is bringing up its sons and daughters as if their lives were dominated by the requirements of landed property. It is blunderingly seeking to perpetuate the psychological attitudes which were necessary to the landed-property régime—the adult childishnesses which hamper the social and economic arrangements of our time.

The middle class—and the working class which now in turn seeks to live up to its standards—is still bringing up boys and girls as if they were not to have the right to choose their own work and their own mates—and hence must be halted in a childish stage of emotional development, so as to accept patriarchal arrangements without protest. We are only beginning to learn to bring up our children so that they may be capable of making their own free and responsible choices in the fields of work and love.

That, briefly, is the historical view of the behavior difficulties which our modern world is manufacturing for itself.

§ 3. Patriarchal Institutions: Arranged Marriage, Homosexuality, Prostitution, Polite Adultery, Sacred Celibacy

The above sketch of patriarchal arrangements was on purpose not definitely placed in time or country, but very broadly ranged over the centuries and nations of the patriarchal past. Now let us consider some specific instances. The difference between the high position of women in Homer or in the legendary materials of Greek drama, and their low position in classical Greek life, indicates the difference between a quasi-matriarchal society and the later patriarchal system. In the earlier social order, women had an independence and dignity that they necessarily lost in the patriarchal scheme. The love stories of Greek legend were stories of love between men and women who were socially free and socially equal. The love anecdotes of later Greek life are characteristically of two kinds: one kind is about love between two men, the other kind is about love between a man and a 'hetaira' or 'companion'—that is, a well-educated and more or less respectable sort of courtesan. These two ancient institutions, homosexuality and prostitution, are intimately related, being products of the patriarchal system. They were institutions, in the sense that they were socially created and served definite social purposes. These social purposes, and the social methods of creating these institutions, are more easily seen in a society which approved them, than in our present-day society which disapproves them and yet goes on creating them.

Greek city-state life had a military organization. In conservative Sparta, where the barbaric modes of life were longest retained, the boys were separated from their families at the age at which we send them first to school; they were enrolled in military companies under the leadership of an older youth, taught to obey orders, endure hardships, and forage for themselves. Cut off completely during late childhood and adolescence from the society of the other sex, they had homosexual love affairs with each other. Homosexual love was socially approved because it made the boys seek to rival one another in military prowess. It thus became a military institution. It served to keep the minds of these boy scouts off what from the military point of view were frivolous matters; girls were despised, and the boys enabled to concentrate all their interests in camp life. Some day they would marry and beget children for the State. They became demesmen at 18, and attained fuller civic rights, including those of office-holding, at a later age. Heterosexual courtship was delayed in the meantime for military purposes. These purposes having been served, a good deal of free choice and courtship for marital purposes was permitted and encouraged as constituting a kind of military eugenics, and marriage appears to have occurred earlier in Sparta for men than elsewhere in Greece. At what was regarded as the proper age (concerning which our information is not precise, but appears to have been at about 25) bachelorhood began to be discouraged and public measures were taken to wean the young men from homosexual to heterosexual love. The marriageable girls engaged in public ritual dances intended to inflame young masculine passions, singing songs in mockery of bachelorhood. In Sparta there were preserved many relics of the earlier freedom of women; they went about unchaperoned, they were trained in their own athletic exercises, they wore clothes which did not impede their movements ('bare-thighed' they were called by a hostile poet); they owned property, as married women they handled a great deal of responsible property transactions, particularly in their husbands' absence at the wars, and they were under no obligation to marital fidelity:—a woman might even, with her husband's permission, bear children to her lovers. As a corollary of these quasi-matriarchal freedoms, they were not given in marriage in childhood, but in the "flower of their age" and "ripe for marriage"; again our information is lacking in precision, but the texts suggest that this was at about the age of 18. The newly-married husband continued to live at his bachelors' club, visiting his wife by stealth at night, and often did not see her by daylight during their married life until she had borne him a child—at which time they appear to have settled down together in a domestic establishment. These marriages were permanent, but, as just noted, a married woman might take a lover, and it appears to have been good form for the husband to show no resentment, the children of these extra-marital love-affairs being regarded as the husband's legitimate children.

Elsewhere than in Sparta, military training was not so early nor so rigorous. Boys in Athens lived at home and went to the gymnasium, which served as a school, instead of away to camp.

They were enrolled in regular military companies at 18, and served two years' garrison duty. They customarily did not marry until after 35—37 is the age approved by Aristotle. The girls, however, in Athens and apparently in Greece generally outside of Sparta, were married off at puberty or as soon as possible thereafter. They had been cooped up in the paternal home until marriage, with no education except in spinning. After marriage a wife remained in her husband's home to manage the servants, except for a little visiting back and forth with other wives, enlivened by wine-drinking, and punctuated by a yearly attendance at the women's religious festival. Her husband went back for companionship to the bachelor club of his youth, in which he retained membership. The discrepancy of age between husband and wife, and the lack of education for women, made any real domestic companionship impossible. In the meantime the man had enjoyed the usual homosexual love-affairs of boyhood and youth—which in the development of manners tended to be politely regarded as merely noble and spiritual friendships, but which were commonly physical as well. His awakening heterosexual interests had been diverted from the plane of normal courtship by the segregation of the sexes in respectable life, and by the existence of prostitutes (dicteriades), whose existence was socially encouraged for the purpose of affording irresponsible sexual gratification. The needs of companionship were to be satisfied in male friendship. It was not necessary to the successful working of the patriarchal family that a man and his wife be companions—and generally they were not. The relations of the ignorant little-girl wife to the middle-aged stranger whom she married without courtship and often without any preliminary acquaintance whatever, were dutiful, and perhaps affectionate in a somewhat daughterly way, but except on the physical plane they did not constitute adult heterosexual love. For the wife there was customarily no permissible opportunity for the expression of adult love-emotions; they would have been quite out of place in an ordinary marriage, and they were punished as adulterous if expressed extra-maritally. She had to remain emotionally in a childish stage all her life.

The man, however, had in the classical period one more and nearer approach to adult heterosexual emotion. This was provided by girls from other cities, unmarriageable according to

Athenian law, who took up and developed the paid dancing-and-singing-girl profession to meet the masculine need for agreeable companionship. They were well educated, they could converse entertainingly, they were 'hetairai' or companions. They became the temporary (sometimes but not often the permanent) mistresses of Athenian gentlemen. The only recorded instance in which a man went so far as to divorce his wife and legitimate his children by a hetaira with whom he lived in regular domesticity so that it constituted a marriage in all but legal form, is that of Pericles and Aspasia. The profession of the hetaira in actual custom lowered itself to meet the ordinary promiscuous sexual demands of prostitution, while the profession of the prostitute raised itself as best it could to meet the intellectual standards of hetairism, and in any case the word 'hetaira' became the polite word for the better-class courtesan or prostitute. These hetairai, then, constituted in fact an intellectually refined sort of prostitution with periods of temporary mistress-ship. And with these hetairai an Athenian male could experience something resembling adult heterosexual love—could at least experience some of the equal companionship left out of marriage and prostitution. He could also experience the emotions of courtship, for here he had rivals, and money-payments were not (or so he was persuaded) the deciding influence in securing the favors of a hetaira.

We have thus in Athenian life an odd rearrangement of the normal love-emotions—as if they had been cut apart and pasted together again in an artificial pattern. Instead of the normally developing interest of the adolescent boy and girl in each other, we have the girls segregated and the boys flirting and courting among themselves, experiencing jealousy, passion and grief, and pairing off for biologically abnormal matings. We have, in the heterosexual realm, marriage without courtship, romance, or passion; and courtship, romance and passion without marriage. Moreover, it is children born of the loveless marriages that are cherished and brought up, not those born of romantic and passionate matings. It is, indeed, as artificial a pattern as it seems; it is artificial in contrast not only with our own customary arrangements but with the general higher-mammalian mating pattern. It was, however, not only a working arrangement but almost the only arrangement under which the patriarchal system actually ever has worked.

If the patriarchal system was to operate without emotional resistance from individuals, they had to be kept in a permanent state of emotional childishness. The males must preferably (preferably, be it understood, from the patriarchal point of view, not from ours) be halted in the homosexual stage of emotional development—which would also advance military interests, as well as serving to preclude heterosexual diversions. They were necessarily permitted or encouraged to heterosexual activities at a later age; but they could be kept more easily under patriarchal control as to their formal marriages if these were also on a childish and dutiful plane. Sexual attraction and courtship were shorn of their dangers to the patriarchal régime by separating them from marriage and divesting them of social responsibility, especially of parental responsibility. Divested of such responsibility they were merely a form of play, essentially childish in emotional content, however apparently adult in physical expression. As for girls, they could be given the adult privilege of maternity only upon renunciation of all other adult privileges; or they might take the adult privileges of courtship and love-choice only if these were not socially responsible actions, that is not involving either permanency or socially protected maternity. So it was that the patriarchal system seemed to work best. So it worked at its Greek best with the further assistance of the patriarchal institution of slavery. Patriarchal civilization whether in ancient China, Persia, Greece, Rome or any of their later imitations, appears to have required the support of homosexuality, prostitution, and arranged marriage, and to have been most stable when further upheld by slavery or serfdom. It is with the former that we are here concerned; and we note that homosexuality, prostitution and arranged marriage appear to have been integral parts of the patriarchal social system; that patriarchal modes of authority are found establishing them as inevitable and necessary institutions; and that a patriarchal civilization has never in history been built up except upon these supports.

CHAPTER III

THE DECLINE AND FALL OF THE PATRIARCHAL SYSTEM

§ 1. The Psychology of Patriarchal Sex-Compromise

Patriarchal boy-love had no necessary basis in any congenital biological aberrancy; it was socially produced. It regularly occurred under the social and economic conditions of ancient civilizations, somewhat as it irregularly occurs in the sexually segregated prisons, armies, navies and boys' schools and camps at the present day—except that it was a socially approved and respectable practice in patriarchal civilization and aroused no neurotic conflicts in the individuals concerned. It involved no permanent renunciation of the heterosexual goal. But it did involve a consciously or unconsciously derogatory evaluation of that goal. Contempt for women hindered psychic progress toward adulthood and caused a turning aside into a by-way of emotional compromise. Thus when at a later age the social code required an abandonment of boy-love in favor of heterosexual practices, these practices—including both association with prostitutes, and legal marriage—were generally and almost inevitably colored and shaped by previous homosexual experience. After such a training the masculine emotions could not easily follow the true heterosexual path of courtship, love-choice and mating to domestic life and parenthood. If patriarchal education had had its due effect in controlling the instinctive feelings, the resultant heterosexual activities would be emotionally curbed and weakened. Such an infantilized and homosexualized kind of heterosexuality was, indeed, all that the patriarchal system could successfully tolerate.

True heterosexual love would have been incompatible with permanent subjection in adult life to parental authority. True heterosexual love involves freedom of choice. It can more or less willingly accept social coercion and censorship in the details of courtship, but in the vital matter of free choice it remains fiercely hostile to outside interference. From the point of view of patriarchal society, true heterosexual love was a wild, primitive, savage, or animal passion—which in a sense it truly is, being governed by the mammalian mating instincts; and it would have been completely subversive of all patriarchal authority. Need we repeat that if young men and young women had been permitted to choose their own mates, the patriarchal system would have crashed? They were prevented from choosing their own mates, first by complete economic dependence upon their parents, and second by the inculcation of permanently childish states of mind in regard to work and love. If they had been able to earn their own livings independently of the family, they would have been free to choose their own mates. If they had chosen their own mates, the power of the patriarchal family would have been shattered. Patriarchal authority thus required an infantilized form of heterosexual love—one sufficiently docile to parental authority. And this infantilized kind of heterosexual love, as expressed in both arranged marriage and in prostitution, had its roots in homosexuality.

The essence of true heterosexual love is a centering of emotional interests in the other sex, in such a way as to lead along the path of courtship to mating, parenthood and family life. There is involved here a high emotional valuation of the other sex and of all the activities which attract and gain the approval and companionship of the other sex. The patriarchal system at this early historical stage transferred the emotional interests of young males from the opposite to their own sex. It was male approval for which they strove. The childish homosexual world of play and fighting was far more interesting to them than the grown-up heterosexual world of work and mating. It was enabled to be so, in defiance of instinctive tendencies to the contrary, by the giving of all power—including education—to men exclusively. The other sex could then be despised as weak and ignorant. The instinctive predisposition of the young male to find young females of especial interest was thus counteracted by the social fact of the degradation of women and by the resultant psychology of masculine contempt for them.

Upon the basis of this socially inculcated male homosexual contempt for women—and upon the corresponding enforced emotional infantilism of women, with its helpless filial acceptance of male superiority—arranged marriage was built up. Not only would the young men and women so reared be socially incapable of free and responsible love-choice—they would be psychically incapable of it. They would, being in this respect emotionally immature, *need* parental authority to guide them, as the trained slave needs the guidance of a master. Their sad blunders when they occasionally tried to act upon their own immature wishes in defiance of parental wisdom, would sufficiently prove the point—just as the foolish behavior of freedmen has proved the corresponding 'necessity' of slavery. The incapacity of patriarchally trained sons and daughters to manage their own matings was the final argument against allowing them the rights of love-choice. Father and mother knew best in these matters! The only marriage relationship for which men and women so trained were fit was the homosexualized and militarized patriarchal family. It was, however, in practice, found needful to reinforce this arrangement either by infant betrothal and child-marriage for both sexes, as in India, or by giving the girl in marriage at or before puberty to a middle-aged man, as in the classical world generally.

The male homosexual contempt for women, and the corresponding emotional infantilism of women, furnished also the psychological bases of prostitution. Sexual attraction was here permitted free play—upon the customary understanding of the complete social irresponsibility of the male and the complete social helplessness of the female. Association with prostitutes was an intermediate stage between homosexual love and arranged marriage. Homosexual love had included feelings of respect for the beloved, and the wish to gain the beloved's approval. These dangerous and socially unmanageable feelings must if possible be eliminated from heterosexual relationships before marriage. Prostitution served the turn very well. It satisfied heterosexual curiosity; it gave heterosexual impulses cheap and easy triumphs; it furnished contrasts with the 'ideal' elements of homosexual love, contrasts which were unflattering to women and which thus helped to 'disillusion' young men of any instinctively grounded ideas of the importance of women. Prostitution was the psychological training-school for arranged marriage.

Oddly enough, however, prostitution also came to serve another and paradoxically opposite purpose. The effort of the patriarchal system to eliminate the dangerous instinctive male tendency toward romantic emotional overvaluation of women, could not quite or always achieve success by these social means. The mating impulse in mankind does not imperatively proceed along fixed instinctive lines as among the lower animals; but its social distortions leave instinctive hungers which crave satisfaction. Thus the instinctive male mating pattern of mankind involves a need of courtship. That is to say, it is prepared for some resistance from the desired female and is adapted to overcome such resistance by wooing. The female resistance or flight serves to increase the male desire; the delays call for the transformation of otherwise unendurable desire into those symbolic and psychic assertions or promises of possession which constitute the parade, the poetry and the romance of courtship. All these have their biological function in fixing the desires of the human male and female upon one another so definitely and enduringly as to make possible the long-term sexual companionship necessary for the bringing-up of children. In patriarchal life the social organization could dispense with these natural inducements to prolonged marital association, having its own socially coercive methods of keeping husbands and wives together without mutual love. Nevertheless there remained in men and women under the patriarchal system a hunger for courtship. It was not to be wholly satisfied among men by homosexual love, in which there was indeed courtship; what was needed was courtship of the opposite sex. This could not normally occur in the negotiations preliminary to arranged marriage—for the essence of courtship is the danger of being rejected. One could court the girl's family; but the girl herself had no say-so in the matter. Such a game lacks zest. Where then, if only as a game, could men find danger, rivalry, courtship and romance in the field of sex? Where could they find the yearnings, the tears, the agonies, the despairs and the raptures to which their biological make-up instinctively inclined then? Arranged marriage was too tame. And nothing would seem at first glance so improbable as that they should find these emotional desiderata in their relations with prostitutes. Yet they did.

The element of dream or fantasy in prostitution-patronage is shown by the fact that the mercenary relation could be psychologically ignored or even romanticized into an element of courtship. The prostitute discovered that she could get more money by selling courtship and romance than by selling mere sexual submission. This discovery raised her to the higher social level of the hetaira, or companion. Doubtless she made this important discovery by accident, since the exigencies of her trade required her to deny her favors to one lover while devoting herself to another. At any rate, she found that repeated denials transformed the most blasé customer into an anxious and ardent suitor, and she improved upon these vulgar facts in order to make herself desirable. She was free, as a legitimate wife was not, to deny her favors. She became haughty, arrogant, capricious; she was as difficult to woo as it was felt that a virgin should be; she managed paradoxically to recapture for professional purposes the allurements of maidenly shyness, evasion and retreat. Older, experienced hetairai instructed silly young harlots in the art of giving men what they really wanted—the spiritual excitements of courtship. And thus all over Greece men sighed in the porticos of prostitutes, wept and tore their hair, talked of suicide, wrote poems to their cruel beloveds; while their wives wept at home, wondering by what magic or witchcraft those hussies had charmed their husbands away from their beds and the household money out of their purses. Poor girl-wives, they were merely beautiful, young, dutifully submissive; how could they guess that these harlots had rediscovered for men's benefit the lost art of courtship? All their witchcraft was in playing upon the instinctive masculine need of engaging in the love-chase.

Yet, so far as the men were concerned, it was only in play—however intensely acted out and with whatever tears and despairs—that they thus achieved the biologically normal masculine rôle. The tears and despairs did not really mean anything. The older harlots had often to remind the young and impressionable ones of that. The tears and despairs should biologically have meant—would in a free society have meant—a passion capable of carrying a man into domestic life and parenthood. But these results were not socially permitted; at least, if they occurred they were not recognized as having any social validity. The children born of such lawless loves were not entitled to parental care and affection. So ran patriarchal law.

Thus prostitution even in its higher reaches of hetairism conformed to infantile limitations. No more than in homosexual love did its ardors customarily subserve the biological realities of mating, parenthood and family life, or constitute an experimental approach toward and preparation for them. On the contrary prostitute-love served as a safety valve, a symbolic and socially 'harmless' mode of expressing emotions otherwise subversive of the patriarchal system. The true patriarchal justification of prostitution was not (as it used to be said) that it protected respectable virgins and matrons from rape, but rather that it protected them from courtship and love-matches—a much more serious danger to the patriarchal system.

Prostitution was thus partly in the nature of a dream or fantasy which approximated the forbidden biological norm in emotionally satisfying symbolic pretense or compromise. It did not, so to speak, exist in the world of social realities, since it had no permitted or recognized social consequences. Its drawback was that it diverted an immense amount of psychic energy from the realm of social realities into such 'dream'-life.

Homosexual love, while a recognized part of the ethical system of ancient civilization in its most militaristic stage, as in Greece, was in opposition to all the sentiments which grew up in a peaceful and especially in an industrial world. The classical world grew somewhat ashamed of it, except in its more refined or sublimated aspects in which it was denied physical expression. As 'Platonic love' it became merely a kind of extravagantly sentimental friendship between men (and subsequently served under Christian auspices as the model for heterosexual relationships in which the physical expression of love was similarly renounced and similarly replaced by sentimental extravagances). The extent to which homosexual love was sublimated into sentimental friendships between men represented in ancient civilization the extent to which men turned to prostitution as a more satisfying compromise with their normal heterosexual instincts. It is understood that these could not as a rule be satisfied in arranged marriage. Thus the 'ideal' aspects of love—sentiments of loyalty, exclusiveness and permanence—were expressed in masculine friendships; its elements of sexual passion, of rivalry and (in illusion, at least) of free choice, were separately expressed in relationships with prostitutes; and its normal social aspects of domesticity and family life were again separately expressed (minus everything else, and plus a recognized 'duty' to the State of begetting children) in legitimate arranged marriage.

This tripartite division of love has still some further variations which will presently be discussed. The point to be noted is that although ostensibly less homosexual than in its earlier stage, this arrangement is still governed by the authoritarian necessities of the patriarchal system and still falls short of an adult heterosexuality which would be incompatible with patriarchal discipline.

It may be asked whether these generalizations are put forward as covering the actual thought, feeling and behavior of the people of the ancient world. There were of course in the ancient world many nations or tribes which preserved more or less of the old quasi-matriarchal institutions, in some kind of compromise with the newer patriarchal forms; and such nations or tribes (we may call to mind the Egyptians) accorded women more respect, and a larger social function. Then there were the socially submerged and backward classes, including slaves, helots, the rural populations and the city poor, who tended to keep some of the older quasi-matriarchal customs or lose the newer patriarchal ones. In some respects the patriarchal customs were an aristocratic luxury, like Chinese foot-binding; poor and busy people had to dispense with them. Again, as these classes achieved power, they tended to reject some patriarchal customs while accepting others as the badge of respectability. Once more, as the leisure classes achieved a more settled security they began to abandon some of their strict patriarchal customs in favor of the looser quasi-matriarchal customs of 'the people'. In Rome the aristocratic form of strict patriarchal marriage was under the Empire almost completely displaced by the older, popular, quasi-matriarchal and freer form. Finally, in the classical Mediterranean world whose centuries we are generalizing upon, there were reciprocal influences between the cultures of city civilizations and of barbaric tribes in all stages of transition from a quasi-matriarchal clan system to a rigidly patriarchal family system. These generalizations, then, refer to certain well-established leisure-class social norms of conduct and feeling, well authenticated in classical literature; but it is to be presumed that states of feeling like our own and actions such as we should approve from our non-patriarchal point of view existed outside the conventions.

We now have to note a further development of the arrangement by which the normal love-emotions of the male were split up into Platonic friendship, prostitute-love and arranged marriage. This is the late classical custom of living with a mistress in a regular domestic establishment over a long period, and cherishing the children so begotten. It is a custom which at first glance appears to reunite the severed parts of love into the normal human pattern. It did so, indeed, in all respects except one. It began with real courtship, it involved real love-choice, it depended for its stability upon mutual passionate love, it achieved domesticity and it did not even stop short of children and family life. Its biological values were thus not as lacking as in temporary prostitute-love. And yet it lacked one important kind of reality. It too, when all was said and done, was merely a dream. The case of St. Augustine as recorded by him in his candid *Confessions* is illustrative.

"In those years", he wrote, "I cherished a girl, not joined to me in legitimate wedlock but sought out in giddy passion, yet one nevertheless with whom I truly kept the faith of the bed; with whom I learned right well by mine own experience how different from orderly marriage agreed to for the sake of children is the compact of passionate love, where though children be unintentionally begotten, yet being born they compel us to love them." This union had endured for years. But socially speaking it was not real. The touch of reality could break it like a bubble. It was high time for Augustine to marry; this was not marriage—it had not been, could not be, recognized by Augustine's family. His devout Christian mother found him a suitable bride; in obedience to her and custom he betrothed himself to the proper little virgin and sent his mistress away. "Torn from my side, that impediment as it were to my marriage, she with whom I was wont to bed, to her my heart clove, cut to pieces, wounded and bleeding. And she went back to Africa, vowing to God never to have anything to do with men again, leaving with me my natural son whom she had borne me"—Adeodatus his name, 'given-by-God'. The years of his proper betrothed still being two short of nubility, he took another mistress while he waited. But he wrote: "Nor was that wound of mine yet cured which had been made by the cutting away of the former; but it burned with anguish, and festered; and when it grew dull, still ached desperately."

The arranged marriage in this instance did not ever take place; instead the Church gained a saint. In a number of respects the incident is uncharacteristic: the legal marriage would ordinarily have taken place; the mistress was usually handed over to a friend; the child of such a broken relationship would be put out to board somewhere, neglected and presently forgotten—such children having no legal rights of inheritance or support. The story, however, illustrates sufficiently the precarious tenure of such domestic establishments. The one important kind of reality which they lacked was social reality; and lacking that they might vanish like a dream at the touch of patriarchal family authority.

One more instance will be given, from late Greek life under the Roman Empire, taken from Lucian's *Dialogues of the Hetairai.* It illustrates the emotional advantages of the hetaira over the wife, through her exaggerated use of the instinctive arts of feminine allurement, evoking in men the whole instinctive masculine repertory of courtship in an exaggerated form; and it concludes on an economic note which may serve to explain to us why Augustine, above, did not defy his mother and marry his mistress.

The experienced Ampelis is instructing the 18-year-old Chrysis. "If you want to make a man wildly in love with you, let him see that you can do without him. When he thinks that he has you all to himself, he is apt to cool down. * * * Come now; I'll tell you what happened to me, not so many years ago. Demophantus was my admirer in those days; the usurer, you know, at the back of the Poecile. He had never given me more than five drachmae at a time, and he wanted to have everything his own way. The fact was, my dear, his love was only skin deep. There were no sighs or tears with him; no knocking me up at unearthly hours; he would spend an evening with me now and then—very occasionally—and that was all. But one day when he called, I was 'not at home'; I had Callides the painter with me (he had given me ten drachmae). Well, at the time Demophantus said some very rude things, and walked off. However, the days went by, and I never sent for him; and at last (finding that Callides had been with me again) even Demophantus began to catch fire, and get into a passion about it; so one day he stood outside, and waited till he found the door open: my dear, I don't know what he didn't do! cried, beat me, vowed he would murder me, tore my clothes dreadfully! And it all ended with his giving me a talent;

after which I saw no one else for eight months on end. His wife told everybody that I had bewitched him with some drug. 'Twas easy to see what the drug had been: jealousy. Now you should try the same drug upon Gorgias. The boy will have money, if anything happens to his father."

The economic moral is in that last little remark. We are now, in late Greek life, not dealing with a legally unmarriageable alien woman. The patriarchal family has no ultimate legal protection against Chrysis; she can become a daughter-in-law—but not in the lifetime of Gorgias's father, who holds the purse-strings. Gorgias has no control of any money except what petty cash he can wheedle out of his father, until the old man dies; he cannot decide his own destinies—cannot choose his own wife. He is an infant under the patriarchal system. And so was that other young gentleman, Augustine. The saint does not go into the economics of his obedience to his mother; but behind the ideal of filial duty there was always the economic power of the family.

It was to necessity as well as to 'duty' that sons bowed, when visiting their socially irregular sweethearts as harlots, or sending away their mistresses when the time came for matrimony. They were often sad at seeing their sweethearts, with whom they had lived in what seemed an ideal union, afterwards pursuing the trade of harlot. "Lesbia, my own Lesbia, that very Lesbia, she whom Catullus loved above all others—my Lesbia—now in alleys sells herself for the obscene pleasure of young Roman gentry." But human nature submits ever to necessity, taking what it can get in the way of fulfillment of its instinctive wishes. Sometimes under the patriarchal regime what youth got was the distorted romance of boy-love; sometimes the fantasy gratification afforded by prostitution; and again the temporary and socially illusive delights of mistress-keeping.

There was also, in some times and places, a further compromise between the requirements of the patriarchal family system and the instinctive demands of human nature, in post-marital and extra-marital romance, or polite adultery. We have seen that it occurred in Sparta, but it is best known to us in its medieval forms. It was a privilege of uncertain tenure, since it ran counter to the patriarchal tradition of property in wives, and was often punished by murder or disgrace. It became during the later middle ages refined or sublimated into a Platonic form, as homosexual relations had been in late classical times, though perhaps not so successfully; at any rate, the Platonic theory gave some social protection to extra-marital relations, which might or might not be in fact restricted by Platonic limitations. But even at its freest it was understood that adultery-love must not be taken so seriously as to disrupt the existing marital arrangements of the parties concerned. As a more or less secret code modifying the ostensible ethical rules of polite society, it furnished a compromise outlet for instinctive emotions—becoming thus another safety-valve of the patriarchal system. It was unlike prostitution, however, in that it involved women of the same social class and often of a higher class; and especially when secretly conducted under conditions of danger it called for the loyalty and courage which had heretofore been associated only with inter-masculine loves and friendships. Thus it recovered for heterosexual love some of the 'ideal' aspects of military homosexual relationships. It was never, in this its most adult form, socially accepted, though it became an attractive theme for poets and story-tellers. It was not socially approved, because it led to elopements which had to be punished with murder or disgrace. It was felt to be tragic in its nature; and only the tamer varieties of adultery which knew their place and could be depended upon to keep it, were socially approved. Thus it might be as tame, as socially 'harmless', as prostitution; and as prostitution tended to become degraded in Christian Europe, adultery rose in favor as being for young gentlemen a more refined diversion, improving their manners more than association with prostitutes, and less likely to result in venereal disease. It also tended to be less expensive on the whole, since the lady's support was already borne by her husband, and the 'presents' which were given to her by her lover need not be—and for reasons of discretion should not be—of any considerable intrinsic value. Furthermore, while a courtesan had motives for flaunting her lovers, a married woman had reasons for concealing the existence of hers, so that the relation was more socially discreet, more compatible in appearance with the ostensible code of sexual ethics.

Now in all these patriarchal compromises with love—prostitution, hetairism, mistress-keeping, and polite adultery—there was ordinarily a limitation of individual male responsibility. Other men shared in the upkeep of prostitute or hetaira, the mistress would be eventually passed on to a friend, the wife was dependent upon her husband. It was a kind of disguised polyandry in which responsibility both emotional and economic was shared between a number of men. It was a relationship therefore which appealed to emotionally timid males as well as to economically dependent ones who were not able to assume wholly or permanently the economic and emotional responsibilities of mating; and the custom served to encourage the male timidity and maintain the male economic dependence to which it ministered.

Furthermore we have to note this. A relationship which is essentially infantile is one which ordinarily does not offer emotional satisfaction to an adult unless its infantility is disguised, glossed over, compensated for by pseudo-adult airs and attitudes. Thus the infantile and quasi-homosexual character of these timidly polyandrous relationships had to be disguised by an exaggerated assumption of adult heterosexual emotions, in the form of an extravagant possessiveness and jealousy. Such possessiveness and jealousy did not lead to the actually responsible behavior which might easily have ensured completeness, permanence and exclusiveness of emotional possession. It was not intended to secure such realistic results, which were not in fact desired. It was rather intended to gloss over the tame acceptance of the actual situation. The more infantile the situation was, the more dramatically exaggerated the pseudo-adult airs of possessiveness and jealousy had to be. The more incapable of adult heterosexual behavior the male was, the more emotionally exacting, suspicious and pseudo-male he became. The inconstancy of women was a necessary article of his emotional creed; and it referred to his own actual plan of sharing his women with other males. It would not do to admit this of himself; he had to attribute his intentions to the external world. Indeed, he was only at home emotionally in a world in which the unfaithfulness of women inevitably occurred. It was easy enough to make it occur and then be surprised and hurt. He had thus proved—by tests calculated to prove it—that his suspicions were true. The tests themselves—neglect of or brutality to a wife or mistress—were justified by the results to which they conduced: the proof that women were inconstant, faithless ever, not to be trusted. And this in turn, as wives and sweethearts sought to adjust themselves to these preposterous tests, led to a preposterous ideal of womanly virtue as consisting of an inhuman or angelic patience and endurance and long-suffering meekness under trial—the Patient Griselda ideal. It was naturally achieved by women less easily in fact than in fiction. The result in fact was more likely to be shrewishness—the normal female response to various kinds of masculine infantilism and unconscious homosexuality.

We have nearly exhausted the descriptive list of the chief masculine attitudes which were created by the patriarchal system and had their usefulness as means of adapting men tamely to the necessities of that system without loss of self-respect. We may repeat here that the patriarchal system was a military family organization suited to a turbulent period of danger and of dependence upon the land as a source of immediate supply of food and clothing—a period, that is to say, of comparative human powerlessness. We shall see how quickly these patriarchal forms begin to break up as mankind achieves greater power through the use of machinery. But we must not leave the subject of masculine attitudes under the patriarchal system without referring to professional celibacy.

Celibacy had obviously an economic basis in the patriarchal system. It was indeed the logical answer to the economic limitations of landed property as a means of support. If human beings were like ants or bees, they would have created a sexless worker-caste. Such sexless workers would have devoted their labors selflessly to the family group, without requiring any sexual incentives or rewards, and would not have burdened the family with any progeny.

With regard to women, some approach to this arrangement was made under the patriarchal system, outside the family by celibate priestesses and nuns, and inside it by spinster relatives. When men similarly renounced immediate and instinctive gratifications they were regarded by others with mixed feelings of contempt and awe. Usually the contempt came first, the awe later if at all; that is, some of those first regarded by ordinary men as fools came subsequently to be regarded as saints or sages, indeed as belonging to the special self-elected caste of heroes to whom no ordinary rules apply. Often these celibates achieved power through service to the State, and celibacy became in time one of the recognized roads to power. Under such circumstances those without other assurance of subsistence would turn to the profession of celibacy as a means of livelihood. Under the Roman Empire, Greece and Rome were infested with professionally celibate—though not necessarily chaste—philosophers, who used the ragged cloak and staff and the highly ethical doctrines of austere philosophic schools as a respectable means of sponging a living and enabling them to enjoy worldly powers and pleasures. Under Christianity these celibate and vagabond professions were organized as brotherhoods of monks and friars, some of which achieved great social usefulness while others remained parasitic.

We have here to consider how the patriarchal system psychologically encouraged the existence, in increasing and finally enormous and overwhelming numbers, of such celibates—regardless for the moment of whether they were as individuals among the useful or the parasitic ones. Learning and teaching were in general associated with celibacy, and these might indeed lead to power; but such incentives would not prevail against instinctive sexual and mating impulses in so huge a number of cases. They could so prevail only if the opportunities for mating were severely restricted in social fact, and if on the whole the masculine psychology of sex were permeated with the homosexual suspicions, distrusts and contempts described above. These suspicions and contempts made it easier for ambitious youths to renounce the instinctive sexual aims. What is frequently thought of as a specifically Christian fear and hatred of sex has its roots in pagan philosophy, and represents the reaction of hurt minds to the facts of patriarchal life. It amounted to a rejection of the current compromises of the patriarchal régime, among which legitimate arranged marriage was logically included along with prostitution. Christian celibacy took its stand upon the basis of sublimated filial and paternal emotions. Obedience to the rule of the actual earthly father was renounced in favor of obedience to the idealized rule of a Heavenly Father; and the obligations of paternal rule over actual children of the flesh was renounced in favor of the obligation of an ideal guardianship and cherishing of all members of the great family of the Church.

Thus in a celibate priesthood vowed to chastity we have the final emotional paradox of the patriarchal system, a substitute parenthood which completes the shattered cycle of the instinctive sexual life. All that has been barred out of legitimate marriage by the patriarchal system is to be found somewhere, in some form—courtship is furnished by prostitutes; romance by adultery; domestic intimacy by kept mistresses; devotion by male friends; and paternal care by celibate priests. No drunken humorist could have conceived a stranger, more fantastic scheme of life. Yet it is logical enough, in the patriarchal system. The sexual instincts, denied simple and direct social expression in courtship, marriage and family life, cast out as unruly by the patriarchal system, return in disguised and compromise forms.

> "They reckon ill who leave me out;
> When me they fly, I am the wings;
> I am the doubter, and the doubt,
> And I the hymn the Brahmin sings."

§ 2. The Patriarchal Débacle

The patriarchal system, being based on landed property, tended inevitably to restrict the privilege of socially protected parenthood to a limited number of inheriting sons and dowried daughters. The superfluous sons and daughters were in one fashion or other thrown overboard to sink or swim. This was less the case among the peasantry who worked their own lands, and could make use of the labors of a large family, than among the aristocratic classes and the city poor; hence the patriarchal family lingered in full strength among the peasantry for centuries after it had begun to break down among other classes. The superfluous sons of the respectable classes became, as we have seen, soldiers of fortune or priests, or members of a new middle class whose interests were hostile to the patriarchal system; and somewhat the same may be said for the superfluous sons of the poor, except that their opportunities as soldiers of fortune, not being socially privileged, tended to make them criminals and vagabonds. The superfluous daughters of the respectable classes might become nuns, and the superfluous daughters of the poor were always in demand as prostitutes—being thus in either case denied the privilege of socially protected maternity.

Yet the economic saving thus effected was in the long run entirely illusory. Many of those thus cast off from patriarchal family protection were unproductive as well as non-reproductive. Priests and nuns had to be provided for, and prostitutes, vagabonds and soldiers of fortune, respectable or poor, did their best to provide for themselves at the expense of others. To maintain them required goods, and what was provided willingly or unwillingly for their support was necessarily withdrawn from the support of families. The economics of the situation are perhaps most clearly to be seen as regards women. The nun on one side and the prostitute on the other took from the family a large proportion of the goods belonging prescriptively to the legitimate wife and mother. Thus her legal monopoly on child-bearing was paid for at a heavy cost. Marriage and parenthood became an ever more severe burden upon both sexes, and in classical times they had already become so unpopular that they had to be urged as a 'duty to the State'.

When prostitution, at the height of the Roman Empire, had become for immense numbers of men and women a substitute for marriage, and when religious celibacy, in medieval times, had become the choice or the doom of other vast numbers of the population, it must be said that these 'protections' of the family were in fact destroying it. The patriarchal family system and its basic mode of production were quite unable to cope with the population problem, except by relying upon war, famine and pestilence to diminish the numbers of mouths to be fed.

The Crusades are a dramatic symptom of the despair, masquerading as faith, which afflicted the dying and convulsed patriarchal régime. The Children's Crusade in 1212—in which some hundreds and thousands of young boys and girls, foreseeing no normal manhood and womanhood at home, set off on the fantastic adventure of rescuing the Holy Sepulchre from the infidel, only to die on the way of starvation and disease, to be eaten by wild beasts, or to be captured and sold into Oriental slavery as eunuchs and concubines—is one of the death-agonies of the patriarchal family system in Europe. It had abandoned under Christianity the polygamy and slavery which still kept it a working arrangement in the East.

The patriarchal system was crashing in Europe when some of the superfluous population found a means of subsistence outside of landed property in trade and then in manufacture. These became a new class, the middle class, which in time was able to create a new kind of social security, offer new social guarantees to parenthood, and put the family upon a new economic basis. It reversed—within the middle class—the psychological relations of the family to property. The reproductive and parental impulses were no longer rigidly limited as to their expression by a static kind of wealth in the form of land; these emotions were rather used as the incentives to economic activities not merely of an exploitive but also of a productive sort. It thereby introduced the modern conception of 'work'. Labor had never been respectable in an aristocratic society in which it was derogated to slaves or serfs. An aristocrat obtained his privileges by inheritance or favor. Work as a respectable means of improving one's lot was introduced by the middle class. And the conception of the possible improvement of one's lot by work led in turn to a repudiation of the aristocratic ideal of castes fixed by birth.

The new economic system developed by the middle class was in a sense not new at all. It had begun in classical times but had been interrupted by the barbaric invasions. In the East it had accommodated itself to and subordinated itself to the patriarchal régime. But in Europe it had to fight that régime to exist. It was progressively destructive to every feature of patriarchal life—to its religion, its politics, its respect for old custom, its authoritarianism, its arranged marriages, its dowry system, its primogeniture arrangements, its segregation of the sexes. And it was able to destroy these because they were not effecting the social stability for which they were designed. The middle-class revolution was successful because the patriarchal system was already a visible failure. As Gibbon wrote of the destruction of the monuments of Rome, and by implication of the fall of the Roman Empire itself: "While the Roman edifices were still entire, the first blows, however weighty, were resisted by the solidity of the mass and the harmony of the parts; but the slightest touch would precipitate the fragments of arches and columns that already nodded to their fall."

In spite of every effort of the triumphing middle class to take on all the cultural traits of the decaying aristocracy, it was unable to restore the broken powers of the patriarchal Church and the absolutist State; and, just as it had to free the slave and the serf, so it was obliged within the family to set the children free from paternal economic and social authority—thus establishing a legal age of majority beyond which parental rule must cease, and giving to sons and daughters the right to marry as they chose. It had to grant this legal and social adulthood to grown-up men and women, because it needed them to be psychologically grown up. It did not need to keep them in permanent emotional subservience to the parental family; it wanted them to have adult work-ambitions and healthy adult heterosexual mating and family impulses as incentives to their activities. It was—for reasons which it did not fully understand—intolerant of the aristocratic compromises of prostitution, mistress-keeping, and polite adultery. It undertook to abolish permanent celibacy as an ideal. It established divorce, reinstituted romantic courtship and love-choice in marriage, and demanded sexual fidelity in marriage not only of women but of men.

Let us take a last look at the patriarchal system in one of its final European strongholds, among the peasantry. LePlay, the French sociologist, dismayed by the shattering of the patriarchal family in 19th-century Western Europe, found it still strong in Russia, and was moved to enthusiasm. "The old parents," he wrote, "finding ample means of subsistence in the nature of their locality, are able to gather around them four generations of their own blood. The father of the family, whose power is justified by his long experience, possesses the necessary ascendancy to hold both youth and ripe age in submission to the Decalogue and to custom. Under this régime peace and stability extend from the family to the entire race"—meaning the Russian State, which at that time furnished to reactionary sociologists a model of stability in contrast to the political distractions of Western Europe.

It was only a generation later that Stepniak found the patriarchal family in decay in peasant Russia: "Their aspiration after independence has not yet directed itself against political despotism, save in isolated cases," he wrote; "but in the meantime it has almost triumphed in the struggle against the more intimate and trying despotism of the *bolshak*, the head of the household. A very important and thoroughgoing change has taken place in the family relations of the great Russian rural population. The children, as soon as they have grown up and have married, will no longer submit to the *bolshak's* whimsical rule. They rebel, and if imposed upon, form new households, where they become masters of their own actions."

In a single generation the wise old patriarch had become the whimsical old despot. Yet he was the same sort of patriarch, doing the same things as before. He had in fact, from our modern point of view, always been a despot; the change was in the children, who dared now to want to grow up. The sons demanded houses of their own to live in with their wives and children—instead of living as children in a four-generation household under patriarchal rule. It was a dangerous desire, and Stepniak pointed out the dangers. These sons went into debt to get those houses of their own. "Only very large [*i.e.*, four-generation, patriarchal] families, which are becoming less common," he wrote, "are able to extricate themselves from the usurer's net in which they have been by dire misfortune entangled. When the liability is divided amongst twelve or more adults [*i.e.*, in the four-generation, patriarchal family], this may compensate for the absence of one or two of their number 'given in bondage', by increased diligence on the part of those that remain. But small families invariably succumb." One or two individuals were in the old days thrown to the wolves, and the patriarchal family troika dashed on!

But, though it was dangerous to let a young man live in a house of his own with his own wife and children, that was the right for which wars and revolutions had been waged, kings tumbled from their thrones and a too-patriarchal Deity from Heaven. It is indeed dangerous for men and women to be adults, but we take it now for granted. It seems odd to us that Le Play should have idealized a family system which produced permanently infantile adults of whom he could thus write without a smile: "When in Russia one asks a man of forty about some fact, he never fails to answer that such information can only properly be given by some one older."

The American, southern mountaineer version of this story is that when one asks a man of sixty such a question, he replies: "You'll have to ask Pappy." But we do not nowadays idealize this adult childishness, we laugh at it or frown at it.

An American woman, Gertrude Marvin Williams, writing of the Hindu form of the patriarchal family system, is more critical than Le Play. "The joint family system", she writes, "is a device admirably suited to the timid man. He postpones indefinitely the wrench of growing up, putting his childhood behind him, and facing the responsibilities of adult life. Through the years he lingers, leaning on his parents and the reassuring intimacy of the family circle." This is the judgment of a new civilization upon an older one—of Western civilization upon a lingering and decadent remnant of the great patriarchal civilizations of the past. It represents the attitude of an age set free by machine power, toward not merely Brahmin India but all of the lingering and decadent remnants of patriarchal childishness in our Western world. Our modern civilization is not a refuge for the timid.

CHAPTER IV

PATRIARCHAL CUSTOMS BECOME MODERN NEUROSES

§ 1. Discarded Mores May Become Modern Art or Heroism

Our argument will proceed to show how patriarchal attitudes of mind, persisting into our modern society, become the social basis of certain neuroses. There is, however, an alternative: these outworn attitudes, which do not fit realistically into our 'actual' lives, may become the incidental graces and solaces of life when transformed into social ritual or art. The scientific exploration of this particular transformation is, however, just beginning; and our detailed discussion of it will appear in a later chapter. It may be said here that socially unacceptable impulses may with complete social approval be expressed in art, and that such expression is not neurotic; also—though the subject cannot be done justice to in a brief reference—that such socially unacceptable impulses may occasionally be expressed in action and be accepted as heroism by society—or by some social group at the time, and by society generally after the death of the person whom up to that time it has preferred to regard as a criminal: John Brown and Stenka Razin, François Villon and Casanova may be adduced as examples, though we may not pause now to justify the choice of their names. The neurotic, then, is one who is unable to fit his socially unacceptable impulses into the existing social scheme by making use of its permitted channels of harmless or useful symbolic compromise-activities for their expression; and who has, let us say, the ill-luck not to find any or a sufficiently large or important social group in need of him as a hero. The importance of art, heroism and social ritual, as regular and occasional mediums for the expression of socially disapproved impulses, is obvious.

The matter is thus briefly alluded to and dismissed at this stage of our discussion, in order to indicate that the precepts of modern psychology do not—as some alarmed readers might feel—inculcate any hard-and-fast rules of conduct which everybody must follow, any one kind of realistic happiness which all must achieve on pain of being condemned as 'neurotic'. There are all kinds of ways of being useful and happy, and some of them lie apart from the beaten path, in the directions of art and heroism. Our argument for the time, however, seeks to distinguish the main-travelled highways.

§ 2. The Contemporary Transition from the Patriarchal to Modern Customs

We have already outlined the required emotional compromises of the patriarchal scheme; and we need only recall that in regard to both love and work they were essentially infantile and homosexual, taking for granted prostitution and bastardy, or sacred celibacy, or arranged marriage and polite adultery—and barring out courtship, love-choice, social equality of men with women, and instinctive family and parental life, except as provided in a limited way in compromise institutions; and as to work, fitting into the hereditary caste pattern which similarly barred out free choice and responsibility.

We have also briefly surveyed the economic and social changes brought about by the middle-class development of trade, manufacture and machine power, and have seen to what a considerable extent these patriarchal compromises have been found cumbersome to the new social order. Without exaggerating the as yet merely partial destruction of all these patriarchal institutions that has taken place in our society, we may say that courtship, love-choice, the social equality of the sexes, and instinctive parental and family life have been brought back into the approved marital scheme, and that work-ambition has been set free from hereditary and caste limitations. Work and love are now substantially liberated, legally and socially, from landed-property and patriarchal-family bondage.

The fact, however, that we are in a transition period means that for multitudes of individuals there comes a change from the old order to the new at some time in their lives—that, having been trained to adjust to the old order, they are then called upon to live in the new.

When individuals have grown to middle-age or beyond before they discover that they are not living in the patriarchal era any more, they may refuse to attempt any adjustment to new conditions. If the discovery comes in adolescence, however, they will take the new freedoms for granted and try to live up to what they can understand of these broader opportunities. If, nevertheless, while accepting the new scheme of life and trying to live in accordance with it, they should be confused by the contradictions between the precepts upon which they have been brought up and the mores to which they seek to adjust themselves, they will frequently muddle their behavior. Here we have the typical cases of patriarchal-family neurosis.

This confusion occurs in innumerable instances to-day in the United States. Our non-patriarchal system is still in the making. Young people from backward rural districts come to towns and cities; young people leave home and go to school and college and into employment; the children of immigrants with a patriarchal background become Americanized and urbanized—and they all find themselves going from a patriarchal into a non-patriarchal world. Indeed, so much of patriarchal education is generally retained even in the upbringing of urban children that the process of growing up involves almost necessarily a violent transition from a small quasi-patriarchal family to a large non-patriarchal outside world. The result is that, even when the adjustment is successfully made, it requires a long time to make. Years of presumably adult life are wasted in the solution of adolescent problems of adjustment to the modern conditions of love and work.

We now come to the question of why the influences of patriarchal education cannot be easily cast off by young people upon their emergence into the non-patriarchal world.

Let us transport ourselves back for a moment into the older patriarchal world. Let us suppose that the only or the eldest son of a family has a strange bent for astronomy; if he had any choice in the matter he would like to devote his life to studying the stars. Let us suppose also that he has taken a fancy to an orphan girl in the neighborhood—no 'suitable' match for him. Sons were given to such odd fancies, under the patriarchal regime, both as to careers and wives. But these fancies were not actually indulged very often. Why not? What prevented the young man from taking up astronomy, and marrying the girl he loved? He might have been disinherited, he might have been cast out with his wife to starve. Yet there was at least a chance of his not being disinherited, and a chance of his making some sort of living in any event. Social tyrannies have seldom if ever been so snugly built up that there was not a way out for those few who dared to look for it. But something deeper and nobler than the fear of starvation restrained him. He would say, perhaps, that it was his love for his father. But we can describe it more precisely than that.

Brought up under a system in which power is inherited from the father, all his childhood dreams of adult independence are associated with the idea of his father's death. When suffering childish defeats and rebuffs of his wishes, he has more than once wished his father dead, in order that he might occupy his father's place and power. He is ashamed of such wishes; he forgets them, repudiates them. And with them he repudiates the associated idea of independence. The education he receives is such as to help him repudiate that idea. It is an education of which we might say that it seems specifically designed to prevent the murder of a father by impatient sons; for it teaches and rewards filial patience, it discourages wayward ambitions, and it inculcates a sense of immense unworthiness in sons, together with an immense awe for fathers. Fathers in Roman times might sell their children into slavery, in Greek times expose them at birth; that was quite all right in patriarchal morality—but the slaying of a father by a child was the most frightful of all crimes. It was a crime which, repudiated from the conscious wishes of the ancient world, nevertheless held a horrible fascination, and was the theme of that world's most thrilling and popular tragedies. It was a great deal on everybody's mind, though of course 'unthinkable' in any specific instance. It was so unthinkable that it made the associated desire for adult independence also unthinkable. One grew up, moreover, to realize that nobody in the patriarchal system had any real adult independence: what was inherited was not so much power as family responsibility—however tyrannically and whimsically it might seem to be discharged. The final reason, then, why the young man dared not choose his work and his wife was that all aspirations toward adulthood were guilty and murderous wishes.

How does this apply to our contemporary situation? Power is no longer associated inevitably with inheritance, but much more now with personal achievement. And inheritance of power, insofar as it is not based on landed property, does not require the death or abdication of the father. Full adulthood can be granted to young people without any diminution of the powers of a father. And ours is the kind of world in which adulthood is in great demand. Yet the mode of bringing up children still largely follows the patriarchal pattern. In a world in which the death of a father would *not* bring any advantage to a son, the old patriarchal methods of preventing father-murder are still being used. In a world in which the triumphs of a son do *not* diminish the powers of the father, the discouragement of ambition still goes on. The patriarchal father was necessarily jealous of his sons. When he heard the younger generation knocking at the door, it sounded to him like his own death-knell. In a world in which the relations of a father to a son can be friendly, their relation is still largely governed by principles handed down from a time when that relation was essentially one between an aging and jealous monarch and the impatient prince who was destined to supplant him.

It is not suggested that modern fathers wish to behave like aging and jealous monarchs, or that they personally feel that way. They are merely seeking to maintain their 'paternal authority and dignity', and 'bringing up their children to be obedient'. The case of daughters in our changing world is complicated by their entrance into work outside the home; but with them too the parents generally pursue a patriarchal policy which does not fit in with modern social needs. They fail to understand that the parental authority and dignity which they seek to uphold is not one which the parental relationship now requires for any social purposes; that the kind of military obedience which they seek to inculcate is not one for which the outside world has much use; and that they fall far short of fulfilling their obligations to their children in attempting to inflict patriarchal discipline upon them. It is their business as parents, nowadays, to help their children grow up to responsible, self-determining adulthood; they not only fail in that, but by patriarchal methods they shame them out of their normal aspirations toward adulthood and leave them confused and helpless upon their entrance into the outside world.

Once, under the patriarchal family system, father and son had opposite interests, and a son could not achieve complete economic and social freedom except through the father's death; this artificially hostile relationship had to be elaborately disguised by extravagant filial pieties and rigidly dutiful sentiments. Behind these fine moral trappings were hidden the secret emotional realities of jealousy and hatred. Those dangerous emotions had to be kept out of consciousness, and they were barred out by shame. Children had to be shamed out of all their aspirations toward adulthood, whether in love or work, if the patriarchal system was to be kept going. And now that the patriarchal system has gone, here among its ruins and in our half-built new world, the moral trappings of those old patriarchal jealousies and hatreds are still preserved, the extravagant filial pieties and rigidly dutiful sentiments still inculcated. The danger—a real danger once—against which these were the protections—no longer exists. The crime which they would prevent is obsolete, one of the

"old, unhappy, far-off things,
And battles long ago."

But the paraphernalia of early patriarchal education still clutters up the modern home.

The time has long gone by when homosexual practices were regarded as the proper solace of masculine youth. The time has barely gone by when the patronage of prostitution was accepted as an inevitable and valuable compromise activity for young male sexual instincts—when a father, for example, took his son at what was regarded as the proper age to a house of prostitution, there to be initiated into the sort of symbolic and imitation sexual manhood with which he was expected to be dutifully content. Prostitution, indeed, still finds a place in our transition civilization but it is no longer taken for granted. Gone, too, as an ideal, and quite generally in actual practice, is the arranged marriage. Polite adultery has a limited intellectual vogue but it is not generally taken for granted among the classes in which it was formerly the most nearly normal outlet of the love-emotions. Nor are young people generally devoted at an early age to celibacy. The old set of artificial landed-aristocratic compromise ideals has been abandoned.

The ideals of the present age are at once more naturalistic and more romantic. They represent a return to the instinctive sexual cycle, within very ancient traditional limitations antedating the patriarchal system, but a return enriched by centuries of cultural experience. Naturalistic as our sexual ideals are, in comparison with those of the patriarchal system, they nevertheless owe much of their emotional variety and beauty to those centuries of desperate adaptation to human danger and poverty. But, having acknowledged this cultural indebtedness to the patriarchal past, we may proceed to discriminate between what belongs to our age and what accidentally survives among us.

Our actual ideals, if we have the liberty to construe them, appear to demand that John and Jane shall marry only because they have found out in courtship that they love one another deeply enough to live together for the rest of their lives in domestic intimacy, with the children of their love; that they live together in the normally exclusive sexual intimacy of lovers, which of course applies as much and as completely to John as to Jane; that they continue their relationship because of their love for each other and for their children, because of their wish to fulfill the responsibilities of love—but not for property reasons, or social reasons, or fear of punishment, or inability on the part of Jane to make a living otherwise; and if these conditions after prolonged and honest efforts at adjustment cannot be met in their marriage, if the relation proves unable to maintain itself by its own inner emotional strength, but is found to be emotionally intolerable, our ideals permit that it be formally dissolved, with due provision for existing economic and social responsibilities (particularly as to children), and John and Jane left free—insofar as these economic and social responsibilities do leave them free—to enter into any other marital relationship which may seem to promise the inner emotional stability lacking in the former.

These ideals—if it is agreed that they are such—are all of a piece, but they are cherished with different degrees of warmth. The belief in divorce and re-marriage (quite aside from those whose patriarchal religion denies such a right, or grants it only under a different terminology) is held in a more or less shamefaced way, though liberally made use of in practice. This is not only because divorce contravenes the lingering patriarchal emotional prejudices and standards of respectability; it is also, apparently, because divorce implies a public failure for which it is felt that the other partner cannot have been wholly responsible—a failure for which the most innocent, injured and well-meaning partner must take some of the responsibility, if only in the matter of the foolish original choice. No such sense of public failure attaches to the mishaps of experimental courtship, however tragic these may seem at the time. That is because courtship has the privilege of being experimental; it is publicly conceded and privately felt by the young people themselves that they may have learned something from the heartbreaks of a courtship romance which turns out badly, something which should enable them to make a more appropriate love-choice in permanent marriage.

All this points to a significant psychological difference between courtship and marriage in our time. Courtship may involve an apparently complete emotional commitment to another person, and even a complete physical commitment—it may involve all but a complete social commitment; yet such private vows may be repudiated upon further experience of the relationship, not without reason, but if with reason then without social censure. Marriage, it is felt, carries with it no such freedom. It is not an experimental love relationship on more realistic sexual and domestic terms. It differs from courtship, which is the private search for and finding of a mate; it is the public fact of being mated. It has a kind of social finality about it, which refers of course to the fact that it is in marriage that children are socially privileged to be born. Courtship, then, is the search for a person with whom one can be deeply and long enough in love to warrant the begetting of children. And divorce, the breaking up of a sexual and domestic intimacy, is thus the confession of a failure or a mistake. It is evidently a makeshift, and psychologically not an ideal at all.

People, it appears, despite the divorce and re-marriage statistics, do not really want a succession of husbands and wives, a succession of marriages. They claim, rather, the privilege of learning by a previous failure or mistake how to make *now* what they feel to be a real marriage. If their wishes could at such a moment reconstruct the past, the former marriage would be transformed into some kind of pre-marital courtship experience, capable of teaching its lessons, but carrying no such social responsibilities as marriage does. Or in its simplest form the wish would run: 'I ought to have known then what I know now!' In a word, the educational period of experimental courtship was incomplete.

A completer experimental courtship period, and not really the makeshift of divorce, represents the wish of those who try marriage again after failure.

And if in the light of this wish we should now restate what appear to be the ideals of our time, they would run somewhat as follows: a courtship period in which one could learn what one needs to know about oneself and love, in order to effect a genuine love-choice—and then the life-long marriage made possible by such emotional knowledge. Such a statement of our ideals may be Utopian, but that is the privilege of ideals; and perhaps this ideal is not as impossible as it may seem. It involves no renunciation of the right of divorce to correct mistakes and liquidate failures, nor any disparagement of its propriety in such circumstances—still less any suggestion that it might ever become wholly unnecessary. It is hardly rash, however, to suspect that our present divorce-rate actually represents deficiencies in the preparatory educational period of experimental courtship, due to the fact that the patriarchal system did not provide any such period or desire any such education. When young people are brought up in the patriarchal way, they may (and often do) require a first marriage to teach them what they should have learned about love in premarital courtship.

§ 3. 'Purity' as the Victorian Disguise of Patriarchal Ideals

We will now consider the bringing up of young people, with reference to their needs of courtship, and the repressive influences of lingering patriarchal idealism. It has been noted that there is no deliberate or conscious intention on the part of present-day parents to inflict arranged marriage, homosexuality, prostitution-patronage, or lifelong celibacy upon their children. Nevertheless the early training of young people, inherited as it is from the patriarchal régime and designed as it was to prepare young people for such childish sexual careers, will be seen still doing its work in producing these psychological attitudes and in unfitting young people for the responsibilities of the adult sexual lives which in our society they are to be called upon to live.

Our age has not inherited its patriarchal morality directly from the frank Graeco-Roman world which understood its purposes and dared face its familiar facts. "We have hetairai for our delight," said Demosthenes in a public legal plea, "concubines for the daily needs of our bodies, wives in order that we may beget legitimate children and have faithful housekeepers." Catullus could introduce, into a complimentary marriage poem written to his friend Manlius, humorous jeers at the forsaken boy-'favorite'. "Your day is over, boy. You served well enough your master's turn, but playtime's done. Now it's Hymen that he serves. Turned up your nose at dairymaids, did you? Off with you to the barber! And you, scented bridegroom, they think you can't keep away from such; but just you show them!" The facts of prostitution and homosexuality, became, indeed, increasingly repugnant to sensitive minds in the patriarchal era; and insofar as people could not persuade themselves that these were trifling faults or follies of youth, they preferred to ignore, forget, or deny their existence. The later Greeks and Romans had already begun to pretend that such practices didn't exist among really nice people. Hypocrisy was rendered as a tribute by the patriarchal system to the austere maxims of pagan philosophy, and presently of the Christian religion. But the facts of patriarchal life were not altered by such a censorship, even in its most rigid Victorian form. Victorian morality consisted largely in ignoring, forgetting or denying the homosexuality which still existed in the sexually-segregated schools, the prostitution which still flourished as the solace of masculine youth, the adultery which was necessary to maintain permanent landed-property marriage. Victorian morality was thus a compromise by the triumphing middle class with the decaying aristocratic régime. The aristocracy could more or less frankly acknowledge the social mechanisms necessary to its existence. But these were not necessary to middle-class rule and they were formally and ostensibly repudi ated; but the repudiation went no further—it was a repudiation in the realm of wishes and not in the realm of facts.

Yet the middle class did undertake to extend the patriarchal ideal of celibacy in a special way. Permanent celibacy was almost as repugnant to the middle class as homosexuality or prostitution; hence its Protestant hostility to celibate religious orders, and its wholesale destruction of their privileges. But celibate chastity could be applied as a stop-gap to replace homosexuality and prostitution before marriage. Such was the Victorian theory—a new idea in Europe, at least as applying to men. Various non-religious incentives were provided to encourage youth to the practice of premarital chastity. One, and a sufficiently realistic one, was fear of venereal disease. This negative incentive, as we have plenty of evidence to show, was not generally sufficient to produce results in actual conduct. Another, and a highly idealistic incentive, was that of 'waiting for one's true love'. Since, however, society (still playing the patriarchal game) might not recognize the love as 'true', and could dismiss the discovery lightly and contemptuously as 'calf-love', this attempt at inculcating a temporary and self-determined male celibacy was generally regarded by masculine youth as a shabby cheat. It was dangling in front of the donkey's nose a bundle of hay which was to be taken away from him at the journey's end.

Still another ideal incentive consisted in the inculcation of the ideal of 'purity' or absence of sexual emotions, hitherto held to be a feminine virtue, as the proper state of all young people. It might seem that this promised little success. Men were socially trained to require such 'purity' of their womenfolk, but women were not trained to demand it of men. They did not ever in large numbers demand it as a pre-marital virtue in men; they were more inclined to laugh at it. Moreover, there was no way of punishing young men for pre-marital 'impurity'. Nevertheless, in the Victorian era, in the middle class, and in Protestant countries, the ideal of youthful 'purity' gained a great vogue.

It is necessary to point out the geographical and temporal limitations of the 'purity' ideal. Its home was Protestant middle-class England. It was in contradiction with the dogma of 'original sin', and its acceptance on the Continent was not extensive. It was, moreover, of such a nature as to seem silly to the aristocratic classes, and to the poor a beatific state practically impossible of achievement. It thus tended to be restricted to a part of the middle class, chiefly in England. America was still culturally an English colony in the 19th century. As rapidly as pioneer conditions permitted, English manners and morals were imitatively taken over. The old rural North European courtship custom of 'bundling', for example, was preached and mocked out of existence. But pioneer conditions long encouraged early marriage, and thus left little or no room or need for the operation of the 'purity' complex as a device for controlling youthful behavior. Gradually, however, this English middle-class ideal was taken over, along with other British manners, and it spread democratically throughout the population. The absence of fixed classes or castes in America, the absence of any landed aristocracy to resist middle-class influences, and the later rapid urbanization of rural standards, gave an unusual degree of uniformity to American manners. So that, at a time—in the early 20th century—when the frightful effects of the 'purity' complex were being discovered in English life, it was still uncritically accepted in American homes. In England it was being subjected to a destructive and largely aristocratic criticism, and lost its moral authority in an overwhelming cynical reaction. In America it has been subjected to a slower skeptical disintegration. We are in America still too near the pioneer early-marriage period to believe in such prolonged infantility as the 'purity' complex provides for youth. Moreover, the middle-class ideal is too definitely attached to normal sexuality to be quite comfortable in the teaching of moral refinements which smack of religious celibacy. Nevertheless, in a half-hearted and almost hypocritical way, because they knew no better method of controlling youth, American parents also have preached 'purity' to their children—with disconcerting results which are now being dealt with by psychotherapists. Historically the 'purity' ideal has been of small scope and short duration; the world at large has preferred to control the behavior of young people by the cynical older patriarchal methods of sexual segregation and punishment. But the 'purity' ideal, so brief and partial in its reign, is important to us because it lies in our immediate social background. It is a late and decadent remnant of patriarchal morals, devastating in its psychological effects upon youth in a non-patriarchal society.

It is psychologically devastating because it involves a contradiction and a lie. It promises to lead away from homosexuality and prostitution-patronage, and it leads to them, without any of the older patriarchal justifications of such modes of sexual life. It promises to lead to the middle-class ideal of a happy and permanent marital life, and it makes this impossible on normal terms. 'Purity' is the old patriarchal homosexuality and prostitution, ashamed of itself, denying its actual goal, infinitely chagrined when it arrives there, and struggling forever in a vain pretense of being the opposite of what it is.

We must now define the 'purity' ideal more precisely. It is an ascription to young people past the age of puberty, clear up to economically adult life, of an infantile lack of erotic interest in the other sex. This prolonged infantilism makes unnecessary the troublesome segregations, chaperonage, and punishments of the older patriarchal régime. The young people can be magnificently and quite inexpensively 'trusted'. It also (in theory only, as we shall see) triumphantly eliminates the offensively ugly patriarchal safety-valve devices of homosexuality and prostitution for masculine youth. Outwardly it achieves a remarkable success.

Some of its apparent successes, however, are due to the fact that its influences are not operating and that other influences are operating. Thus, when the goal of matehood is clearly in sight and the path to it not blocked by insurmountable obstacles, the heterosexual emotions are instinctively and cautiously as well as recklessly selective; the responsibilities of love-choice involve their own delays before a decision which is felt to be final; the sexual union is associated with the responsibilities of permanency and of children, is not lightly or casually entered into, and may without any social coercion be voluntarily postponed until both man and girl are well assured that this is a permanent mating; while the essential and incidental processes of the later educational and the early economic career of the young man lend themselves readily to use as a part of the courtship-pattern of display, rivalry, and the love-chase. Our inherited sexual instincts brook a great deal of delay in the attainment of their goal, and take easily to the most elaborate and circuitous roads and efforts, provided that they appear to be and actually are roads and efforts leading to that goal. Thus young people who are not in the least 'pure'—*i.e.*, not at all lacking in normal adult erotic response to the attractions of the other sex—may nevertheless be remarkably 'chaste', without any outward compulsion, if selective courtship is sufficiently interesting and promissory of a not too long delayed marital happiness. This kind of unforced youthful 'chastity' (the word is put within quotation-marks, because it carries medieval meanings which do not strictly belong to the state here indicated) is not a tribute to the 'purity' ideal, but a proof that it has failed to be taken seriously. Such young people are using their normal sexual instincts to secure their happiness. 'Pure' young people have no normal sexual instincts to use, and invariably (without exception, so far as the records go) make sad failures of their attempts at love-lives.

For this 'purity', or absence in post-pubertal life of adult heterosexual emotions, though immediately convenient to parents in the management of their children, is not attained without a special kind of repressive education. The post-pubertal boy and girl are organic mechanisms driven by the power of endocrine influences through the selective courtship pattern of behavior toward mating and family life. These instinctive tendencies are so strong that only the most powerful of social influences can counteract them. And the social influence here used is the ancient patriarchal one of shame.

Under the early patriarchal régime boys were shamed out of being interested in girls, but were allowed to have homosexual love-affairs. They were shamed out of the wish to court respectable girls on their own initiative, but were allowed to compete for the favor of prostitutes. It was not assumed that they had no sexuality at all. It was not assumed even of those devoted to religious celibacy. Some of these might feel a 'vocation' or call to a celibate life; but others had to scourge and fast sexuality out of themselves.

The newer 'purity' ideal, however, was an assumption that young people—at least, nice young people—did not have any sexuality whatever, up to marriage. They were brought up to believe that right-minded and 'clean-minded' boys and girls did not have erotic emotions and desires. When they inevitably found that they themselves had such emotions and desires, they were ashamed. They were ashamed of themselves for having normal sexual emotions, and they repudiated these emotions, denied their existence, pretended to themselves that they were not the horrid little beasts which they seemed in fact to be. And these normal sexual emotions, thus psychologically blocked from any sort of appropriate fulfillment in action, regressed to a childish level and expressed themselves in a socially permissible exaggerated filial devotion to father or mother, or in exaggerated brotherly and sisterly affections. Boys were, indeed, commonly told to 'treat every girl as if she were your sister'. Innocent homosexual relationships, that is to say intense friendships with young people of the same sex, without much or any physical expression of affection—the old Greek Platonic love-affairs in a more thoroughly censored form—were encouraged. A basis was laid in the earlier years for the repudiation of heterosexual emotion by the discouragement and shaming of natural childish curiosities about sex—the very tone of the reply in which information was refused indicating that sex was a 'nasty' subject. Sex was thus associated with that other 'nasty' subject which is a normal matter of great interest in early childhood, the defecatory and urinary functions. Children were shamed out of their interest in that 'disgusting' matter, and they were encouraged to put sex in the same 'disgusting' category. No wonder, then, that these 'purity' teachings had their due effect. These 'clean-minded' little boys and girls, ashamed to have 'dirty' thoughts, grew up into 'clean-minded' young men and women ashamed to have normal heterosexual desires.

It was not intended, however, that they should remain permanently in this angelic state. They were not devoted to a lifelong religious celibacy. They were supposed, at the proper age and in the proper circumstances, to fall in love, get married, have children, and live happily ever after.

But it was not easy for angels to become suddenly human. Sex did not cease to be 'disgusting' when it was permitted in marriage. Often the later childish discovery that their own parents actually had such 'disgusting' relationships had been a frightful shock. The sexual realities of marriage were, to such a well-brought up young woman, often revolting. For the young man, trained to 'think of all women as he did of his mother and sisters', the incest-barrier was unconsciously operating as a barrier between him and his bride. The most thoroughgoing successes of the teaching of youthful 'purity' thus resulted in sexually frigid wives and impotent husbands.

The impotence and frigidity alike might be restricted to the marital relationship. The unconscious incest-barrier would exist only under circumstances of such moral or social respectability as called forth the automatic reflex of 'purity in thought and deed'; elsewhere, in non-respectable relationships, the sexual emotions could find expression. Thus for men there was a psychological outlet for the sexual impulse with non-respectable women, who might be prostitutes, or merely not of his own social class, the daughters of the poor, whom he was under no inner compulsion to 'treat as if they were his mother and sisters'. Here we have, as can be seen, kinds of behavior similar to those which were lawful and customary under the old patriarchal régime; but in modern society, in which they do not fit, they are not 'manners and customs', but neuroses.

Under the old patriarchal régime a similar distaste of refined wives for the sexual embraces of their husbands, often combined with what seemed a strange penchant for lower-class lovers, had been commented upon by satirists and moralists. They were especially attracted by professionally 'brutal' males—gladiators, bull-fighters, prize-fighters—or 'rough' and 'common' men in general. "Hippia, though wife to a senator, accompanied a gladiator to Pharos and the Nile, and the infamous walls of Lagos", wrote Juvenal; and the poet then remarked, with the effect of a parable, upon the different attitude of wives towards the rough facts of a sea-voyage in the company of their husbands and again in the company of their lovers: "If it is their husband that bids them, it is a great hardship to go on board ship. Then the bilgewater is insufferable! the skies spin round them! She that follows her adulterer, has no qualms. The one is sick all over her husband. The other dines among the sailors and walks the quarter-deck, and delights in handling the hard ropes." And why, asks Juvenal, is your fine lady so excited over her darling Sergius? He is frightfully ugly—"but a gladiator!" It is this that makes him to her "as beautiful as Hyacinthus".

In modern times, similarly refined wives, disgusted at respectable marital embraces, have been known to seek out those of lower-class, non-respectable or 'brutal' males, whether chauffeurs, bootleggers, gigolos, or, according to popular humor, icemen. In place, however, of the ancient attitude of moral scandalization, we tend now merely to say 'neurotic' of these inwardly compulsory sexual preferences, which, however much brazened out, give much distress and unhappiness to the women who are afflicted by them. They lack, in our eyes, the dignity of 'sin'. Under the patriarchal system they may have been the only opportunities afforded to wives for satisfactions not to be expected in arranged marriage. But under the modern system of courtship and love-choice, such satisfactions are to be had, in normal and unexaggerated form, in marriage; and not to be able to find them there, to be capable of finding them only in the society of degraded people or those not entitled to the respect due to a marital partner, is awkward, ridiculous, pitiable—and hence neurotic.

These fruits of 'purity', however, are doubtless not so opportune as the corresponding masculine forms of behavior. Wives suffering from this type of neurosis cannot all be Messalinas in practice and must often content themselves with reading those popular works of scandalous fiction which offer them rape and other pseudo-masculine brutalities in mere fantasy. Very common, however, according to medical and psychiatric literature, is wifely frigidity, the sexual childishness due to early teachings of 'purity' and sex-disgust. There is reason to believe that frigidity was quite common among wives throughout the patriarchal period; but being part and parcel of the sexual psychology of infantilism which upheld the patriarchal system, it was regarded as a virtue: it is in our modern times and in the light of our modern demand for adult behavior that it becomes ranked as a pitiable neurosis.

Common also and for the same reason is the inwardly compulsory male habit of extra-marital sexual gratification. Prostitution is said to be more patronized by married than by unmarried men. For 'purity', having failed miserably in its promise of marital happiness as the reward of an angelic youthful sexlessness, leads ultimately to the irresponsible sexual relationships which it was rashly guaranteed to obviate. It leads back into the patriarchal squirrel-cage treadmill, the vain effort to find love in its symbolic substitutes. Only, in our time, these patriarchal forms of behavior have lost their social validity and have become neurotic.

The 'purity' ideal in its heyday was accused by social critics of increasing the ranks of prostitution with middle-class girls, not forced there by poverty but by shame. The respectable Victorian girl, if we may believe the extensive fictional literature dealing with her, was likely to feel that an actual physical surrender to the normal impulses of sexuality, if not sanctioned by marriage, served to exclude her from the company of 'pure' women, leaving her no option as to her future life—she was 'bad', and she had to take up some form of prostitution, vulgar or polite. These cases, while lamentable in fact and touching in fiction, are perhaps of less social importance to us now than the spread, among respectable women who retained their 'purity', of what was essentially a prostitute psychology concerning marriage.

In a world in which women were thus at a social disadvantage, and in which a surrender to normal heterosexual emotions was likely to prove a fatal error, they learned to use their sexual attractions cold-bloodedly to enhance their social and economic positions. It was, under the socially acceptable guise of 'purity', the ancient prostitute trick which we have seen the experienced hetaira Ampelis teaching the 18-year-old Chrysis, new to her profession: "If you want to make a man wildly in love with you, let him see that you can do without him." It is an instinctive feminine wile, used here in an exaggerated way for economic purposes. The Greek hetaira dared not let her emotions run away with her in a world in which women were so much at men's mercy; no more did the Victorian Miss. The Greek hetaira slept with other men to show her indifference; the Victorian Miss showed her indifference still more conclusively by seeming to be an angelic being to whom the idea of sexual surrender to any man was unthinkable—until the proper price was paid. In both cases sex was used as a means to an economic end. That is prostitution psychology.

It would be idle to blame women for behaving that way in a world in which they faced ruin as the penalty of a misstep—faced it so truly that 'ruin' became the common term for sexual surrender to a man outside of marriage. It was not neurotic for Victorian damsels thus to use their 'purity' as a prostitute uses her charms, to gain some degree of security. But in a world in which honesty is increasingly required in relations between the sexes, not least of all in the courtship period, the lessons handed down from Victorian grandmothers are increasingly useless and mischievous to young women because they unfit them for making honest and happy marriages. It is not now a socially approved practice for a girl to 'capture' a man whom she does not love as a husband; there are now more respectable ways of making a living. It is increasingly felt that what she owes to herself is to find a mate whom she can love and live with happily. She cannot do this without being emotionally honest with herself and with the men among whom she will find her mate.

Love has its own instinctive evasions and playful deceits to gain its own ends of increasing attraction and stimulating pursuit—its path is not the short and narrow path of intellectual truth, but a sufficiently devious one; yet love has its own kind of truth to emotional purpose, which it must follow if it is love. The profound and fundamental feminine distrust of men is still a prostitute's necessity; but it is more and more a barrier to women's happiness in normal life. Distrust of the other sex, and of one's own sexual emotions, is, however, an essential part of the ideal of 'purity'. The teaching of 'purity' to girls trains them only for a prostitute-like bargaining for social security with their bodies in arranged marriage, a thing no longer respectable.

To the extent, then, that 'purity' is still inculcated in girls to-day by well-meaning but mistaken parents, it trains them to be neurotic prostitutes, gold-diggers, or alimony-hunters; but it unfits them to be happy wives.

§ 4. The Difference Between Neurosis and Psychic Health

We must pause to emphasize once more the difference between neurotic and non-neurotic behavior. The difference is, as Freud has pointed out, "entirely a practical one, which is determined by the available capacity for enjoyment and accomplishment retained by the individual".

There is in our discussion no intention to regard any kind of behavior as neurotic in itself, without respect to the social background. Homosexuality, prostitution-patronage, and the other kinds of behavior here under review, are not neurotic in their proper patriarchal setting, where they involve no mental conflicts. They may be silly, cruel, and otherwise offensive. But the question of whether they are neurotic depends upon whether they are such compromise formations issuing from mental conflicts as are bound to impair social usefulness and personal happiness; and that depends in turn upon the behavior-code of the epoch (see Chapter XVI, § 1).

Marrying without love, courting prostitutes, keeping mistresses, scattering bastards and leaving them to their fate, and indulging in polite adultery, were patriarchal norms of conduct—are still patriarchal norms of conduct in patriarchal countries. However preposterous and undesirable they may seem to us, these practices had their sufficient social justification within the structure of patriarchal society. That was the way the patriarchal system worked. These practices could only become neurotic as the result of fundamental economic changes, which result in withdrawing social justification and approval from them. They are nowadays neurotic only insofar as they hamper social usefulness and prevent personal happiness.

Perpetual celibacy and chastity, for example, are not neurotic insofar as they still find shelter and justification in old patriarchal religious institutions, or in newer social-service formulas on the same model, which enable the celibate to be comparatively useful and happy. We are entitled, if we wish, to despise such ways of being useful, to smile at such ways of being happy; but we are not entitled to dismiss as neurotic any such usefulness and happiness as may be found to exist. The plain fact of our age, however, is that it does not afford such shelter and such justification to large numbers of celibates. Monasteries and nunneries are no longer centers of learning and art; no longer to any considerable extent avenues to power. So that most celibates are nowadays unable to feel proud of their celibacy. Nor is chastity in our middle-class world a permanent treasure; it is in general, in adult life, felt as a disability. The late patriarchal institutions which gave an honorable shelter and a real social function to celibacy and chastity have dwindled to a minor scope in modern society. Most of the world's work is now so arranged as to have simple sexual incentives and rewards in monogamic family life. It is increasingly true that the realm of social effort is comparatively meaningless to such people as are not appealed to by these incentives.

The same argument may be made with regard to prostitution and prostitution-patronage. There are still submerged elements of our modern population who take these for granted as ways of life. To the behavior of individuals in that situation, it would be ridiculous and unjust to apply the term 'neurotic'. They have no choice of a more normal kind of sexual life; and in these symbolic substitutes for love they get the best satisfactions which life has to offer them. But with the growth of western civilization, these submerged elements of our population are dwindling, and our generalizations apply more and more universally.

Our middle-class industrial and trading system (except in some of its less modern or more piratical forms of industrial exploitation, as for example in 'seasonal' labor, cattle-herding, lumberjacking, the manning of ships, and a few others) takes a universal marriage and family life for granted, and is built directly around these institutions as a center. And not only does the modern system work best with a population which conforms emotionally to this sexual arrangement, but it is affected injuriously by almost every personal maladjustment in the sexual realm. The man who is happily mated and takes satisfaction in his family life is found to be the man who pays his debts, the man upon whom an extension of the credit system unprecedented in history can be built up. The disruption of an individual family represents almost invariably a series of economic losses and injuries to others. Marital disruption represents unpaid bills, loss of efficiency in industry, an addition to the turn-over cost of labor, and it may mean among the economically insecure part of the population a temporary or permanent problem of vagrancy, as well as possibly requiring social assistance for the wife and children. When a poor family breaks up, it may take, as social workers have learned, the efforts of half a dozen state and social agencies, the court of domestic relations, the juvenile court, pensions and institutional aid, to repair the social damage. The institutional care of deserted children has been found in certain instances to take ten times as much money as was required in wages to keep the family going. Juvenile crime has also to be added to the bill. The fundamental importance of domestic and family happiness in our middle-class industrial and trading régime can hardly be overestimated.

And it is for these among other reasons that the patriarchal remnants of homosexuality, prostitution, polite adultery, and other forms of infantile sexuality are socially inconvenient—so much gravel in the delicate machinery of modern economics, so many obstructions in the realm of normal social expectations. In being such, they impair the social usefulness of the individual.

And in lacking their ancient social justifications, they afford no plausible grounds for the individual self-respect which is essential to happiness.

A single comparative illustration will be given before we proceed. The young man who is 'crazy about a girl' finds that it makes a difference to society-at-large, and to his relations to that society, whether the girl is a night-club prostitute or a respectable girl who is a possible marital mate. Under the patriarchal scheme the prostitute-affair would have been approved or taken for granted. In our modern world it is the courting of a possible wife that is approved or taken for granted. Thus if the young man day-dreams at his work, his faults will be the more readily forgiven by a considerate employer, if his mooning falls into the category of approved courtship. The same day-dreaming, but of a kind more remote from and hostile to the realities of his life, will in itself arouse his employer's alarm and distrust, and these will be confirmed if it is found that he is leading an 'irregular' life. Day-dreams which are a part of love in the world of reality will presumably lead to socially approved conduct—to becoming, as a married man, a steadier and more ambitious worker. Those day-dreams, on the contrary, which are part of a love-affair that is an escape from the world of reality or a defiance of it, may lead to unsocial behavior—not impossibly to theft, discharge, vagrancy, and violent crime. Prostitution being no longer taken for granted as an essential part of our social system as an adjunct to respectable marriage, the young man who has opportunities for play with and courtship of respectable girls but finds the society of prostitutes preferable, is to-day more and more suspect of being psychologically limited in some way, inwardly barred from normal sexual relationships and ultimately unassimilable in normal social life. He is suspected, not any more of 'sinfulness', but of being neurotically afraid of the realities of normal sexual life. A case in point from the psychopathic records of a criminal court:

This 20-year-old youth had never taken any interest in girls. He had dutifully accompanied his sisters to parties, and had obligingly served as an escort for their girl friends. He was a very quiet, a steady, well-behaved (and perhaps we may say an exceptionally 'pure') young man, having given "little thought to girls". His business duties brought him in contact with a man who was the proprietor of a road-house; going there as the man's guest, he became acquainted with a prostitute employed as an entertainer. (From this point our own interpretations and comments will be italicized.) *The normal enterprise required in courting respectable girls, a kind of enterprise which he lacked, was not necessary here;* she made the advances. *The barriers of his sexual timidity being thus broken down,* he "began to make love to her madly." He also "spent money lavishly upon her, and in a few weeks had dissipated all his savings. *Spending money on a girl is in the realm of normal courtship socially approved; and in that realm it need take no exaggerated form. Here, however, because money-spending had to serve in lieu of the courting enterprise which he did not possess, his need of this symbolic gesture of possession became egregious and impossible to satisfy by any realistic means.* He "took to borrowing and soon found himself heavily in debt." *Prostitute-love did not make him more ambitious; on the contrary,* he "neglected his work," and "soon became demoted and finally discharged by his employer." *Because this was a socially disapproved kind of love,* he failed to find any sympathy at home: "His family scolded and punished, and he very soon became ostracised by the rest of his family." Being now without a job and without any realistic means of getting money, *he was free to dream of getting it in large sums by quick action; and being unable to think of going to the girl without money,* he planned and executed two gasoline-station robberies one night: He was caught, fortunately before he had blundered into murder. He showed some "feeling of relief at being caught". *He was waking up from his dream.* In what happened further he was very fortunate. Instead of being sent to prison for from ten to thirty years, he "was placed on probation, a position procured, his family given some instruction upon the psychology of adolescence, and arrangements made for taking care of his debts." Two years later we find him (*normally*) in love and engaged to be married, twice promoted at his work, and with a large savings account.

This instance serves incidentally to illustrate the circuitous routes by which neurotic people often arrive at adulthood; but it is given here in order to illustrate the factual character of the word 'neurotic' in relation to modern prostitution-patronage. 'Neurotic' is a specifically descriptive, not a merely disparaging term. It is not a new way of saying 'bad' or 'immoral'. The boy was neurotic in his original lack of interest in girls, neurotic in his 'purity'; this was, although not at the time perceived to be such by his patriarchally-minded family, a limitation upon his usefulness and happiness. It was merely a later stage of this neurosis—not an inevitable later stage, but one of several that were possible—when he fell in love with a prostitute, lost his job, and committed a crime. The early 'purity', the later prostitute-patronage, were manifestations of the same neurotic maladjustment to reality. If we speak, then, of prostitution-patronage as neurotic, it is not by way of using scientific terms to express a moral disapproval, but to indicate the fact of maladjustment in the realms of social effort and personal happiness. In a world which increasingly grants instinctive courtship and love-choice to men and demands normal sexual happiness as a stabilizer of marriage and of family life, the preferential or compulsory resort to prostitution is increasingly found to be a neurotic evasion of life's realities.

We shall next show this to be true also of polite adultery.

CHAPTER V

PATRIARCHAL CUSTOMS BECOME MODERN NEUROSES
(*Continued*)

§ 1. Polite Adultery as a Modern Neurosis

The term 'polite adultery' will be used here to indicate any extra-marital sexual relations which involve *a tacit or express agreement that they are not to be taken seriously.* Polite adultery is not intended as the beginning of, or as an experimental approach to, any permanent and socially recognized mating between the two lovers. *Polite adultery recognizes the permanence of the existing marital relationships of the partners, and promises not to disturb them.*

The term thus usefully serves to distinguish such emotionally evasive and irresponsible relationships from unconventional matings in which all the emotional and social responsibilities are accepted by both partners, but in which legalization is for any reason actually impossible or socially unnecessary. The term also *excludes* the confused experimental approaches of unsatisfactorily married people toward a new and real mating. And it *excludes* impulsive and emotionally sincere surrenders to extra-marital sexual attractions, the emotional importance of which may after the fact be found too slight to interfere with existing marital relationships, but which it is presumed would be followed by honest matings if they continued to seem emotionally important.

In practice the classification may not be easy. A relationship may be polite adultery for one of the partners, and for the other an attempt to find a real mate. A relationship may begin as polite adultery, but become serious and lead to a marriage. Or it may begin in emotional sincerity and through loss of courage on the part of one or both of the lovers they may then accept the limitations of polite adultery. The distinction is one of inner purpose and outward tendency.

Other extra-marital sexual relations tend, not always successfully, and sometimes through the paths of crime, toward an openly acknowledged mating. *Polite adultery tends, by its secret gratifications, to make possible a continuance of emotionally unsatisfying marital arrangements.* It was held by the aristocratic code—and is still so held by such surviving intellectual relics of the patriarchal régime as Count Keyserling—to be more honorable for a wife (the husband's divagations being taken for granted) to seek sexual and romantic satisfactions in adultery, than for her to break up an unhappy marriage. It is a pre-adult code suited to the necessities of landed-property marriage. But *it definitely implies arranged marriage, and contentment in quasi-infantile and irresponsible sexuality,* such as has become increasingly incompatible with modern self-respect. It represents only a symbolic and unrealistic attainment of adult sexual aims, and its childishness has no longer any social necessity to recommend it. Like homosexual love, like prostitution-love, adultery-love becomes increasingly a neurotic trait, insofar as it represents a personal inability to adjust to the existing opportunities afforded, however clumsily and painfully, by divorce, for real mating in marriage. As a mode of evading emotional realities, and a socially disapproved one, it interferes with the usefulness and happiness of the individuals who are inwardly compelled to its usages.

To be sure, imaginative literature has a vested interest in adultery-love and a traditional duty of defending it against current morality and law. A story-teller such as the present writer may not without loss of caste appear to join forces with the custodians of law and order in any attack upon the desperate makeshift happinesses of oppressed human beings. If it were true that we in our day had wholly escaped the patriarchal past, if divorce and remarriage were really possible to all unhappily married people, and still more if they had ever really had a chance to grow up emotionally to a point of being able to make healthy love-choices in marriage, then story-tellers might with a better professional conscience make use of the psychological apparatus which finds these furtive snatches at illusory happiness in polite adultery to be usually neurotic. The psychologist, however, is under no such professional disabilities; having found the patriarchal-type marriages neurotic when they persist into our age, he has no hesitation in finding equally neurotic the secret holidays by which patriarchal-type marriages are maintained and made tolerable.

It may be noted also that the story-teller's professional hostility to law and order, particularly in the sexual realm, is one which has been exacerbated by centuries of the patriarchal tyranny. It was in a world in which marriage tended to be a biological monstrosity that he learned to romanticize adultery. But our modern world has increasingly permitted to legal marriage the biologically normal freedoms which gave beauty and dignity to adultery—its unforced love-choice, its emotional self-determination from beginning to end. Now that marriage is founded upon free choice, adultery is no freer; it is less free, in its polite forms, in that it must deny its seriousness, evade its responsibilities and turn its back upon its future. Marriage can now be more whole-hearted than adultery. It is now adultery that represents a tame compromise with the world. The romance of adultery was a gift of the patriarchal régime. Only when the world interposes its authority between Tristram and Iseult, only when Lancelot and Guinevere may not be husband and wife in reality—in a word, only when biological love is a social crime, is adultery poetic. The modern Tristram who does not ask Iseult to divorce King Mark and marry him, because he does not want to lose his cushy job as King Mark's secretary; the modern Guinevere who does not divorce King Arthur and marry her Lancelot because she does not want to lose her social position as King Arthur's wife—these in comparison with their originals are rather shabby heroes and heroines. Perhaps they are not so much afraid of giving up their present security; perhaps they merely do not believe that love lasts long enough to make it worth while. If art is to plead for them, it can scarcely be on old-fashioned romantic grounds. Different grounds must be sought, and H. G. Wells has undertaken to find them in one of his novels, *The World of William Clissold.* Clissold in explaining his own polite adulteries frankly renounces the desperate dignity and tragic beauty of medieval romance. "It is a fundamental convention in the romantic version of life that when a married woman takes a lover she prefers him to her husband. In three quarters of the illicit love affairs in such a great centre as New York, London, or Paris, this is not true. It is probably even less true than the converse proposition about men. And the mere suggestion to most of these modern women rakes that they might go off and live in blissful union with the lovers they have been adoring would, I believe, be quite sufficient to end the affair for them. I cherish no illusions about my relations to the goddesses for whom I have been a worshipped and worshipping god, dear friends though they have been to me. For only one of them have I been the anti-husband. For most, I have no doubt that if the husband's life or prosperity or pride had been seriously threatened I should have been sacrificed with about as much regret as, let us say, a once worn dinner dress that he found too frank and discreditable, or a pet dog he did not like."

What, then, is the specific appeal of these petty adulteries? Says Sir William Clissold in the novel: "I do not think these modern women want men very badly; they want love. Usually they are married women or women already possessing lovers. But their man is masterful and oppressive, or he is negligent and wandering in his attentions, or preoccupied and dull. Mr. Smith or Brown reminds our lady too plainly, too flatly, that she is just Mrs. Smith or Mrs. Brown. He ceases to make her a goddess for his adorations. In a life of thin, unexacting routine love also becomes a routine. She has no sense of glorious giving, no sense of self-escape. But when she steals away to a lover all that is changed. You can hardly call her an unfaithful wife, for when she steals away she is no longer a wife. She ceases to be Mrs. Smith or Mrs. Brown. That is the gist of the whole thing. As her lover ceases to be Mr. Jones. They both keep holiday from these commonplace verities. They go out of the world. She becomes as much a goddess as Diana visiting Endymion. As Mrs. Brown she would no doubt be betraying Mr. Brown, but as Diana in a secret cave remote from the things of everyday life she betrays nobody. Restored to her self-respect, to her belief in her possible loveliness, she can return to her too casual and negligent husband with a pleasant sense of dignity preserved and equality restored." And again Sir William is made to refer to them as "little opium doses of love".

This candid defense is a sufficient characterization. It is all old patriarchal stuff—these are tame substitutes for the realities of love, comforting pretenses, masquerades, patchwork arrangements to console people for the emotional deficiencies of unsatisfying marriages. No doubt polite adultery makes such marriages more tolerable—provides the delights of illusion—serves as an opiate to deaden the ache of biological love-hunger—and is in these respects more exciting than the novel and the movies. No doubt also there are common emotional difficulties in marriage which may after a fashion be dealt with by indulging in extra-marital sexual adventures—not that these solve the marital problem, but they restore the wounded self-respect of people who lack the enterprise necessary to face and solve their marital problems. To conceive marital problems as insoluble is a patriarchal frame of mind. From a modern point of view it would be called a timid or cowardly frame of mind; evasion of such problems in extra-marital sexual adventure represents the highest flight of courage possible to that frame of mind.

Moreover there is no doubt that polite adultery may serve to provide a psychic liberation from loneliness—breaking down the barriers between mind and mind at the same time that it breaks down those between body and body, and giving (whatever else it may fail to give) the consolations and delights of spiritual intimacy, so often never achieved in the tame and cautious man-and-woman friendships permitted under the patriarchal régime. This use of polite adultery appears also to point to the emotional deficiencies of patriarchal marriage as its origin. It is a curious reflection upon the state of social relations between the sexes, and one explicable only in the light of patriarchal traditions, that men and women should be so much strangers to each other, so afraid of one another, that it is necessary for them to have sexual relations in order to be friends. We are reminded of the cautious approaches of strangers in savage life; in order not to treat one another as deadly enemies, it is necessary for them to go through a ritual ceremony designed to allay their reciprocal fears. In order really to trust one another, it may be necessary for them to drink a little of one another's blood—or anything to give them the sense of oneness.—

"They have looked each other between the eyes, and there they found no fault.
They have taken the Oath of the Brother-in-Blood on leavened bread and salt:
They have taken the Oath of the Brother-in-Blood on fire and fresh-cut sod,
On the hilt and haft of the Khyber knife, and the Wondrous Names of God."

It would appear that we are still savages in this respect; that patriarchal traditions have carried down to us the old savage fears which make men and women strangers to one another, and that the mutual communion of sexual passion is sometimes necessary in order to permit the free and generous outflowing of mutual tenderness and sincerity which we might suppose to be our human birthright. In so far as sexual relations may be necessary to dispel the fears that men and women have of each other, they may well be a civilizing influence in social relations; but the state of fear itself is a relic of patriarchal and of savage times, and it is maintained only by the patriarchal psychology of sexual segregation. In a world in which the only intimate relations between men and women were sexual, friendship between men and women would necessarily find in sexual adventure its only opportunities. It would not have seemed in the least strange in early patriarchal times, but it is now beginning to be a little amusing, that men and women should find themselves unable to begin a fearless and tender friendship except in bed.

Realistic literature, observation, and self-examination all reveal that modern people are not in general really at ease in their polite adulteries, however these may be explained and justified. Such modern people have usually discarded the notion of 'sin' in connection with extra-marital adventures, they often have elaborate intellectual justifications for their behavior, and they frequently have behind them a social group which amiably tolerates or even takes for granted their divagations. Yet they are quite generally found upon intimate acquaintance to be getting very little happiness out of their 'little opium doses of love', and they frequently give every evidence of being miserable and tormented men and women. That is because these essentially thwarted and irresponsible relationships cannot satisfy their deepest emotional needs. The result is that they behave inconsistently, sometimes with reference to the assumption that these are light and casual affairs, and again with reference to the deeper wishes the existence of which they have just denied. They are constantly having their feelings hurt by the failure of a 'light' lover to take the relationship seriously; yet if he takes it too seriously they are alarmed and pained. They are, in fact, governed by contradictory motives; they are trying to find love, and at the same time to evade the emotional responsibilities of love.

Patriarchal society, accustomed to the emotional waste of these proceedings, to the social and economic inconvenience which they cause, and regarding them as inevitable, has established in aristocratic manners and inculcated in aristocratic art a convention of tolerance of these as 'human weaknesses'—a tolerance practiced to the extent that segregation of the sexes has failed to achieve its purpose and punishment by murder is socially impracticable. Middle-class society, unable to reinstitute the segregation of the sexes and unwilling to countenance private murder as a punishment for adultery, has nevertheless never been content to regard adultery as inevitable. Even where its own device of social ostracism has quite broken down, there remains in our middle-class world a shadow of emotional disapprobation, even in its most worldly tolerance, with regard to men and women who find themselves unable to live happily within the marriages of their choice and who play at adultery in the patriarchal fashion.

There is to be noted an interesting discrepancy between the general social attitude at its most tolerant toward adultery-love, and that of most of our fashionable novelists and poets, who by contrast are fulsomely sentimental. Our novelists and poets, following patriarchal tradition, still generally seek to make tragic heroes and heroines out of adulterous wives and husbands; in order to do so they have to pretend that the ancient patriarchal barriers still exist and that there are no divorce courts—or they have to take the mere frowns of neighbors and relatives at the idea of divorce with the seriousness which was appropriate in patriarchal times when those neighborly and family frowns represented law and order and were the threats of disgrace and death; all this gives to the writings of such novelists and poets a quaintly old-fashioned air. Sometimes these writers seek to gloss over this out-of-date and timid sentimentalism with an aristocratic and homosexual cynicism, drawn from patriarchal idealism in general and sometimes echoing the Fathers of the Church, concerning the emptiness of love, the futility of the flesh and the vulgarity of sex. Current public opinion is considerably more robust; even upon the level of amused gossip it concerns itself with the psychological realities of these situations.

One more aspect of polite adultery may be briefly commented upon here. There are instances in which married couples by open agreement indulge in extra-marital sexual affairs, and regard themselves as superior to and more modern than other people because they not merely tolerate their divagations in each other but give them sympathy and encouragement. They pride themselves upon their absence of jealousy. In some instances these situations represent an unwilling adaptation of either the husband or the wife to the other's wishes, the theory of freedom being devoutly proclaimed as a means of 'saving face'. In some instances the arrangement is no doubt mutually satisfactory. It is probably more socially satisfactory that people thus halted in an infantile and homosexual stage of psychological development should thus adapt heterosexual marriage to their inner wishes, than that they should over-compensate in the direction of heterosexuality by homicidal jealousy. But these exaggerated freedoms, like the exaggerated demands for exclusiveness of morbidly jealous husbands and wives, are symptoms of pre-adult sexuality. Why, indeed, should they pride themselves upon their lack of jealousy? They are attaining an inner and usually unconscious satisfaction of their homosexual wishes by their mutual infidelities. They are not consciously homosexual, and hence do not seek a direct satisfaction of their wishes through overtly homosexual practices; the indirect union with others of the same sex which they achieve by their liberal marital arrangements subserves the same wish in a symbolic fashion. Their 'modern' marital understanding effects a socially discreet compromise between the respectable appearances of ordinary heterosexual marriage and their unconscious wishes, which could not be gratified without more of a break with social conventions. When conventions demand heterosexuality, and the inner wish is homosexual, then heterosexuality must be used to serve the homosexual wish. This false heterosexuality, this unconscious homosexuality disguised as heterosexuality, is to be found at the heart of many sexual arrangements which are put forward by their practitioners as ultra-modern.

§ 2. Tolerance the First but not the Last Word of Science

It may be said by some readers: 'If this is Science, then it is just as intolerant as Religion ever was.'

This supposed intolerance consists partly in pointing out that certain unconventional sexual freedoms, which the individuals concerned prefer to think of as peculiarly modern and enlightened, are really very ancient; that they corresponded precisely to aristocratic patriarchal conventions which had their raison d'être in the maintenance, by love-without-marriage, of the institution of marriage-without-love. It is perhaps unkind to deprive people of an intellectual rationalization of their inwardly compulsory practices, to deprive them of the sense of dignity and superiority which these rationalizations have afforded them. It is particularly unkind in these days, when such rationalizations have gained considerable intellectual currency. On the principle of making an emotional living by taking in each other's washing, the rationalizers have handsomely assured each other in print that their stale old patriarchal compromises are splendidly modern. It would doubtless be more kind not to intrude cold historical facts into this warm atmosphere of consolation. But such comfort is the function of Art, and perhaps of Religion, not of Science.

But Science is charged with a further intolerance in ascribing the anachronistic practice of these patriarchal conventions to 'unconscious homosexuality'. And here, it is true, modern psychology may accidentally and unintentionally lend itself to the service of religious intolerance. *People whose unconscious homosexuality takes the form of an overcompensation in the direction of an exaggerated fear and hatred of homosexuality, and an intense intolerance of every departure from what they have assured themselves to be the safe norm of monogamic marriage,* may hail the attempts at scientifically descriptive nomenclature in modern psychology as so much justification of their anxieties, and may use these terms as clubs and stones wherewith to hunt down others whose unconscious homosexuality takes a different form. This is unfortunate, but it is not easily to be helped at this stage of public education. Except for such explanatory passages as this, and perhaps in spite of them, the present work would be, or will be, taken as furnishing helpful hints to sexual-heresy hunters. Its aim, however, which is to affix the correct descriptive term of 'unconscious homosexuality' to certain patriarchal conventions, cannot be fulfilled if certain ostensibly modern unconventions are not shown to be identical with them.

It is true, however, that the ascription of homosexuality, unconscious or otherwise, to individuals, has an emotional color in the public mind not intended to be conveyed by the psychologists who use the term. This emotional coloration is a relic of an old historical situation. The later patriarchal religions, notably Christianity, found homosexuality associated in overt forms, along with human sacrifice, with the earlier religious cults which occupied the transition era between savage and patriarchal life; and they persecuted it with fire and sword, though they eventually made their own terms with it, chiefly by accepting it in its sublimated and more or less socially useful forms. The accusation of homosexuality was once almost identical with the accusation of heresy; and people have been burned at the stake for it. One of the vulgar terms for overt homosexual practices is derived from the name of a medieval heretical sect by whom it was supposed to be practiced. The lingering brutalities of social intolerance toward homosexuality are partly the remnants of that ancient religious struggle; while the mingled self-pity and self-superiority traditionally found among overt homosexuals, the curious mingling of smugness and martyr-like airs, may perhaps owe something to those ancient fires. It would be a pity if the patiently analytic and descriptive efforts of modern psychological science were used in order to renew these ancient persecutions. But at least it may be said that modern psychological science does not propose to send anybody to the stake, or excommunicate anybody. All modern psychological science can do is to offer its help in the understanding of human nature. And in finding an unconscious homosexuality in various quasi-heterosexual arrangements, it is furnishing us the knowledge which will be for many the means of achieving normal happiness. But it cannot enforce normal sexuality upon mankind; it can only help individuals to stop fooling themselves.

Finally, the charge of intolerance against modern science comes to this: that it proposes to iron out all the variety of human nature, and force all individuals into the same presumably 'normal' mould. So gigantic a task, and one requiring so many centuries of effort, is out of the question. Nor do those who are undertaking to apply modern psychological knowledge in education, correction, and other administrative ways feel that they know enough about the possibilities of human nature to have a fixed pattern in their minds to which all individuals should conform. It is true that in dealing with unhappy and maladjusted people, whether children, adolescents or adults, they find themselves able to restore many of them to happiness and usefulness precisely by aiding them to achieve adult heterosexual attitudes. In this sense modern psychological science is engaged in a campaign against infantilism, including homosexuality in its conscious and unconscious forms, and including every other form of infantilism which is found to interfere with adult usefulness and happiness. And weak though these efforts are when matched against the gigantic forces of tradition, poverty, ignorance and the economic injustices handed down from the patriarchal world, yet it may be said that modern psychological science offers its aid in that war. It is not in love with the world as it stands or with human nature as it is found, and it does conceive immense possibilities of change. More than one institution still standing from patriarchal times will fall before that war is over, before our modern world has become really modern.

The tolerance against which modern psychology is supposed to offend is more often than not the defense-reaction of those who have some special privilege to defend, generally of an infantile nature. This may be in the realm of religion, property, or morals. Here it is the special moral privileges that appear to be in danger at the hands of science. The scope of this book does not permit us to deal extensively with overt homosexuality, or any of the other infantile perversions and substitutions and fetishes which clutter up the heterosexual impulses of individuals. But it may be said that tolerance toward them is the first word of modernity. We shall never accomplish our own modern social purposes in an atmosphere of intolerance. It was imperative, as we emerged from the baleful lights and grotesque shadows of the old struggle between patriarchal civilization and transitory barbarism, that there be an intelligent mediation between the misunderstood victims of these archaic infantilisms and their overcompensating misunderstanders, such as would reconcile them in a knowledge of their common humanity. This religious or artistic task was, so far as the intellectual world was concerned, nobly accomplished by Havelock Ellis, in his many-volumed *Studies in the Psychology of Sex*. There is not a sexual oddity which he has not labored to make us understand as an exaggeration of some aspect of normal human emotional life. He has thus become par excellence the teacher of tolerance to our generation. He has become our lay father-confessor. He has eased our minds of the burden of our sexual infantilisms by revealing their relation to the scheme of life. That has been good for us. It has constituted a tremendously valuable catharsis. Where patriarchal religion has turned away from the task and traditional art has blundered and failed, he has used the instruments of science to perform their function. But in concentrating so much upon matters where, it would appear, we are in need of spiritual consolation, he has inadvertently given to the intellectuals of our generation a one-sided notion of the scientific attitude toward sex. It is only since the balance has been restored by studies initiated under Freudian influences, that we can realize the curious absence in these volumes of any proportionate reference to family life. The fact that children are born and cared for does indeed make its appearance in those pages, but an inhabitant of another planet would gain no adequate notion of the central significance of that fact in our sexual arrangements. The *Studies* were, for that matter, written in the spirit of 19th-century intellectual revolt, at a time when the abuses of the disintegrating patriarchal family system had put 'the family' in disgrace; in the endeavor to escape from these tyrannies, the social facts were sought to be analyzed into disparate impulses. Thus we gain from the *Studies* a notion of sex as a variety of responses of the human organism to a variety of stimuli—not, as we currently understand it, as a series of reactions along a path of development from infancy to adult life. Hence it is that the accidental stopping places in this process of development have been given by the sage an importance which well-nigh if not altogether obliterates any view of the adult goal. Love as an impulse which finds a completer fulfillment in marriage and family life than in the excitements of courtship; courtship as an educational process preparatory to love-choice and mating; and the aberrations of homosexuality, fetishism and the rest as the results of an outward or inward blocking of the path of sexual development—these simple and obvious generalizations, so important to us now, are lost sight of. Perhaps the sage felt that they could be taken for granted; there were many to celebrate the joys of hearth and home, and all too few to dare give utterance to these other

"long-dumb voices,
Voices of innumerable generations of prisoners and slaves,
Voices of the diseas'd and despairing and of thieves and dwarfs,
Voices of cycles of preparation and accretion,
And of the rights of them that others * * * are down upon,
Of the deform'd, trivial, flat, foolish, despis'd,
Fog in the air, beetles rolling balls of dung.
* * * forbidden voices, * * *
Voices indecent by me clarified and transfigured."

True enough; and yet so impressively has the sage done his work that it perhaps needs now to be said that sex is, after all, not essentially homosexuality, or sadism, or fetishism, or undinism, or any of these quaint childish matters; it is first of all the biological impulse which brings men and women together in love and courtship and marriage and family relationships. And the modern attitude toward sex is not mere tolerance of its curious infantile divagations, but an understanding of this normal sexual cycle and of how it may be successfully and happily traversed without halting forever in its early stages or blundering off the track and being unable to find the way back. The modern attitude, that is to say, is one which recognizes that there is something to do for people after you have persuaded them to forgive themselves their silly little sins; something to enable them to find and enjoy the great normal sexual happinesses of mankind—now after long ages being more generally made available to them by our machine age—free courtship, love-choice, matehood and parenthood.

If modern science, then, seems intolerant toward the sexual peculiarities which we have learned not to be afraid of, it is not really so. It takes tolerance for granted and makes no special virtue of it. But if tolerance is read to mean 'Leave people as they are—give your blessing to all the cruelties and absurdities of infantile sexuality'—then those who are using modern psychological science must confess that they are, indeed, trying to change people, trying to rescue them from their quagmires and blind alleys and set their feet upon the path toward biologically normal usefulness and happiness. Is the physician intolerant toward the sick man whom he desires to cure?

But the question may be put in this form: 'Is your modern psychological science so intolerant that it can recognize nothing but a psychic sickness in anything aside from the so-called normal biological path?' The answer is: 'No.' The question of psychic sickness—of neurosis—is, in the words of Freud, an entirely practical one, determined by the facts of personal misery and social uselessness in their degree. The questioner may be referred to the first section of the previous chapter, concerning Art and Heroism, and to the subsequent discussions there promised of the kinds of usefulness and happiness which lie aside from the simple biological path. Those who are unable or unwilling to adjust themselves to the biological cycle in which most people find their lives' satisfactions, have still the opportunity in our civilization of making themselves socially useful in unusual ways, and of deriving such happiness as they can from those achievements. In the sense in which they may be said to have been sick, they have thereby achieved their own kind of cure. Modern psychology wishes to learn from them; it does not propose to change the Hero and the Artist into something they do not wish to be. It is only to those who are failing in usefulness and happiness that its ministrations are offered. But our modern civilization is different from patriarchal civilization, and its demands in the matter both of Heroism and of Art will require special consideration when that point in our argument is reached.

Perhaps it is a mistake to interrupt our argument in order to reply to objections which may be advanced by those who anticipate incorrectly the conclusions at which it will arrive. In any case it is hoped that these replies have cleared the atmosphere of some doubts and suspicions, so that we may proceed.

CHAPTER VI

PATRIARCHAL VS. MODERN CHILD TRAINING

§ 1. 'House-Breaking'; and Shame

After these preliminaries we are perhaps in a position to discuss the origin and development of the patriarchal-family neuroses in our modern society.

Wherever we turn, to doctors, teachers or administrative officials, we find the maladjustment of individuals to our modern society ascribed to faults in their upbringing, to definite errors in their early education. The nature of these parental errors is now generally agreed upon. What we have to point out is that these errors are simply ancient patriarchal virtues out of place. In effect, however, these ancient patriarchal modes of education serve to halt emotional development in an infantile stage.

We will begin with what is perhaps the earliest problem with which parents have to deal—the 'house-breaking' of infants. Our simian cousins, it appears, solve their sanitation problem by occupying a family nest only for a single night, and then moving on to another; within a month or so the family (or horde) has made the rounds of its accustomed food-territory, and returned to the neighborhood of the old nest—now cleansed by wind, rain and insect activities. Köhler was unable to train his young chimpanzees in any habits of cleanliness with regard to their excremental functions; his punishments only increased their interest in their forbidden play. In contrast with the cat family, which lived in permanent caves and dens and had to keep them clean, the simians never acquired any instinctive habits of cleanliness in this respect. Man has no such instinctive habits; but when he commenced to live in caves or permanent habitations, it became necessary for him to enforce a code of cleanliness, which he appears to have done through a socially inculcated disgust at excrement. The earlier, then, that children could be taught such disgust, the more convenient it was for their elders.

The psychological development of the individual would, if not interfered with, carry his interests away from his own body. The effort to hurry this development by disgust is not without an inner psychological effect. The interests renounced in the realm of consciousness are retained permanently in the unconscious mind, and are expressed in symbolic form. Every savage tribe has some ceremonial dealings with filth, often in the practices of witchcraft and generally in medicine. The 'nasty' medicinal recipes which were handed down almost to modern times in Western civilization were derived from Egyptian medical practice, and date from savagery when filth had a magical value of its own. Scatological humor is another symbolic expression of these repressed infantile interests. By itself, and under social conditions in which sexual impulses had some degree of freedom, the anal disgusts appear not to have affected sexual attitudes.

When, however, in late patriarchal times, sexual interests and curiosities began to be severely repressed in children, the anal disgusts furnished a psychological basis upon which sexual shame was built up. Sexual and anal matters were thus in late civilized life confused, as apparently never in savage life. And because of the social requirements of infantilism in the patriarchal era, this infantile confusion of sexual with anal taboos was encouraged. Both within the loveless arranged marriages and outside in prostitution-love, it was better (for patriarchal purposes) if sex were held in contempt, regarded as 'dirty' and on the plane of defecation. The resultant sexual frigidity of wives did not matter; it was, indeed, approved as the correct attitude of a respectable or 'pure' woman. In sexual relationships outside of marriage, it made easier the psychic separation between the physical impulses of love and the emotional states of devotion and responsibility which lead to domesticity and family life. Sexual intercourse could be regarded as, for men, a vulgar necessity, having nothing to do with the mating cycle. And the anal disgust with which sex was viewed enabled the women who were the partners of these extra-marital indulgences to regard themselves as low creatures, the inferiors of 'pure' wives. All this fitted in with the economic and social necessities of the patriarchal régime.

Quite obviously it does not fit in with the economic and social necessities of the modern world, in which men and women marry for love and can only be held together in a domestic and family relationship by love. The 'purity' of the Victorian wife has become the neurotic frigidity of the modern wife—a sickness of which she is ashamed and which, if she can afford it, she turns to a psychiatrist to cure. If uncured her neurosis may lead her from one divorce to another, or through a nightmare of sexual disappointments and misadventures; it may mean the loss to her children of their father, through divorce or desertion, or the spoiling of their lives by domestic quarrels and scenes, and in any event it will mean the lack of an atmosphere of domestic harmony in which they can grow up happily and wholesomely. This ancient patriarchal virtue of sexual shame has become a modern neurosis.

It would doubtless be possible to keep the childhood training in anal disgusts, without any corresponding sexual disgusts; but so far as we know this is possible only by the savage method, to be observed to-day in Melanesia and Samoa for example, of over-compensating against disgust in the sexual realm by a social stimulation of childish curiosity and experiment in this direction. To us such savage children seem sexually precocious; and what is from the middle-class point of view a similar sexual precocity is to be found in Western civilization among backward agricultural populations and among the poorer urban working classes so far as these have not adopted middle-class standards. These sexual precocities in the form of early adolescent, pre-adolescent and childish sexual observation and experimentation, though shocking to the middle-class mind, may have under such circumstances a social value precisely in compensating in the sexual realm against anal disgusts. But this is at least doubtful.

This overcompensation by sexual precocity against the influences of anal disgusts is, in any event, a socially expensive one. It is responsible for a great deal of illegitimacy and the spreading of venereal diseases. Even if these problems could be solved, the difficulty would remain that sexual precocity runs counter to middle-class morale, and that in a democratic culture these practices cannot remain naïve, but because of their conflict with accepted mores becomes the occasions of neurotic maladjustment. It might be supposed that middle-class mores would change in this direction as they have recently shown some signs of doing, except that the educational requirements of our civilization call for free courtship rather than for free sexual relations in adolescence. The savage method of overcompensating in the sexual realm against the effect of anal disgusts, while not to be undervalued in its place, has inevitably a diminishing rôle in our civilization and cannot be regarded as a general social solution of the problem presented by the sexual-disgust neuroses.

On the other hand it is not necessary in our civilization to keep the anal-disgust education which so confuses and hampers our sexual development. Modern sanitation, urban plumbing, has made it increasingly unnecessary for us to use the savage mechanism of disgust in the house-breaking of children; and when we have dispensed with that savage mechanism we have no need for the savage overcompensation in the sexual realm. We can now deal with the early educational problem of domestic sanitation in an objective and unemotional way. This is now being done by intelligent middle-class parents. Children are growing up who are trained objectively in civilized manners in these respects, without any sense of disgust or shame in connection with any of their bodily functions. It is already observable that such young people display less interest in scatological humor; having no need of that more or less socially approved form of relief for repressed bodily interests, they do not find the mention of anal matters particularly laughable. This will be regretted by those who have found a field of social usefulness in so-called Rabelaisian humor —their audience is diminishing. In such young people, moreover, there is no foundation for sexual disgusts. They will be spared the frigidity and impotence, or the compulsion to find 'low' partners for the sexual act, which are among the consequences of sexual disgusts inculcated on an anal basis in childhood.

These repressed anal interests, furthermore, together with heterosexual shame-repressions, are the foundations of some forms of overt as well as of unconscious homosexuality. In adult sexuality the childhood diffusion of pleasure zones gives way to a specific kind of genital precedence; in homosexuality the development is halted in an infantile stage. To be technically exact this statement would have to take account of physiological details in both sexes which we must leave to books which deal with those matters. It is sufficient here to point out that the freeing of children from the burden of anal disgusts has in our civilization an enormously favorable effect upon their chances of adult happiness in love and marriage.

§ 2. Eating; and Compulsion

The two most important of the psychic mechanisms used by the patriarchal family in the training of children were shame and compulsion. Children were shamed or forced into certain socially approved patterns of behavior. We have discussed certain uses of the shame mechanism in connection with children's education in domestic sanitation. We will now discuss the use of the compulsion mechanism in regard to eating.

The problem of anorexia, or lack of appetite, does not arise in savage life, where the food supply is limited, and kept only with difficulty up to the level of necessity. A hand-to-mouth existence makes good appetites. In patriarchal times, when the food problem was solved, at least for the fortunate classes, by agriculture and by storage of supplies, appetite could be whimsical, uncertain and delicate—certain foods could seem repulsive. But any tendency on the part of children to display these tendencies only gave the patriarch an opportunity to exercise patriarchal discipline. The child's plate—as some people can remember—was filled, and he ate it empty under the stern parental eye; his gorge might rise but he ate the food and ate it all lest worse befall him in the way of punishment, which under the patriarchal régime could be frightfully severe. 'Finish your dinner.' 'Eat what is on your plate.' 'You will eat what the rest of us eat.' These were commandments not to be disobeyed.

Now, however, that frightfully severe punishments for children are out of vogue, the situation which they repressed emerges as a familiar problem of childhood, and special means have been sought to deal with it. The difficulty has been found to be largely psychic, found to lie precisely in the attempt to apply the patriarchal methods of compulsion. That is, minor physical causes produce a temporary lack of appetite which if ignored would soon disappear; but when food is anxiously pressed upon the child he develops a more or less permanent disgust for it; and the conflict between him and his parents becomes a trial of strength and a means of getting attention. The situation is exacerbated by parental anxieties over the child's health—anxieties which could not so easily arise in the large families characteristic of patriarchal times. The maternal care which in the patriarchal era had to be spread over the diseases and accidents of six, eight or a dozen children in the time left from cooking, baking, brewing, sewing, mending, washing, etc., is now in middle-class homes concentrated upon a few children or upon one. A kind of domestic military-executive capacity suitable for the family-regiment of former times is, without the former military punishments to effect enforcement of its decrees, brought to bear upon the new recruit, and the result is mutiny.

It is, however, more important to the small family that an individual child retain its health than it was to the large patriarchal family. There are certain food-values which it is imperative that a child should get, and when he fails to respond to 'Eat your vitamines, darling!' the modern parent is at a loss. In this situation our modern Medicine Men are called in, and they bewilder the parent by trying to teach her a new and non-patriarchal method of getting her children to eat the right foods. The new method is bewildering because it involves a complete repudiation of parental compulsion. It seems to the parent to consist of the wild anarchy of letting the child alone. It does, indeed, base itself upon the modern psychological assumption that a child's normal appetite is adequate to its needs, and that the way to restore an appetite to normality is to remove the special conditions, physical or psychic, which keep it from being normal. While thus dealing with origins it does not worry about the symptoms which are the effects of such causes; and by thus appearing indifferent to the symptoms, it bewilders those parental minds which are ignorant of causes and are accustomed to dealing only with effects.

An illustration of this modern scientific attitude toward the problem is furnished by an article by Dr. C. A. Aldrich, of the Children's Memorial Hospital in Chicago, on "The Prevention of Poor Appetite in Children". It may be quoted in some detail, inasmuch as it is not only an account of the new methods in dealing with this particular problem of anorexia, but serves also as a good description of these new psychological methods of influencing human behavior in every field. All that has been found out about the problems of children is being transferred rapidly to our human problems in general, as we shall see. Meanwhile, without losing sight of their literal application, let us take Dr. Aldrich's instructions on the cure of 'psychic anorexia' as constituting for our purposes a kind of parable on psychic maladjustment in general.

"Not only is this condition serious from the standpoint of the child's nutrition, but the oft-repeated battles at mealtime have a bad effect upon his mental equanimity. * * * How can a serene atmosphere surround a child who three times daily is urged, threatened, petted, spanked, or hectored into eating his meals? Not infrequently the parents, as a result of these trials, need psychiatric treatment more than do their 'won't eat' children. Possibly this is due to the fact that in this more than in any other behavior disturbance, the child is likely to have the upper hand in the strife. He can always secure the honors of the day by vomiting. * * * About five years ago, therefore, I began to try to raise a brood of youngsters who would be glad to eat.

"At the outset it was assumed that all animals are born with an appetite, and that the problem ultimately resolved itself into doing all those things which would stimulate this appetite, and omitting those that would tend to destroy it. From the first it was appreciated that psychic influences would probably play an extremely important rôle in prophylactic treatment, because appetite is largely a psychic function." The method is to begin in earliest infancy. Mothers and nurses are instructed "never to urge their children to eat, except under express orders", but to report refusal. On refusal being reported, they are told to reduce feedings and look for some physical upset, such as a cold. The traditional way of meeting such a situation is thus described: "Instead of reducing the diet, the mother became determined in her efforts to feed the baby, and from this unpleasant struggle over the bottle at a time when the child was physically not fit to eat, the child developed an aversion for food on a psychological basis. He first learned to associate unpleasantness with food. If left alone with appetite as a guide, the baby in a few days would have been ravenously hungry, and would have made up for lost time; but forcing him to eat gave rise to a psychological aversion that dulled the returning appetite, and the basis for a prolonged illness was established." Besides physical causes, such as colds and other infections, teething, car-sickness, and (physical) food idiosyncrasies, there were found to be psychic causes of temporary loss of appetite, including "change of attendant and the arrival of a new baby in the household of a hitherto only child".

Omitting various specific directions, we find that the children were taught to feed themselves as early as possible, and that "In the main, the child was humored as to choice of food. This is not to be interpreted as meaning that he was allowed to eat anything he pleased. But where there was a choice between two foods, the one that the child liked best was most often used. It was not considered advisable to make the child eat everything 'so that later on he would like everything', because in the writer's experience this really means that the child is more likely not to enjoy eating anything, the repetition of struggles resulting from insisting on especially disliked food tending to produce a psychological distaste for all food." On the other hand, sudden and marked changes in the character of food were avoided by such devices as giving the baby "an occasional bottle from birth, often enough so that they remembered the bottle as a friend, not a stranger"; and mixing vegetable with cereal, if the child at first objected to the transition, and giving cod-liver oil and orange juice "from the first weeks of life so that the babies could accustom themselves to the change early". Upon this foundation, it was insisted that "pitched battles over meals" be avoided, as "nothing could be worse for the child's nutrition than repeated emotional strife at mealtimes".

The difficulties in carrying out this regimen were found to lie in the parents, not the children. "Some undoubtedly tried to leave their children alone at meals, but just couldn't do it. Many parents are so constituted [we would add, by the patriarchal family tradition] that they have to see to it that what their children do is done *because* they supervise it. They need a lot of education. * * * In this community—as in many others, I suppose—when I began this work, practically all the 'enlightened' were dominated by the idea that children must be made to eat the definite set formulas prescribed by their physician, nurse, government-health bulletin, or what-not agent." [One is reminded of Plato's description of child-training: "he cannot say or do anything without their setting forth to him that this is just and that is unjust; this is honorable, that is dishonorable; this is holy, that is unholy; do this and abstain from that. And if he obeys, well and good; if not, he is straightened by threats and blows, like a piece of warped wood"—the patriarchal method of education.] "Instilling the ideas here presented", says Dr. Aldrich, "was, therefore, particularly difficult. It was hard to make people understand that I was doing this because I wanted my formulas to be eaten, not because I did not care what the children ate."

It will be equally hard to make people understand that modern psychological science, upon a foundation of healthy early habit, prescribes free and responsible choice in human behavior in general, because it wants certain results to follow, not because of indifference to results. It seeks to avoid continued parent-child strife over behavior problems because that is a way to secure bad and not good adjustment to adult standards of living. It wants to avoid creating psychological distaste for the necessary food of life. It wants to protect and maintain our instinctive appetites. It is not afraid of those appetites on the one hand, nor on the other does it believe that they have to be enforced by social compulsion. It believes that the social purposes of our times are such as can be harmonized with the instinctive purposes of life.

§ 3. Growing Up; and Infantile Fixations on the Parents

In savage life the services of the child in food-getting and other tasks are needed by the family and are utilized as soon as possible—at what seems to us the incredibly early ages of six, five, or four. The child, moreover, finds these tasks, though laborious, more interesting and honorable than anything else life has to offer, and accepts them eagerly and proudly. There is little formal teaching of adult duties; everything is learned by observation and lending a hand. The parental example, reinforced by that of other adults of the family and tribe, inculcates adult behavior. Already, however, in savage and barbaric life, there can be seen a tendency for the elders to monopolize certain adult privileges, and to yield them only reluctantly to the young.

In patriarchal civilization this postponement of adult life

becomes one of the chief features of the social arrangement. Various adult privileges are withheld from the young as long as possible. Child-training thus becomes not a period of growing up in social responsibility but a period of enforced abstention from such social responsibility—learning to 'keep one's place' as a minor. *Nine-tenths of patriarchal education consists in showing respect to the elders.* A young person's growth in social adaptation is thus, under the patriarchal régime, one of manners, and these manners are manners of subservience. They do involve the performance of tasks; but *these tasks are performed for the convenience of the elders, and at their behest.* To be unduly forward in the performance of tasks is as great a breach of patriarchal family discipline as to be slow in obeying commands. 'Who told you to do that?' A young person must wait until he is told, before he may act. His relation to tasks is therefore not immediate or objective; *it is only his task because it has been given to him by an elder.* He does it, not because it needs to be done, not because he is skilful in the doing of it, and least of all because it pleases him to do it—he does it to please those in authority. Every task thus has a highly personal aspect; it is incidental to, and a demonstration of, the proper relationship between the old and the young. And since the parents are the interpreters to the child of tribal authority, work becomes a filial duty.

The military aspect of such patriarchal education is obvious; and it has been pointed out that there were good social reasons for such military family discipline in its time. But that time is now passing in Western civilization. The parents are no longer the sufficient interpreters of the social purposes of the group; and the family army which they ordered about has dwindled. They are tin-pot generalissimos now, in command of a squad at most. Their notions of tribal welfare are at variance with one another in the same community, and the children who learn to please them are likely to have to unlearn their lessons when they emerge from the family into the larger social world. Moreover, the dwindling of the family and the narrowing of its functions has left them with only a few opportunities for the exercise of their patriarchal modes of discipline. This is especially true of the maternal parent, to whom the earliest training of children was given over. With so many children and so many duties in the patriarchal past, she was bound to do a healthy amount of neglecting. LePlay, the mid-19th-century idealizer of the patriarchal family as he found it in Russia, described the conditions which encouraged early marriage and (as we should say) prevented emotional fixations of the children upon the parents. A young man of an age to marry must get married, he pointed out, because otherwise his position in the community is, through neglect by his own family, "in some respects unendurable; for instance, it is impossible for him to get suitable clothing. His sisters-in-law are naturally occupied in the first instance in looking after the linen and clothes of their husbands; the prime interest of his young unmarried sisters is the preparation of their trousseau; the old mother, when still living, is absorbed in superintending family affairs, or in the cares of her husband and grandchildren; she can hardly attend to an adult unmarried son. Thus, even if he were not naturally drawn to it, he must seek in marriage the way out of a false position, and thus lighten the charge he inflicts upon other members of the community." A young man had to get married, if only in order to have shirts!

Yet this apparently healthy patriarchal family organization, when carried down into modern times, becomes the ground of 'mother-fixation' from which blossom some well-known modern neuroses. It produced similar results, occasionally, in the period of transition between quasi-matriarchal savage institutions and patriarchal ones—but these results were regarded merely as examples of splendid filial devotion. Thus Herodotus tells a story of two Argive youths, Cleobis and Bito. "There was a great festival in honour of the goddess Hera at Argos, to which their mother needs must be taken in a car. Now the oxen did not come home from the field in time: so the youths, fearful of being too late, put the yokes on their own necks and themselves drew the car in which their mother rode." They got the old lady there on time but the effort killed them; they were accordingly looked upon by the Argives as the best of men, and statues of them were sent to Delphi.

With the decay of patriarchalism, such fantastic recrudescences of mother-worship occur also in our society. We find an impressive though less athletic example quoted by Professor Leta Hollingworth: "An old mother died recently at the age of 113 years, living with three bachelor sons, aged 81, 74 and 70 years respectively, 'who said they had never married because they did not want to leave their mother.' These three bachelor sons ran the farm. The youngest, aged 70, whom she called 'the baby', did the housework. A married son, aged 77 years, lived only a few miles away. Although these 'boys', as they were called in the neighborhood, were known to be among the richest residents of the locality, they kept the home place as much like old Ireland as possible, 'to please mother'. No telephone bell marred its quiet; there was no radio; they kept no motor car." We do not in our society set up statues to such devoted sons, nor do we honor such son-consuming mothers. Instead we psychoanalyze them, and in our intellectual plays and novels hold them up to scorn and obloquy. Indeed, when it was recently proposed to erect a statue in New York City to the authoress of *Little Lord Fauntleroy,* a host of middle-aged men, who in their helpless boyhood had been forced by their mothers to wear long curls and velvet jackets in imitation of that precious little 'mother's boy' hero, wrote so indignantly and vituperatively to the newspapers in condemnation of the project that it was dropped. Our society has no use for a kind of mother who keeps children in bondage to herself personally. They belong to the world.

The world, however, to which they belonged in patriarchal times was so wholly an extension of the patriarchal family that children were prepared for it by the cultivation of just these filial and highly personal loyalties and obediences. They could transfer their unquestioning devotion, their helpless subservience, their dutiful lack of initiative, successfully to the service of the great families (Peisistratidae and Alcmaeonidae, York or Lancaster, Guelph or Ghibelline), or the family-like organizations (Reds or Blues in Constantinople, Arian or Athanasian), which ruled the State and the Church. The medieval 'mysteries' of trade were conducted on the same patriarchal family principle. One was trained in the family for a dutiful, uncritical, blind and helpless sonship to the father-leaders of society. This blind and helpless filial quality was extolled as the prime virtue of ordinary citizens. They did what they were told, hated all those with whom their family-organization might be at war, killed and died for it, not knowing what it was all about. Theirs not to reason why—.

This state of affairs, though not yet by any means entirely obsolete in modern politics or even in business, is manifestly an archaic drag upon the democratic tendencies of our age. In general these infantile loyalties are called upon only in war and in warlike activities. The normal procedure of peace can make but little use of them, finds them hampering to progress. Insofar as our transition era has actually attained modernity it dispenses impatiently with these infantile qualities in adults, and calls for a training of children which will lead them to think and act for themselves when they are grown up.

It is, however, in the domestic realm that our modern world has become most acutely conscious of the hampering effects of patriarchal education. Marriages need no longer be contracted as a matter of filial duty; and the parental fixations which were once of use in keeping such loveless marriages intact, now on the contrary make them unstable. The young man and the young woman who have become the victims of these parental fixations find themselves unable to enter successfully into the essentially democratic relationship of modern marriage. Men go about seeking a mother-substitute, women go about seeking a father-substitute. The unconscious identification of the loved person with the parent may introduce the incest-taboo into the emotional relationship and cause impotence or frigidity. These effects are observed not only by psychiatrists among the middle-class but by social workers among the poor. A marriage will be spoiled by the fact that the husband or wife is more deeply attached to the parental family (compare the universally popular mother-in-law joke); it is from her parental family or some member of it, perhaps her father or brother, that she seeks advice upon all occasions. The breakdown in outward social life of patriarchal institutions, which deprives the husband of the authority and dignity which the social system could once assure him, leaves him frequently at the mercy of the infantile family attachments of his wife. The converse is also notably true; the husband remains too much of a son to his mother to be ever wholeheartedly a husband to his wife. These marriages, which require responsible love-choice for their stability, being thus inwardly weak, and lacking the outside social props furnished by the compulsions of the patriarchal system, go to pieces under the stress of economic accident, as well under the shock of sudden prosperity as under the disintegrating effects of sickness and lack of employment. The children may be thrown upon society, or they may in default of parental care become delinquent in various ways. Their unsatisfied need of loyalty to a parent may conduce to their being, if girls, exploited in prostitution, or, if boys, to their becoming members of a criminal gang. For, interestingly enough, the pimp and the criminal gang leader are the nearest modern peace-time representatives of the archaic patriarchal boss which they have been trained to require.

It is not, however, only in the domestic sphere, in the failure of patriarchally trained children—which means, in effect, the children of loveless marriages—to make successful adjustments to modern love-marriages, that these difficulties have been recognized. The patriarchal home is now so out of tune with modern society that the break which comes upon the emergence of the child from the home into the larger world of school or employment is notoriously a critical time in the life of our young people. It is typically the time of neurotic breakdowns, which bear fruit in sexual delinquency, criminality, alcoholism, drug-addiction and suicide. Adolescence represents the danger-point in modern individual life, precisely because of the sharp transition it affords between the patriarchal home and modern society. It is then that the weaknesses of patriarchal training, its uselessness and mischievousness as a preparation for modern adult life, stand revealed.

A variety of far-flung administrative activities, recently co-ordinated in the 'Mental Hygiene' movement, have furnished us with data upon individual psychic maladjustment, which in every instance points to bad parental training—that is, to patriarchal methods—as a cause. In kindergarten or play-school, in public and private schools, high school, college, industry, there are studies being made of the maladjusted. The maladjustment may prove to be physical, a deafness or poor vision which can be corrected by medical attention; or it may consist in a comparative lack of intelligence—though I. Q. tests need not be regarded as final, nor as implying congenital and irremediable defect. But when the difficulty does not lie in these directions, it is always found to be due to bad parental influences. These bad parental influences are summed up in rough-and-ready fashion as being almost invariably a too-stern father or a too indulgent mother.

Indulgence and sternness are not really as mutually exclusive as the terms would suggest; it would be equally correct to speak of over-indulgent fathers and over-anxious or despotic mothers. But for convenience we will use the terms as they are ordinarily given. But the paternal sternness and the maternal over-indulgence are remnants of the old patriarchal system, and both were necessary in their time. Paternal sternness, however excessive it may now seem to be, did prepare the children for the world into which they were growing up. Maternal indulgence was limited by the demands of a large family and the larger scope of women's work inside the patriarchal home; and it was brought to a close by the early marriage of daughters and by the removal of sons from the home at an earlier age. But now that the world has changed, these patriarchal attitudes prove poisonous to children. We will deal later in detail with characteristic situations, including especially education, and will there observe the effects of paternal over-sternness and maternal over-indulgence as shown in specific case histories. Here we may content ourselves with quoting a generalization made by Professor C. Mildred Thompson, dean of Vassar college: "*Cherchez la femme* is the advice of the French cynic in any puzzling situation. I had not been long dean before I learned, in the face of a problem, to look first for the parents. Two to one, a neurotic mother or a despotic father is at the root of the difficulty."

§ 4. Why Are Contemporary Parents Still Patriarchal?

For a moment we will turn from the child to the parents. Why is the father so often stern? Why is the mother so often reluctant to let her children get free from her? To say merely that this is the 'patriarchal tradition' is to leave out of our historical explanation the living emotions which that tradition justifies in parental minds. The father is, to put it simply, over-stern because he is unhappily married. He is unhappily married because he was brought up in the patriarchal tradition, because he never grew up psychically to the point of being able to make a responsible love-choice which could be the basis of an enduring marriage. He may have married 'sensibly' to suit his parents, or as the result of a blindly rebellious attempt to escape from their dominance, in a transitory romantic infatuation. He may be cynical or resigned, he may commit secret or flagrant adulteries, or he may be extremely Puritanical. But the absence of any internal bond of love to hold his marriage and with it his family life intact makes him all the more distrustful of human nature and all the more a believer in compulsions. It is not because he has heard it in a sermon or remembers it from his father's lips that he believes so devoutly that human nature is prone to waywardness and that any child will go to the devil if not watched, ordered about, regulated and punished; it is because his own marriage has nothing in it of healthy love to hold it together. He has to be the stern and watchful God in his little universe. *The force of the patriarchal tradition is in the tissue of ignorance, misery and failure in love that goes on from generation to generation.* It is to break this chain of ignorance and misery that the efforts of child guidance are now directed—to free the child from these unhappy influences and enable him to achieve a successful adjustment to the realities of life and love.

We may ask again, why is the mother so often reluctant to let her children get free from her? Because she is not in love with her husband, or not in love with him in an adult way. And that is because she has been brought up in the patriarchal way, because she has never grown up psychically to the point of being able to experience the emotions of adult heterosexual love. She remains in an infantile stage, with parental fixations or unconscious homosexual wishes to interfere with her marital life. She turns to her child for emotional satisfaction, exploits the child's affection and obedience, and if the child is a boy homosexualizes him by making him a pet or 'mama's lover', so that he is incapable without the severest struggle ever to grow up to psychic manhood.

Two social institutions are important as deflecting these emotional currents away from the home and sparing children their worst effects. One is divorce, the other is work outside the home for mothers. Divorce brings frequently enough its own penalties to the children, but it saves them from the harshness of a father to whom they represent the chains which bind him in an unhappy marriage. Work for mothers outside the home in our transition era brings also its own penalties to children, but it saves them from the concentrated maternal managerial attentions.

The problem of work for women outside the home is one which is not yet, as will be shown later, satisfactorily solved in our society. The economic careers of women are interrupted by domestic and maternal responsibilities, their return to the world of outside work is made difficult. Work of sorts does indeed exist for middle-aged women in our society, but it lacks not merely the authority and dignity of home-management but also the emotional excitements which family life normally provides. Middle-aged working-women without families, finding life alone in a hall-bedroom intolerable, often prefer the social solaces of women's lodging houses. Mrs. Cecil Chesterton, describing her own researches in the slums of London, says:

"The older women * * * who frequent lodging houses are semi-permanents. These semi-permanents have regular if poorly paid work. They are office cleaners, jobbing laundresses, daily cooks at cheap restaurants. The money they pay per week for their bed would rent a room in a poor locality, but * * * there is one overwhelming obstacle to such a mode of life. For the single woman well on to middle age, to live alone is to court a desolation of spirit that saps vitality. The loneliness of such a situation is intolerable. Few of these old women have friends, or men acquaintances; they sustain their hold on life through the younger women whom they meet at the lodging house. They feed their emotions on the emotions of these others, gaining a spurious excitement from their tragedies and amusements.

"It is not only in the public lodging house that you find this particular phenomenon. You will find elderly spinsters and childless widows in all grades of society preying upon the vitality of the young. Lack of occupation, in these latter cases, intensifies the desire for sensation and, whereas the office cleaner is content to observe her younger and attractive sisters, the middle-class woman of certain, if small income, with nothing to do, actively oppresses her unfortunate friends and relations. The same morbid condition is noticeable in widows and sons, and with them that sense of superiority which comes from male appreciation. In such cases it is the daughters who pay; for the mother to sustain emotional contact with life [through them], leaves very little opportunity for their privacy of feeling."

The decay of the patriarchal family as an economic institution, as a center of production, a factory presided over by the housewife, and the failure of our society thus far to provide the idle housewife with outside work as dignified and as interesting (for there is no sense in idealizing our economic arrangements), has left her at least in the middle class with nothing to do with her energies except manage and spoil her children's lives. If she is unhappily married, if she has been reared in the patriarchal way and is not psychically adult, she will inevitably make use of this opportunity. "There is probably not a person in this room whose life has not been shadowed in some way by unwholesome parental attitudes", said Dr. Esther Loring Richards, associate professor of psychiatry at Johns Hopkins University, to the Chicago Woman's Aid. "Take the matter of adolescent emancipation, for example. Fifty years ago it was considered pathologically unnatural for any daughter to 'refuse to see her parents through'. This meant that she gave up hopes and ambitions and plans and resigned herself to a program that year by year became more drab and circumscribed. In middle life she found herself alone in the ancestral home, surrounded by faded heirlooms and devoid of friends, who have long ago been obliged to leave her behind in the journey of life. Or there is the daughter who was told she could marry only on condition that she made her family life beneath the parental roof. Or there is the son who struggles for years to run the family business according to methods his father found successful in 1888. Should these uncanonized saints rebel and attempt to live their own lives, terrible scenes ensue. I know a 60-year-old father who went to bed and stayed four years because his 30-year-old son moved to a neighboring town in order to carry on his business to greater advantage. A clever and brilliant teacher of 42 wrote me not long ago, 'I should like to come down and visit you, but mother makes such a fuss when I leave her, and always does something to make herself sick.' This woman has been separated from her mother only during her four years at college, and even then that devoted parent hounded her with daily letters saturated with accusations of neglect and selfishness. A telephone employee, superintendent of a city exchange, told me that at 32 years of age she had never bought a pair of shoes for herself. She didn't have the courage to select her own clothes because of the storm of ridicule and abuse she would receive from her mother. To meet the conflict of this family situation, she became a headache invalid. I have struggled in vain for six years to persuade two intelligent and genteel parents to allow their two daughters of 30-odd years to have checking accounts. These dear old souls still follow their children to the front door with rubbers and measure out their cascara at night." And Dr. Richards commented: "In attempting to salvage this adult wreckage, the physician is again confronted with facts of selfishness, jealousy, self-pity, and spite reactions, complacently rationalized in the phrase 'parental love'."

Thus the individual neuroses found to be afflicting so many middle-class mothers and injuring the lives of their children, turn out to be symptoms of our transition from the patriarchal régime. They are due in the first place to the inability of men and women trained in patriarchal sexual attitudes to make satisfactory marriages; and in the second place to the failure of our machine age to provide satisfactory terms for their re-entrance into the industrial world outside the home—something better than mere slave-jobs, work sufficiently attractive in the social power which it represents and possibly in the opportunity which it may provide of getting vicarious emotional refreshment from the lives of young people—something to lure them away from the empty field of their traditional usefulness and authority. If, on the other hand, modern industry should continue to reject the services of older people, it is quite possible that family life after a period of intense individualism should reconstellate itself into a larger group. That is to say, it is quite possible that our present two-generation style family life represents an emotional rebellion against the tyranny of the elders; and that after the elders have learned their lesson, after the spell of the patriarchal tradition is broken, when King Lear has got over his delusions of grandeur, and Mother-in-Law has learned not to interfere, they may be welcomed back into the family circle, and find there a real usefulness and a sufficient dignity.

In the meantime the situation recalls the persistence among insects of instinctive behavior under circumstances in which the results are merely ludicrous or pathetic. Major Hingston in his fascinating book, *Instinct and Intelligence,* describes in an illuminating passage the actions of a spider building a web, the main structural supports of which he, the observer, taking the part of an unkind Fate, was experimentally breaking. It would have been only the work of a moment, he remarks, for the spider to adjust to this situation by restoring the broken strands; but she could only go ahead with her work in the good old way, regardless of whether the structural supports were there or not. "Construction continues," he reports, "though the snare rapidly becomes a tangle. The spider, however, seems quite satisfied. * * * It just carries on, blindly and hopelessly. On it goes, round and round, * * * always fixing threads in the wrong place. At every turn its difficulties increase. More and more confusion follows in its architecture. Nevertheless it sticks to its duty. * * * Satisfied with the work, it seats itself at the center, surrounded by the hopeless tangle of its lines." We are shown a drawing of the intended web, taut and shapely, the one toward which her instincts urged her; and then another picture of the actual web, shapeless and meaningless and useless—so much like so many human lives in our transitional period, that one is impelled to take it as a symbol of the results of the blind operation of traditional behavior under altered economic and social conditions.

§ 5. Education; and Inherited Social Limitations

A great part of the power of the patriarchal scheme of life lay in the social benefits which could be conferred directly by parents upon their children through the operation of the hereditary principle. Aside from the transmission of land and the power and wealth which it represented, these benefits were chiefly in the nature of hereditarily transmitted trades and crafts, in which both privilege and training passed from father to son. It is true that our transition era still retains the hereditary principle with respect to property, and that power and privilege in the realms of economic exploitation are inherited, though without any formal class monopoly of them. But our technical and general knowledge has long since burst the old family bonds.

Reference has been made earlier to the fact that in the 17th century the obstetrical forceps, the first form of the instrument now in use, was invented and handed down as a professional secret in a family of man-midwives, the Chamberlens. Hugh Chamberlen, in 1672, in the preface to his English translation of a French obstetrical treatise, "made the then incredible statement that his father, his brothers, and himself had long attained to and practised a way to deliver women in difficult labors without hooks, where other artists used them, and without prejudice to mother or child". The forceps had in fact been invented by his grandfather. "Many years had still to elapse before the secret of the

Chamberlens leaked out." It was not until the early 18th century that forceps of this type became generally known and used.

A picture of the Chamberlen forceps, hidden under a floor by a member of the family, and accidentally found, is shown by Dr. Singer, together with pictures of the earlier obstetrical instruments, the "dangerous and brutal" *Speculum matricis,* and that "even more terrible and powerful instrument, the *Apertorium,* provided with a sharp edge by which the mouth of the womb was violently cut or torn". Passing over the horrifying immorality of dooming countless women to tortures and death by keeping the new instrument a family secret, we merely note that in patriarchal times fathers did have special and valuable knowledge to hand on to their sons. What a son can learn nowadays from his father in any technical realm is out of date in comparison with what can be learned from other sources. To advance a son's interests a father must now abandon all the traditional paternal pretensions to being the best authority upon anything; for the facts of modern life will not back up his pretensions.

Wisdom now resides outside the home; and fathers and mothers must themselves go to school again, or make continual efforts to keep abreast of modern knowledge, if they are to serve even as trustworthy interpreters of modern knowledge to the child. Indeed, so broad is the field of knowledge that the parent generally turns over his ancient rôle of instructor in facts to the school teacher, though he retains the patriarchal privilege of handing out ultimate wisdom in the realms of politics, religion and morals, and sometimes in those of dress and manners.

Our schools and colleges are under the necessity of mediating continually between the politics, the religion, and the morals taught to young people as absolute by their parents, and the different concepts of politics, religion and morals which they find held in the outside world. Sometimes the educational authorities must also mediate between parental notions of clothes and manners and those of a changing society.

In all these conflicts between absolute parental standards and different social standards in the world at large lie possibilities of neurotic maladjustment for the child. It will be illuminating to our discussion to consider some of these conflicts in detail. We may begin with clothes and manners. The importance of these to young people is first of all in their being a bond of likeness to or equality with the social group; and second in their being a part of the apparatus of courtship. As Professor Leta Hollingworth says: "*whatever is in vogue* as to costume, hair-dressing, cosmetics, manners, and speech constitutes sex appeal for the generation then on the scene. The boy or girl who is 'swell', 'snappy', 'en vogue', is the one who stimulates the greatest response. What style or vogue is, and how it changes from year to year, are large questions of aesthetics into which we need not enter here; but it is fatuous for parents to suppose that they can set the style for their adolescent children, or can press the latter into the mould of fashion that prevailed in their own youth. The mother of to-day [1928] who insists that her daughter wear long skirts, long hair and whalebone corsets dooms the girl to failure in the sphere of sex attraction, if docile, or to desperate rebellion, if self-assertive. Neither of these unhappy conditions is to be desired. Each generation knows what constitutes attractiveness for its members, and will fight to achieve it. Only the unwholesomely meek will follow obsolete patterns.

"When we consider these facts, it becomes apparent that a large place must be assigned to clothes in the life of the adolescent boy or girl engaged in courtship. The clothes must be 'right', or acute misery ensues. A considerable amount of delinquency among adolescents, especially among girls, is directly traceable to the intense craving for the 'right' clothes. Young adolescents who earn, tend to spend too large a part of their money on clothes, in the interests of attracting the opposite sex."

Clothes and sex-attraction may not seem to belong under the heading of education, but that is because we have permitted education to be so largely divorced from life. Properly regarded, education is a preparation for adult life; and clothes and sex-attraction, as a part of courtship, are quite in place in any discussion of education. Clothes and sex-attraction, moreover, lead us directly to the question of morals, with which education is supposed to be concerned. The fact is that the mother who attempts to keep her children from following the current fashions is trying to manage her children's sexual destinies. She is afraid to trust them to manage their own love-lives. She is seeking to play the old patriarchal game in a non-patriarchal world. She is unable to give them any assistance in growing up; she wants them to remain infantile, so that she may choose their husbands and wives for them. For her to concede her children the right to dress like other boys and girls would be to concede them emotional independence from her.

The difficulties of college girls in making the ordinary social adaptations called for in such an institution is ascribed by Dr. Karl Menninger, Mental Hygiene Counselor at Washburn College in Kansas, to a home training in "excessive prudishness" which has left them "unfitted for the real contacts of every-day social life". He tells of Gertrude, who was "turning from unpopularity among men to the love of Jesus." "I wish", she said, "some one would tell me why it is that I have no social life, no dates, and practically no girl friends. It must be my fault; the others chum together all right." The fault was found to lie with her home life, of which she gave this account: "Naturally my mother is against all the things the young folks do—she is over-solicitous, always opposing something. She is opposed to dancing, for example, and to modern styles, so that I always come in six months late on any fad. When skirts were long, mine were half-way; when they were short, mine were still half-way. She never favored my getting my hair bobbed until this fall [1927?]. That's always where I am—that's me, or I should say, that's my mother. And what can I say? I am just dominated by her. She is always saying she is afraid she will dominate me and doesn't seem to realize that she already does, but other people see it. I think and act just as she does, and it makes me so old. I can't enjoy the chatter and gossip of the other young folks or make myself like them or be liked by them."

"My last case", said Dr. Arthur H. Ruggles, formerly Consultant in Medical Hygiene at Dartmouth college, speaking before the American Student Health Association, "is that of a girl who was brought up in New England by very Puritanical parents. She was taught that dancing is sinful and card playing even more so. Intellectually she was very capable and got on fairly well at college until her junior year. She made few friends, but those few were very good friends. She could not, of course, take much part in the social life of the college because she could not dance or play cards or even be present where such things were being done.

"In her junior year, the question of smoking among the girls came up. Unfortunately the newspapers got hold of the affair and made a good deal of it, so that it was rather forced upon the college authorities as an issue." (We may take this to mean that the parents learned what was going on in their daughters' social world, asserted their traditional patriarchal powers, and the college authorities felt obliged to surrender to them and make an administrative pretense of sharing their rural moral horror, thereby losing their own real authority with the students—an incident typical of our transition period.) "The girl I am telling about was perfectly horrified to learn that such a thing was going on. Her reaction was tremendous. A meeting was held to discuss the subject and she got up and said that it was not a question of policy at all—it was a question of right and wrong; that if this sin continued, her class and her college were certainly headed for perdition, and she felt that she must raise her voice in protest against it. Of course she was subjected to a certain amount of sneering and jeering from some of her college mates, and she began to feel herself a social outcast. She was on a committee with some of the people who disagreed with her and she felt she should resign from this committee. She really made a great issue of the affair.

"At the same time she was having other difficulties. Through some of her friends, she got rather interested in dancing and sometimes found herself wondering whether it might not be permissible as a wholesome athletic exercise. This gave her the feeling that she was a traitor to her father and mother, who were making sacrifices in sending her through college. To add to her conflict, she was taking a course in the philosophy of religion and some of the ideas expounded in it were directly at variance with those of her parents. The broader spirit of these new teachings interested her, even fascinated her; and here again she could not help feeling that she was disloyal to her father and mother. It became a question to her mind of either giving up college and with it the ambition of a lifetimes or playing false to their teachings. The situation was too much for her and she had reached the point of deliberately making up her mind to commit suicide as the only way out of her troubles."

It may be asked, are the psychic difficulties in the educational field solely those which concern the conflict between the standards of the parental home and those of the outside world? And do they always, directly or remotely involve the sexual problem?

The answer appears to be 'yes'. Latin and trigonometry would seem to be incapable in themselves of producing neurotic breakdowns. Sometimes an I. Q. test reveals an incapacity for doing certain kinds of work—though, indeed, after a test which appeared to show an abysmal mental incapacity for college work, a girl freshman (reported by Dr. Menninger) was so helped by a single talk with the Mental Hygiene Counselor that she "improved promptly after the interview, passed in everything, took up the French she had dropped, and registered for the sophomore year!" Again, the I. Q. test may show a student as fully capable of doing the college work, yet he may fail in all his examinations and leave school; as happened in the case of the boy who told Dr. Ruggles that his father and older sister had always run his life for him. "I always had to do things exactly as they said, especially just as my father said. He has to know exactly where I'm going and what for, and everything like that." He did not study, and cut his classes very liberally; his behavior seemed "an echo of this old home situation and of his resentment of parental autocracy". There are, indeed, physical difficulties; but "One man has an injury to his back or gets a sinus infection, and it does not bother him particularly; another man is quite upset about it". The difference is in the psychic background. There are also economic problems which aggravate physical and psychic difficulties; "a casual survey of a number of colleges", says Dr. Ruggles, "has made it clear that there are a small percentage of men who are really in need of rest and food, who are carrying on a little athletic program of their own in taking care of somebody's furnace or shoveling snow from somebody's paths, and at the same time not getting enough to eat. It is not to be wondered at that some of them break under the strain." But the difficulties which typically arise in the educational career are those which reveal a patriarchal situation at home.

This case of Dr. Ruggles's will represent half of the neurotically maladapted youngsters: "His mother was neurotic, his father * * * a domineering, dictatorial man. All the boy's life, his mother had spent her time trying to protect him from the verbal attacks of his father, so that there had been constant conflict in the family. The boy had grown up in that atmosphere of conflict, and was extremely unstable emotionally. He had wanted to go to a certain college, but his father had forced him to go to another. After he got to college, he did what a boy of his type is bound to do—he over-reacted to his new freedom. At home his every action had been dominated, and now that he was his own master, the pendulum swung too far in the other direction. He smoked too much; when he drank, he drank too much." And this case of Dr. Menninger's will fairly represent the other half: "He had had only two 'dates' since coming to college and had taken no part in athletics. Card playing, liquor drinking, pool playing, and similar activities, were all taboo." He day-dreamed continually, suffered inferiority feelings though regarded as a snob, was disappointed in the school, had difficulties in history and mathematics. "He is the son of a very successful, but taciturn and surly autocrat. 'What my father thinks is as good as a command.' "

The girls, *mutatis mutandis,* react in the same way to the new social world of college. Excessive patriarchalism at home may cause them to wear loud clothes, steal, be suspected of sexual misdemeanors. Or on the other hand they may behave like one of Dr. Ruggles' cases, of whom her sorority sisters reported that she "wouldn't take part in anything, go to any parties, walk with any man, or go anywhere alone. She's so afraid at night, she won't go home alone, won't go in or out of the house without some older girl. She's just impossible." She was a good girl by 5th century Greek or medieval standards. But times have changed.

The assumption by parents of patriarchal attitudes of ultimate wisdom and authority keeps their children infantile. But where then, if not to the parents, shall children turn for wisdom and authority? There is in our modern world no ultimate wisdom, no final authority. But there is increasing help and guidance in the outside world, and the effort of modern parents must be to make their children able to take it as they need it by free selective choice. Thus to emancipate the child from dependence upon his parents involves a surrender by them of the reverence once thought rightly due them from the child. It involves a progressive attachment of the child's respect—always by free choice—to such outside sources of wisdom and authority as he can find for his own needs.

The patriarchal attitudes, so hampering to the development of young people to adulthood, are generally a matter of inflicting old-fashioned conventions upon them. Yet the patriarchal spirit may be equally manifested by 'advanced' parents who force sectarian modernistic, futuristic or rationalistic dogmas upon their children in the realms of religion, politics, morals, manners, and health-practices—and with the same results as have already been described. The published case-histories seldom deal with such situations, since they are not so representative as the others. As one comes upon them among the intelligentsia they are frequently mitigated by such intellectual resources as enable the troubled adolescent to find some roundabout and satisfactory solution for his emotional conflict between the duty of following 'superior' parental teachings and the desirability of conforming to popular usages. If this does not occur, the 'superior' parental teachings may constitute a barrier between the adolescent and social and sexual adulthood, through loneliness and the sense of queerness; he may behave snobbishly, while feeling himself to be a martyr. The danger is of course that actual social persecution may encourage the formation of persecution delusions. On the other hand, the adolescent instead of despising society at large may take the other course of despising his 'superior' parents, and may over-compensate in the direction of the most stupid conventionality and formalism in politics, religion, morals or manners. If it is vegetarianism that has been dogmatically inflicted upon him by parental authority, he may avoid vegetables altogether and restrict himself to what he has heard scornfully described as 'dead animals'. If he has been brought up in a narrowly revolutionary parental atmosphere, he may go into Wall Street. If 'advanced' ideas of sexual freedom have been forced upon him, he may be found later clinging to the most antiquated or Puritanical principles of sexual behavior. It is evidently not a good thing for a young person to have to despise his parents, or else (in order to be loyal to them) despise society at large. Either way lies the danger of neurosis.

Such a painful dilemma would not arise if he were given the right to choose for himself, according to his own needs, what guidance he will follow. It is not intended here to be suggested that society at large is always right and parents are always wrong; on the contrary, parental standards may be truly superior to those of the general social environment. If the child is permitted to choose, he will always be inclined to choose to follow parental standards. But the right of choice involves 'the right to be wrong'. There is for modern parents an important distinction between those things which everybody would agree with them in holding to be true and those things which they hold to be true but which are disputed by others. Thus as a parent I can tell my child that two times two is four or that London is the capital of England, without there being any question of opinion about it. But though I may hold it to be true that Jesus died to save us (or that Jesus is a myth), this is not to be told to children as though it had the same quality of universally accepted fact as the facts of arithmetic and geography; for it has not. I may deeply and sincerely believe that the Republican party is responsible for American prosperity (or that there is a class struggle in which the workers will eventually destroy capitalism and establish a workers' commonwealth); but my children will later hear other opinions to the contrary—I could write feelingly upon this subject, remembering how literally in childhood I took my father's dogmatic political statements, how foolish I felt when I discovered that they were not believed by other adults whom I was bound to respect, and how great difficulty I had not only in re-establishing my respect for my father, who appeared rather ridiculous, but in forgiving him for having taken advantage of my filial confidence and caused me to make an arrogant little fool of myself!—It is doubtless hard to break with the patriarchal position, hard to surrender the parental privilege of saying what is what about everything in heaven and earth. But one can learn to say, of matters in social dispute: 'This is what I believe; but there are many other people who think the opposite. I think they are mistaken, and they think I am mistaken, but we must agree that each has the right to make up his own mind about these things. You will have lots of time to decide for yourself what you think about them.' It is even possible to say, when a child identifies himself too readily and warmly with a parental opinion: 'You see, there are reasons why other people think and feel differently about these things'—and give those reasons, adding, 'Of course, they could make out a stronger case for themselves than I can for them. Some time you will have a chance to listen to their arguments, and see what *you* think of them.' This non-patriarchal attitude gives the child not merely the privilege of disagreeing with his parents without despising them, but also that tolerance toward views which he regards as mistaken which will enable him to live in a social group with which he is in partial disagreement without any feeling of insecurity. If, given free choice, he prefers to follow parental guidance and reject such social conventions as are in disagreement with it, he will do so serenely. The conflict between parental views and those of the social group will be seen objectively; it will not be a conflict within his own breast.

To be sure, these conflicts between special parental and conventional social views can be postponed if the child is brought up in a sectarian atmosphere, in a racial, religious, political or idealistic community in which the whole social group has exactly the same views as the parents. But this is merely to delay the discovery that there is a larger world outside the home, and to intrude into the beginnings of adult life problems which should be solved in adolescence. We have spoken for the sake of convenience, moreover, of the general social conventions as though they were really general. This can be true only in a society far more stable than ours. In America especially there is really no such thing as a generally accepted convention about anything—not even about styles of clothing, which have changed again in certain respects before they have reached the periphery of their public. There are no generally accepted conventions in manners, and all books of etiquette are both misleading and out of date. There is no generally accepted convention about drinking. There is none about the degrees of physical intimacy permissible in courtship. That is not only because America is being so rapidly changed by certain influences of the machine age, but also because these changes are so profoundly resisted in some respects by the special patriarchal traditions of particular 'racial' groups. All that can be said is that young people tend more to behave in the same way than do their elders. But this chaotic conflict of conventions old and new, decaying and experimental, is the final reason why special parental attitudes should not be dogmatically enforced upon children. We cannot permanently shelter our children from other people's different modes of life. We cannot slice off a little corner of the world and teach our children to adjust to that. Sooner or later the barriers will be broken down and these hitherto sheltered young people will be plunged into the confusion. They need to be prepared to deal selectively with new influences. *Since we live in a changing world, our stability must be in our possession of powers of choice.*

The ideal of modern education has been lucidly stated by Margaret Mead in an argument against dogmatic sectarian codes:

"Instead, we must turn all of our efforts to training our children for the choices which will confront them. Education in the home even more than in the school, instead of being a special pleading for one régime, a desperate attempt to form one particular habit of mind which will withstand all outside influences, must be a preparation for those very influences. Such an education must give far more attention to mental and physical hygiene than it has given hitherto. The child who is to choose wisely must be healthy in mind and body, handicapped in no preventable fashion. And even more importantly, this child of the future must have an open mind. The home must cease to plead an ethical cause or a religious belief with smiles or frowns, caresses or threats. The children must be taught how to think, not what to think. And because old errors die slowly, they must be taught tolerance, just as to-day they are taught intolerance. They must be taught that many ways are open to them, no one sanctioned above its alternative, and that upon them and upon them only lies the burden of choice. Unhampered by prejudice, unvexed by too early conditioning to any one standard, they must come clear-eyed to the choices which lie before them."

This modern attitude, however, needs to be distinguished from the feeble and timid evasion of responsibility which is sometimes sought to be dignified by the noble name of 'tolerance'. The modern attitude is neither a confession that we do not know what is best for young people to do, nor an expression of indifference as to how they behave. Tolerance is the method, not the goal. For modern applied psychology has its goal, and its goal is psychic health. The dice of tolerance are loaded. By giving free choice, we seek to ensure healthy choice. Much has to be done in the way of promoting a basis of physical health and of social health (the abolition of poverty, for instance) before this program can bear its full fruits. Call it intolerance, if you wish. Science is intolerant toward physical disease, toward poverty (which is a social disease), and toward psychic disease. It is intolerant in the sense that it brutally says that this prettily flushed cheek is a symptom of tuberculosis,—those luxuries symptoms of a deranged social system,—that apparently insouciant piece of youthful bravado the symptom of a painful neurotic conflict. Our modern Medicine Men can recognize the presence of the invisible bacterium behind the rosy skin, the wastage of poverty behind the parade of national luxury, and the hovering spectres of Fear and Anxiety behind the carelessly tossed curls. Let us not be deceived, they have a program for us, and if they propose to give youth 'free choice' it is because that is the best way to get youth to behave wisely. Let us, they say, show you the difference between psychic health and psychic sickness, between permanent infantilism and the path up to adult life, between being a self-miserable social nuisance and a useful and happy man or woman—and then, my dears, do just as you please!

CHAPTER VII

SOME IDEOLOGICAL OVERCOMPENSATIONS

[Exaggerated or False Ideals—As to Parents and Children]

§ 1. 'The Abolition of the Family'

Before we go on to discuss love, courtship, marriage and family life in the modern world, it will be necessary to consider some of the social theories by which contemporary thinking is more or less guided. The historical origin of these social theories will be pointed out, and it will be suggested that they are in the nature of emotional propaganda to overcome a 'cultural lag', and that their value consists rather in detaching people's sentimental attachments to the past than in affording true prophetic visions of the future.

Mankind has been notoriously reluctant to adapt its ways of thinking to changed economic conditions. When patriarchal agriculture diminished the food-anxieties which had generated the magical rites of the hunting period, the sentimental attachments to the old sexual sorceries by which food animals were supposedly encouraged to propagate, still lingered on in men's minds; and the later patriarchal religions conducted campaigns of cultural propaganda against their 'heathen beastliness'. Lately, and indeed ever since the patriarchal régime began to show signs of breakdown, there have been cultural campaigns against patriarchalism, in favor of a variety of concepts of modernity.

These chapters will deal for the most part with the latter attempts at adjustment. But one at least of the former will be included, since it is still influential in our own time.

These social theories have undoubtedly served the purpose of helping people to break with the past and accommodate themselves with less emotional strain to current actualities. It is difficult and perhaps impossible to evaluate social theories justly in so rapidly changing a world as ours; and it may be premature to say of any social theory that its day of usefulness is past. Nevertheless there are grounds for believing that the value of certain theories is such as puts them into the category of religious consolation or aesthetic wish-fulfillment.

In the realm of practice, moreover, the objection to these campaigns of cultural propaganda is that they are likely to be overcompensatory in their zeal. In going to extremes they find themselves back where they started, for extremes have a way of meeting. The Devil is fought with his own fire, and what ensues is simply a new form of Devil-worship. The war against witchcraft produced an Inquisition which was practically a new witch-cult, believing in the same theories and practising the same insane cruelties in the name of Christ.

In the same way, or so we shall try to show, certain rebellions against patriarchal family life are in fact dominated unconsciously by patriarchal ways of thought; they seek escapes from the patriarchal family by idealizing it out of immediate recognition, and when we have followed these mutineers around Robin Hood's barn we find ourselves safely back again in the patriarchal camp. This is true not only of the older idea of abolishing the family, but of the newer idealizations of the machine age as one which frees woman from the home and maternity through wage-labor. We will take up the earlier idea first.

So unsatisfactory have been many of the results of child-rearing in the patriarchal home, especially in its disintegrating forms, that social idealism has from time to time envisaged some Utopia in which the child-rearing functions would be taken over entirely by the State. The classic example is Plato's Republic, in which the children were to be put into a State nursery at birth, the nursing mothers not knowing whether it was their own children or others that they suckled, but all of one age-class being called fathers and mothers by those of a younger age-class—the Private Family being thus abolished entirely. Plato's Utopia was, like the celebrated Platonic ideal of love, merely a refined and theoretically expanded version of military-homosexual institutions which harked back to the period of barbaric conquest—in this instance of the Spartan boy-camps. It represents that distrust of human nature in general and of the sexual instincts in particular which is characteristic of the patriarchal attitude. It represents a final attempt in theory to extend the patriarchal system logically over society as a unit.

The modern State—which is still in many respects what the ancient State was, a political extension of the patriarchal family—has taken over many of the educational functions of the family. In cases of breakdown of parental care the State has undertaken the parental rôle by establishing institutions for the care of orphaned or abandoned or maltreated children, where the Platonic ideal can be observed in practice. The results have justified Aristotle's shrewd comment: "How much better is it to be a real cousin of somebody than a 'son' after Plato's fashion!" Institutional life at its best has been notoriously drab and barren in comparison with ordinary family life. Institutional life has been found to fail in developing individual powers, and in furnishing incentives for growing up. It has characteristically turned out spiritless creatures, who do not know how to get along in the outside world.

These results have been very instructive. They have revealed to what an extent our social and economic life in general is centered in the family, and only capable of being adjusted to by those who have been brought up in a parental home. So true is this that the best modern institutions for children now model themselves upon the parental home, and try to give what it should give. The most successful of them appear in every possible respect to be furnishing ideal family life, so much so that the appearance would be deceptive to the casual observer. Even at their best, however, these institutions, when they replace the private home *entirely,* are regarded as makeshifts, as poor substitutes for a real home with real parents. And real homes and real parents are known to be so important to the child's development that it is more and more the practice that only as a last resort are homes broken up and children taken from their parents. Homes have to be very definitely found to be demoralizing to the children, parents have to be given up as hopelessly incapable of improvement, before the best modern practice countenances such an extreme measure as destruction of the family union.

The modern factory system, by making use of the services of women, has afforded us a partial demonstration of the tendencies of the machine age with regard to the home. Since women-workers who have babies cannot take them to the factory and are too poor to hire private caretakers, day-nurseries have come into existence to a limited extent. The appearance of this institution was hailed by extremists in the pre-war feminist movement as promising in its ultimate extension to free women from the bondage of home-making. Its actual makeshift character at present is indicated in this description by Queen and Mann: "It is utilized rather frequently when the mother's earning power is more marked than her ability as a housekeeper, and when no funds are available for keeping the family together unless the mother works. It means, however, that she must rise early, prepare breakfast and take the children to the nursery before she goes to her place of employment. It means that after working hours are over, she must call for the children, take them home, prepare their supper, put them to bed, wash and mend their clothes, besides attending to her own personal needs. Clearly no woman can be expected to do all this unless she possesses unusual strength and ability." As a result, the day-nursery tends to become a place where mothers are instructed in "child care, cleanliness, cooking, sewing, buying and other domestic functions. Some nurseries even provide laundry facilities where mothers may do their own washing. Frequently mothers' meetings are held, and occasional visits are made to the homes."

Thus in practice, as distinguished from extreme feminist theory, *the day nursery is being used in our machine age as a help to homes in difficulty, and not as a means of displacing the home.* Subsequent machine-age theory and practice, moreover, has aimed at a more direct aid to these distressed homes, through mothers' pensions. "There are many", say Queen and Mann, "who believe that an adequate system of mothers' pensions would reduce the need for day-nurseries almost to the vanishing point." Between 1911 and the present time the mothers' pension movement has spread rapidly in the United States, so that all except the backward Southern States provide such legislative assistance to homes. This assistance was at first intended only for the homes of widows, but, says Grace Abbott, "the trend of recent legislation is toward a broader application of the law, giving the benefit of the aid to all dependent children if the circumstances are such that in the interests of the child the home should be maintained and assistance is necessary to secure that end".

This matter involves a question of fundamental modern attitudes not only toward the home, but toward the rôle of woman and the claims of wage-industry upon her services. Other aspects of the question will be discussed later; here we need only observe that *the actual tendency of social legislation in our machine age is toward the protection of the home, and the recognition of its services as practically irreplaceable so far as children are concerned.*

It is interesting also to note that in Soviet Russia the same legislative tendency has triumphed in practice over a powerful ideological resistance. For various reasons, the taking over of the functions of the home by the State has been generally a part of State Socialist idealism. The establishment of a Socialist Republic in Russia gave an opportunity for social experiment in that direction—immediately in the necessary care of infants orphaned by civil war, and prospectively on a larger scale in ordinary life with a view to freeing women workers from domestic cares. The actual Russian Socialist experience in the care of orphans is instructive. Because of the poverty of the early Soviet régime, the Foundling and Orphans' Homes were not as representative of the highest standards of hygiene and trained care as was later possible; nevertheless, they seemed to offer real advantages over the ignorance, dirt and superstition of ordinary peasant homes. It was expected that the State Institutions would demonstrate the superiority of scientific care to maternal ignorance. However, the statistics of infant mortality in the institutions were discouraging; and the workers in charge reversed their course, abandoning in practice the Platonic ideal. Dr. Lebedeva, head of the Department for the Protection of Motherhood and Infancy, explained: "We use, and will continue to use, the method that proves best in actual practice." The method that proved best with orphans was putting them into carefully selected private family homes—where twice as many of them lived. Said Dr. Lebedeva: "If we had better equipment, better trained personnel in our institutions, it might have been different. But under our present conditions there is no doubt that the home offers a more stimulating environment for the development of the infant than the asylum. Not only have we decreased the death rate in this way, but we have insured normal development to a much larger proportion of babies, since in almost every case our asylum-trained babies were both mentally and physically backward."

This account of the Russian Soviet experience is given by Jessica Smith, who remarks: "I had been somewhat puzzled by the discrepancy between the pictures that had been painted for me from time to time by members of the Communist Party and organizers in the Genotdel [Working and Peasant Women's Department of the Communist Party] of the beautiful homes for babies and children they would build in the future, where the children would be taken away from their mothers completely, and the actual policy of the Mothers' and Babies' Department."

The actual policy is thus the same as in Germany and America, and is more energetically pursued in some directions, the need being greater. Propaganda is extensively used, one poster showing "a mass demonstration of babies out for their rights, being harangued by a gesticulating infant from the platform, bearing banners demanding 'Protection from flies!', 'Dry, clean diapers!', 'Our Mothers' breasts!', 'Fresh Air and Light!', 'Midwives, not Babkas!', 'Healthy Parents!' ". The day nurseries, to which working mothers come and feed the nursing babies three times during the day, are educational agencies for the training of mothers. Social insurance is used for the same purpose as mothers' pensions. Homes are preferred to institutions, and in the latter "more variety and color are being added to the surroundings as science and experience teaches that even the most hygienically perfect environment and sanitary care may not give the varied stimuli of the home atmosphere to the child's dawning intelligence".

The general European and American tendency has been until recently to regard the historic patriarchal form of the family as identical with the human family institution—and to regard the progressive destruction of the patriarchal family as a destruction of 'the family'. Often this has been deplored, less often welcomed. But it appears that the family has an educational function thus far indispensable to society. *The current tendency of Western civilization is to protect the family from further destruction, in the interests of the child, and to rehabilitate it in conformity to the exactions of our culture.* These efforts on behalf of the family represent not merely a sentimental popular protest, but the result of social experience and scientific study.

We do not know what some unknown future may bring, but we do know that the family is an economically efficient child-rearing organization which society is at present too poor with all its available wealth to replace. If public education of the young in the United States were reorganized on the model of our best experimental schools, it would require (according to Arthur E. Morgan, president of Antioch College) all the funds now spent to maintain an army and navy, in addition to those now used for educational purposes. The stupendous cost of replacing the remaining educational functions of the family by efficient collective methods can be faintly realized. The economic efficiency of the family in child-rearing is perhaps best illustrated by the enormous social cost of picking up the pieces when an individual family completely breaks down in its task. From two to a dozen social agencies, public and private, with their corps of trained workers, and the assistance of the courts, may be called upon to attend to tasks of child-rearing which could have been accomplished not only more successfully but less expensively if the family had not broken down. Nor is that the whole story of the expense. The family as a child-rearing institution can be much more highly subsidized than it is now, and still save billions to society.

In the Utopian novels of H. G. Wells there is a recurrent suggestion of the abolition of the private family and the care of children in some kind of State kindergartens. In Utopia the considerations of economic expediency adduced above would of course not apply; and since the completion of the economic revolution brought about by modern machinery would abolish poverty, these economic considerations are not final. Let us agree that society will some day, through the removal of the need of war-armaments, be rich enough to have the most expensive kind of public education for children. The question then remains whether there would still be private homes to which children would return as an emotional base; or whether, as in Plato's community, children would be left in the State nurseries as soon as they were weaned, growing up without knowledge of who their individual parents might be. Such a condition as the latter is conceivable, but it seems to require that the individual parents should be too busy with other important work to attend to their own children, and that other men and women should somehow find child-rearing their most important work. This also is thinkable, on the analogy of baking; parents need not bake bread for their individual families, they can leave that to the baker. But this does not explain why the children should not know their own parents, nor the parents their own children. That is most explicable as a mere emotional reaction to the evils of patriarchal family life—a wish to 'crush the damned thing'. As such a wish-fulfillment it would legitimately belong to the province of art, but need not detain us further as a social prophecy.

However, there is another possible reason for such an institution. It would be in order, it would indeed be necessary, if men and women ceased to live together (or with anyone else) as husband and wife for a long enough period to bring up the children they had begotten and borne. If there were no private homes, that is to say, there would have to be public homes for children. This condition would be the result either of men and women being prevented by adverse social conditions from living together (a state of affairs unimaginable in Utopia), or it would be the result of their not wanting to live together. Now there are some people who feel that way; they believe they can have healthy children, but they don't feel able to live in a domestic relationship with anybody for very long. Indeed, so great are the difficulties in making a successful emotional adjustment to the more responsible aspects of sexual love, that anyone may be discouraged from fantasying himself or herself a successful parent. It will free the sexual and romantic fantasy-life if the imagination can repudiate the parental responsibilities by shunting them off upon the State. This can hardly be done in a self-respecting way in actuality—though Rousseau managed to persuade himself that he was acting in the best interests of his child when he left it at an orphanage. But if such an opportunity of evading parental responsibilities as the actual world provides is too undignified for our fantasy-life to make use of, it will be all the more welcome when it is provided in the flattering terms of Utopian art. It is seen that a possible world, and one sufficiently beautiful, could grant our wish to evade individual parental responsibility—could get along without asking us to perform the difficult task of remaining in love with the children's other parent for years and years and years! Thus relieved by art of our secret fear of being emotionally inadequate to parenthood, assured that our wish to evade responsibility is really a kind of superiority, and that we are merely ahead of our time, we feel better. That is the religious function of art, to grant absolution to our weaknesses and to fulfil in fantasy the wishes that cannot be satisfactorily fulfilled in actuality. But this is art, not science. For if the argument be that people in general do not want to live together in love as husband and wife and as parents caring for their children, then it is quite certainly wrong. They are afraid they may fail. They frequently need all sorts of reassurances to give them courage and self-respect. They need to have their fears forgiven by art. But the wish to take adult parental responsibilities is instinctive.

Our human private-family habit could doubtless be changed under social pressure; there is hardly any way of life, however violently contrary to our instinctive proclivities, which has not been dutifully and sentimentally accepted by masses of mankind. If our civilization really tended by compulsion in the direction of replacement of private families by State nurseries, the history of mankind gives us little reason to doubt that we should eventually accept such an arrangement as proper and regard all others as immoral—so much so that our high priests and prosecuting officials would be sending people to prison for the 'obscenity' of preaching or secretly practising private family life instead of the approved touch-and-go promiscuity. The tendency, however, is not in that direction. Modern social purposes in child-rearing need no such elaborately artificial support as State parentage; these purposes can be harmonized with and largely accomplished through what appear to be our instinctive proclivities toward mating, parenthood and family life.

§ 2. 'The Absence of Parental Instincts in Men'

Any reference to 'instinct' brings us at once into an atmosphere of violent and inconclusive scientific disputation; there are several quite different meanings attached to the term 'instinct', and none of these has any general scientific acceptance. We must therefore pause here and say what is meant in these pages by the word as applied to human behavior. The instinctive human proclivities here referred to are not asserted to be on a par with the comparatively inflexible and unvarying responses to stimuli in lower animal life; nor is there any suggestion that we can rely upon our instincts to the extent of abandoning purposive social control through habit, custom and law. Indeed, those who profess to believe our natural instincts a sufficient guide undoubtedly construe as instinct much behavior that is actually social custom; and they would probably be horrified and disgusted at the spectacle of human lives lived literally according to their prescription. It is, moreover, as a school in which some of our primal instinctive proclivities are trained to yield precedence to others in the interests of civilized life, that the family institution has its fundamental social value.

The existence of any parental instincts in either sex (as distinguished from early maternal reflexes) has been denied. Maternal care of children, however, is generally conceded to be instinctive; but it is ordinarily supposed that any parental instinct for children is so lacking in men that social compulsion is necessary to maintain the family. It is in this form, as bearing most closely upon our thesis, that we will take up the argument. Do men have to be socially compelled to take care of their children?

The habits of the anthropoid apes have sometimes been appealed to as evidence for and against male parental instincts; but the fact is that we know scarcely anything about the domestic behavior of our simian cousins. Reference to the family arrangements of savages shows them to be guided by very elaborate and obviously artificial customs which have been interpreted as necessary social compulsions exerted upon the male in order to make him assume paternal responsibilities. These customs, however, may with equal justice be regarded as selective compulsions which not merely encourage paternal behavior under some circumstances but discourage it under other circumstances—as we shall see.

Any 'instinctive behavior pattern' to be observed in human life will necessarily be affected by traditional social habits of repression and sublimation. To speak of human behavior as 'instinctive' can only mean that it constitutes a comparatively simple, universal and uniform response to stimuli. Thus, except under the influence of powerful inhibiting forces, it is the ordinary tendency of adult males and of young children, living in conditions of or approximating domestic intimacy, to become emotionally attached to one another and to behave in what we call a 'paternal' manner on the one hand and a 'filial' manner on the other. The 'paternal' behavior will include tenderness, guidance, correction and protection as simple responses to the stimuli of childish needs and helplessness. The 'filial' behavior will include appeals for such tenderness, help and protection, and some degree of docility toward such correction. Whether these responses would occur if there were not previous training of both the adult and the child in family or social life is like asking whether lungs would ever learn to breathe if there were no air. And all this responsive 'parental' and 'filial' behavior of adult male and child can occur without legal or institutional pressure—though it is ordinarily encouraged and rewarded by the child's mother. If such 'parental' behavior is normal in bachelors in boarding-houses, it is none the less normal in the fathers of children. We may say, then, that parental care is an instinctive propensity in fathers, as distinguished from such non-instinctive and social mechanisms as tax-paying (for, among other purposes, the care of children in schools, etc.), or alimony and the couvade.

Anthropologists have surmised with great probability that the couvade (a custom according to which the husband is put to bed as if it were he who had just given birth to the child) may be among other things a means of emphasizing and securing paternal responsibility. To the local Medicine Men it must seem as though it were this ceremonial which created paternal responsibility, and not the mere vulgar fact of domesticity. Yet the rest of the world bravely dispenses with that social construction, and we find that fathers in a state of contented domesticity do love and care for their children without it! Perhaps other social mechanisms to enforce paternal responsibility are really more in the class of the couvade than we realize. We have laws compelling men to support their wives and children, and special courts to which wives and mothers may appeal for the enforcement of such laws. Yet a contemporary sociologist, Ernest Mowrer, has computed statistically the results of various modes of attempted adjustments of family discord (including non-support cases) from the records of social agencies in Chicago, and finds that there are "fewer cases of 'adjustment', or showing successful treatment, where there has been contact with the Court of Domestic Relations than could occur by chance. * * * The chances for successful outcome, *i.e.*, ending in adjustment or no record of discord—are better, therefore, if the treatment does not take the family to the Court of Domestic Relations." This has proved so true that only apparently hopeless cases are now brought into court. "On the question of court intervention", says Joanna Colcord, Superintendent of the Charity Organization Society of New York City, "there has been in desertion and non-support cases almost a right-about-face; the best social practitioners now say, unhesitatingly and unequivocally, that they take cases into court only as a matter of last resort, after case-work methods have been tried and have failed. In no other case where court action is undertaken by one individual against another does the relation between them remain unchanged. One could not conceive of a business partnership failing to be annulled by one partner who brought suit against another, yet we expect the marriage relation to survive this. As a matter of fact, such is its vitality that it often does. But many times the result of court action is only to deaden once and for all the tiny spark from which marital happiness might have been rekindled."

We must omit here a consideration of the circumstances under which domestic relations are satisfactory or unsatisfactory to those immediately concerned, except to say that they involve sexual adjustment, which is in turn dependent upon the capacity of husband and wife for adult emotions. The point under immediate notice is that social efforts to compel responsible paternal behavior are in our culture confessedly on the whole a failure; and that on the other hand, satisfactory domestic relations bring about parental responsibility with no need for other social compulsions. The domestic relation is itself without doubt in certain respects a social construction; but it has natural bases of physical and psychic response which justify us in distinguishing it from social constructions pure and simple. . . . Doctor William Healy, director of the Judge Baker Foundation, quotes an interview of an American woman, a student of the problem of illegitimacy, with Castberg, the originator of the Norwegian law giving children born out of wedlock the same rights as any others. "She asked: 'Are you not lowering the standard of ethics for women and are you not eliminating the family as the unit of society?' The old Viking shook back his hair and brought his fist down on the table and said to me, 'No, absolutely no. That is nature, the love of the man and the woman to care for their own child—you cannot break that up.' "

There is much to be said for the view that the effect of social custom and law upon the family relationship has been directed toward selectively inhibiting the emotions of paternal responsibility. Among certain animals the impregnation of the female is instinctively followed by a domestic life together. Among human beings at any level of culture this domesticity *may or may not* occur—custom, taboo and law requiring that it *shall* occur in socially approved cases, and equally requiring that it *shall not* occur in others. The girls of the Trobriand Islands near New Guinea, as described by the anthropologist Malinowski, live premarital lives of complete sexual freedom, but they must *not* have babies until after they are married. Nor in general do they. "Gomaya, one of my early informants, had a relation with a girl called Ilamweria. She became pregnant and gave birth to a girl, whereupon Gomaya abandoned her. He was quite convinced that she had never had relations with another boy." (In fact, physical fatherhood does not exist according to the religious tenets of this matrilineal people.) "It was enough that there was prenuptial motherhood, which is considered reprehensible by the natives. For Gomaya this was a sufficient reason to give up his matrimonial plans with regard to this particular girl." Had they been married before the birth of the child, Gomaya would have ceremonially taken the child in his arms, and henceforth would have been required to help bring it up. But it was not a socially approved birth, because it occurred before marriage, and so Gomaya was required to repress any impulses of tenderness and to refrain from any protective behavior toward his child—or rather, he was forbidden to live on such terms of domestic intimacy with mother and child as would have elicited in him such responsive paternal behavior.

For one social reason or another, paternal behavior is thus selectively discouraged all over the world. Nevertheless, in defiance of law and official tribal morality, though not of actual custom, domestic establishments outside of marriage are often set up. The result, concerning which there is an abundance of testimony, is that the children of these illicit unions are treated with the same tenderness by the father as if they were legitimate children whom he is 'obliged' to love; these 'love-children' are only abandoned later under social pressure—and not always even then.

Among the many testimonies to the emotional ties of natural fatherhood under conditions of domestic intimacy following love-choice, is that of St. Augustine, quoted at length above (Chapter III, § 1). He paid candid tribute to the power of instinctive parental love to resist the claims of social 'duty' in his description of "the compact of passionate love, where though children be begotten against our wishes, being born they compel us to love them". It was in spite of social duty as construed in those patriarchal times that he kept his illegitimate child by his side, when in obedience to social duty he sent his mistress away.

Social custom and law have thus, except in approved instances, operated purposefully to discourage paternal tenderness and care and the domestic arrangements which would encourage parental behavior. Marriage as a mode of determining the inheritance of property has been a social instrument by which all except socially approved children were denied so far as possible the love and care of the father. Marriage has been for some thousands of years in respectable property-owning society, up to modern times, an institution hostile to all the natural emotions and fearful of their intrusion. The Central Australian marriage system seems merely to caricature the essential distrust of human nature implicit in respectable property-transmitting marriage throughout European history: as described by Spencer and Gillen, Father A contracts with Father B to the effect that *when* B's daughter (a mere infant, but already betrothed) is married, *and* bears a daughter, and *that daughter* becomes of marriageable age, *she* shall become the wife of A's son! This is the most triumphant and conclusive exclusion of instinctive sexual choice upon anthropological record. The Greek system as smugly defined by Demosthenes is scarcely less artificial—"hetairai for our delight, concubines for the daily needs of our bodies, wives in order that we may beget legitimate children and have faithful housekeepers." Human nature is remarkably docile under social coercion, but it is difficult to keep one's emotions so neatly partitioned off into separate categories. Nowadays we call it a 'split libido' and regard it as a neurosis. Under the social pressure of property institutions, instinctive mating has been in the patriarchal past, as we have seen, cut off wherever possible from its biological ends in parenthood and family life, while domesticity and responsible paternity have been as far as possible stripped of their biological preliminaries in free courtship and love-choice. The historic mutilations and deformations of the natural pattern of play, courtship, selective choice, reproduction and family life, have furnished the conditions under which the existence of such a pattern could be plausibly denied. To have admitted its existence would have been to admit the artificiality of those social arrangements.

The Trobriand Islanders have a matrilinear organization in which the son inherits from his maternal uncle; in order to support this social arrangement they have to deny religiously that the mother's husband is any relation to the son; and they then have to deny that sexual relations have anything whatever to do with the production of children! It is not (*pace* Malinowski) a matter of naïve ignorance, but a matter of strict dogma; they dare not intellectually accept the obvious facts of physical paternity, even when these are brought to their attention—they only become angry.

The patriarchal system has labored under a similar intellectual disadvantage of having to assert that its artifices were laws of nature. Hear the wise Aristotle repeat the profound patriarchal dictum: "The male is by nature superior, and the female inferior; and the one rules, the other is ruled." It is "according to nature" that the freeman should rule over the slave, he says, the man over his wife, the father over his children. "For the slave has no deliberative faculty at all; the woman has, but it is immature." Professor Aristotle also regarded it as economically and politically expedient that wives should be only half the age of their husbands at marriage; and he was innocent of any suspicion that this particular arrangement might conduce to the 'natural' superiority of the husband over the wife.

If the philosophers of the patriarchal era could so easily persuade themselves that 'what is ours is natural', it was likely enough that the poets and prophets who hailed the breakdown of patriarchal institutions should, like Rousseau and the Romantics generally, idealize 'Nature' and renounce the 'errors of civilization'. We are now undergoing a reaction in our day against those enthusiasms. It was too confidently believed that if young people were only set free to choose their own mates without parental interference, their marriages would be happy and stable, and their children well brought up. That has not proved to be the case. But 'freedman' psychology is scarcely normal. And before we despair of our freedom, before we hark back wistfully to the good old days when we did what we were told whether we liked it or not—married the wives our parents picked for us, and were not expected to be faithful to them, scattered our bastards here and there, because it didn't matter, and brought up our lawful sons to the same tune under social compulsion—let us consider whether our instincts might not be a better guide to usefulness and happiness in this as in other matters if we were in a state of adult psychic development and health.

It is the belief, then, of modern psychological science that we have in men as in women parental instincts which can be trusted, as a part of the whole natural mating cycle, to provide all the emotional incentives necessary for the task of child-rearing, without legal compulsion. These instincts do not of course furnish us with the knowledge of how to adapt our educational methods to the demands of civilization. But the denial of the existence of paternal instincts is a patriarchal dodge to get us back into the fold; it is counter-revolutionary patriarchal propaganda. The next step in such propaganda is the denial that mothers have any maternal instincts; and the final step would be to deny that babies can learn how to suck milk without being ordered to do so by Church and State. The real aim of such pseudo-scientific pretenses that social coercion is necessary in the domestic realm is not to make parents love their children; it is to keep them from loving any but 'legitimate' children—it is an attempt to preserve the institution of family property from the dangers of instinctive parental love.

§ 3. 'Never, Never Hug the Baby!'

Before we get too far away from the theory of the 'abolition of the family' it would be well to discuss a related form of exaggerated idealism which has at least a momentary intellectual currency. Just as the evils of patriarchal family life aroused a desire to 'crush the damned thing', so the evils of contemporary neurotic mothering have aroused a desire to do away with mothering entirely. The ideal of abolishing the family by State Parenthood, however, as we have seen, was only jumping from the patriarchal frying-pan into the patriarchal fire. And the contemporary idealism which seeks to protect children against neurotic mothering by abolishing mothering altogether, or by restricting it by formal sets of rules based upon fear, may only serve to create worse infantile fixations upon the mother.

The exaggerated revolt against mothering has its most distinguished and fanatical propagandist in Dr. John B. Watson, inventor of the theory of 'Behaviorism', and author of a book (preluded by a series of articles in a woman's magazine) on the *Psychological Care of Infant and Child.*

The present writer is incapable of estimating the scientific value of Dr. Watson's experiments within the realm of behavior-study, but it may be taken for granted that they constitute a real contribution to knowledge. However, any intelligent reader is capable of seeing the complete lack of connection between Dr. Watson's careful and exact experiments and his passionate denunciations of mothering. His book is an indignant and almost broken-hearted defense of children against the evils of 'coddling' in infancy, and with much that he says there can be no possible quarrel by any intelligent parent. But his hatred of neurotic mothering is so intense as to be reckless and in places more than a little foolish. His heart is always in the right place—he is for the child's right to grow up. "When I hear a mother say 'Bless its little heart' when it falls down, or stubs its toe, or suffers some other ill, I usually have to walk a block or two to let off steam." Does him credit, too, as a human being. But he is still merely letting off steam, still merely expressing his violent indignation, when he comes back and writes: "I sometimes wish that we could live in a community of homes where each home is supplied with a well-trained nurse so that we could have the babies fed and bathed each week by a different nurse." He has not tried the experiment—though the conditions in orphanages, and the experiences of orphan children who live in a succession of homes, suggest that the results might not be favorable—but he is sure it would work out splendidly. Here he doesn't have to experiment in order to 'know'—he speaks from the depths of emotion.

Indeed, hospital experience appears to have definitely shown the unwisdom of Dr. Watson's views. Dr. Dorian Feigenbaum in a psychoanalytic paper on child care calls attention to a report in *Kosmos* of an address by a German pediatrist, Professor Ibrahim, regarding the methods of preventing deaths among institution infants whose mothers, during the war, worked in munition plants or behind the line.

Until a few years ago, says the report, children in public institutions, deprived of their mothers' care, fell into a state of decline which received the name of 'hospital disease' or 'hospitalism'. Its symptoms were loss of appetite, cessation of growth, intestinal disturbances, nervous restlessness and sleeplessness, and inclination to catarrhal and glandular disorders. In spite of the modern equipment and thorough care received in such nurseries, the children died. It was observed that they did not appear to want to live, and lack of love was assigned as the cause of their deaths. Man (said Ibrahim) is not a machine that can be fed with fuel and run by a time-table; the new-born child is no soldier to be put through a barrack routine—"it wishes to receive attention as *I* and be treated as a personality. The smallest human being is—happily!—the greatest egotist." Until a few years ago it was impossible to keep babies alive in institutions; "success came first recently when it was recognized that the reason for hospitalism was lack of love, and individual nursing was substituted for promiscuous or mass nursing." Each wet-nurse has a limited number of nurslings, and she must treat them "as her own, individually and lovingly". The more, said Ibrahim, that we realize the importance of mothering, the less we shall have of the horrors of hospitalism. To what has been done in this direction he attributes the decline in mortality in children's hospitals.

To go back to Dr. Watson.—Mothers really should, he says, be rotated, a different one every two weeks, like nurses "in well-regulated homes". But the same mother may be tolerated if she is sensible. "There is a sensible way of treating children. Treat them as though they were young adults. Dress them, bathe them with care and circumspection. Let your behavior always be objective and kindly firm. Never hug and kiss them, never let them sit in your lap."

Exaggerated as these prescriptions and proscriptions are, they are indubitably well-meant. They are intelligible when understood as a protest against the constant babying of children which goes on in some households. They are, it is true, quite beside the point of really intelligent child-training. Children are not 'young adults', and it would be absurd if they were really treated as such.

What is meant is 'Don't treat them like dolls'. But who treats children like dolls? Parents who are psychically infantile themselves. Dr. Watson suggests that it is because the mother has to have some one to 'love'. He assumes that 'love' is bound to be neurotic and silly. "No matter how much she may love her husband, he is away all day; her heart is full of love which she must express in some way. She expresses it by showering love and kisses on her children." Does she, indeed? Not by a jugful. She doesn't indulge in neurotic 'love'-tricks unless she is neurotic. If she is psychically adult enough to be in love with her husband, she doesn't take out her love inappropriately on her children—even if her husband is 'away all day'. And if she is psychically infantile, she will victimize them just the same even if her husband is at home continually. These adjurations and injunctions are unnecessary to psychically healthy parents. For psychically healthy parents will be able to give their children the reassurance of love and of petting—which they do need, in spite of Dr. Watson—without harming them. For they will be loving the child *as a child* and not as a substitute-lover. They will not be gratifying their ungratified sexual emotions in their maternal hugs and kisses. In fact, psychically healthy parents will be able to break all of Dr. Watson's rules with impunity. The child will feel the difference. A hug or a smack (the taboo on kissing children on the lips being accepted on hygienic and not sex-alarmist grounds) from a psychically healthy mother will produce none whatever of all the frightful consequences in later life so solemnly enunciated by Dr. Watson. And on the other hand, every one of these rules may be strictly obeyed by neurotic parents, with neurotic results just the same; a honeyed pseudo-maternal tone can be full of saccharine sexuality, a flirtation with pseudo-maternal glances can enslave a child, where genuinely maternal hugs and kisses will leave him emotionally free. Dr. Watson fails to perceive this fundamental distinction. He allows, as a kind of despairing concession to maternal weakness, "a kiss once on the forehead when they say good night"—"if you must". He regards all maternal caresses as necessarily poisonous, that is to say, in a terminology he does not use, neurotic; and all he can think of is to forbid them, and to try to scare the mother into abeyance of her mischievous maternal habits by talking about the way she is 'conditioning the reflexes' of her children. "She is starved for love—affection, as she prefers to call it." True enough, of neurotic mothers. "It is at bottom a sex-seeking response in her"—very true. But the mother who is not love-starved and unconsciously sex-seeking, who has achieved emotional adulthood and is enjoying a healthy love and sex life in her marriage, is to be trusted to bring up her children without any fear that her maternal caresses are going to blast her children's lives.

Not only are Dr. Watson's rules irrelevant to child-training in a home where the parents are psychically healthy and adult in their love-lives, but they are all too likely to be useless to neurotic parents. Children can be emotionally exploited by neurotic parents in the name not only of Religion, of Duty, or Morality, and of Love, but—not with equal ease perhaps, but with the marvelous ingenuity of which the unconscious mind is capable—in the name of Science, of Freedom, of Freud, and of Dr. Watson. It is never difficult to construe the Tables of the Law so as to give sanction to one's own neurotic wishes. Thus, in the following passage, what Dr. Watson seeks is to secure objective 'conditioning of the reflexes' without unnecessary maternal interventions: "It [the infant] should be taken up at 7 o'clock, sponged lightly, dressed and given its breakfast at 7:30; then allowed to romp until 8, then put upon the toilet for 20 minutes or less (until the bowel movement is complete). The infant from eight months onward should have a special toilet seat into which he can be safely strapped." Etc. But one anxious mother, by carrying out these excellent suggestions with, as she believed, complete exactitude, merely succeeded in giving her child an emotional fixation (or should we say a conditioned reflex?) with regard to that 'special toilet seat', so that he could not function in this respect at a neighbor's house. This was neither an accident, nor an inevitable result of the application of these quite judicious rules. It was the result of the unconscious purpose with which they were applied by the mother. Consciously, she wished to protect her child from the preposterously exaggerated attention of a whole tribe of neurotic female relatives; unconsciously she wanted to make her child completely dependent upon *her own* care. She 'rationalized' her purpose as a desire to be the scientific and 'sensible' mother whom Dr. Watson seeks to conjure out of the void. She became it with a vengeance, she brandished Dr. Watson's book at the relatives, she barricaded the nursery door with Science; until there was left to the poor child only a 'kindly firm' mother (keeping herself at a tantalizing distance from her child, and never, *never* kissing it!) and the presiding ghost, shall we say, of Dr. Watson: the most secure and reassuring thing in all its childish universe being the special toilet seat! She had succeeded in enslaving the child and herself to a scientific apparatus which in turn enslaved them to each other. To be sure, that was not what Dr. Watson intended; but it shows where an exaggerated fear and hatred of maternal coddling is all too likely to land you—right back in maternal (or paternal!) coddling, so disguised in scientific verbiage, so thoroughly 'rationalized', so buttressed against criticism, as to be almost impregnable.

Dr. Watson should not be blamed for this particular misuse of his ideas. But his own emotional attitude is exaggerated to such a degree as to detract seriously from the public usefulness of his book. That is a pity, for despite the short-sightedness of his views, they include true standards of child development, and some very valuable new suggestions—as for example in the matter of the child's clothing.—"(Why buttons should ever have been placed in the exact center of the back on any child's dress is more than a psychologist can explain.)"—The subject of instruction in sex is also very admirably handled. Indeed, there are so many fine things in this book that one regrets the necessity of exposing its follies. Even these, its outbursts of frantic rage against maternal caresses and its anxiously absurd laws for their prevention, being dictated by emotions of sympathy for the child-victims of neurotic mothers, can be forgiven. They have been brought up here at all only because this particular emotional excess fits all too well the neurotic patterns of a great many people; having suffered from coddling in their own childhood, they believe they have in Dr. Watson's book full scientific justification for rushing to the opposite extreme in bringing up their own children. They have to be told that avoidance of parental caresses will not make neurotic parents into healthy ones; that Dr. Watson is mistaken in his over-emphasis upon that point; and that children do need to be sure of their parents' love for them.

CHAPTER VIII

SOME MORE IDEOLOGICAL OVERCOMPENSATIONS

[Exaggerated or False Ideals—as to Women and their Independence of Men]

§ 1. 'Woman as a Free Worker'

The ideological overcompensations next to be discussed concern both men and women, but they will be considered chiefly as affecting women. The first of these has already been alluded to—the extreme pre-war feminist theory which, taking note of the increase in the work of married women outside the home, goes on to envisage a state of affairs in which careers in the realm of wage (or salaried) labor will be the normal goal of all women, instead of the restricted career of wifehood-and-maternity. Thus far, except in its emotional emphasis, there is nothing in this social theory to arouse our suspicions. It is true—to rehearse briefly some aspects of the industrial revolution—that the invention of modern machinery has taken a great deal of what used to be 'women's work' outside the home; and that if women are not to be idle and parasitic they must follow it into factories and offices.

The women of the working class have had little or no choice in this matter; they have been obliged to work outside the home. There has been for them no need for a social theory as an encouragement to their venturing outside the home; they have gone out of the home into the factory under the lash of necessity. And they have done so, not as a means of keeping their self-respect, not as a way of doing their duty by society, not as a way of keeping from stagnating in idleness; when they have gone out to work, it has been for the sake of their homes, to help provide food and clothing for their children and money to pay the rent. From their point of view it has been a way of making the best of a bad situation; they have to neglect their homes in order to help maintain a home at all—they have to neglect their children in order to keep them from starving and freezing. For they are not able to replace their own services in the home by servants paid for out of their wages; and day-nurseries and such other aids as may be furnished by the State and various social agencies are more educative than substitutive in value. Thus the statement of this social theory of work as women's goal is strictly a middle-class overcompensation against parisitism. The idea of work as a *goal* would be repudiated by working women; to them it is a *means to an end,* and the end is love, marriage, children and home-making.

But in practice, as distinguished from theory, the same is true for the young women of the middle class. It is through having careers—or starting out to have them—that they are likely to find their best opportunities for achieving their instinctive goals of mating and maternity. Thus we can see one excellent reason why this social theory should have attained popularity among middle-class feminine youth. If the time has gone by (and it has) when marriage was for men an immediate economic advantage, if a girl could no longer sit in the shelter of the parental home and wait for suitors, then an economic ambition was for a girl the best kind of marriage-insurance. Work brought her among men; her capacities for self-support allayed their economic anxieties; and, once given propinquity, her instincts and theirs achieved their ends in marriage and children. Thus the theory of the economic independence of women served benevolently to disguise the girl's ancient search for a man to be the father and protector of her children. Nor have we any quarrel with these unconscious deceptions and self-deceptions, especially so long as they serve a biological purpose and fulfil the individual wish for happiness. It is insofar as they serve other ends, religious or artistic, in reconciling women to their lot, that they may come under criticism here.

The fact is, as noted above, that in America the pioneer or free-land period has passed. The discovery and settlement of America afforded to European peoples a period about three centuries long in which the social conditions of land-bound patriarchal society could be escaped from by pioneers, and in which the existence of a frontier, of free land for the taking, relaxed economic tensions throughout Western civilization. The importance of the pioneer background in contemporary American culture cannot receive adequate attention here; but it may be said that its most significant effect upon the mating situation was in lowering the marriage age for men and in making a wife and family economically desirable assets for a young man. The disappearance of the frontier changed this state of affairs, tended to raise the marriage age for men. Other effects of machine production, especially the general abolition of apprenticeship, have on the other hand tended to lower the age at which young men could marry. But wives and children are not immediate economic assets in an industrial society, as they were in pioneer days. However, the machine age has opened up to women other ways of making a living. It was doubtless necessary that they should learn the gratifications that work provides in itself, aside from its uses in maintaining a home.

But though careers of a self-expressive nature may be truly gratifying in themselves, there is no doubt that scrubbing floors for example is more gratifying when it is one's own floor that is scrubbed than when it is the floor of an office-building. To tell scrubwomen that they have been 'liberated' by the machine age from the toilsome drudgery of private home-making into a wider field of social usefulness would be silly; nor would the scrubwomen be taken in. But there is a large section of the population which is distinctly middle-class in culture and yet so economically insecure that it belongs otherwise to the working class; and to the intelligent young women of this group the social undervaluation of their sexual capacities which they suffer is such that they must get what satisfaction they can in an over-valuation of their industrial careers. They are distinctly not wanted as childbearers; their capacities in that direction are alarming rather than gratifying to the young men with whom they associate. They are not wanted as wives by young men who cannot afford to get married. In patriarchal times marriage was subsidized; the girl was given a dowry, and her parents or brothers acted as matchmakers in her behalf. But now these patriarchal devices are broken down; the girl must shift for herself, and find her own husband. She is in somewhat the same position as a dowryless girl in patriarchal society.

Such a girl had to reconcile herself to the prospect of going husbandless and childless. She was given the opportunity of doing useful social work, either in the parental home as a spinster, or in a religious institution as a nun. To enable her to accept these limited satisfactions in lieu of marriage and motherhood, their importance was emphasized, perhaps we may justly say magnified. 'Family duty' and 'the religious life' were the terms under which a continuous cultural campaign was waged, with the purpose and effect of reconciling large numbers of women to the loss of the adult sexual rights of love, mating and motherhood. The modern social theory which magnifies the importance of women's work in factories and offices serves the same purpose, though in our society it is not intended to reconcile them permanently to such a condition. It is used as a temporary consolation, and it is in practice combined with another patriarchal compromise.

Of the girls for whom there were no dowries in the patriarchal régime, not all remained old maids in the parental home or became nuns in religious institutions; a great many became prostitutes, hetairai or mistresses. They were thus permitted to have a sexual life of a sort, though one devoid of responsibility. They could not have socially recognized matings, and they bore children at their own risk. Without attaching to the modern girl worker any undeserved stigma of prostitution, we may recognize that society tends to grant her similar sexual freedoms, along with the privilege of work. She is not condemned to a *permanent* career of secret and irresponsible sexual gratifications; these are *temporary* alleviations of her lot. Nor has the gloriousness of these sexual privileges been as publicly celebrated as the glory of working for wages. Nevertheless when any publicist or novelist has spoken a kind word about these necessitous compromises, it has been hailed by a large number of young people eager for some idealization of a situation which they face or already find themselves in. A kind of unofficial censorship prevents the free public expression of the immense amount of private idealization of 'sexual freedom' which exists in our society. But the fact is that large numbers of young people for whom there are no immediate prospects of marriage do console themselves with irresponsible sexual gratifications for a period of years. This has always been true of young men in patriarchal society, and now it is becoming increasingly true of girls. They feel, however, the need for intellectual justification and still more for emotional reassurance as to these incidents, which are in themselves so full of emotional frustration. This need is partly met through novels and poetry. It is, as has been said before in these pages and will be urged later at length, the function of art to provide such religious consolation. But that is not the function of science. And a social theory which is used to glorify these poor substitutes and compromises is not scientific but religious or artistic.

What modern psychology has to say about these socially frustrated love affairs is that they generally represent infantile and not adult forms of sexual behavior; and that the important thing about an individual instance is whether or not it is a step upward along the path of development toward adult life—whether it is educational, and if so whether at too great an emotional cost to the individual. Young people can often bear robustly more emotional misadventure than can well be realized by older people who have forgotten their own youth. They can bear misadventures which teach them what are their real emotional goals and make them better able to achieve such goals. But again they may be permanently discouraged from such adult achievement.

And it is here that we have to consider the effect of a social theory which obscures the importance of the adult goal of sexual happiness in marriage and parenthood. Its effect is to 'save face', to reconcile young people to emotional compromise, to disguise failure. *It needs to be said that useful wage-labor, enlivened by occasional secret sexual love-affairs, probably punctuated at intervals by abortions, without prospect of permanency and without hope of mutual responsible parenthood, is not a glorious or even a satisfactory career for a young woman. It is merely a combination of patriarchal nunship with patriarchal hetairism.*

(The phrase might be more striking, but would be quite *unjust*, if it ran 'a combination of patriarchal nunship with patriarchal harlotry'; for the comparison is not with the mercenary character of irregular patriarchal amours, but with their temporary character. Sexual companionship is in itself deeply satisfying, but the less so when it is prescriptively forbidden to have any permanence. It is, or may be, a normal stage of courtship, and as such it does not limit itself to the passing moment but looks forward to and may grow into marriage and parenthood. It is when the sexual relation is limited to companionship cut off from deeper issues that it is merely a pseudo-modern hetairism.)

It would have been unjust to 'blame' the young people who accepted the tawdry compromises of the old patriarchal régime. A half-love is better than none; and we have the testimony of the poets as to how much passion and sincerity could be put into their frustrated loves, how much beauty and sweetness as well as despair and bitterness could be found there. It would be as unjust and as stupid, nowadays, to 'blame' young people for taking their pseudo-modern half-loves. Our poets and novelists bear testimony as to their passion and sincerity and beauty. But we may question their modernity. We may say that insofar as our machine age fails to grant opportunities for adult sexual relations to its populations, insofar as it condemns them to a revised version of patriarchal compromises and frustrations, it is still patriarchal, still incompletely modernized.

The task of modern psychology may here seem unkind; but it must needs strip the idealistic disguises from a familiar situation of necessitous compromise. Perhaps if we can recognize our half-loves for what they are, we will individually find it easier to achieve adult relationships; and if economic circumstances still stand in our way, perhaps our discontent will help in bringing about the further modernization of our economic arrangements.

Many of these considerations will seem already out of date. They apply perhaps more especially to a pre-war stage of young feminine idealism. The post-war stage, as expressed in current poetry and autobiographical fiction, is one which is marked by a larger experience of work outside the homes for wages and a greater experience of sexual 'freedom', but marked also by a complete absence of idealistic illusions about either. The younger generation of women now beginning to find a voice in literature is frankly discontented with the terms upon which both work and love are open to them.

Meanwhile, we are perhaps in a position to recognize any theoretical idealization of woman as a wage worker, which is at the same time a depreciation of the importance to her of mating and maternity, as being the old patriarchal swindle upon human nature. Its aim is to make her a contented wage worker while she is being robbed of her sexual rights. Doubtless this bunco-game served an excellent social purpose in getting girls out of the dying patriarchal home, "the girl's prison and the women's work-house", as Shaw called it; doubtless it may be better to be a bachelor-girl hetaira for a while than an old maid forever. "You never know what is enough unless you know what is more than enough", as Blake said, and "the road of excess leads to the palace of wisdom". But now that they are out of the old patriarchal home, the problem is for them to get back into the home on modern and self-respecting terms; and it does not help them to pretend otherwise.

§ 2. 'Free Motherhood'

It has been shown that one of the characteristic features of the patriarchal régime was the stigma put upon the illegitimate child and its mother for economic reasons. It is correspondingly a feature of our developing non-patriarchal society that it tends to remove this stigma; it strikes at the root of the cruel patriarchal convention by requiring the father of children to help support them whether they are begotten in or out of marriage. It is true that this obligation of partial support is in many instances limited or nominal; and that it is not highly enforceable by law in the absence of domestic relations between the father and mother. The most advanced laws on the subject are that of Norway (1916), which "gives to a child born out of wedlock the same right of inheritance that is given a child of legitimate birth" ["except in the case of peasants' farms"]; that of Sweden (1918), which "gives no right of inheritance from the father except in the case of 'betrothal children' but places the responsibility for support on both parents"; that of Russia (1918) which provides that "Children descending from parents who are not married have equal rights with those descending from parents living in registered marriage"; and that of Minnesota (1917), which declares that its purpose is "primarily to safeguard the interest of illegitimate children, and secure for them the nearest possible approximation to the care, support and education that they would be entitled to receive if born of lawful marriage." In 1922 the National Conference of Commissioners on Uniform State Laws (U. S) approved and recommended to the States for adoption a uniform illegitimacy act, the principles of which have since been incorporated into the laws of several Western states, and which has influenced legislation in other states. It declares: "The parents of a child born out of wedlock and not legitimated owe the child necessary maintenance, education, and support." It makes the father liable for the expenses of the mother's pregnancy and confinement. The obligations of the parents to support the child under the laws for the support of poor relatives are also made to apply to children born out of wedlock.

The illegitimacy problem is an extremely complicated one, not to be summed up in a phrase. It is partly a question of protecting the State against the burdens of support of illegitimate children by placing their burdens on the father and mother—the latter being by these same laws restrained from the policy of abandonment which has come down from the patriarchal régime and is still in vogue in some patriarchal countries, as in Latin America, where foundlings are left at religious institutions. This is one break with the patriarchal past. The new laws, by recognizing the rights of illegitimate children to parentage, implicitly recognize the rights of men and women to become parents outside of marriage, upon the same terms or as nearly as possible the same terms of responsibility as within marriage. That is another break with the patriarchal past. These laws, by recognizing (in greater or less degree) the right of children born out of wedlock to *inherit* from their parents, repudiate the economic purpose of the cruel patriarchal discriminations exercised on behalf of the family institution. That is one more break with the patriarchal past; in Sweden the peasants, whose property is in land, have secured exemption from these inheritance laws, and in Soviet Russia the peasants have bitterly complained of them—so that we may recognize that these new laws are characteristic of a society which has passed beyond the landed-property stage of economics.

These laws, as in Sweden, tend to rehabilitate the old pagan and rural institution which is sometimes (but erroneously) called 'trial marriage'; it is really a form of engagement or betrothal in which sexual relations are conventionally permitted; the engagement could be broken at will by either party before pregnancy occurred but not afterward, and it became a marriage and was socially recognized and legally ratified as such when a child was born. It may for convenience be called here 'sexual betrothal'. This pagan sexual-betrothal custom has lasted (Havelock Ellis reports) in Northern Europe from pre-Christian times among various parts of the population, chiefly but not always rural. In Sweden, according to Ellen Key, the majority of the population begin married life in this way; in Denmark a large number of children are conceived before the unions of the parents are legalized; in Germany ante-nuptial conceptions take place in nearly half the marriages, and sometimes in the majority; it was the 'island custom' of Portland, England, until well on into the 19th century, and it has been reported as common in many "or perhaps all" parts of England; in France the custom among the urban working classes resisted the influences of the Latin patriarchal tradition, so that in the late 19th century it was stated that in an average Paris arondissement nine out of ten legal marriages were the consolidation of 'free unions' [sexual betrothals, rather], and early in the present century it was said that at least half the marriages were of this kind. This betrothal custom tended to be restricted to (or to disguise itself in manners which purported to be restricted to) courtship conventions which, says Ellis, "while allowing the young couple to spend the night together, in a position of more or less intimacy, exclude, as a rule, sexual intercourse." This custom of 'courting in bed' was imported into America by various North European rural peoples early in colonial history; as 'bundling' it was mocked out of vogue, as Professor Calhoun shows, by English and urban influences, and had to compromise with artistocratic conventions of chaperonage; nevertheless it gave a naturalistic basis to courtship which has been retained in American culture.

The pagan convention of betrothal with full sexual privileges, and the right to break off before but not after pregnancy occurred, has also been carried down to the present times in America among rural and working people; and the legal marriage after pregnancy has occurred has often been enforced by the girl's father or brothers by threats of violence, giving rise to the phrase 'shotgun weddings'.

In the conflict of cultural conventions—when the sexual freedom of betrothal could be construed by an unscrupulous or fickle suitor in the light of the patriarchal tradition of virgin brides, as a proof of the girl's being merely a harlot and worthy only of desertion—the old custom would die out as a social convention; and the unsatisfactory nature of enforced marriages would lead to the abandonment of such attempts to maintain masculine responsibility in such betrothals. The mixed character of the American population, leading to misunderstandings between lovers as to the extent of the responsibility of the man in sexual relationships, has caused a general abandonment of the old custom. Nevertheless, among social groups in which there is a common cultural basis and hence a greater possibility of mutual understanding and trust between lovers, the privileges of an engaged couple are often tacitly taken to include sexual intercourse; and in many groups in which sexual intercourse is otherwise regarded as morally reprehensible in an unmarried girl, it is no derogation of her respectability if it occurs during an engagement or even during a series of different engagements. Dr. G. V. Hamilton's study of two hundred American husbands and wives revealed that "almost a third of the men and women [23 out of 100 men, 36 out of 100 women] had enjoyed sexual relations with their mates before marriage"; the proportion of husbands who had had sexual relations with their wives before marriage amounted to half of those born in 1880 or earlier, and declined with each age-group until it was only a little more than a quarter of those born in 1891 or later—which would suggest that the increasing cultural heterogeneity of the population was having its effect in discouraging these betrothal privileges.

(The decline in betrothal sexual relations by age-groups in Hamilton's cases was concomitant with an increase in the numbers of the women who had illicit sexual relations, before or after marriage, rising from 45% of those born in 1880 or earlier to 60% of those born in 1891 or later, and finally outdistancing the men in this respect: thus 80% of the men and 45% of the women born in 1880 or earlier had illicit sexual relations before or after marriage, while only 51% of the men born in 1891 or later had such illicit sexual relations as against 60% of the women in this younger age-group. *The decrease of betrothal sexual relations was thus accompanied by an increase in illicit sexual experiences of women outside of betrothal.*)

It is, however, precisely the pagan responsibility of the male for children born as a result of betrothal sexual relations which is given legal enforcement by the new illegitimacy laws, as against the patriarchal tradition of male irresponsibility. The new laws may thus be said to presume that entering into sexual relations constitutes implicitly a pledge by both the man and woman to bear between them their full responsibilities for any children they may bring into the world—a pledge which is a kind of natural marriage, and which the law undertakes to enforce as far as it can.

Since natural marriage also includes domesticity and ties of enduring affection, the law cannot in their absence give the full benefits of parentage to illegitimate children; but the presumption is that these should have been mutually promised, and that the failure of sexual partners to face and accept these mutual responsibilties puts them in the class of the ignorant, the reckless, the parasitic, the feeble-minded or the badly brought up, who must all be treated as children and wards of society. These as a matter of fact constitute a large proportion of illegitimacy cases, the bulk of those with which courts and social agencies have to deal. They involve young people who are lacking in the social responsibility or the personal caution or the intelligence or perhaps merely the knowledge necessary equally for successful adaptation to social codes or successful violation of such codes. The two main groups of illegitimacy cases to which the new laws apply are: (1) those representing natural marriages suffering from patriarchal injuries, which are sought to be rehabilitated legally in defiance of patriarchal tradition; and (2) those which represent the misadventures of children, fools and the socially disorganized.

But there is another group which needs to be taken into consideration. It is numerically small but of some sociological and psychological importance since it has given a special twist to contemporary thought on this subject. It is hardly represented in the statistics or the case-histories of illegitimacy, for it does not arise from culture-clashes, poverty, feeble-mindedness or social disorganization. It appeals to our interest not at all as pitiful but on the contrary as rather heroic. It is (3) the small group of women who have babies without being married, because they want them and do not want husbands. We may, indeed, go behind the returns and inquire if these ostensible reasons are the real ones; yet the importance of these cases is not in what may be the truth about the individual motives, but in the appeal which these reasons, genuine or not, have for the contemporary mind. Thus it might be that the real reason is that the father of such a child is already respectably married to some other woman; or that he does not want to marry the mother of his child; or that she has lost hope of getting a husband, and takes what she can. The pretence of not wanting to have the father of one's child as a husband would thus be a means of 'saving face' for herself, or for the man, or both. But the question is, why should the pretense, if it is such, be more 'face-saving' than the truth? Why, on the other hand, even though it be true that a woman merely wants a baby, should she not pretend that she wants the baby's father as a husband but cannot have him? Why does that situation merely appeal to public pity and the other to a kind of alarmed public admiration? Why is the plea of 'maternal-wish *minus* mating-wish' more effective before the bar of public opinion than the plea of inability through adverse circumstances to fulfil both the mating-wish and the maternal-wish?

Harking back to the unmarried mother of the first great group described above, she who became pregnant in the expectation of marriage, we find that her maternal instincts are so entwined with her mating instincts that when the mating instincts are frustrated by her lover's abandonment of her, her maternal instinct is also often temporarily checked in its outflow—so that she may abandon her child, or wish to give it away, or, if it is not yet born, have an abortion. What she wants is child-and-husband, and the two wishes are so much one in her mind that she often finds it at first impossible to love her child when her own mate-love has been repudiated. Under these circumstances it becomes the effort of the social agencies (or of her family, if it is sympathetic) to encourage her maternal impulse so that it can carry on without the help of mate-love. They do this in the interest of the child, which needs maternal care, and of society, which cannot provide efficient substitutes for that care; but they also do it on the girl's behalf, for when her maternal instinct has recovered from its temporary depression, as it almost invariably does, she wants her baby. But in the meantime the injury and insult of mate-desertion has to be compensated against, and the privilege and glory of maternity is talked up as though maternity were the most important and indeed the only important thing in the world.

Here for example is a letter sent by Judge Ben B. Lindsey "with a gift of flowers, to a young girl from one of Denver's best homes. Because of my urging she had consented to have her baby [instead of an abortion], at whatever cost to herself, and had just given birth to it." Here is the way maternity has to be talked up to girls who have no mates to give the adventure its full biological meaning: "To a brave, pure, sweet little girl whose suffering and nobility in doing what God and Nature would have her do rather than the cowardly thing thousands not half so good have done, more than atone for any mistake of conduct she ever made, and entitle her to all the love and respect that any girl in the world was ever entitled to; and which endear her, besides, to one who is very proud of her and her folks—for a brave, plucky fight."

Obviously this is in the nature of religious consolation—and a good job, too. The cool public report of social agencies that 'the girl was encouraged to take an interest in her child' covers a great deal of warm private eloquence. Bernard Shaw set the key for it in that speech of John Tanner's in *Man and Superman*: "Good Heavens, man, what are you crying for? Here is a woman whom we all supposed to be making bad water color sketches, practicing Grieg and Brahms, gadding about to concerts and parties, wasting her life and her money. We suddenly learn that she has turned from these sillinesses to the fulfillment of her highest purpose and greatest function—to increase, multiply and replenish the earth. And instead of admiring her courage and rejoicing in her instinct, instead of crowning the completed womanhood and raising the triumphal strain of 'Unto us a child is born: unto us a son is given', here you are all pulling long faces and looking as ashamed and disgraced as if the girl had committed the vilest of crimes." And to the girl, Violet, herself: "I know, and the whole world really knows, though it dare not say so, that you were right to follow your instinct; that vitality and bravery are the greatest qualities a woman can have, and motherhood her solemn initiation into womanhood; and the fact of your not being legally married matters not one scrap either to your own worth or to our real regard for you." If Violet, the object of all this eloquence, had really been unmarried, she would have appreciated these consolations; but as it is she is indignant—for they imply to her that she is regarded as either a poor unfortunate or a plain fool, in having a baby without a mate to share in the responsibilities of child-rearing.

Now it is obvious that girls who expect to have husbands-and-babies are in no need of the anticipatory consolations of a social theory which assures them that having babies-without-husbands is a glorious thing. For such a social theory to gain any wide emotional acceptance, so that it can be appealed to in support of individual cases of unmarried motherhood, there must be many women who cannot expect to have husbands. That, indeed, happens to be the social fact. It was true before the war, on account of economic conditions; and it was true on a huge scale in Europe after the killing and maiming of so many young men. A decrease in marriage opportunities means an inevitable increase in illegitimate births. If the discrepancy between the numbers of women and of possible husbands were to be expected to remain at the immediate post-war level (because of a future filled with continuous wars), or to increase because of bad economic conditions, then we should have to face the prospect of abandoning our system of monogamous mating; but the claims of polygamy would have to be urged against those of the husbandless-mother system. Polygamy is at least a workable system under such conditions. The polygamic marriage requires no subsidies from the State, as husbandless maternity usually does. The theory of unmarried motherhood is rather an emotional overcompensation to a bad economic situation than a valid prophecy of future social conditions. For that matter, the proportion of early marriages, and the proportion of marriages of women during the child-bearing ages, have all increased steadily in the United States from 1890 to 1920. This leaves us, as a motive for any widespread condition of voluntary motherhood combined with voluntary abstention from marriage on the part of women, only a peculiar sexual psychology. In the social theory it masquerades as feminine 'independence'; but we are obliged to choose between two possibilities—first, an unwillingness on the part of women to confine their sexual relations to a husband (a wish which could be as well satisfied in polite adultery, under cover of marriage); or second, the absence of the normal desire for a sexual relationship.

Here, indeed, we have the answer to our riddle of why a few examples of alleged voluntary husbandless motherhood have such an effect of arousing an alarmed public admiration. The implication is that a woman who is sexually indifferent to men has nevertheless under the 'pure' compulsion of the maternal instinct submitted herself to the biological process which is poor Nature's clumsy and obscene method of bringing about eventually a child! And, to paraphrase Gilbert:

> If she's content with a maternal love which would certainly not satisfy me,
> Why, what a most particularly pure young woman this unmarried mother must be!

If it is not exactly immaculate conception, it is evidently the next best thing.

It is, then, to Puritanical traditions that this theory of 'free motherhood' appeals. It is for this reason that it makes a more reputable and 'face-saving' public defense than the admission that one has been more passionate than discreet in one's love-life. The plea of preferring not to enjoy a mated love-life with the man deliberately chosen as the father of one's child, if true, would amount to a confession of some sort of sexual infantilism. It is unhappily true that in patriarchal marriage the satisfactions of maternity were often enough the only ones that a woman could reasonably expect to find, and she had to make the most of them. Legally married, she was nevertheless deprived of mate-love. There were patriarchal voices in plenty—notably of the Church—to tell her that she had the better part, that motherhood was enough, that the vulgar satisfactions of mating-sexuality were well foregone. And so our modern celebration of 'free motherhood' turns out to be an echo of these ghostly patriarchal voices!

It may appear to be inconsistent with this exposure to reiterate that every civilization has room for exceptions and that admiration need not be grudged to any kind of heroism. For 'heroism', as we choose to call it, fulfills a social function akin in its nature both to religious and to aesthetic consolation. People are entitled to identify themselves with the heroes and heroines of imaginative literary works, or with the living or dead heroes and heroines (or saints) whose differences from common mankind seem to shed a beneficent light upon their own peculiarities of temperament or situation. They are thereby made less lonely, they are comforted and cheered. But we are entitled to call them ideological over-compensations. Both religious and aesthetic consolation have their true dignity and justification in fulfilling in a necessarily exaggerated way in the realm of fantasy, needs that *cannot* be fulfilled in the realm of everyday actuality. If they *can* be fulfilled in actuality, it is cowardly and neurotic to accept a fantasy substitute.

CHAPTER IX

STILL MORE IDEOLOGICAL OVERCOMPENSATIONS

[Exaggerated or False Ideals—as to Sexual Freedom and Responsibility]

§ 1. 'Sex as Amusement'

Normal selective courtship begins in play. This play, which in civilized society is not overtly sexual, represents the first experimental post-pubertal contacts with the other sex. It is at first general, not highly personal. It affords opportunities for emotional development through experience, and its companionships in their progression give rise to instinctive comparisons. Selection proceeds, and becomes more personal. The individual is learning to love.

This selective courtship process, if not socially thwarted, leads on to mating and thence to parenthood.

In patriarchal society, however, with its peculiar displacements and rearrangements of the incidents of the sexual cycle, the segregation of the sexes prevented any instinctive courtship between two people who were to be married. If instinctive courtship occurred at all for the girl, it could occur only after marriage had given her (as it did in some patriarchal societies) the right to associate with men in general. She thus first enjoyed *after marriage* the companionship of the other sex at large; and her behavior followed, within socially prescribed limits, the normal developments of instinctive sexual selection. That is, what she at first enjoyed was the multiplicity of social contacts with the other sex. These experiences developed her emotional nature, and the instinctive comparisons to which they gave rise were selective. Her companionships became more highly personal. She was learning to love—something which being abruptly put to bed with a man of her family's choice could never teach her. It might happen, indeed, that in these comparisons her own husband came off best. It was perhaps not impossible—though it was held so by medieval love-logic—that a woman should love her own husband. More probably, or so the evidence goes to show, she would fall in love with some other man. She might, from fear of death or disgrace, repress or sublimate this love. If not, she entered into sexual relations with her lover. Patriarchal society very frequently gave her tacit and sometimes express permission to do so.

Now this entering into sexual relations here marks the arrival of the individual at the stage of mating. In the absence of social regulations to the contrary, these lovers would have an instinctively exclusive sexual union, which they would believe or hope to be permanent, and their announcement of their belief or hope to the world would constitute a marriage. In the normal sexual cycle, the achievement by selective courtship of a mate is the instinctive guarantee of a union lasting long enough to provide nurture for children. And in this faith they would have children.

But in patriarchal society, a socially arranged marriage and probably parenthood also had preceded this instinctive mating. The woman was tied. Modern society would permit divorce and re-marriage in spite of these complications. But in patriarchal society the property considerations which had originally brought about her marriage were still paramount. She might, indeed, furnish a theme to legend, poetry and drama by running away with her lover and making it a natural and real marriage in defiance of religion, duty, poverty and danger. More usually she surrendered to patriarchal society. But she would be disappointed in her lover for tamely acquiescing in that surrender; or ashamed of herself for having been lacking in courage. At any rate, the glory of their love would have departed. She would take another lover, of whom she would never be tempted to entertain such outrageous hopes. She would never again be 'such a fool' as to love like that. And in lieu of these outrageous hopes of love, sex would remain an agreeable pastime. There was no reason, moreover, why these pleasures should be shared with only one lover, since they could be had with men in general. So she might become a devotee of what is known as 'light love'.

That is to say, the mating impulse when thwarted in its instinctive aims by social coercion tends to regress to an infantile stage —that stage of impersonal play and of promiscuous experimentalism in which it began, retaining only the adult mode of sexual intercourse as the medium of such childish play. It differs from the earlier stage in that its play and its promiscuity are not a step upward toward adult love, but several steps down from adult love.

These steps down from adult love are taken to avoid psychic pain, to escape the almost unbearable consciousness of defeat in life's prime instinctive purpose. The instinctive purpose is repudiated, and purposelessness is set in its place.

The regression may not be permanent. When it is the result of individual defeat by Nature or by Chance and not by Society, it is usually not permanent. Imaginative literature has avoided dealing with such regressions because they are felt to derogate from the dignity of the hero or heroine. That a man or woman, suffering from grief because of the loss of the loved one through death or through permanent (or even merely prolonged) separation, should seek relief from such grief in 'light love', in sex-relations shared promiscuously and merely as an amusement, is horrifying to tender minds. Yet it notoriously does occur in real life with great frequency. Moreover, it serves the purpose of psychic pain avoidance. Like all anodynes it has its dangers. The individual may be ashamed of such a regression, particularly as it seems to mock at the previous professions of grief and at the sentiments of eternal fidelity with which they were accompanied. A regression of this sort may leave a residue of psychic poison in the form of self-distrust to paralyze later attempts at adult love. But if the social standards of behavior are such as to excuse (as they traditionally do for men) such regressions, or if a sense of humor leads the individual to look back upon them as comic rather than as tragic contradictions in his or her nature, they may be psychically harmless. Sexual regression may be said, with due recognition of its dangers, to be Nature's own method of cure for sexual grief. It does, or may, relieve the intolerable tension of a love which has lost or failed of its object. And it very frequently serves as a new start, from scratch as it were, toward adult love. And upon this understanding it tends to be condoned by modern society. Indeed, it is only when the individual lacks the courage to start anew that the regression is permanent. And it is social coercion in general which robs individuals of that courage and reconciles them to the permanent acceptance of 'sex as amusement'.

We may now generalize to this effect: In apparently every society, whether savage, patriarchal or modern, there is an express or tacit permission to certain adult groups, classes or individuals to indulge in sexual relations under circumstances in which marriage and parenthood are forbidden or out of the question. In savage society these permitted practices have usually a religious significance, in patriarchal society an economic significance, and in modern society a psychically medicinal significance. In all these instances, 'sex as amusement' is a regression, due to failure or social thwarting of the mating impulse.

We are leading up to a consideration of an important modern instance of this kind of regression, through social thwarting, at the end of adolescence. It is a relic of patriarchal society, and represents economic and social situations not yet fully modernized. These social and economic aspects of the subject will be reserved for later consideration. What we are now to consider is the tendency in some quarters to accept this lingering patriarchal sex-compromise of 'sex amusement' as being a normal and desirable 'freedom' for boys and girls, and one which only moralists and prudes would object to.

In this connection savage adolescent sexual custom is appealed to as an example and model. In many savage tribes boys and girls are socially permitted and encouraged to have sexual relations during the long period between childhood and marriage. Our young people, it appears, to a great extent take the same liberties. Would it not, then, the question is asked, be sensible to give them social permission and encouragement to that effect?

The nigger in this woodpile is not, perhaps, readily apparent. But it is the same old patriarchal swindle. The sex-relations which are thus so handsomely offered to young people may be a better bargain than the neurotic 'purity' which they are offered by other messengers from the camp of dying patriarchalism. But these Greeks that come bearing gifts are trying to take their real freedom away from young people—their freedom of courtship, which threatens to destroy patriarchal property-marriage altogether. The ultimate aim of this offer of 'sexual freedom' is to restore the segregation of the sexes. That, however, remains to be shown.

In savage life there is a profound cleavage between the realms of men's and of women's work and interests; and during the long period of years between puberty and marriage, sex-relations serve to bring boys and girls together in acquaintanceship and companionship and thus pave the way for adult love. These sex-relations are at first hardly more than exploits to satisfy a childish and egotistic pride. "Both boys and girls", says Saville of the New Guinea Mailu, "keep tally of such intrigues: (1) by making knots in a piece of string; (2) by cutting notches in trees * * *; (3) by placing in line on the ground the sucked fruit of the pandanus. This fruit ripens only during *lioro* time, when dancing and night-reef fishing are in full swing." These affairs, pursued so indefatigably in such numbers, are nevertheless the beginnings of personal courtship. Malinowski inquired of his Trobriand Islanders what a girl and boy said to each other upon the occasion of their first love-making. Literally translated, the conversation is said to run: *She*—"Whether sweetheart-thine I?" *He*—"Yes! sweetheart-mine thou—very-much desire-mine; time, time, we copulate; very-much-face-yours-beloved-by-me face-thine cross-cousins!" [*Cross-cousins* used figuratively means 'suited to each other'.] *She*—"No desire-mine you-get-hold one woman new-woman; thou-indeed I." ["I don't want you to get a new girl; just you and I."] These meetings will be secret at first; but "a couple who have lived together for a time and found they want to marry, as it were advertise this fact by sleeping together regularly, by showing themselves together in public, and by remaining with each other for long periods at a time."

Political ambitions or parental motives may interfere with these matches; for descent is here reckoned in the matrilineal line, a man is no relation to his children, and a chief can only hand over privileges to a favorite son if that son is married to his (the chief's) sister's daughter (or with this daughter's daughter), that is to say in cross-cousin marriage. The social interferences with these primitive courtships are well described by the Dutch novelist Laurids Bruun, in *Van Zanten's Happy Days,* a novel in which the details are apparently authentic records of savage custom in Pelew Island, a little north of western New Guinea. Here, as in the Trobriand Islands, the bachelors sleep in their club house, and when a girl arrives at the age of puberty she begins to sleep there with one and then another of the youths. "They do not change partners as often as might be expected. As a rule, the matter is settled for the woman from the very first day of her entrance into the Common House [Bachelors' House] * * *. The young girl is immediately surrounded by unattached youths of about her own age, swarming and buzzing around her like bees. Flattered and pleased with the attention shown her, she looks round the gathering and quickly chooses one to be her partner, in what is to her the most serious business in life. * * * Having chosen her mate, she sleeps on his mat in the Common House until one of two changes occur. If the connection leads to strong infatuation, so that the man becomes afraid of losing her—for example, by the advent of a new and dangerous rival—he hastens to buy her from her father; in other words, to marry her, upon which they both remove from the Common House, where every one has an equal [sexual] right. If, on the other hand, one or other of the parties does not come up to expectations; or if the man cannot or will not pay the price which for the sake of her family and the honour of her *totem* is demanded for her, then a respectable girl, knowing the respect due to her, gives her laggard suitor the cold shoulder and turns elsewhere." It may be that "the rejected suitor makes things nasty for her in some way or other, which, however, is considered very bad form * * *.

"Affairs are thus managed among the more sensitive and decent young people, who possess a certain amount of proper pride. But it may, of course, also happen that a girl sticks to her first choice, regardless of his inability to buy her; unless he is more sensible than she, and gives her up in order to marry a woman whose price is more in accord with his fortune. If not, it cannot be denied that an illegitimate connection is established which can have unfortunate consequences.

"Things may be all right for a time; but one day her father becomes impatient and informs his daughter that he cannot wait any longer for the capital which she represents to materialize. She must make her decision.

"The poor suitor presents himself in desperation to make the best offer he can, only of course to meet with an uncompromising refusal, at the same time having the purchase price flung in his teeth.

"Every well-bred Mahura girl would then bow to the inevitable and to her duty. She allows her poor suitor to disappear out of her life, * * * and chooses a new mate, this time with her brain instead of her heart, aided perhaps in her choice by her parents.

"Sometimes, however, things do not go so smoothly. I know one case—Toko told me about it—in which, to appease her father, the girl dismissed her fiancé and chose another suitor. But the latter was merely a dummy, whom they [she and her lover] had persuaded to act the part of lover before the public at the evening meal round the fire. At night he disappeared, and the girl continued sleeping on her old suitor's mat, a fact which could never reach the ears of her father, for all that happens in the Common House is most jealously guarded by its inmates.

"The new arrangement worked successfully for a while but when the latest official fiancé, who was in all respects a suitable match, made no effort to claim the girl for his wife, the old man again took his daughter to task.

"Again she posed as the obedient daughter; again she obeyed her father's commands, dismissing the second suitor—she could not waste all her youth in the Common House, where she would soon be one of the eldest—and choosing a third, also a good match. But he was only another dummy, playing the part for his friend, the poor suitor, and the girl still slept regularly on her lover's mat.

"And so it went on, until at last the father was forced to the conclusion that his daughter was less attractive than he had thought, for none of her suitors offered to buy her. Since there was nothing wrong with the family *totem,* he reasoned, it must be the girl who had some hidden fault.

"After a painful cross-examination, the only material result of which was a good thrashing for the girl in revenge for his disappointment, the old man made the best of a bad job, and resolutely lowered his price * * *.

"Again a period of waiting. When the old man saw the girl still remaining on his hands he resigned himself to a certain loss, and, as a last resort, of his own accord approached the poor suitor.

"The latter stood willingly and honorably by his original offer; they became man and wife, and, according to Toko, lived happily ever afterwards.

"This story of true love * * * had, however, a sequel.

"I fully believe what was said, that they were very happy—obstinate people, on the whole, are happier than others—but one thing is certain, they never had a child: for now that it was desirable, it was found impossible. The reason for this melancholy fact lies in the use of a certain practice [*i.e.*, abortion], fully permissible for an unmarried native girl, but which among civilized people is considered a serious crime, and punished severely, regardless of the stage of development at which the act is committed. A case such as the foregoing [*i.e.*, the lovers' stubborn resistance to parental plans] is, however, a rare exception; as a rule, affairs relating to the matrimonial market run smoothly and respectably."

Thus, already in savage life, at the very beginnings of patriarchal authority, the impulses of courtship are hampered and thwarted by alien social and property considerations. And we are perhaps now in a position to recognize that the apparently simple tradition of 'sex as amusement' is really a social compromise. Insofar as these apparently promiscuous sex-affairs represent genuine, inwardly determined shiftings of sexual interest, they are simply incidents of experimental courtship, a quite serious emotional concern of youth, and not at all an amusement. They are made an amusement only by being cut off from their biological purpose in mating and parentage. In obedience to a social dictatorship which overrules the mating-wishes of the young people, they are obliged to repress their instinctive sense of the seriousness of love-making; they must take lightly the thwarting of their mating-passion, and console themselves with another bedfellow. It is bad form to take these sex-affairs so seriously as to evince hurt feelings or jealousy when they are ended for social reasons.

Miss Mead gives from Samoa an example of a girl who thus contravened the mores in taking sex-affairs too seriously. Mutu, "a widower and a sophisticated rake", had an affair with his niece, Moana, who was outside of bounds for him because their relationship was within the so-called brother-and-sister class. "This incident, not common in Samoa, because of the great lack of privacy and isolation, would have passed undetected in this case [she was living at his house], if Moana's older sister, Sila, had not been in love with the uncle also. This was the only example of prolonged and intense passion which I found in the villages. Samoans rate romantic fidelity in terms of days or weeks at most, and are inclined to scoff at tales of life-long devotion. (They greeted the story of Romeo and Juliet with incredulous contempt.) But Sila was devoted to Mutu * * * to the point of frenzy. She had been his mistress, and still lived in his household, but his dilettantism had veered away from her indecorous intensity. When she discovered that he had lived with her sister, her fury knew no bounds. * * * When he later on announced his intention of marrying a girl from another island, Sila again displayed the most uncontrollable grief and despair, though she herself was carrying on a love affair at the time."

Miss Mead goes on to say: "Cases of passionate jealousy do occur, but they are matters for extended comment and amazement. During nine months in the islands, only four cases came to my attention, a girl who informed against a faithless lover accusing him of incest [this was Sila, whose story has just been given], a girl who bit off part of a rival's ear, a woman whose husband deserted her and who fought and severely injured her successor, and a girl who falsely accused a rival of stealing. But jealousy is less expected and sympathized with than among us * * *."

The last of these four cases of Samoan jealousy is given in detail. Lola had gone to live with relatives, "a very high chief's family, in the next village. * * * But she had only been established here a month when another chief, with a young and beautiful taupo [a kind of 'princess'] in his train, came to visit. The new chief and the whole party was lodged in the very house where she slept. * * * The Don Juan of the village was a sleek, discreet man of about forty, a widower, a *matai* [holder of a title], a man of circumspect manner and winning ways. He was looking for a second wife and turned his attention toward the visitor who was lodged in the guest house of the next village [the visiting 'princess', that is to say]. But Fuativa [the village Don Juan] was a cautious and calculating lover. He wished to look over his future bride carefully and so he visited her house casually, without any declaration of his intention. And he noticed that Lola had reached a robust girlhood and [so he] stopped to pluck this ready fruit by the way, while he was still undecided about the more serious business of matrimony.

"With all her capacity for violence [for Lola already had a bad reputation as quarrelsome and insubordinate], Lola possessed also a strong capacity for affection. Fuativa was a skilled and considerate lover. Few girls were quite so fortunate in their first lovers, and few felt such unmixed regret when their first love affair was broken off. Fuativa won her easily and after three weeks which were casual to him, and very important to her, he proposed for the hand of the visitor [the 'princess']. * * * The rage of Lola was unbounded [aggravated by the fact that, in order that the marriage might not fall through, Fuativa had been by connivance given an opportunity to seduce the unwilling 'princess'] and she took an immediate revenge, publicly accusing her rival of being a thief and setting the whole village by the ears. The women of the host household drove her out with many imprecations and she fled home to her mother. * * * She was now in the position of the delinquent in our [civilized] society. She had continuously violated the group standards"—not the least important of which was the rule that sexual affairs must not be taken too seriously, or as more than a passing amusement. "The young people of the village branded her as the possessor of a *latu le aga* ('a bad heart'), and she had no companions. * * * When I left, she was living, idle, sullen, and defiant in her long-suffering mother's house." Thus by the final punishment of ostracism by her age-group is the Samoan girl taught to take sex with the socially requisite degree of lightness.

The correspondence at so many points of this savage custom of taking sex as an adolescent amusement with some modern adolescent behavior to the same effect may suggest that it has come down as an unbroken tradition through the ages; and that the breakdown of patriarchal sex-segregation is restoring a more ancient custom, with the parked automobile taking the place of the Bachelors' House as a shelter for adolescent sexual affairs.

There is, however, a less romantic explanation which consorts better with the facts.

(1) The rural custom of 'sexual betrothals' (see Chapter VIII, § 2), as handed down particularly among northern European peoples from pagan times, applied to an early age-class of young people on account of early marriage. Thus these might occur at 15, 16 or 17, ages which now tend to be adolescent and not adult. While these betrothals might be broken off if pregnancy did not result, they were in no sense irresponsible sex-play. They were preceded by 'bundling' without overt sexual relations, and the initiation of these latter constituted an engagement to marry.

(2) The culture-clash brought about by the extension of patriarchal institutions and ideals caused this custom of sexual betrothal to be not only cruelly exploited but completely misunderstood as irresponsible sex-play. What appears to be a reversion to savage adolescent custom is rather an agricultural early adult custom, not yet fully adapted to contemporary standards of later adulthood, and seen through patriarchal eyes.

We are, ineed, able to classify contemporary American adolescents who are found to be practising overt sex-relations, in simple historical-psychological terms, as follows:

(A) Young people in remote rural communities where adulthood is by social standards reached early. These sex-relations, except as they may be exploited by outsiders or vitiated by young male emigration to cities, are a form of engagement or at least of serious courtship resulting in early marriage. The young people are not neurotic in these practices because they are conforming to well-established social customs. But awareness of different social standards may make them ashamed of themselves and neurotic.

(B-1) The extension of the patriarchal ideas of male irresponsibility has given a kind of covert social sanction to adolescent male sexual exploit, with the girls as persons for whom no responsibility is felt. These adolescent Casanovas are not 'young savages' but miniature bucks and blades and gallants whose ideas hark back to the aristocratic past, sowing their wild oats with the assurance that they are within their masculine rights. Their experiences in sex are typically either with prostitutes or with women or girls who are felt to be socially or morally inferior—'tough' girls who have already lost their 'chastity', servant girls, and girls of (socially-presumed) inferior 'race' or nationality—all of whom are for these reasons unmarriageable and fair game for sexual exploitation. These adolescents, according to strictly patriarchal and not savage ideas, look forward to marriage with a 'pure' girl, like their great-grandfathers. They are not neurotic in these practices because they are unaware of doing anything more than is expected of a manly young fellow after the age of puberty. Their neuroticism will come later in attempts to adjust themselves to an adult world which does not work on patriarchal lines. They may, however, learn to repudiate their patriarchal ideas and see the girls who have been the objects of their exploitation as worthy of their respect and marriageable.

(B-2) Adolescent girls with a social background of early adulthood and sexual betrothal may enter at first with serious intentions into sex-relations with the boys above described, unaware that in doing so they are classifying themselves in their partners' estimation as 'tough' girls. They may then in discouragement or defiance accept this label and pursue their sex-affairs for amusement (if the shock has thrown them into neurotic mental conflict), or even for gifts and money as amateur prostitutes. When, however, they are able to realize their situation without shame, they try to adapt themselves to different methods of courtship—a thing difficult to do, not because of the demands of their own sexuality so much as the inability to get rid of the label of 'bad girl' without removing to another community.

(C) Repressed adolescents of both sexes, coming upon these examples of overt adolescent sex-relations, and more or less propagandized to join in them, may do so as a revolt against or escape from parental tyranny or a compensation against parental neglect and bad home conditions which afford insufficient assurance of their being loved or wanted. These repressed adolescents are below par in their sexuality and it is for this reason that they snatch so recklessly at what appears to be adulthood. These are the neurotics; but though their desperate attempt to escape from the prison of an enforced childhood through the gateway of sex-relations often increases their neurotic difficulties—not to speak of getting them into other troubles—it is sometimes the best solution which they can by themselves without intelligent adult guidance achieve: and is not to be regarded as more dangerous subjectively (though it may be more dangerous practically) than the earlier stage of adolescent neuroticism. Moreover, it may get them into enough trouble so that they will receive some intelligent adult attention—a paradoxical consideration not to be overlooked.

(D) Feeble-mindedness as a matter of fact accounts for a considerable proportion of overt adolescent sex-relations.

(E) Culture-clashes bring about another and accidental sort of overt adolescent sex-relations, through a misunderstanding of the modern freedom of association of boys and girls—a misunderstanding in particular of the convention of 'petting.' The boys and girls who do not grow up in a modern environment but come upon it from homes in which they have been secluded from social relations, tend to lump together the few cases of overt sex-relations of which they hear with the universal convention of 'petting', and to believe in all good faith—like many of their elders—that overt sex-relations are universal among the boys and girls of their age-group. This misunderstanding is helped along by the modern adolescent freedom of language and frankness of reference to sexual matters. (Incidentally, this accounts for some lurid youthful literary accounts of adolescent life, written by very inexperienced youths.) The reaction may be one of shock and disgust; or these boys and girls may feel called upon to live up to what they understand to be the current adolescent custom. More generally they do not know quite *what* to think about it all—they just blunder along. In their attempt to adjust themselves to more liberal standards of sex association than they have been accustomed to, through misunderstanding, by inadvertence or accident, or in emotional confusion, they overstep the very liberal adolescent conventions of petting into overt sex-relations and flounder about for a while in the excitements and worries which these provide, before they adjust themselves to modern adolescent conventions. Since that—adjustment to adolescent conventions—is all they are trying to do, they deserve sympathy and assistance in their effort and it would be absurd to magnify what is only a social blunder into a moral issue. They have, as it were, blown their noses on their sleeves—and bad enough they feel about it. A true kindness is to look the other way. Certainly these are not the protagonists of either a savage or an ultra-modern morality. They are, often pathetically, just trying to do what's right; and if our modern conventions of sex-behavior become standardized sufficiently for the publication of a book on the Etiquette of Sex (I think I will write it myself), they will turn to the chapter entitled 'What Is Expected of You at Sixteen—(1) if a Boy—(2) if a Girl' and learn the rules by heart in deep thankfulness.

"What kind of girl, then," says Professor Phyllis Blanchard, "is she who is victimized by this new freedom of modern youth, who finds that her trust in her boy companions has been misplaced and that they have taken advantage of her condition? Ordinarily, this is a type of girl whose home training has ill prepared her for assuming direction of her own conduct. The girl who has grown up with boys, at home with brothers or at co-educational schools, is aware of masculine attitudes. She knows where 'necking' leaves off and sexual seduction begins. The girl who enters a co-educational college from the shelter of a convent school, or from a home in which she has been guarded from contact with boys, is the one who does not know how to make the proper use of liberty. Her desire to be popular, when she is for the first time on familiar terms with the opposite sex, leads her to bestow favors too freely, to accept proposals which her more sophisticated classmates would refuse. She gives the impression that she is inviting sex experience when in reality she is only trying to imitate girls of more worldly experience.

"Some of these girls from a cloistered early environment become serious 'problems' in the student personnel of large co-educational universities. In one college, an unexpected pregnancy brought a convent-bred girl to a private conference with the dean of women, in which she admitted some recollection of conduct, after she had had a few drinks, which might have caused her condition. She had not realized the danger at the time, because of her unrealistic sex education. In another university, the disciplinary committee was called upon to consider the case of a girl who had returned to the dormitory at a flagrant morning hour, dishevelled and incoherent. She had gone for an automobile ride with some other girls and boys, but had become frightened when they parked and entered into rather vigorous love-making. She ran away from the party, only to find that it took hours to walk back over a distance the car had traversed in minutes. At home she had never been permitted to go out with boys, and remarked that she did not understand how to act toward them."

(X) This classification would not be complete without some reference to the (mythical) young people who are the heroes and heroines of certain anecdotes which are circulated among the older generation. Even if true, they would merely represent items in our list of adolescent neurotics. But some of these anecdotes, referring particularly to girls, offer alleged statistical proof of their sexual casualness in the form of an attribution to them of cold-blooded contraceptive preparedness for miscellaneous sex-encounters. These statistics, if true upon such a scale, would indicate so complete a change from the familiar characteristics of adolescent female sex-attitudes, so vast a degree of realistic forethought, so entirely candid a facing of possibilities, so utterly drastic a transplanting of the erotic content of the dark unconscious into the daylit conscious mind, and so overwhelming a distrust of the other sex, that this revolution in adolescent female psychology would overshadow any merely moral implications it might possess. Insofar as such tales are circulated not in disparagement of the younger generation but as an admiring tribute to it, they represent the imaginative wish-fulfillments of middle-aged and elderly people who were patriarchally cribb'd, cabin'd and confin'd in their own adolescence.

(Y) Finally, it should be noted that many alleged instances of overt adolescent sex-relations are not adolescent cases at all, but early adult cases. These terms are necessarily vague, but 'adolescence' becomes meaningless when extended to the age of 25. It depends upon circumstances, but some young people are fully adult at 21 and some at 18 and their sex-behavior does not come at all within the adolescent category.

(Z) Besides these classes of early betrothal, survivals of patriarchal exploit, neurotic revolt, feeble-mindedness, social accident, and pure myth, there may exist some class as yet, however, not authentically reported, of boys and girls far from the mating age who are intelligently successful and emotionally happy in overt and irresponsible sex-relations on the democratic savage pattern. Until these are really known to exist, they need not be considered.

The correspondence, then, of such contemporary adolescent overt sexuality as exists, with the savage adolescent pattern, is not so close as has been supposed. There is, besides, an important difference in the fact that one is conventional and the other unconventional. Whatever we may think of the savage adolescent custom, it is approved by the adult savage world. The adolescent savage boys and girls who have overt sex-relations are neither feeble-minded youngsters who are unable to understand or live up to the conventions of their world, nor youngsters in neurotic rebellion against the conventions of their world. They are in their world perfect young gentlemen and young ladies engaged in getting acquainted in the politest way they know, and their closest likeness after all remains to the conventionally modern rather than the unconventionally modern adolescents of our society. The accepted 'petting' convention of modern adolescence is more like youthful savage custom (see Chapter XII, § 1) than high-school sex-intrigues can be, because both of the former are accepted customs and nothing to worry about. In our culture those youngsters who haven't sense enough to worry about their sex-affairs find themselves out of their depth in pregnancy, abortion and venereal disease, and are brought into the Juvenile Court; while those who are intelligent enough to avoid these dangers are, with the patriarchal exceptions noted above (in B-1), unhappy about their behavior, which if chronic is found by subsequent psychotherapeutic investigation to have been neurotically determined and to be egotistic rather than sexual in its motivation.

The readiness to believe in the universality of overt sex-relations in adolescence, and the proposal that they be given full social approval, are both marks of patriarchal-mindedness in disguise. The patriarchal mind can be detected by its incapacity for realizing that heterosexuality is something which requires time and experience for its development to the point of sexual mating. The patriarchal mind used to put children to bed together and call it marriage; now, trying its damndest to be modern, it proposes to put children to bed together and call it 'freedom'. If the bed were in contemporary civilization the only place where young people could get acquainted, the proposal would have its merits: and we should, like the savages, have to accept the abortive methods by which such adolescent bed-fellowship is prevented from burdening the adolescents and society with babies. These will be discussed presently. But if the adolescent need is to get acquainted, we have in modern life our own ways of promoting its fulfillment. We have friendship and play and 'petting'.

The patriarchal male, however, is both shocked and bewildered by the custom of 'petting'. He is accustomed to divide girls into two categories, the 'chaste' and the 'unchaste'. He has his patriarchal uses for both. The 'chaste' or 'pure' girl knows or is presumed to know nothing whatever of sex, and to have had not the slightest erotic contact with men. The patriarchal male knows how to treat such a girl—he respects her and keeps his hands off her and may eventually marry her, expecting her to come to his couch as pure as the driven snow and just as chilly. He knows what to do with the 'unchaste' girl, too—he amuses himself with her without any care as to the consequences for her; and he expects her to be ready to accede without coyness to his demands. But the intercategorical modern girl who is neither 'pure' according to his definition nor yet apparently 'unchaste' in deed is a puzzle and a torment to him. He doesn't know how to treat her. If he is too respectful, he feels that he is being a fool; and if he takes too much for granted, he may get slapped.

The patriarchal mind tends in this humiliating situation to reassure itself by asserting that there is something unnatural about the modern 'petting' girl. Chastity is all right and unchastity is all right, too, but this betwixt-and-between behavior seems to the patriarchal mind the most frightful of all possible perversities. The 'petting' girl is expected to come to some very bad end, probably raving insanity; and it is all the more bewildering when she, having emotionally educated herself in her own fashion, chooses a mate and loves him in a quite normal and healthy way.

(It is important here to distinguish between the 'petting' behavior which belongs to adolescence and the adult neuroticism which cannot get beyond the 'petting' stage to actual sex-relations. We are here considering the adolescent girl and her bewildered patriarchal critics.)

The reverberations of this patriarchal perturbation are heard in literature. Americans with their agricultural background were more used to free association of the sexes than to sex-segregation, and to them adolescent 'spooning' was a commonplace. But the French, when peasant custom forced its way up into respectable society, had to invent the term 'demi-vierge' for this astounding phenomenon of a girl who would not fit into either of the two convenient and mutually exclusive patriarchal categories. It was Owen Johnson, possibly tutored by French influences, who seems first to have made in literature the troubled discovery of a condition which in life was quite familiar, sounding the gong of alarm in 1913 in a novel called *The Salamander*. Actually the girl 'played with' fire and was not burnt by it! With this began the pseudo-scientific literary assimilation of normal adolescent 'petting' to various homosexual and frigid types. It was comforting to the patriarchal mind to believe that *something was the matter* with these girls. In that regard, however, science has failed to back them up. "We have been taught to believe", says Professor Phyllis Blanchard, "that such forms of sex expression, which are usually termed perverted and abnormal, are not only morally wrong but also that they are dangerous for physical and mental health. Psychiatric observation suggests that mere participation in these experiences is not in itself injurious unless indulged in to such an extent that it interferes with the necessary regimen in respect to food, rest and sleep." (What a blow, to hear that Science's adjuration to the petters is only: 'You really *must* get *some* food and sleep, my dears!') "It is when conscientious scruples, born of early [patriarchal] teachings, give rise to feelings of guilt and anxiety," Professor Blanchard continues, "that we may expect a reaction upon mental health. When the girl begins to think in the [patriarchally] conventional terms of *misconduct* rather than *conduct*, emotional conflicts are apt to develop. The impairment of health is usually due to these emotional conflicts concerning the experience and not to the experience *per se*."

The proposal, then, which we have been so patiently considering is to take away the emotionally educational adolescent right of 'petting' and insist that young people accept the patriarchal notion that if a girl is going to permit some 'liberties' she has no right to draw the line at sexual intercourse—'if she's goin' to act that way, she's gotta come across'. The result of a general acceptance of this proposal would be to build up again the ancient patriarchal categories of 'pure' and 'impure' girls. The former would be robbed of their right to an emotional education in free adolescent association with boys; the latter would be robbed of the right to marriage and socially protected maternity. That is the patriarchal nigger in that woodpile. Fake 'sex freedom' merely harks back to the patriarchal system.

There is more to be said, however. The patriarchal theory, as we have seen, divides women into two classes; one is shielded by segregation from any sexual contact, the other thrown open to ruthless sexual exploitation. Underlying this arrangement is a theory inherited from savage culture, that free association of the sexes in adolescence *means* sexual intercourse. And patriarchal society, which shields its respectable girls from the pains and dangers of the abortions which are a corollary of adolescent sexual freedom, has no hesitation in pushing its unrespectable girls into these pains and dangers. Savage society democratically accepts them for all girls.

Now the savage use of sex-relations in adolescent play and courtship is made possible (though it should be noted that Malinowski finds it still a mystery among the Trobrianders) through ways—known apparently in every savage tribe (often as a woman's sex-secret, not known to men), as well as in every civilized society—ways in which pregnancy is avoided, as it seems to them, or, more strictly speaking, ways in which pregnancy is regularly interrupted by medicinal means at so early a stage that it appears to constitute avoidance of pregnancy. The path of youthful savage dalliance thus requires for its successful pursuit the possession, at least by witch-women known to the girl, of a certain 'magical' technique. It also requires good luck. All savage medicinal abortifacients, insofar as they are not merely symbolic and as worthless as they are harmless, are powerful poisons. The toll which they exact of pain and death can readily be imagined, though anthropological literature is uninformative on this point. But death and pain are commonplaces of savage life, and these are hazards to be readily accepted in the sexual career of savage girls, as they are frequently enough in the sexual career of civilized girls. There is, moreover, in savage as in civilized life, the possibility that regularly repeated abortions at an early stage of pregnancy will bring about an organ-habit of automatic miscarriage at that stage; a tendency which may give apparent authenticity to the more symbolic and non-medicinal kinds of pregnancy-'preventing' magic if subsequently used.

This secret sex-lore of savagery, divested of its respectability and not very much if at all improved scientifically, has been handed down through the patriarchal era and is now available with some later additions to the adolescents who wish to demonstrate their adulthood without biological consequences. Not only does the technique in many respects bear the mark of its savage origin, but it is currently used with an accompanying frame of mind which is very near to belief in magic—a frame of mind in which wishes and not facts are important. Some of the means which are believed to offer immunity from the biological consequences of sexual intercourse are, it is true, as modern in origin as the 17th or 18th century. But some of this adolescent immunity-lore is very ancient, most of it undependable, some of it dangerous; and frequently enough the most enterprising of these adolescent adventurers in sex are the least modern in their technological equipment. Armed with stray fragments of this traditional lore, often with what amounts to scarcely more than a wish-belief that 'nothing will happen', these boys and girls enter upon their adolescent amusements. Upon the girl falls the final and often the entire responsibility for nothing happening; and it is frequently not until she has been tutored by painful experience that she does anything more in that direction than hope for the best or refuse to consider the possibility of anything to the contrary—or, which is quite frequent, resolve to commit suicide if 'anything' *should* happen. Maladjustments of the reproductive organs, and other local conditions, may give her temporary or permanent immunity from pregnancy; or the same results may be reached as the result of venereal infection. Even when her lore of prevention is fairly adequate if used with unremitting care and forethought, these qualities of mind are not characteristic of adolescence and are still less characteristic of irresponsible and neurotic sexuality; so that it is usually only a question of how long it will be before some inevitable rashness, indifference, forgetfulness or over-confidence will oblige her to have recourse to cruel and inexpert and dangerous attempts at abortion. If these fail, she may become one of the statistics of unmarried motherhood—unless, as in savage Oceanica, her parents help her to conceal her plight.

If such totally unexpected motherhood arrives, the un-adult nature of the sex-play which preceded it may be illustrated by the girl's frequent unwillingness to marry her erstwhile playfellow, even if he is willing to marry her; for she is not in love with him. In preparation for such a contingency, the tradition of 'sex as amusement' encourages her to the display of a kind of sexual sportsmanship, which consists of not demanding any responsibility of any sort from her partner. Then if she should 'get into trouble', a contingency which she sees as through a glass darkly, nobody will be to blame except Nature, who has played a cruel joke upon her. But the grim consolation of being a victim of one of Nature's little jokes is appropriate only when the situation calls for it—such considerations are not intruded into the earlier stages of sex-play. Until the contrary is proved, her dubious stock of sex-lore is supposed to give her equality with the male sex in its happy immunity from 'consequences'.

This idea of male freedom from such consequences has a traditional background that is worth looking into. It does not merely have reference to the fact that men do not have to *bear* the children they may beget; it is, beyond that, a social construction, being freedom from any obligation to *take care of* the children they may beget outside of wedlock. Thus the 'sexual freedom of men' meant in patriarchal times a social permission to abandon illegitimate children. And this freedom from sexual responsibility was at that time shared by his extra-marital partners. In late patriarchal times, and still to-day in patriarchal countries, the foundling home relieves extra-marital sex-relations of all responsibilities. In the light of the death-rate of such institutions, this amounts to a polite way of giving the mothers and fathers of illegitimate children the privilege of killing them. And this privilege, taken for granted in earlier patriarchal times, is the foundation of the theory of sex as amusement. Sex as amusement is simply the old patriarchal safety valve; it exists to reconcile people to the loss of their biological rights of responsible courtship, love-choice, mating and parentage. It assumes that the privilege of parentage is limited to loveless legal marriages arranged to safeguard property; it assumes that love has no right to determine serious mating, to become marriage or result in children. Sexual intercourse eviscerated of its deepest emotional meanings, divorced from reality, robbed of hope, is flung to the boys and girls as a toy to amuse themselves with. In patriarchal society it was well understood that this meant the killing of such children as were accidentally born of such play.

In a Restoration comedy, when the servant announces to the young hero the woman with whom one of his illegitimate children has been put out to nurse, the young man of fashion replies: "Pox on her! could she find no other time to fling my sins in my face? Here, give her this [*Gives money*], and bid her trouble me no more;—a thoughtless two-handed whore! she knows my condition well enough, and might have overlaid the child a fortnight ago, if she had had any forecast in her."

Modern society, by insisting not only upon the mother's but increasingly upon the father's responsibility for such children, has knocked the foundation from under the patriarchal tradition of sex as amusement. By placing the illegitimate mother and father economically at least in the relation to the child and to each other which they would occupy if their sexual relations had been a part of courtship, it assumes courtship to be the only socially acceptable grounds for sexual relationships. Whether they intend it or not, the young people who use sex as an amusement have legally obligated themselves to joint parental responsibilities for a possible child.

The current theory of sex as amusement assumes, to be sure, that modern and scientific methods of preventing conception have eliminated the risk of pregnancy and thus justified an attitude of emotional irresponsibility in sexual relations. This is a convenient assumption, but (and I speak as an ardent advocate of public education in modern birth-control methods) it is a mistaken one. A candid and informative discussion of different birth-control methods is prevented here by the Comstock law, but it may be said that the most modern, scientific, emotionally satisfactory and effective of these techniques are such as require "energy, self-control and persistence", and are moreover of such a nature as not to be readily available for use by adolescents (see also Chapter XII, § 2). The fact is that the sexual adventures of adolescent girls are not well safeguarded against pregnancy by the archaic and uncertain methods at their disposal. The fact is further that such young adventurers not only have to but do largely depend upon 'luck'; and that their 'luck' quite generally in the long run fails to serve them. Then, to quote the recent manual of birth-control to which H. G. Wells has written an introduction, "they proceed to take poisonous doses of drugs" —exactly like the savage girls described above. "They become the prey of vendors of so-called 'Female Pills' and of other quacks who claim to cure 'female irregularities'. Sometimes the enormous doses of poisonous drugs succeed in terminating the pregnancy; usually they only succeed in ruining the health of the mother. Sometimes they kill her without in any way disturbing the pregnancy.

"But when drugs have failed, there is still one final resort"—surgical abortion; and such are the conditions under which this operation is performed (it is legally regarded as a criminal one, unless required by grave considerations of health) that it is likely to be performed unskilfully. Hence it is quite common for it "to be followed by a condition of sepsis of the genital tract". This *may* lead to death, but "more frequently a condition of chronic infection of the genital tract results, which not only leaves the woman a permanent invalid but makes it impossible for her ever to bear another child."

These conditions are described as occurring quite generally in *marriages* which depend upon archaic methods of family limitation. Dr. Hannah M. Stone quotes from a study of 1,655 married women, who had had a total of 1,434 induced abortions, varying for the individuals from one to as many as 40. Exact statistics are naturally unobtainable, but Dr. William J. Robinson estimates that "the number of induced abortions performed now annually in the United States reaches a figure which is somewhere between two and three million." There are (1920 census) over nine-and-a-half million women of childbearing age (15 to 45 years) in the United States. Two million abortions a year among ten million women would on an average give one in every five such women an abortion in each year. What proportion of these abortions occur outside of marriage cannot be estimated; but it is incorrect to suppose that the adolescent girl adventurers in sex are so much better informed than their mothers, and so much more gifted with 'energy, self-control and persistence' in the use of modern techniques of contraception as not to bear a considerable proportion of this burden of abortions. Judge Lindsey found that of the 495 Denver girls of high-school age who confessed to illicit sexual relations, one out of every twenty had failed to avoid pregnancy. "How many others", he asks, "chose the abortionist and said nothing?"

Let us not pretend that the younger generation is more

'modern' than it is. To the extent that in adolescence it practises 'sex as amusement', it comes indeed, especially under alcoholic influence, startlingly close to the savage and childish wishful belief in the biological meaninglessness of sex-relations, and tends to use no contraceptives whatever. Where there is a complete emotional irresponsibility in sexual behavior, either in adolescence or in adult life, there is very commonly also a complete physical irresponsibility. Only lovers who, in marriage or out, are capable of the emotional responsibilities of love, are also generally capable of taking responsible attitudes in the matter of avoiding abortion. The risk of abortion, like the risk of venereal disease, is in fairly direct proportion to the irresponsibility of the sexual relationship; and the best insurance against both is love-mating with its normal prelude of courtship. Sexual relationships which are not a part of emotionally sincere approaches to mating, which are indulged as irresponsible amusement, still generally involve the savage makeshift of abortion and still pay the savage toll of useless death and meaningless pain.

The current pseudo-modern theory of sex as amusement has to ignore this as an unpleasant fact, which would mar the happy mood of irresponsible sexual play. It is true that pain and perhaps death are among the things that love must face if it dares to go on to completion in parenthood. But love was ever conceded to have its tragic aspects—it is only from the picture of irresponsible sexual amusement that these shadows have been censored out. From the minds of two lovers whose love-making is part of a sincere courtship, the thought of tragic possibilities is never far absent; for the thought of tragedy can be borne by love—it is only to sex-play that it seems so irrelevant and its advent so shocking. The play-view of sex is really founded upon the quasi-infantile pretense (a required religious belief among some savages) that sexual intercourse and childbirth have nothing to do with one another. To this infantile wish the realities of life not only do not correspond but are in the long run incapable of being made to correspond by any but the most consistently efficient use of the most modern methods of prevention; and this consistent efficiency in the use of such methods is very regularly defeated by unconscious wishes and intentions of an instinctive nature. The fact is that the adult male and female instincts are not satisfied with sterility; and through the connivance of the unconscious mind, through 'forgetfulness' and 'carelessness', these conscious shifts are defeated. The effort of the instincts to achieve fulfillment may go no further than the abortionist's table. These unconscious blunderings toward parenthood under the ban of conscious intentions to avoid it, represent the poor and pitiful efforts of adult emotions to get satisfaction in this infantile realm of sex amusement. In truth it is not easy for people to achieve the frame of mind necessary for the unperturbed enjoyment of sex as irresponsible amusement, except among savages, children and morons.

The appeal to savage adolescent sexual customs has confused the issue by classing together two situations, which we will now disentangle. One is an adolescent situation, the other a post-adolescent early-adult situation. It is frequently difficult to distinguish these in real life, since adolescence may merge into adulthood with its own problems still unsolved. However, (1) the adolescent situation is the one in which the instinctive need is for a free range of association with the other sex, so as to allow the emotional nature to develop through experience, and so as to give leeway to the selective process with its increasing emphasis upon personality. It begins in promiscuous contacts, and ends, through emotional education by them, in the capacity for mate love. (2) The post-adolescent or early adult situation is a different one. It consists in finding social opportunity for carrying out the mating impulse in marriage and parenthood.

The adolescent situation thus is one in which the problems concern psychic progress toward love. The early adult situation is one in which the problems concern the social-economic chances of marriage and parenthood. And the use of 'sex as amusement' has an entirely different significance in these two situations. (1) In the first situation, the presence or absence of overt sex-relations is irrelevant to the problem of psychic progress toward capacity for love. Sex-relations as such do not promote such psychic progress, and lack of sex-relations does not hamper it. If sex-relations are the only form of social intercourse between the sexes, as they tend to be in savage adolescent life, they serve the purpose of getting the boys and girls acquainted with each other. Modern adolescent play and 'petting' do the same thing. These modern forms of association between boys and girls are not 'substitutes' and certainly not 'abnormal' substitutes for overt sex-relations; they are the direct realities of comparative acquaintance, which rather than sexual intercourse fulfills the instinctive needs of adolescence. Thus the social encouragement of sex-relations in a society which already encourages free acquaintance would solve none of the problems of adolescent youth. Such overt sex-relations, when they do occur between adolescents in modern society, usually complicate their problems instead of simplifying them. So far as adolescents are concerned, the proposal to 'give them complete sexual freedom' is insincere —at least nobody proposes that they shall be encouraged to beget and bear children during adolescence, in or out of marriage. Sexual freedom, however, is not complete without the rights of mating and of parenthood. It seems to be agreed that adolescent boys and girls are too young to bear these responsibilities and that they should by all means be socially discouraged from undertaking them. It is thus not at all sexual freedom they are offered but merely sexual irresponsibility. They already have the privilege of irresponsibility in this adolescent period, upon more realistic terms. They have irresponsibility as long as they stop short of overt sex-relations. The extension of irresponsibility to sexual relations is a realistically dubious gift and psychically a step away from and not toward adulthood. It means, if it means anything, that they are to be encouraged to dissociate sex and mating, sex and parenthood; that sex-relations are to be made merely a childish toy. For whose benefit?

(2) In the early adult situation, 'sex as amusement' represents a defeat by society of the mating impulse. These young adults do not want 'sex as amusement'. They want to get married. But they lack social-economic power to do so. Lingering patriarchal arrangements condemn them to what seem meaningless delays. Insofar as these delays do not seem meaningless, insofar as they represent wider opportunities of love-choice and deeper capacities for love, they may be accepted by young people as a kind of prolongation of adolescence. But when they are merely social baulkings of a sexual impulse that has arrived at the mating stage, they are not accepted. The mating impulse may with difficulty be sublimated for a time. It may be repressed, with results in neurotic illnesses of all sorts. Or it may and frequently does take what it can get—which is precisely what

medieval love took: sex-relations without any prospects of marriage and parenthood. Young people do accept this lack of prospects. They take sex-relations as casually as they can. These sex-relations are nevertheless often informed by and symbolically expressive of all the feelings of matehood which these lovers must formally renounce. To the girl, in spite of her denials and protestations to the contrary, such a relationship is often in her secret thoughts equivalent to a secret marriage; and it may remain for her a kind of dream-marriage until some incident makes her too acutely conscious of its realistic limitations: the incident may be merely a striking one of 'socially necessary' hypocrisy before their families, which she sees as a symbolic repudiation of their mateship; or it may be a 'socially necessary' abortion, which is to her a symbolic repudiation of parenthood. The glory has departed from their love; he is not a hero in her eyes nor she a heroine in her own. They have not defied fate together. The love-affair ends in mutual recriminations, and she takes another sweetheart. The time between now and possible marriage must be passed somehow, with jobs and men. Hurt in her deepest wishes, she seeks the healing which regression offers. Impersonal sex is the cure for heartbreak, and now it is available to girls as well as to men. From this childish level she may and usually does climb back again, perhaps not without shame, but gaining courage and faith, until she is capable again of mate-love—perhaps again to be defeated and discouraged before she finds a relation which she and her lover can make real in marriage and parenthood.

To the young woman and the young man in their times of discouragement and humiliation, there comes the gospel-theory of 'sex as amusement'. It assures them that they don't want to get married and have babies, and that they are not the victims of their youth and poverty, but gay young adventurers. It relieves them of the shame they feel for their regressions into quasi-promiscuous and impersonal sex-relations; and insofar as the importance of these has been hideously exaggerated by their early religious training, this new gospel may be necessary to their mental sanity. But it seeks to persuade them that they do not ever want to grow up. It takes away the tragic pain of sexual defeat by repudiating the goal of sex; it hides away the mating purpose and puts purposeless sexual amusement in its place. It reconciles them to their lot in a society which is still in its economic and social theory and practice at this point more patriarchal than modern. It reconciles them, that is to say, to a state of affairs in which marriage is not to be undertaken until the man is in a position to support a wife and children, and in which that 'position' lies perhaps indefinitely in the future. It is for this reason that the lovers must hide their love, tell lies about it, betray it, until at last, outraged in their deepest feelings by these renunciations, they separate and console themselves with 'sex as amusement'. That, then, is the other nigger in the woodpile. 'Sex as amusement' is to be a means of reconciling young adults to the abnegations of love forced upon them by lingering patriarchal ideals of marriage and property.

A word, however, should be said in behalf of the 'sex as amusement' theory. It has been treated seriously here; but it is sometimes not intended as seriously as that. The wretchedly unhappy exemplars of it here adduced from the realm of fact may not be the ones that are in the minds of those who cherish it; their exemplars reside, eternally happy, in the realm of fantasy. So long as this is understood, that 'sex as amusement' represents an imaginative escape from reality, it may pass without criticism. For people suffering from patriarchal repressions, people caught in patriarchal man-traps of marital duty, people overwhelmed with patriarchal religious notions of the sinfulness of sex, people weighed down by the responsibilities or aching from the griefs of adult love, this infantile dream of 'sex as amusement', without a yesterday or a tomorrow, free from hope and fear, may afford relief—the same relief as is afforded by these regressions in actuality, but without their practical drawbacks. It would be unfortunate if we had no such imaginative escapes, incapable as most of us are of living consistently upon an adult plane. All such dream-worlds have, moreover (though here the use of the term may appear odd) the function of religious consolation, giving absolution through fantasy-fulfillment to repressed impulses. Havelock Ellis, in recommending Casanova's *Mémoires,* asks: "If then childhood needs its pure fairy-land, and youth its fairy-land of impossible adventure, what fairy-land is left for adult age?" Obviously the fairy-land of sex, into which Casanova can lead us. "Is it not a part of its attraction, and indeed that of all fairy-lands, the existence of a different code of morals? It seems to me that this is so. But precisely in that lies the moral value of such literature. Indeed the whole question of the moral value of art—that is to say, of aesthetic enjoyment—is really involved here." Walt Whitman urged in his own behalf and in behalf of such artistic freedom in general that "the soul of a man or woman demands, enjoys compensation in the highest directions for this very restraint of himself or herself, level'd to the average, or rather mean, low, however eternally practical, requirements of society's intercourse. To balance this indispensable abnegation [in the real world], the free minds of poets relieve themselves, and strengthen and enrich mankind with free flights in all the directions not tolerated by ordinary society. * * * Only understand that the conventional standards and laws proper enough for ordinary society apply neither to the action of the soul, nor its poets." Emerson has expressed the same spiritual need for fantasy-compensation against the narrowness of reality in his poem "Mithridates":

"I cannot spare water or wine,
Tobacco-leaf, or poppy, or rose;
From the earth-poles to the line,
All between that works or grows,
Every thing is kin of mine.

"Give me agates for my meat;
Give me cantharids to eat;
From air and ocean bring me foods,
From all zones and altitudes;—

"From all natures, sharp and slimy,
Salt and basalt, wild and tame:
Tree and lichen, ape, sea-lion,
Bird, and reptile, be my game.

"Ivy for my fillet band;
Blinding dog-wood for my hand;
Hemlock for my sherbet cull me,
And the prussic juice to lull me;
Swing me in the upas boughs,
Vampyre-fanned, when I carouse.

"Too long shut in strait and few,
Thinly dieted on dew,
I will use the world, and sift it,
As you spin a cherry.

O doleful ghosts, and goblins merry!
O all you virtues, methods, mights,
Means, appliances, delights,
Reputed wrongs and braggart rights,
Smug routine, and things allowed,
Minorities, things under cloud!
Hither! take me, use me, fill me,
Vein and artery, though ye kill me!"

§ 2. Religious Asceticism as a Protest Against 'Sexual Witchcraft'

A religious reaction to sexual irresponsibility has been to go to the opposite extreme and declare that sexual intercourse is permissible *only* when it is used with the intention of producing children, and is otherwise sinful. This notion, though it still lingers among the intellectually backward part of the population, chiefly as a form of hypocrisy, is nevertheless so out of date that we need not trouble to attack it. But it will be, on the other hand, profitable to analyze it sympathetically along historical and psychological lines, and see how it arose and what emotional plausibility it has had to sensitive minds.

The savage use of medicinal means by which sexual relations are freed from their consequences has been found even among such primitive peoples as the now extinct Tasmanians, and there is some reason to believe that it may date back to the neolithic and possibly the paleolithic period. These practices, which were apparently associated with primitive sex-magic and animal-fertility cults and were one aspect of the power thus claimed to 'bind and loose' the fertility of all Nature, were handed down into medieval times by the witch-cult which had survived from primeval life.

It is important for us to realize some of their historical associations, which still profoundly affect our lives to-day in adverse ways.

The practice of sexual intercourse without biological consequences in childbirth was once apparently a religious magical practise, supervening upon the still more primitive ritual slaying of new-born children to propitiate the food-giving powers of Nature. The means by which childbirth was avoided was regarded as magical, and the practice itself was magical in its original purpose. In the view of later patriarchal religion it would be, as it professed to be, the result of a compact with the Devil, the archaic animal-fertility god of Europe. We must remember, then, the association of these professedly magical sexual practices and means with the polymorphous-perverse sexual tendencies of the decadent pagan 'return to savagery' in the long débâcle of Mediterranean civilization which occurred as the result of continual war, wide-spread famine, and chronic social hopelessness. The new cult of Christianity—which was in many respects a desperate attempt at sanity in a world gone childishly silly, hysterically cruel and almost insane with anxiety—had to take, or at least did take, the stand of separating the spiritual aspects of love from all its physical aspects, which latter were habitually degraded, in marriage as well as without, to a level of superstitious infantilism disgusting to sensitive minds in search of gentleness, serenity, and mutual trust. Early Christianity thus put a premium upon the asceticism which seemed to be the best or the only way of life in which freedom of the spirit from disgust and self-loathing could be attained. This prescription was at first extended to the marital state, where complete abstinence from the sexual expression of love, a love-life upon an exclusively spiritual plane, was exacted. There is no doubt, moreover, that this kind of spiritual love, in contrast to the anxiety-ridden, infantile sexuality of their previous pagan careers, was found agreeable by many Christian converts, and that in such a physically ascetic life they found delights of mutual understanding, helpfulness and peace. The same experience has been testified to in modern times by many a former 'loose-living' man and woman who found not merely peace but spiritual love for the first time in religious chastity, and the reality of the experience and its practicability for some natures need not be questioned. (Other natures, to be sure, like that of St. Augustine in his youth, though wretched [*miser*] enough in their sexual lives, and longing for release into spiritual love, could only pray, with him: "Give me chastity and continency, but do not give it yet"—being afraid, with Augustine, that God would hear their prayer "too soon, and too soon deliver me from my disease of incontinency; which my desire was, rather to have satisfied than extinguished".) With the entrance of Christianity into the field of practical administration of the Roman ruin, however, it had to make terms with marriage.

St. Paul's stand in this matter is often misunderstood. He was mediating between human nature and the extremists who wanted to prohibit marriage to Christians, or at least sexual relations in marriage. He said: "It is good for a man not to touch a woman" and "I would that all men were even as I myself". Then, as a practical psychologist and administrator, he said: "But every man hath his proper gift of God, one after this manner, one after that", and as for the unmarried and widows, "if they cannot contain, let them marry: for it is better to marry than to burn"; but as for the married, "Let the husband render unto the wife due benevolence; and likewise also the wife unto the husband. * * * Defraud ye not one the other, except it be with consent for a time, that ye may give yourselves to fasting and prayer; and come together again, that Satan tempt you not. * * *" It was an early Christian custom to have a 'spiritual bride', a virgin living in the same domestic establishment for the sake of spiritual love but without sexual relations. Here also Paul mediated in a practical way to prevent scandal. Moffat's modern translation of this passage will be more illuminating than the St. James version: "if any man considers that he is not behaving properly to the maid who is his spiritual bride, if his passions are strong and it must be so, then let him do what he wants—let them be married; it is no sin for him. But the man of firm purpose who has made up his mind, who, instead of being forced against his will, has determined to keep his maid a spiritual bride—that man will be doing the right thing. Thus both are right in marrying and in refraining from marriage, but he who does not marry will be found to have done better."

The celebrated or notorious Pauline commandment, "Wives, submit yourselves unto your own husbands, as unto the Lord", was not intended as a degradation of women but as a specific permission to have sexual relations in marriage without fear of their being a sin against Christian holiness; the marital sexual union is to be regarded as sanctified by identification with the mystical union of Christ and the Church, and the commandment continues: "Husbands, love your wives as Christ also loved the Church."

Thus we see Christianity accepting the sexuality of the marital state as a necessity of practical administration, though with reservations in favor of chastity. The problem, however, of the use of sexual relations in the marital state for the mutual 'benevolence' judicially advised by St. Paul, continued to be a trouble to Christian doctrine. It was felt needful that it be permitted as an expression of spiritual love, and not of mere pleasure—in which respect it was regarded as no better than fornication. The distinction is not as absurd as it might seem to the modern mind in revolt against Churchly repressions. It is a distinction understood by all lovers, by whom sexual relations are felt to be either expressions of a complete psychic union involving mutual trust and responsibility, or else emotionally worthless. The distinction is an instinctive one with a profound biological significance, and refers very simply to the fact that sexual relations are productive of children who will need parental care. Thus the Church was psychologically correct in its later emphasis upon the begetting of children as the 'purpose' of marriage and of sexual relations—though it has been ignorant and brutal enough in its application of this maxim.

In order, however, to understand this ignorance and this brutality, we must refer back to the historical conditions under which the Christian attitude was formulated. Paul says nothing directly as to the duty of begetting children—that is a later Christian development. But he does refer (in the Epistle to the Ephesians) to the mysterious pagan practices of sexual witchcraft, for that was ideologically their nature, by which sexual intercourse might be indulged as a pleasure without the responsibility of child-nurture, through making the relation infertile. In one part of the letter, now distinguished as Chapter V., he (or whoever wrote the letter which is ascribed to him) dealt with the subject of sexual morality, defending marital relations in the Pauline manner already indicated in the previous quotations, by identifying the sexual union with the mystical union of Christ to his Bride the Church, but warning these Christians and former idolaters against the sexual practices associated with idolatry; "for ye were sometimes darkness [once heathen], but now are ye light in the Lord: walk as children of light". He has spoken in plain words against fornication and whoremongering, but when he comes to these idolatrous sexual-witchcraft practices he speaks more allusively, but as of matters which his readers will understand: "And have no fellowship with the unfruitful works of darkness [that is, of heathendom], but rather reprove them. For it is a shame even to speak of those things which are done in secret." He then comforts them metaphorically for their past heathenish sexual practices, assuring them that by Christ's light even the darkness and spiritual death of heathendom are transformed into light and life.

Now these 'unfruitful works of darkness' thus referred to were modes of abortion, or, to speak of them in the terms in which they were understood by those who practised them, mysterious and magical modes of effecting the infertility of sexual relations. They were partly spells and prayers to archaic sexual deities, or to archaic forms or functions of the familiar Graeco-Roman-Oriental deities; partly ritual practices only symbolically relevant to the purpose; and—so far as they were in fact effective—they were the use of poisonous medicaments, either internally or (since they were very powerful poisons and might cause death) as ointments rubbed into the skin, sometimes combined with violent massage. These, if effective, and if not causing death, would produce convulsions and by effecting an early miscarriage would restore the menstrual flow at its regular time. They were, however, in these early stages of pregnancy not popularly understood as abortions but as modes of magical 'prevention' of pregnancy. They were, moreover, not regarded as simply medicinal; they were a part of the worship of heathen gods—in fact a kind of heathen 'sacrament' by which the worshipper was united with the heathen god. Even in their medicinal aspect they were magic, dating as they did from a pre-scientific system of thought according to which "a drug was not a chemical substance taking effect naturally on the human system, but something into which a supernatural virtue had been magically introduced, in order the more easily and efficaciously to be brought to bear upon the patient". They were thus related antithetically to the Christian sacraments. They were, in fact, regarded as a form of devil-worship.

This mode of dealing with the population problem had, apparently, as said above, supervened upon the primitive mode of killing undesired infants at birth. The killing of such infants had itself tended to become not merely a necessitous practice but, if only by way of emotional self-justification, a religious practice in primitive times.

In early Greek times, the killing by exposure and neglect of undesired children was an accepted social convention, having in Sparta a pseudo-eugenic purpose. "A father", Plutarch tells us, "had not the right of bringing up his offspring, but had to carry it to a certain place called Lesche, where the elders of the tribe sat in judgment upon the child. If they thought it well-built and strong, they ordered the father to bring it up, and assigned one of the nine thousand plots of land to it; but if it was mean-looking or misshapen, they sent it away to a place called Apothetae (the Exposure), a glen upon the side of Mount Taygetus". The limited amount of Spartan land is obviously here the real consideration. The women, moreover, "used to wash their newborn infants with wine, not with water, to make trial of their constitutions. It was thought that epileptic and sickly infants were thrown into convulsions" and strong ones "hardened" by it. The ancient Celts invented a polite moral justification of the same necessitous practice; we are told, says Frazer, that they submitted the question of the legitimacy of their offspring to the judgment of the Rhine; "they threw the infants into the water, and if they were bastards the pure and stern river drowned them"—a custom so widespread as to be invoked by Frazer as the origin of the Biblical story of the infant Moses set adrift in an ark of bulrushes. In Aristotle's time there was evidently a strong revulsion of feeling against infanticide. "As to the exposure and rearing of children, let there be a law that no deformed child shall live, but where there are too many (for in our State population has a limit), when couples have children in excess, and the state of feeling is averse to the exposure of offspring, let abortion be procured before sense and life have begun".

The archaic method of infanticide has been urged in our time by an anti-feminist writer, Anthony Ludovici, in preference to what he terms the "coldly calculated" contraceptive methods of birth-control; deliberate infanticide would, in his opinion, "restore an enormous amount of lost *joie de vivre* and innocence to the life of millions of people." The practice, however, would not appear to have contributed largely to the *joie de vivre* of the ancient world; parents were obliged, it would appear from their literature and legend, to console themselves with the fantasy that the exposed infant would not be devoured by wild beasts, or brought up (as was permissible to the finder of such an exposed infant) to slavery, but found and reared by some kind-hearted peasant, eventually to become a great hero or king. If the exposed child were, however, a girl, it does not appear that even poetic fantasy could envisage a happy life for her, since she was probably doomed if rescued to a life of public prostitution.

The problem was a real one, set by the food-producing limitations of the patriarchal landed-property régime; nor did abortion seem much preferable to the alternative of infanticide, inasmuch as it was characteristically abandoned by the medical profession to the witch-women (as the treatment of venereal disease was to magicians in classical times, and later to quacks). Abortion remained a dangerous and uncertain resource; and for Christians it was out of the question because it was so involved with idolatry.

The Christian hatred of idolatry was not merely a theoretical objection to the nonsense of worshipping graven images; it was a profound and upon the whole a civilized horror of the mental degradation of savage superstition and of the cruelties inextricably intermingled with idolatry. Bernard Shaw has accurately expressed that civilized Christian horror in the heroic speech of his Lavinia in *Androcles and the Lion:* "* * * when these men drag me to the foot of an iron statue that has become the symbol of the terror and darkness through which they walk, of their cruelty and greed, of their hatred of God and their oppression of man—when they ask me to pledge my soul before the people that this hideous idol is God, and that all this wickedness and falsehood is divine truth, I cannot do it, not if they could put a thousand cruel deaths upon me."

The horrors and abominations of idolatry were matters of common Christian knowledge and belief. In every anxiety-crisis of the ancient world, as in wars and famines, there was a tendency to lapse into the archaic religious practice and propitiate the offended gods of Nature by offering up the first-born, as for example in Phoenicia to red-hot iron arms of Moloch. These sadistic practices of ritual infant-killing were, at least in popular belief, deliberately cultivated down to a late date by the witch-cult. And it was to witches, or hags who had the dark repute of witches—the descendants as it were of the ancient priestesses of savage Nature-worship and the repositories of their archaic feminine sex-lore—to whom women must go for the mixtures of cabalistic nonsense, pseudo-medicinal carrion and filth, and poison, which promised them the occult power of leading sexual lives without pregnancy resulting. They were the same to whom women went for magic love-philters, for magical means of killing their rivals, and for poisons to poison their husbands with. It is not strange, then, that the Church should have forbidden these 'unfruitful works of darkness' to her children, and that the attempt at 'spiritual marriage' without sexual relations should have been made.

The later doctrine, however, of the duty of unlimited procreation does not represent the early Christian view. Family limitation was a customary practice in the Roman world under economic conditions in which there was little general assurance of future care for any child. The Christian attitude at this time may be described as one of taking a great deal of infant mortality for granted, from the 'natural' causes of disease and poverty. But the Church did not cynically rest content with that. It also undertook to promote Christian knowledge and self-restraint to keep families within reasonable limits. In this recipe the Christian knowledge was no less important than the Christian self-control. It represented an attempt to replace the heathen lore of pregnancy prevention by a naïve Christian science, through the supposed discovery (which would be true in only a few cases) that marital relations could be indulged during certain parts of the month without pregnancy occurring in consequence. Since this supposed avoidance of biological consequences was effected without the use of devilish arts, it was obviously intended by God in order that husbands and wives should be able to use sex for the apostolically permitted purpose of mutual 'benevolence'. The fact that this method (still with the same medieval naïvete recommended by Roman Catholic priests) required sexual abstinence at other times, and was thus a practical application of the primitive Christian chastity-ideal within a limited field where it was not beyond human power to be exercised, gave it all the ear-marks of authenticity. It was to some extent unofficially buttressed by another recipe, one which is in contradiction to Pauline doctrine, but which would spring naturally from the anxiety-state in which marital relations were had by women who feared pregnancy; this was the belief that deliberate frigidity in the woman during the sexual act would prevent conception. This lack of sexual pleasure could be regarded as the next thing to actual chastity, hence spiritually meritorious, and hence a divinely appointed means of family limitation. We are by now, in Christian sex-superstition, far back along the road to the silly savagery against which Christianity had been so noble a protest. We need not follow this road to the end and indict Christianity for all the convenient compromises it made with paganism, for all the savage cruelties and silliness into which it lapsed. But we may observe that it was only gradually forced through a series of logical but absurd steps into the frightful abomination of approving the begetting of idiots, and into abject surrender to the modern Mammon-worship and Moloch-worship of industrial greed and militaristic Statecraft, through encouragement of unlimited families of children to be used up as child-labor and cannon-fodder. It should be noted, moreover, that the old pagan methods of abortion were not called by that name; that these pagan methods were believed to be magical and devilish means of preventing conception. The contemporary priestly fear and hatred of modern scientific contraceptive methods harks back to the traditional Christian hatred and fear of sexual witchcraft. It was against poison and idolatry that Paul uttered his warnings, against infernal sacraments in which the soul of the devotee was sealed to the Horned God of animal fertility, against devil-worship and its cloud of cruelties, perversities and insanities. Paul, who wrote, "Let the husband render unto the wife due benevolence: and likewise also the wife unto the husband", might have welcomed the modern scientific methods which make that due benevolence possible without anxiety. But some of the clerical followers of Paul strangely enough prefer abortion to birth-control. One wonders what kind of epistle Paul would have written to them.

It is interesting also to observe the tragic predicament of the sexual life in the Christian era.

In earlier savagery, the killing of unwanted children had not been tragic, since tragedy is not inherent in circumstances but in the defeat of rational hope in the mind that observes them. Selective infanticide was to the savage mind a mere economic necessity, and the mind ever adjusts itself to the laws of necessity. Nevertheless, an essentially tragic question was bound to arise when it was discovered that there was a connection between the sexual act and childbirth:—the question, 'Why must children be created only to be killed?' And here, as always, religion took up the task of justifying the ways of God to man. In primitive life this task was accomplished by obscuring the issue—by dogmatically denying the fact of any connection between the sexual act and the creation of children. Religion fell back, that is to say, upon an earlier state of felicitous ignorance, belonging to the period when man was hardly more than an anthropoidal ape with a brain incapable of reasoning so far from cause to effect. Primitive religion asserted the sacred truth of the early fantasies by which pregnancy was explained as the occupation of a woman's body by an ancestral spirit.

There are still savage tribes who dogmatically believe this to be true. They are intellectually at a stage of development in which they are capable of recognizing the actual cause of pregnancy, but they refuse to see it and grow angry when it is pointed out to them. The religious theory of ancestral-spirit impregnation (in the sense of occupation of the womb) is among them built into a matrilinear social organization in which a woman's husband is 'no relation' to his wife's children. Property descends from a woman to her children and from a man to his sisters' children. This social organization, which appears to be (though the generalization is disputed on evidence from the American continent) a universal characteristic of early savage life, would be shattered, as it was in Europe, by the recognition of paternity. The belief in 'no paternity' also subserves another important feature of savage life, the universality of which at the matrilinear stage has also been asserted and disputed, but which is present in the savage societies most thoroughly studied:—the sexual freedom of young people before marriage, within the limits prescribed by the incest-taboo. The savage dogma of 'babies without sexual intercourse as a cause' implies, of course, 'sexual intercourse without babies as a result'. The sexual relations of these young people are thus freed by savage religion from the burden of a sense of responsibility such as arises in civilized society. This freedom from responsibility, however, can be literally true only for the young men. The girls have to keep from having babies, for, in some savage societies at least, unmarried motherhood is as socially disgraceful as in civilized life. The sexual freedom of the unmarried is in fact, even though not in theory, subject to the restrictions ideally laid down for those *past* the approved "age of generating" by Plato in his *Republic;* after prescribing an age-class incest-taboo, he says: "we will allow the men liberty to cohabit with any woman * * * and so likewise the women to embrace any man * * *: all this liberty we will allow them, after we have enjoined them to attend carefully, in the first place, if anything should be conceived not to bring it to the light; but if by any accident it should be brought forth, to expose it as a creature for which no provision is made." The disgraceful accident of unmarried motherhood is in some savage societies liberally concealed through the adoption of the child by a relative.

In the Trobriand Islands, where the religious dogma of 'no paternity' is devoutly accepted, the sexual affairs of the unmarried are so usually devoid of consequences in childbirth—exactly as they should be according to the savage theory—that Malinowski after years of residence and study there, remains mystified, and asks: "Can there be any physiological law which makes conception less likely when women begin their sexual activity early in life, lead it indefatigably, and mix their lovers freely?" The answer to this riddle of youthful freedom from the biological consequences of the sexual act is less mysterious in other savage groups. Concerning the unmarried sexual life of the Mailu, perhaps a hundred and fifty miles away from the Trobriands, on the southern coast of eastern New Guinea, the missionary Saville tells us: "Parents are said to be very shocked and to reproach their children severely, but it must be a kind of winking 'shock', for my informants agree that mothers and aunts assist the girls in certain fasts (*sora*) at certain times, and after the girl has taken salt water, an aunt prepares medicine (*iapa*), reckoned to be a preventive, and gives it to the girl, and the mother, at the request of the girl, prepares roasted food for her instead of ordinary boiled food! What this *iapa* is neither my wife nor I, after many years' residence among these people, can find out; all our informants agree that such 'medicine' is taken and believed in by the natives as possessing the property desired. They cultivate here a fish-poisoning plant * * * used by Malay girls 'as an abortifacient' * * * but I doubt its being used here for that purpose. Native men say that *iapa* is water in which certain leaves have been boiled. Girls have admitted to my wife that such a thing is taken, but individually assert entire innocence as to what it is or how prepared. Both married and unmarried girls take it. * * * Young married fellows accuse their wives of having taken this *iapa,* and thus account for their not having children. Marriages are often broken off in that way. We have heard of" [certain] "flower-buds being eaten with ordinary food to bring about sterility, also the anointing of the body and head with a preparation made from leaves. Illegitimate children are very rare." These are the primordial methods of savage sex-witchcraft. Since they are in fact abortifacients, though reckoned as preventives, their use requires expert knowledge, if they are to be effective, as they appear to be. The savage girl must necessarily know some of the physiology of sex beyond the sexual act; but these are women's-witchcraft secrets, unknown to men. "Not only", says Saville, "is there a professed ignorance on the part of men as regards feminine concerns, but I think it really exists. There is so much secrecy in feminine affairs that one could easily imagine the existence of a feminine club or secret society within our savage community. I doubt whether a husband or wife gets to know the 'self' of the other." So that this happy savage insouciance about sexual relations turns out to require a religious dogma of immaculate conception, working conjointly with secret feminine arts of abortion. There is plenty of evidence that the knowledge of the facts of sexual impregnation is merely repressed from savage consciousness. It is a case of not letting the right hand know what the left hand doeth. The men are encouraged to a completely irresponsible sexuality, and the burden of avoiding undesired consequences falls upon the woman. This arrangement is not unknown in civilized life.

In savage life, however, this sexual witchcraft is not to be understood as constituting simply a practical science known to women and withheld from men. It has its practical and effective aspects, but these are psychologically immersed in symbolic anxiety-relief of magic. Some and perhaps most of the means thus used are practically ineffective and only to be explained by savage symbolism. Thus the particular flower-buds eaten by Mailu girls have the property of astringency and could thus be regarded as a safeguard against pregnancy: the illustration is hypothetical, but on the lines of savage medicine as handed down from Egyptian to Graeco-Roman and medieval medicine. Any realistic knowledge of the physiological facts involved would be repressed by the religious dogma of non-sexual spirit-impregnation, and replaced in consciousness with dependence upon the wish-fulfillments of magic. Savages, like farmers in the old maxim, live on hope. We are thus plunged into a mental darkness in which the wish counts more than the observed fact. Savage psychic robustness to the evils of life is a robustness founded upon a hopeful disregard of unpleasant facts; and this applies especially to their sexual lives.

"It has been said", remarks Dr. Singer, "that, 'save the blind forces of Nature, nothing lives or moves that is not Greek in origin'. The saying needs modification, for there is a thing which still lives and moves which is not Greek in origin, a blind force which is not a blind force of Nature. It is the force of Superstition, of that age-old belief that Nature will give us something for nothing, which is expressed by the word 'Magic'." Not exactly 'something for nothing', but a reality for a symbol, a fulfillment in return for a wish properly expressed. The Wish has command over Nature by symbolic means; it becomes the all-powerful magic Will which the powers of Nature must obey. It is a childish dream-world, that of sexuality, using powers of life and death that it does not understand.

This savage dream-world of sex had been inherited by the classical world. It was temporarily shattered by the reconstruction of society along patriarchal lines. Among the sorts of power taken away from women or at least forbidden to them, were their archaic magical powers, including sexual witchcraft—which was henceforth obliged to lead a more or less subterranean existence, until social anxieties brought it once more into general use. The savage theories of sex were on the whole repudiated; but in certain respects they may be described as having been reconstructed to fit patriarchal convenience. Sexual irresponsibility was abolished only to a certain degree and within certain bounds. Religion no longer required the denial of male paternity in the physical sense; but it still permitted the male to refuse social paternity to any undesired or superfluous child—including of course any child born out of wedlock. But even when born in wedlock, the superfluous child—being, in the Platonic phrase, "a creature for which no provision is made"—was condemned to perish by infanticide. For a time in the clear hard light of pagan realism these necessary measures could apparently be taken deliberately by parents and justified by philosophers. But before Christianity the outraged human spirit had begun to ask the tragic question, 'Why must children be born only to be slain?' The only evasion of that tragic question was through recourse to the dangerous practices of abortion, practices which were then involved with the most archaic and degrading superstitions and surrounded by an atmosphere of secret abominations.

It was in this situation that the new Christian religion put the tragic question in its most fundamental form: 'Why should a child be *begotten*, if it is to be denied the right to live?' The ethical concern behind the Christian attitude was the same as that which to-day underlies scientific birth-control. But the day of science was yet far off, and the only way in which Christianity could purge itself of the cruelty of irresponsible sexuality was by the program of chastity—later modified in certain ways, as we have seen, in the attempt to adapt its requirements to the mutual-love purposes of marriage.

The tragic question which Christianity dared ask is one which patriarchal society in general had not the courage to consider; it sank back into the savage sexual dream-world. Unable and unwilling to adopt the Christian recipe of chastity, it shut its eyes to the consequences of its irresponsible sexuality. Doubtless patriarchal society did the best it could under the circumstances, in which sexual love was impossible without forgetfulness of its inevitable results. But, however put out of sight and out of mind, these remain the skeletons in the closet of patriarchal civilization, the pitiful and shameful secrets which lie hidden in the most respectable patriarchal marriages. There is a final touch of horror in the tenderness with which the inevitable deprivation of life was administered to the superfluous offspring of these marital embraces—as when the new-born infant was drowned in *milk*, or the mother's breast smeared with opium to carry the suckling peacefully into its eternal sleep. We may ask, did no thought of these consequences ever shadow the nuptial bed? And perhaps the proper patriarchal answer would be that those who could not help thinking about such painful things should not marry but go into monasteries and nunneries. These were the conditions of sexual life, and husbands and wives had to accept them. They lacked the savage religious dogma which dissociated sex from reproduction, but they had the savage ability to refuse to think about unpleasant things.

Such adjustment to adverse social conditions of life, however, is only to be had at a price. We know to-day that the fear of bringing into the world children who cannot be properly cared for, and the fear of abortions, produce sexual frigidity in women. If we have, as some doctors believe, an overwhelming preponderance of sexual frigidity in women, that may be regarded as an inheritance from the patriarchal inability to make conditions for the sexual life such as could in their entirety be faced by the conscious mind. Modern contraceptive methods are not yet all that might ideally be desired, but *they do enable people to live sexual lives which they need not be ashamed to think about.* And, conversely, those to whom sex is *per se* a shameful subject stand suspect of having the best reasons for feeling that way about it.

CHAPTER X

A FAIR WARNING TO ALL

[The possibility of exaggerated or false ideals in these pages]

§ 1. The Dangers of Ideological Overcompensation

This somewhat formidable term, 'ideological overcompensation', has been used here as suggesting the common method of origin of various extreme theoretic ideals which are not superficially similar. All of these theories have arisen out of emotional states—which, while it should put us on guard as to the possible weaknesses of such theories, is thus far nothing against them. But it is characteristic of emotion which reaches the point of anxiety that it has to satisfy itself in symbolic action regardless of the practical irrelevance or mischievousness of such action. We have suggested that such anxiety states were more or less responsible for all the extreme theoretic ideals here discussed.

Some of these theories have expressed the wish to escape, by turning round and going in the opposite direction, from things hated—like Plato's proposal to abolish the Family by merging it in the State, and the Christian ascetic revolt against sexual irresponsibility. Others, by favorable interpretations of painful situations, have sought to reconcile our minds to them—like the ideal of woman as a 'free worker' and that of 'free motherhood.' These also rush to opposite extremes from a thing hated, but have the additional element of construing present realities so as to make them less humiliating. Both are, as we have tried to show, so irrelevant to realistic purposes, and sometimes so mischievous, that they are false guides to action.

Nevertheless, so long as they remain in the field of thought, not as preludes to action but as imaginative consolations and wish-fulfillments, they have a religious or an aesthetic function—so that our drastic criticism of them on realistic grounds has always been followed by a defense of them as psychological safety-valves. They are, in their own realm, useful precisely because they are *not* practical.

It may be difficult, but it is always desirable, for us to test our theoretic ideals to discover whether they are (as they may seem) guides to realistic action, or (as is always likely) something in the nature of religious consolation or aesthetic wish-fulfillment. If they turn out to be the latter, we need not abandon them, for they will continue to have their uses as emotional relief; but we will cease to mistake them for the kind of wishes which are to be put into action.

Now it will probably not have escaped the reader that many of the psychologists whose discoveries and views are here being more or less systematized, and certainly the writer of this book, have emotional attitudes about the habits of thought and action here described as 'patriarchal'. The question then arises, may not the views here promulgated be a kind of rushing to an opposite extreme, or a kind of Pollyannish self-comforting in regard to the state of the world? If Plato can be accused of these self-deceptions, are any of us immune from them?

None of us are necessarily immune from them. And it is a healthy exercise to suspect the presence of fictitious elements in this present view, as in all others. In watching for them, we may protect it against them. But even that watchfulness is no final guarantee of its validity. Its validity is authenticated only by its continuous correspondence to the facts of life. It is not, however, a reproduction of the chaotic flux of fact; it is an attempt at combining historical, biological and psychological interpretations of fact into one interpretation, which is then applied to the facts to see how well it fits. It is not a dogmatic but an experimental application of the interpretation to the facts; it will doubtless require correction—and, as hinted at the outset, the particular attempt at systematization which this book represents may be in many respects premature.

Some of the facts of psychology here set forth represent comparatively new discoveries. Many of what used to be considered facts of human nature have turned out not to be facts at all but false dogmas about facts. It does not invalidate the modern view of human behavior to bring up exploded patriarchal dogmas as if they were facts that had been overlooked. It does not invalidate the modern view to present infantile wish-fulfillments as if they were facts. But it is open to any critic to bring up obdurate facts that may have been conveniently overlooked in the passion of generalization, or—more drastically—to point out infantile wish-fulfillments which may be here masquerading as facts.

Any view of human behavior must necessarily pass both these tests. But the testing should be reciprocal. Test your own familiar convictions as to the facts of human nature by these new discoveries and generalizations. Suspect your own convictions, protests and incredulities first. Ask *why* you believe what you believe. Attribute infantile motives to your mind, experimentally—you will be astonished to find out how often they will turn out to be correct. Adjure *yourself* in the spirit of Cromwell's words to Parliament: "I beseech you, brethren, in the bowels of Christ, to believe it possible that you may be mistaken!" It is more than probable that you are mistaken about a great many things.

On the other hand, it is when you find yourself accepting too readily such conclusions as these advanced here that you would do well to pause and question them. For their authenticity cannot be guaranteed in advance, they can only be subjected to the test of further experience, and you take them, not upon the word of the present writer nor even of any of the authorities upon whom he relies, but upon your own responsibility as a truth-seeker.

It may make easier the task of doubt and the obligation of facing the possibility of having been mistaken, if we reflect upon these words of Guglielmo Ferrero's: "Since it is theory, then, which gives facts their value and significance, it is often very useful even if it is in part untrue; for it throws light upon phenomena to which no one had paid attention, it forces us to examine from various angles facts which no one had been studying, and impels us to undertake investigations of wider scope, destined to have more fruitful results."

§ 2. 'Adjustment to Reality'

There is, however, a special danger in our present view of behavior. It lies in an over-estimation of 'reality'. It has been seen that the difference between psychic health and neurosis is a practical one, consisting partly in the degree of capacity for enjoyment of life and partly in the degree of capacity for social adaptation and hence usefulness. Both these standards are, however, in being 'practical', dependent upon temporal conditions. The contemporary realities to which we necessarily seek to adapt ourselves are, it is as well to remember, not eternal verities; and conformation to a definition of psychic health is ***not a religious ideal.*** It is, indeed, well for us to retain some mental independence of the 'realities' to which we seek to adapt ourselves. It is well to question the validity of these 'realities'. It is well, even when we have accepted their validity, to respect the reluctance with which our adaptive efforts are made. In our eternal reluctance there may be and probably is something of equal value to the human race with our temporal adaptations.

Illustrations are easy. We have noted that in the savage society of the South Seas with its socially prescribed customs of light love, anything resembling adult sexual exclusiveness, as denoted by jealousy, becomes 'neurotic'. The philosophers of that region argue that sex is not to be taken too seriously—an opposite conclusion from the one which the philosophers of our culture reach. Among ourselves, the fantasy of South Seas promiscuity is a mere dream of escape from the 'realities' of our life, or else an attempt to dignify our sexual promiscuities with the romantic accessories of an alien cultural purpose. But the philosophers of the South Seas could quite as readily argue that the desire for adolescent sexual exclusiveness, when found in their culture, is a mere 'dream of escape' from the 'realities' of their culture, or an attempt to justify the folly of jealousy. What both sets of philosophers mean is that their culture suits them and that they accept its purposes.

But we in our present inquiry have sought to go beyond that. We have attempted to find a kind of absolute:—a search never without its dangers. We have sought to find it in historical and psychological development. In historical development we find that the savage culture of our ancestors has given place to that which we now cherish. In psychological development we find that the sexually undifferentiated emotions of the child give place to the heterosexual emotional fixations of the adult. We conclude that while the savage's standards of behavior may suit the savage, and the child's standards of behavior be suitable to the child, our civilized adult standards represent a superior achievement. Nor is this merely another way of saying that 'what is ours is better'. For by the tests of historical and psychological development we are able to discover that many sorts of socially accepted 'civilized and adult' behavior are not very civilized, being governed by patriarchal property-anxieties, and not very adult, being in fact infantilisms in disguise. It would be useless, in practice, to make these discriminations, if we had not been enabled by modern machinery to transcend these property-anxieties. It is upon the basis of the modernity we have actually achieved that we are enabled to criticize and repudiate patriarchal compromises.

But this is not merely a fact; it is also a faith—the faith that our machine-given power to transcend patriarchal property-anxieties is not an accident nor a momentary blessing from which we must presently relapse into the welter of the ancient struggle against famine and poverty in the ancient ways. It is thus implicitly a belief in Science and in the ability of mankind to use Science for other purposes than those of self-destruction. There is not much sense in learning how to live happily if we are never to have the chance. There is not much sense in trying to bring up our sons and daughters to adult standards of love if the 'realities' to which they will in fact have to adapt themselves are the casual and purposeless fornications and whoremongerings inevitably characteristic of a world at war. We should merely be giving 'counsels of perfection', or in other words talking through our hats.

We are thus committed implicitly to revolutionary social views, though not necessarily to any specific revolutionary procedure. This book is an account of a middle-class revolution, which is as yet incomplete. It is now seen in a half-way stage of compromise with the aristocratic institutions which it has half destroyed. It is not within the province of this book to show how half-patriarchal our modes of government and industry are; that will have to be taken for granted on the basis of observation and common sense. But we are committed—by the very views which require us in the interests of psychic health to adapt ourselves to current realities—to discrimination among these current realities as to *which are dying and which are being born.* When it comes to bringing up our children, the discrimination is still more cogent. In order to adapt ourselves to a changing world, we have to know in which direction it is changing. To make clear that direction is, indeed, the purpose of this book. But, however realistic are the observations upon which such views of change are based, they are always an act of faith. And since this faith operates in and upon the world of current realities, it is an act of creation. We have the task of helping to bring into full life the modern world which is still half shrouded in the cerements of a dying patriarchal order.

There is a danger in this, but it is not so great a danger as that involved in the folly of taking current realities at their face value. *It is the latter danger which modern psychology now runs.* Psychology is being found useful—and it is being used to bolster up the dying patriarchal régime. We need not complain of this. We are not yet so far out of the woods that we dare dispense with our paraphernalia of coercive order. But we can and should realize that modern psychology is taking its place along with modern artillery as a defense of the existing social system as a whole, in *both* its modern and its savage-patriarchal aspects.

When psychologists are serving institutions they are no longer pure scientists, they are practical people engaged in maintaining order. Under these circumstances it is remarkable how much independence and courage they display—an independence and courage, indeed, that is generally commensurate with their scientific knowledge. It is true that, for example, a candid public discussion of the homosexuality of sex-segregated schools need not be expected from the psychologists who are just now coping with that problem in their jobs in such schools; a candid public discussion of the neurotic qualities, ranging from patriarchal fussiness to sadism, which are to be observed pretty generally in the employing class, is not to be expected from the psychiatrists who are engaged in industrial studies; nor are candid public discussions of inferiority-feelings as a military virtue to be expected from army and navy mental-experts. This is not usually because they are dishonestly concealing something from us; it is usually because they are sufficiently patriarchal to take these current realities for granted.

If the distinguished psychologist Professor X. and the eminent psychiatrist Dr. Y. had happened to be Medicine Men in Yucatan at the time when it was the religious custom to throw a young girl into the sacred pool to drown as a propitiatory offering to the gods of rainfall, it would not have occurred to them to consider whether or not the action was sadistic; nor would their training have encouraged them to inquire even whether it was useful. They would have been able to discover that those girls who went shrieking and struggling to the edge of the precipice were badly brought up. They would have conceived their scientific duty to be a study of the situation which would yield the knowledge as to how to bring up girls so that when they were thus honored by being chosen as the bride of Chacmool, they would enjoy the prospect and go eagerly or at least cheerfully to their doom.

If you think that this is unjust to the distinguished psychologist Professor X. and the eminent psychiatrist Dr. Y., it is because you do not know the gentlemen. They are not in the least unkind, they are certainly not sadistic; it is merely that they take current realities for granted. They assume that the demands of society are always correct; and they use their expert psychological knowledge in the service of current social ideals. It is necessary—though it may and should hurt their feelings—to test their complacent assumption of the correctness of social ideals by considering their behavior when transposed into a society in which social ideals now abhorrent to us were once accepted by all the best people. Such examples are afforded by 'suttee' and other kinds of human sacrifice for 'the good of the tribe'. Early in the 19th century a runaway sailor named John Jackson, who lived for two years among the Fiji islanders, saw men led along and buried alive in the holes where the posts of a chief's house were being set up. One man he observed standing in the hole with his arms round the post and his head still clear of the soil. As Frazer relates the incident, when the sailor asked why they buried men alive at the foot of the posts, he was told that the house could not stand up if men did not continually hold the posts up; and that if the men sacrificed their lives in endeavoring to hold the posts in position the virtue of the sacrifice would induce the gods to uphold the house after the men were dead. No doubt these men went willingly to their doom, so strong was the social control, so effective the sense of duty—and so useless the attempt to resist or evade. They would have been heretics, blasphemers, traitors and cowards, had they developed conscientious objections to their sacrifice. So also with the multitude of wives who have ascended the funeral pyres of their husbands, according to the good old custom which served to appease the wrath of the ghost and keep it from troubling the community; and the trains of attendants, male and female, young and old, who have accompanied great kings into the realm of death—no doubt they generally went willingly and with a befitting sense of the nobility of their doom. Sweet and proper it is to die for the good of the tribe. The virgins in ancient Yucatan who were sacrificed annually to the god of the water-spring, in order that there might be no drought, had doubtless a solacing sense of the great privilege of dying that the tribe might live. Yet it might have happened that in some instances the sense of self-preservation, the instinctive desire to live, was so strong that it remained unsubdued and was in conflict with the social demand that they die. In that case it might have produced a neurosis. The person in question would not be able to admit anything so frightful as disbelief in the theory of sacrifice—no, but even though believing it his duty to die, he might have developed a neurotic paralysis of the legs which would have made it impossible for him to ascend the place of sacrifice. He would wish to, of course—but he just couldn't; and he would feel very bad about it. In the case of a queen who was required to set an example of piety to her subjects, so that it would have been disgraceful for her to be carried struggling and shrieking to the funeral pyre, it might have been the duty of the Chief Priest or Medicine Man to talk her into a proper state of mind and body for the great event. That functionary would not have had at his command the scientific methods of our Professor X. and Dr. Y., but it is not difficult to imagine him assuring her that she was simply afraid—though not really a coward, because her self-respect would require her to go through with the sacrifice. And it is conceivable that as the result of such a sympathetic talk she might have faced the facts of her mental conflict and recovered the use of her legs, thereupon making the supreme sacrifice with courage and dignity. A triumph for the Medicine Man, and one which if it ever occurred should have increased his prestige in the eyes of the rulers of the tribe. It would have been no part of his priestly function to question the validity of human sacrifice; he might have private doubts, but he would lose his prestige and his place and probably his life if he ventured to express them. It was not his duty to dream vain dreams of an ideal society, but to 'adjust the individual to the existing environment'.

To our Medicine Men of to-day, war may privately seem open

to doubts of various sorts. But in an emergency they cannot (or do not) abdicate their social function. When soldiers develop neurotic objections to getting killed, the psychologist and psychiatrist are pleased to have this new field thrown open to them, so as to widen our scientific knowledge. Here is what they find: "Faced with almost certain slaughter if he obeys his orders, or believing such to be the case, there arises within many a soldier a conflict between his instinct of self-preservation and his sense of duty. His instinct will drive him to flee; his sense of honor, his training as a soldier, his pride, his love of country and of an ideal—the social bulwark—demand that he obey. For many the situation is intolerable. Auto-suggestion—memory of a previously broken leg or of some other injury—or external suggestion—the sight of wounded being taken to the rear and safety—may enter in and there develops, as a compromise, a hysterical paralysis, or a blindness, a deafness, an aphonia [loss of voice], etc.—a fear reaction, albeit a reaction in general unconscious." It is no part of the function of our modern medicine man to indulge his private doubts, if such exist, as to the social usefulness of the sacrifice from which the man thus seeks to escape. It is his business to restore the patient to military usefulness—to send him out to be killed. First diagnosis, then treatment. "On his arrival at the hospital, it is found that there is nothing organically wrong with the patient. The leg is paralyzed or the eyes are blind, but with no organic injury to account for the condition. Treated as malingerers, called yellow or cowards, patients of this type are lost. Other conflicts are precipitated that further incapacitate. Treated for what they were, the nature of their difficulties intelligently explained to them, their feeling of disgrace, remorse, inadequacy, failure combated on the ground that they were not disgraced, that they were not in reality yellow, but that in the first test in a [mental] contest they did not fully understand they had failed through an unconscious response to a normal instinct, a large per cent. of these patients in the A. E. F. recovered and, with regained self-respect and confidence born of greater knowledge of themselves, returned to the line and 'went through', many making the 'supreme sacrifice.' "

That is to say, the psychologists and psychiatrists dutifully became the accomplices of the war-lords, one of whom, Winston Churchill, First Lord of the Admiralty, thus candidly describes his own activities: "At the Ministry of Munitions we were the bees of Hell, and we stored our hives with the pure essence of slaughter. It astonishes me to read in these after years the diabolical schemes for killing men on a vast scale by machinery or chemistry to which we passionately devoted ourselves." We need not complain of our psychologists and psychiatrists becoming the accomplices of the war-lords, since that is their social function in society to-day. But we may ask them not to feel obliged to be more hard-boiled than the war-lords themselves. If they admit that they are servants of the social order, doing their duty, they can be forgiven, as the war-lord, the soldier and the common hangman are forgiven; but if they take upon themselves a priestly office, and give their blessing to the merely current realities which they serve—if they undertake to say to the soul of man, 'This is all there is—there isn't any more,' then they are voodoo-doctors.

There is, it must be admitted, a certain amount of voodoo-doctoring in the current practical use of modern psychological knowledge—an inevitable tendency toward proclaiming this the best of all possible worlds, an inclination to lapse into smugness if not into actual cowardice. It is all the more to the credit of the mental experts that there are so many who range themselves with the prophets and not with the priests—for a mental expert finds that he has to be inescapably one or the other.

"All our work in mental hygiene", says Miriam Van Waters, "proceeds on the theory of bringing about an adjustment between the individual and his world. This raises the age-old question: To what shall we adjust? Shall we seek to have our children adjust themselves to our city streets, our exploited amusements, our industrial civilization, our weakened homes, mechanized schools, shallow moral standards? In short, to our disintegrating systems of family and social control? Or shall we seek to provide them with new goals? The very fact that to-day so many young people are in conflict makes us pause to ask ourselves: Are our children at fault, or do our institutions require modification? Do our social workers really desire to have youth completely adjusted to the present situation?"

And Dr. Frankwood E. Williams asks: "What have we to offer youth? Is it ourselves? Is it that we wish to make youth like ourselves? Have we of our generation succeeded in solving the problem of living? Have we the recipe for successful, full, generous, happy living?

"As a matter of fact, if one looks about among those of one's own generation and the older generation, one finds that most people are not living successful, full, generous, happy lives. One finds that most people are living very narrow, pinched, ungenerous, distorted, twisted lives, and that they are full of fears and anxieties and insecurities. Have we the recipe? Is it that we wish to make youth, to compel youth, to be like ourselves? Have we such pride in the way we have managed some of the problems that have come to us? Are we proud of our jealousies, our rivalries, our dishonesties, our ungenerous and suspicious attitudes towards others? Are we proud of our domestic life, our sexual life, our spiritual life? Are we proud of our success in handling political problems, of our industrial competition, with its false values—which is a product of our generation—of our methods of handling delinquency, of our methods of dispensing charity, our methods of dealing out justice in the courts? Are we proud of the methods employed in handling international disputes, of our suspicions and fears of things we do not understand, our false pride and braggadocio?

"These are things that represent us. They are us! They are the product of the ability of our generation to manage life. Are we to coerce youth into accepting this product and all that it implies? But this is not all. Youth might suffer us these things. There is a more serious score against us. Not for a long time has a generation failed so signally as ours—our generation and the one just ahead—in the management of life. Has any generation ever failed more completely? We have only recently finished slaughtering several million youths. It was our generation that slaughtered these youths. * * *

"In the face of this, how dare we talk of coercing youth into adopting our standards of life, our ideas, our attitudes, our methods of dealing with emotional problems? And yet, that is what we seem prone to do. * * *

"There are things which are not settled. Ethics, Morals, Religion—these are not static things that are made and fixed and that we can accept and hand to a younger generation. Ethics, Morals, Religion are dynamic things, growing things. Instead of coercing youth into accepting these things at the stage to which we have been able to develop them, forcing him to accept our partial product as final, we should, realizing the potential nature of these things, permit that youth should have his own opportunity to continue growth and development in these fields.

"We say we want him to carry on our ideals, but we are not even sure of the soundness of our own ideals. Why not let him have a chance to form his own?"

These represent the efforts necessary to be made in this field to keep the standard of 'adjustment to reality' from degenerating into a shibboleth in the service of a dying patriarchal order.

CHAPTER XI

DELAY AND FAILURE IN REACHING THE HETEROSEXUAL GOAL

§ 1. Juvenile Delinquency (Boys)

One more broad question must be discussed before we go on to deal with modern courtship and marriage. There is a lingering symptom of patriarchal-mindedness in our society, which takes the form of anxiety lest young people be too much attracted to those of the other sex. By such readers our section dealing with the pseudo-modern ideal of 'sex as amusement' will have been totally misunderstood. The fact there insisted upon that the sexual relation is willy-nilly a responsible one, will appear to them only another way of saying that it is 'dangerous' and that the attractions which lead to it should be shunned or repressed. That was far from being the point of that discussion. It was a theory of irresponsibility which was being inveighed against—not the pitiful efforts of young people to achieve matehood, against frightful social odds, and without even being permitted by a false education to know what it is they are instinctively trying to do, let alone encouraged to take pride in the effort and use the resources of our civilization to achieve their goal.

Patriarchal morality has always been afraid of heterosexual passion. That was inevitable, for the reasons which we have been studying in considerable detail. Heterosexual passion was the enemy of patriarchal society. "It is meet", says the great philosopher-poet of antiquity, "to * * * scare away all that feeds love and turn your mind to another object, distract your passion elsewhere and not keep it * * * [lest you] lay up for yourself care and unfailing pain. For the sore gathers strength and becomes inveterate by feeding, and every day the madness grows in violence and the misery becomes aggravated, unless you erase the first wounds by new blows and first heal them when yet fresh, roaming abroad after Venus the Pandemian ['go to a prostitute,' Lucretius means], or transfer to something else the emotions of your mind." Because of love, we are assured, "their estate runs away and is turned into Babylonian coverlets; duties are neglected and their good name staggers and sickens." Wise as Lucretius was, he was not wise enough to imagine a world without arranged marriage, a world in which heterosexual passion and not property considerations could be the basis of marriage. Euripides put the anxious prayer of all sober-minded antiquity into verse when he made one of his choruses cry out:

> "Loose not on me, O Holder of Man's Heart,
> Thy golden quiver,
> Nor steep in poison of desire the dart
> That heals not ever."

The patriarchal-minded, who cannot realize that the world has changed, are still to-day afraid of heterosexual passion. They believe, like the ancient philosophers, that all crimes and follies spring from the fatal attraction of the sexes for each other; and their remedy is still, as of old, a kind of psychic emasculation and refrigeration of mankind and womankind.

They have to be told that they are mistaken; that the patriarchal emasculation and refrigeration of the sexes has succeeded all too well; and that our crimes and follies spring in large measure precisely from these psychic malpractices. They have to be told that our modern world needs more, not less, heterosexual passion to make it go round smoothly.

We may as well begin with the subject of juvenile delinquency. There is a common but quite erroneous belief that juvenile delinquents are such because of an excessive or precocious interest in the opposite sex. Quite the contrary is true.

We present here a brief digest of some revealing though very incomplete reports on young delinquents furnished by the Judge Baker Foundation, which "studies educational, vocational and conduct problems of young people". These are in most instances cases of incipient criminality. We have taken in order all those cases which concern boys in the first series of reports. The information is arranged here so as to bear emphatically on the question of sexual development, and our own interpretations of and generalizations upon the data are put in italics:

Gregorius, aged 16 (I. Q. 98). "At 11 years he first appeared in court for petty larceny, and there followed repeated appearances for begging, stealing, staying away from home for days at a time, truanting, petty burglary, and receiving stolen goods." *Now was this because Gregorius was too much interested in girls, or too little?* He himself said: "I do not care for the pleasures that boys seek with girls because in the first place if a boy thinks of that he's done for, and he's no good." *The facts appear to be: that he had no maternal help in learning the love of woman* (his mother having died in his early infancy); *that his father did not set a standard of adult masculinity for him to emulate* (his father, as unusually intellectual immigrant workingman, had never been able to support his family:—an older son lived with relatives, a younger daughter had been placed in a foster-home, and the father and Gregorius lived together in one room, where the father cooked, kept house and even did the family washing); *and that the boy's late childhood and early adolescent sexual impulses had to express themselves through the quasi-homosexual channel of gang-exploit* (he learned to steal with them *as* he learned to swear—"If you don't [swear] they call you a mama's boy"). Gregory's father had been a radical in his youth and had been in prison for anti-governmental activities; the boy *also* talked "against the government", and was "communistic". When placed in a succession of foster-homes, Gregorius was disliked because of this talk and the intellectual braggadocio with which it was uttered. He was also disliked for asserting the superiority of his own race to Americans—*an attempt to compensate himself for the inferiority of his position. Because* his father was intellectual and had ambitions for him, the boy wanted an education. But he was discouraged by his *economic* position: "I used to try to make plans, then I'd see my position and I would forget." *His sexual regression took the forms of* laziness and excessive bodily dirtiness. *Work and cleanliness are both direct approaches to the heterosexual realm. His sexual emotions were rigidly repressed, with the result that* he "never worried about sex affairs, though the boys talked a good deal about girls". Subsequent history: He returned home and went to school, where he did not progress. The next summer he was sent on a six-weeks' cruise in the Summer Navy School, where "he enjoyed the drill and got into no trouble of any kind". *He was not grown-up enough, however, to adjust himself to the more adult heterosexual incentives of civil life, for* the next year, when he had a good job after school hours where he was "completely trusted", he "was not at all attracted by the girls who worked in the office—indeed when they joked with him he seemed rather to disdain them, and never seemed in any way silly in his attitude toward them"; *and* "in the middle of the year, apparently without any reason, he suddenly gave up this job. He did not seek any other in its place, and his father was forced to ask some financial help from the child-placing agency. They were able to obtain for Gregory a scholarship, which carried him through the rest of that school year." He was nearly 20 years old, *and he wanted to remain a child.* At some unstated date, when in company with a boy friend, he again stole, and was arrested and put on probation. *The friendliness with which he was treated has helped to convince him that* "the United States Gov't. cannot be beat"; *but he is still afraid of girls* ("if a boy thinks of that, he is done for"), *and protects himself against the adult rôle by* dirtiness and negligence of appearance—his father complains that "He did not take good care of the few clothes that he had", and his wilful and exaggerated bodily dirtiness led to a bad case of scabies. *Though* a possible criminal career, which might easily have ensued if the boy had been sent to a "reform school", has been averted, *Gregorius seems at this point not yet safely grown up* (Case 1).

Winthrop, aged 16 (I. Q. 116), of respectable New England family; in court twice, once for burglary and again for breaking into a garage and stealing an automobile. *Since automobiles are popularly associated with juvenile sexual enterprise, and since juvenile thefts so frequently involve automobiles, here is an opportunity to inquire whether car-thefts are caused by interest in the other sex.* Winthrop, we learn, "has not been immoral with girls". "His stealing and truancy have been under the influence of one young fellow who is 'the biggest all-round crook' he ever heard of. * * * In answer to the question: 'Why do you go with him?' he says, 'I don't understand that myself. Everything seriously wrong I have ever done has been his idea.'" Winthrop says that his crowd "is very little interested in girls and that there is no bad sex talk and no bad pictures. 'They don't go in for that sort of thing.' " They are addicted *instead* to *quasi-homosexual* gang-exploits which include burglary and larceny. Subsequent history: Winthrop joined the Army, giving a false age. He remained in the service three years, "stood high in his examinations, and has a splendid record for conduct". *We do not know, however, how he will succeed in adjusting to civil life* (Case 2).

Five similar cases are presented together for comparison (comprising Case 3), and the report remarks: "Concerning attraction to girls, we learn that in four cases this was not undue or premature. Indeed, in several of the cases it is specifically stated that their relationships with girls were very normal and wholesome. In two cases there was sex stress and some occasional immorality with girls. While one would not imply that this proportion has any statistical value whatever, yet it may be stated that among delinquent boys one finds that in very small measure have they been immoral with girls. Less than 5% of 2,200 boys up to 18 years, repeated offenders, in our Chicago and Boston series, had been immoral with girls, according to the best knowledge obtainable—and undoubtedly this figure is not far from the truth." *Indeed these proportions do have significance, as we shall see.*

Douglas, aged 12 (I. Q. 138), of good American family; he has "a mania for stealing". This boy was under the impression that sexual relations were practically universal among the boys and girls in junior high school and high school. He said that "so far as he knows he is the only boy who doesn't do it". *It would appear that the poor child was frightened of what he felt to be a kind of manly duty or obligation now devolving upon him, and that he substituted for it a kind of 'manliness' (theft) to which he felt more equal.* Theft was associated with sexual ideas about girls, and with auto-erotic practices; he said of the latter, "It's that starts me thinking about stealing". He had learned stealing from a boy who talked much about sexual relations with girls. He feels "restless at times 'and then I feel that I have got to take something, no matter what it is.' " Subsequent history: He was sent home; a theft immediately occurring was ignored, and since then his conduct has been "entirely satisfactory". Conditions in the school have changed, as a result of investigation, social effort, and particularly the formation of boys' and girls' clubs. "Two or three of the worst boys have moved away. The girls who formerly used to do bad things don't do them any more and there is practically no talk about it." Douglas at 14, *though* intellectually very precocious, "does not go with any girls". *The information given does not indicate whether or not he is recovering from his sexual shock as thoroughly as he might—whether or not he is going to remain permanently afraid of girls* (Case 5).

John, aged 17 (I. Q. 88); previously paroled for repeated delinquencies, and now up for theft. "He has never shown any interest in girls until, just recently, he has been meeting them in parks." *This feeble heterosexual interest (feeble because on the easy and emotionally unenterprising plane of sexual relations with 'bad' girls without the necessity of courtship) is ineffective in straightening out an already established infantile pattern of sexuality.* For John, gang-exploit has led straight into homosexuality. "He never was in anything that was bad until they moved to a certain neighborhood in X. That was where he first knew Mack, and through him knew Wall. * * * All these boys used to hook school and they got him started. * * * Concerning what particular things went on in this crowd we learn that they had 'some awful bad pictures' [*i.e., 'bad pictures' might connote those suggestive of sexual acts, but 'awful bad' ones are apparently those representing homosexual or other perversions*] and that they all were involved in homosexual affairs together. * * * In the industrial school he heard much about it, too; lots of the boys used to do it there. * * * The fellows would go into each other's beds and they would get whipped for it." *Other boys have grown up emotionally despite such influences or practices; but the record suggests a regression to a sadistic level:* he was arrested for "serious tampering with a railway signal", and "twice he set fire to the school". Subsequent history: He was sent to a State Industrial School for older boys, ran away, was arrested for burglary, attempted a sexual assault on a 6-year-old niece, and was then sent to a reformatory; paroled, he made no effort to get work, and was sent back. He "does not in the least mind being a prisoner and makes no effort to shorten his term" [by good behavior]. "He seems to be ambitionless." The report comments: "It is doubtful if he has had in all these years even a dozen hours of individualized attention at the hands of any expert who knows the basis of conduct disorders" (Case 6).

Tom, aged 9 (I. Q. 89), of poor immigrant family; an active, merry, freckled child, somewhat gifted as a singer and dancer, who plays truant and begs, lies and steals his way till he is picked up and sent back home. "Late one afternoon an agency visitor, who was on a large ferry boat in the harbor, heard a childish voice saying, 'Come on fellers, let's have a song and dance.' Turning around, she recognized Tom," who ran and "crawled under a seat. She followed and dragged him out unresisting." He has a "sweet voice and good ear for pitch and rhythm". He started running away to follow bands and parades before he was six. *Such indefatigability may seem to deserve a happy ending in electric lights on Broadway, but we are in the realm of realism, not of romance. Yet oh! that it were possible to make an artist out of Tom—for the likelihood of his being made into an ordinary respectable citizen seems slight enough.* We learn that "there has not been any evidence whatever of bad sex habits". "He hears a lot of bad stuff when he's away, and the bad words that he hears come up in his mind sometimes. 'They come up in my mind, but I don't say them. Then I feel like firing rocks. I get as mad as anything.' " He has, *however*, a habit of soiling with feces the bed and his own clothes. He used it as a means of getting excused from school day after day, so that he could go to the movies. *One may suspect that his sexual impulses have regressed to an early-infantile anal plane, and that this accounts for his complete break with organized society* (Case 7).

Olaf, aged 15 (I. Q. 107), accused of theft. He denied the specific charge, but "frankly acknowledged stealing with the crowd" to which he belonged. "Olaf's companionship since he was 13 has been almost entirely with boys who make up a crowd that consists of about twenty members ranging from 12 to 16 years of age." "Olaf states that he has never gone much with girls; he has never been immoral with them." The boys of his crowd "loaf about the street until late at night. Of course there has been plenty of bad sex talk among them, we hear, but we never had the slightest intimation that they were in bad sex practices together or that they had any association with or interest in girls." "Not only the main, but apparently the sole bond that held these boys together has been the recounting and committing of delinquencies"—including jumping railroad trains, petty street stealing, running away to other towns, stealing from stores, breaking and entering. Subsequent history: Olaf was arrested several times, and then joined the Navy, giving a false age. *We need not be surprised to learn that* he got along well *in that patriarchal institution, one of the few that still provides an honorable shelter and a useful career to males of pre-adult sexuality; nor need we be surprised to learn that,* after a prolonged illness with fever and an honorable discharge, *he was still unable to meet the adult demands of civil life—so that* he was arrested on charges of larceny and of being implicated in a homicide, of which latter he was acquitted. "For a while he tried to keep away from his old companions", *but life on any but an infantile plane was too hard for him,* and "soon he took to drinking", and then "disappeared and when next heard from was in a reformatory in the middle west, where he now is" (Case 8).

Sam, aged 15 (I. Q. 96), illegitimate, father unknown and mother dead, stepfather cruel; held as a vagrant. He had been put out in foster-homes since he was six years old, but had always failed to adjust to them. He stole, lied, and was destructive. He was markedly auto-erotic. "It appears that he never had any special chum or was influenced particularly by any other boy or that he associated at all with girls." The report comments: "One must consider him in terms of sheer inferiority feeling based particularly upon the fact of his illegitimacy, which he has long known." Subsequent history: more vagrancy and probably stealing; enlisted in the Navy, giving a false age, and did well there, but was discharged after six months; shipped on a whaling voyage, then re-enlisted in the Navy, which he likes: "In the Navy you don't have to work very hard." "The call of the ocean has got me. I guess it comes through my father; he was a captain once." The report comments: "Note [as an example of compensation against inferiority feeling] that this boy has invented for himself a father who not only gives the respectability of paternity, but who lends glamour to the career which he has chosen." He "denied venereal disease and immorality"; says he did "correspond" with a girl, "but she got in trouble" [with some other fellow]. The report comments: "Often he gets on by virtue of being bolstered up by régime and a circumscribed life." Also: "it was clear that he needed a social setting that might offer conditions under which he could live satisfactorily." And "one fairly asks if there are not many constitutional inferiors who maintain their places in the ranks and get along very well indeed in army life". *We see that it is no accident that modern civilization so often shunts off into these patriarchal byways such youths as do not respond to the normal incentives of civil life; these institutions, it may be repeated, are almost the only surviving, honorable and useful relics of a patriarchal past which worked best with masses of what we now call 'constitutional inferiors'* (Case 10).

Joseph, aged 13 (Yerkes-Bridges test, 119 [adult intelligence]), father recently dead, mother sickly and over-fond; a habitual truant from school. He hates school. "It gives me a headache and a bellyache, makes me dizzylike." The school, it appears, is such as to justify rebellion; but too much maternal indulgence and sentimentalism (his mother couldn't bear having her boy away from her) *turned Joe's normal and healthy rebellion into* a home-staying pattern. "Outside of the hours when he is at school or supposed to be at school, Joe is practically always at home." He knows "one little club of boys. They are good; they won't stand for anything bad, not even smoking". Subsequent history: Joe was sent to a disciplinary school, but truanted and sold papers. He was then sent to a correctional institution—*everything in fact was done that might have ruined him, except that Joe's impulses were all blundering toward adulthood*—then paroled, and sent to a farm. Here *by a lucky chance* there was a small school with informal discipline; he liked it, did not truant, and got good marks. His silly mother was with difficulty kept from bringing him back to her side. *Separated from her, Joe began to grow up emotionally and take a normal interest in the other sex.* "Joe developed a friendship for a girl in another class and bought her presents. This was a frank, open and nice affair." Coming home and failing to get work, he enlisted in the Army, giving a false age, was sent to Germany, and returned. "He never liked the discipline of the Army"—*because he was too adult to need it; but he was adult enough to adjust to it.* He appears to be able to get along in civil life (Case 11).

Jack, aged 15 (I. Q. 89), regarded by the police as "probably the most hardened young criminal in southern New England". He had left school and gone to work at 14. He "cries if his mother weeps, and always gives in to her immediately if she resorts to tears". He is often afraid to sleep alone. He has run with a gang for several years. He and some others were recently arrested breaking into a store with a kit of burglar's tools; and "investigation brought to light the fact that this crowd, of which Jack was thought to be the leader, had, during the previous year, been involved in a large number of burglaries, audaciously planned and heretofore supposed to have been the work of experienced criminals". Jack says he wanted to prove to the gang that he was "game". As to girls: "the crowd will be out together on the street and will meet girls, 'tough nuts', and pass them and call out, 'Say kid.' Then they will begin to talk and all go round together. Says he has done bad things with girls two or three times. He tells us particularly about two 'tough ones,' they call them the oil twins because their name is something like that. But he doesn't care about girls and that sort of thing is no temptation to him, he just does it with the gang. With these fellows he has been to burlesque shows; 'that's about the worst.' By paying the usher half a dollar they have been permitted to go back to the dressing rooms. He says there have been no bad sex affairs between the boys themselves." *It requires very little enterprise to go with girls who are known to be 'tough', and boys who are really afraid of girls and quite incapable of normal courtship can demonstrate their 'manliness' in this way to the gang.* Subsequent history: Jack was sent to a farm, but became homesick and ran away to his home and mother, crying, and saying, "I am never lonely where you are, Ma." He went to work, but quit his job on account of [unexplained] ridicule by other employees. He wanted to go West, and was sent to a farm ranch. He was overworked, and a better place was found for him, where he got along well with employer and companions. Later he joined the Army, and wrote: "I don't mind it much for I am learning a good trade." Back in civil life he became a good worker, *but still* "showed no interest in girls or women." *However,* his mother now being dead, he wrote to the agency visitor, "I'll have to adopt you to be my Mother, the sweetest name in the world, that is if you do not mind. * * * Love and kisses. A million kisses for you." He was now 20 years old. *His emotional interests had never been detached from his mother; but by way of this mother substitute, he seems to be slowly growing up toward an adult interest in girls of his own age-class* (Case 13).

Harry, aged 10 (I. Q. 92), deserted by mother and boarded out since a baby; complained of because dishonest and destructive, "setting fires in dangerous ways", and a truant. He had been taunted as a child for being an "outcast". He was excessively auto-erotic. "Even in the first grade the boys would swear, and they did bad things together. Always in school he heard about these things." As to fires—he had a friend named Billy M.: "Once he [Billy] was out in a field and he had a little girl with him 'and he made a fire and he was undressing her there.' Harry says he saw him. 'Billy was trying to burn her and a cop came along and he ran away like the dickens and he pushed her into the fire and her clothes were on fire.' * * * Two little girls who played at Miss Weir's have undressed and wanted him to play doctor with them and to get into bed with them, he says. But he told them it was naughty * * * it is what Billy M. did that put it in his mind to make fires." Subsequent history: Harry was placed in a home in the country, where at first he gave only slight trouble. His foster parents "felt that he was an unusually clean-minded boy". But later, at 12 years old, he became a nuisance through his uncontrollable restlessness, attention-getting stunts, and gossiping. He was suspected of being mentally deficient and psychopathic. He was sent to a school for the feeble-minded (his I. Q. was now only 75). From there he at last succeeded in running away, and went back to his foster-home in the country. His foster-mother had moved away, but her nephew took the boy in. [There were other children, *but the report unaccountably omits mention of a mother or housekeeper.* At any rate, Harry was "fond of the family".] Harry proved helpful, cheerful and obedient (his I. Q. went up to 85). It was agreed by psychiatrists that "the boy now presented nothing whatever that suggested psychopathic tendencies". *He appears to be growing up out of a dangerous childhood regression to an infantile and sadistic level of sexuality. It would be interesting to know more about the different foster-maternal and foster-paternal influences under which he was at first unmanageable and later docile* (Case 14).

William, aged 15 (I. Q. 128), father dead seven years ago, mother a "nervous wreck"; in trouble for habitual stealing, lying and truancy. His mother "tried to be his comrade". "He has never been to dances, and has shown no interest in girls." His first theft was "immediately after" a boy friend "told him about sex affairs". Another friend, with whom he was involved in the theft of an automobile, "is immoral with girls", but William himself "has never gone with girls or had anything to do with them". Expelled from high school and then from preparatory school, he was committed to a correctional school. There he "set about trying to be of service to the younger boys. He was much concerned about the problem of immorality among them. He seemed very religious and much concerned about his mother now"—he had cruelly played upon her love for him to get money out of her before. Subsequent history: He was returned to the correctional school, then paroled to a denominational preparatory school, then placed in an all-year tutoring camp where he gradually got over his tendencies to dishonesty, and was finally allowed to go home. His mother had had to go to work, and was in better health, and "she no longer nagged". At 19 he was the ranking student in a preparatory school, and giving "no trouble whatever". *The origin of his sexual regression in his filial situation seems fairly obvious* (Case 16).

Richard, aged 17 (I. Q. 97), of prosperous New England family; a habitual delinquent, now up for robbery. "He would rather steal than eat." "He maintains that he has never had any sex experiences either with boys or girls. Of course he has heard some talk, most of it in the correctional school, but he has never gone in for that sort of thing. He has no curiosity about it, and never has thought much about it at any time." Subsequent history: sent to a reformatory, paroled, arrested in Canada for the theft of an automobile and sent to a penal institution. The report comments: "Before long this young man will be released at about 22 years of age, having been under daily observation, in institutions supported by public funds, for over six years, and he will probably come out, as nearly all others come, repressed, hardened, and in many ways made worse by the miserable things that go on in prison life and, what is most curious of all from our standpoint, in any fundamental way still unstudied and unknown" (Case 19).

Edward, aged 15 (I. Q. 96), a habitual delinquent, "engaged in considerable stealing for the last three years". His father was forced to marry his mother after she was pregnant, and he subsequently deserted her. The mother is irresponsible and dishonest. The boy has heard her thefts talked about, and once saw her stealing something in a store and being caught at it. Since the age of 11 he has lived with an uncle. Formerly he welcomed his mother's visits, but recently he has been morose and irritable after seeing her and apparently indifferent as to whether he saw her or not. Yet he remains "loyal" to her; "he preferred to wear a cheap suit of clothes that his mother had bought for him during this last year than wear the much better clothing with which his relatives had provided him." But "he never speaks of her". Direct questions brought out his painful knowledge of his mother's character, and he then talked more freely. He said that "when he has the opportunity to steal he thinks of her and he feels reckless, as if it didn't matter if he stole". *Shame about his mother has repressed his sexual emotions, and* he is not interested in the sex talk he has heard. Subsequent history: Placed in a succession of foster homes, at first he stole, but later was trusted "absolutely". *He has found a solution of his mental conflict about his mother;* she has behaved badly to him, trying to exploit him, threatening him and seeking to get his wages without doing anything for him, *and he has emotionally repudiated her—and has taken his latest foster-mother as a substitute-mother.* He keeps this woman's picture in his room, calls her his 'Ambition', and buys her little presents. He is saving his money in order to buy a farm for himself. He is now "a different-looking boy". *He has cut the Gordian knot, and is growing up* (Case 20).

Here, then, to sum up, are 18 unselected cases of boy delinquents; 13 of them have had no sexual relations with girls, 3 of them have had such relations with 'tough' girls as a part of their gang prowess, 1 has had sexual relations under undefined circumstances, and 1 is not reported upon; 9 were 'not interested in girls or sex'; only 1 had a girl friend; 13 had a deeply emotional relationship to a gang and to particular gang-fellows; 1 had learned homosexual practices, 1 was apparently anal-erotic, 2 were sadistic; 4 joined the Army or Navy, and 3 got along there better than in civil life; 7 had obvious defects in their parental influences, 2 began to improve when they escaped from bad maternal influences, 2 found substitute mothers, 1 a substitute father, and 1 invented an imaginary hero-father. In no single instance was heterosexual passion the cause of juvenile delinquency, and in the few instances of physical heterosexual relations the quasi-homosexual gang emotions were paramount—it was something to boast about to the gang. The one instance in which a 'girl friend' is a figure in the report is that of a boy whose sole delinquency was truancy from a poor school; and the appearance of the girl friend in his life is a prognosis of his successful growing up. All of these cases represent halts in development toward sexual adulthood—halts and turnings aside for the most part into the quasi-homosexual byway of gangdom.

The boy-gang is a patriarchal institution. It dates back to ancient Sparta and earlier. Here is Plutarch's account of the gang in its Spartan heyday. Boys were not brought up in families, "but as soon as they were 7 years old, Lycurgus ordered them all to be taken by the State and enrolled in companies, where they lived and ate in common, and were associated in play and work. The boy who was wisest and fiercest in fight was made captain of his company; they looked to him for orders, obeyed his commands and submitted to his punishments, so that even in childhood they learned how to obey. * * *

"Of reading and writing, they learned only enough to serve their turn; all the rest of their training was intended to teach them to obey cheerfully, to endure hardships, and to win battles. As they grew older, their training became more severe; their heads were close-clipped, and they were accustomed to going barefoot, and to playing for the most part without clothes. They wore no tunic after their twelfth year, and were given but one cloak a year. They were dirty, being without baths or ointments, except on certain days, as a luxury. They slept all together in troops and companies, on beds of rushes which they themselves had picked on the banks of the Eurotas with their hands, for they were not allowed to use a knife. In winter they mixed the herb called lycophan with the rushes, as it is thought to possess some warmth.

"When the boys reached this age [12], they were favoured with the companionship of lovers from among the young men of repute. * * * The lovers of the boys also shared in their honour or disgrace; it is said that once when a boy in a fight uttered a disgraceful cry, his lover was fined by the magistrates. * * *

"[The boys' leader,] the Eiren, a youth of twenty, commands his company in their battles, and in the house uses them as servants to prepare his meals. He orders the bigger boys to carry logs of wood, and the smaller ones to gather potherbs. They also bring him what they steal, some from the gardens, and some creeping slyly and cautiously from the men's dining-tables; but if a boy is caught he is flogged for being a clumsy thief. * * * There is a story of a boy who had stolen a fox's cub and hidden it under his cloak, and rather than have the theft detected let it tear out his bowels with its claws and teeth, until he died. This may be believed from what the Spartan youths do at this very day, for I myself", says Plutarch, "have seen many of them die under the lash at the altar of Diana Orthias."

The boy-gang, then, in early patriarchal times, was a pillar of the State. Now its heroic code of honor has fallen to be only the thieves' code of 'never squealing'. The story of the stolen fox-cub would be told admiringly to-day only by some romantic glorifier of Apache-life. "Only ten years old he was," said Bli-bli, staring into his absinthe [we are quoting from an imaginary British translation of an imaginary French yarn] "but he died like a true nark. He thinks the bottle of nitric acid might sell for ten centimes, so he ups and pockets it. And it had just broke in his pocket when the gendarme comes by. There was the stuff burning him to the bone, and he not giving a sign, but answering the gendarme as innocent as you please, and he dying there on his feet—a game lad, what?" No, it rings hollow. The trouble is that we do not nowadays think it smart for little boys to steal, however heroically. Nor do we think it admirable for them to have homosexual love-affairs. Yet such is the nature of that patriarchal institution, the sex-segregated boy-gang, that stealing and homosexual love are part and parcel of it, in its decadence as in its prime. Some of these gangs have Platonized their homosexuality into passionate friendships. Mack or George is the admired boy-friend who must be imitated in everything he does, followed breathlessly into burglary, or even into joyless and rather shameful exploits with 'tough' girls. We do not want this patriarchal-régime juvenile behavior, but we still encourage the patriarchal-régime boy-gang by a kind of patriarchal education which teaches boys that girls are to be avoided. By our fear of heterosexual interests in boys we maintain a quasi-homosexual mode of juvenile life that leads as of old to the gang-exploit of theft.

We must make our choice—adult heterosexual standards, or infantile anal-erotic, sadistic and homosexual standards of life. Our armies and navies cannot take and discipline all our sexually infantile male population.

§ 2. Juvenile Delinquency (Girls)

The patriarchal régime did not organize girls into gangs, and gang-life is not a feature of delinquency among girls to-day. Sex-segregation, however, was an important aspect of patriarchal-régime girlhood; and sex-segregation still to-day produces among girls its ancient results of sexual infantilism, some of which result in delinquencies. It would not be difficult to show, from various studies that have been made, the relation of theft, truancy and pyromania to sexual regressions. This, however, would only parallel the case-studies of boys which we have just reviewed; while the circumstances are different, the effects are the same. It will be more to our point to take up those delinquencies among girls which involve sexual offenses, and show that these are the results not of sexual precocity but of failure to be adequately heterosexual.

This generalization does not, of course, apply to cases in which a girl has too rashly entered into what in a previous passage (Chapter X, §1) has been referred to as the old pagan and not yet obsolete custom of 'sexual betrothal'—that is to say, sexual relations as a part of the privileges of a pledge to marry—and in which her partner has avoided his responsibility and deserted her when she became pregnant. Her behavior, in a country of conflicting sexual mores, may have been indiscreet, or it may in certain circumstances mean a mere ignorant gullibility on her part; yet it has been, emotionally, an adult performance. She has found, or so she has believed, a mate, and has accepted what she regards as guarantees of protection for herself and her child. The most advanced legislation undertakes, indeed, to enforce these guarantees. Her behavior is thus an 'offense' only insofar as her ignorance or gullibility may have burdened society with her care and that of her child.

Western civilization, however, has tended to delay marriage for girls far beyond the patriarchal nuptial age of puberty; and this is particularly true in urban regions. The age of practical marriageability therefore sets a downward limit to 'sexual betrothals', and sexual relations entered in to by girls below this age, being practically cut off from any reasonable expectations of marriage, are regarded as social offenses. This age-threshold varies with the marriageable age, but there is a tendency to raise it to include the educational period or roughly the 'teens, and to consider sexual relations by an unmarried girl during this period as juvenile delinquency. This view does not always jibe with the facts, especially when a girl in her 'teens has 'finished' her education and become a wage-earner. If she is old enough to support herself and old enough to be legally married, is she not also old enough to go about the business of getting mated in the way which may appear to her the most likely to succeed? There is a frequent difference of opinion here between the social workers and the girl. The social workers' view of the situation is influenced by the many instances in which such realistic wooings have not been successful. It is naturally the failures which come within their province. In using published accounts of female juvenile delinquency we are obliged to accept the social workers' view of these situations; the proof of the pudding has been in the eating, and the fact that the social workers have been called in is proof that in these instances the girl is a 'juvenile delinquent.' We must turn to the more catholic observations of Judge Lindsey and Miriam van Waters for illustrations of youthful wooings which include sexual relations and yet turn out well. Judge van Waters gives an account of a wooing that was not recognized by either of the young people as such until that view of their behavior was sanctioned by the Juvenile Court. "Maggie was a rollicking, buxom girl of 17", who became pregnant while on probation. She "concocted a story of nameless attack", but [N.B. to the Reader: stop, draw a long breath, and prepare yourself for an abrupt introduction to really modern methods of social work!]—"the Court commented on her strength, her bravery, her resourcefulness, and gave her two weeks in which to find the man and bring him herself, unaided, to court. Surprised, but not daunted, the girl succeeded. The man proved to be a soldier with a temperament much like her own; on careful examination, physical, mental, and social, he was proved to be a fit husband and was permitted to marry Maggie." The reader may also be able to provide illustrations of unconventional but successful wooings from observation or experience.

Social workers, indeed, are increasingly obliged to recognize that instinctive efforts to achieve mating, though along socially forbidden paths, are nevertheless frequently crowned with success. Van Waters speaks of girls who 'make good' by plans that run counter to the wishes, routine and expectation of the social workers—that is, "those who 'make good' in spite of us." This type, she remarks, "is of profound sociological significance". "How many of us know girls * * * who have taken the bit in their teeth and run away from us, later to emerge decently clothed, resourceful, industrious, successful and adjusted to life beyond our fondest hopes. Recently I visited some thirty state institutions for the training of delinquent girls. Most of the superintendents reported stories of rebellion, escape, followed by the inexplicable 'making good'. Many commented on fortunate marriages contracted because the girl strayed in forbidden places, dance halls, piers, rinks, cafés and other loafing places of Prince Charming. We are more familiar with this type of fortuitous success in boys than in girls, boys who flee from us to navy, army or wild west. Many a candid probation officer will tell you that she has met with it in girls."

Bearing these exceptions in mind, we may then exclude from our consideration of 'offenses' such youthful sexual betrothals as we are aware of only because they happen not to have been ratified by success. It would be absurd to regard solemnly as an offense against society the same behavior which next door or down the block has been though unknown to us the prelude to a socially approved mating.

We are left, then, with sexual offenses which may reasonably be called such, as involving emotional irresponsibility. It may seem that the question has been begged by this delimiting of its scope; but that is not to be helped, for there is nothing to be gained by pretending that emotionally sincere and adult sexual behavior is a real offense against society, however unfortunate may be the consequences to the individual. The scope of our inquiry, however, has not been delimited as much as it might seem to be. It includes, as a matter of fact, practically all of the sexual delinquencies of girls which come up for public consideration.

It includes, to begin with, a great deal of prostitution. There is no doubt that poverty is the prime cause of prostitution, and that its ranks are always kept filled by the pressure of need. But there is a kind of sexual infantilism which takes readily to prostitution without much or any pressure. It is not an excessive interest in men or in sexual pleasures which leads such girls to the practise of this profession, but rather a lack of capacity for adult sexual interest in men and an emotional indifference to the sexual act, frequently marked on the physical plane by a complete frigidity. "The beginning of delinquency in girls", writes Professor W. I. Thomas, "is usually an impulse to get amusement, adventure, pretty clothes, favorable notice, distinction, freedom in the larger world which presents so many allurements and comparisons. The cases which I have examined (about three thousand) show that sexual passion does not play an important rôle, for the girls have usually become 'wild' before the development of sexual desire, and their casual sexual relations do not usually awaken sex feeling. Their sex is used as a condition to the realization of their other wishes. It is their capital. * * * Mary begins by stealing to satisfy her desire for pretty clothes and 'good times', then has sexual relations for the same purpose. Katie begins as a vagabond and sells her body just as she does occasional work or borrows money, in order to support herself on her vagabonding tours, sexual intercourse being only a means by which freedom from school work is secured. In the case of Stella the sexual element is part of a joy ride, probably not the first one. Marien treats sexual life as a condition of her 'high life', including restaurants, moving pictures, hotels, and showy clothes. Helen said, 'I always wanted good clothes.' To the young girl of this class sexual intercourse is something submitted to with some reluctance and embarrassment and something she is glad to be over with."

This group of psychosexually undeveloped girl delinquents includes also many who are not prostitutes though they may become such by force of circumstances, and whose motives are quite different from those described above. Tillie, for example, a 14-year-old (I. Q. 116) studied by the Judge Baker Foundation (Case 9, Series 1) was described as "obsessed with sex ideas". She had stolen money from her family to buy pretty clothes; but her sexual affairs began in genuine affection. She "met some sailors in the park and on the streets after school and walked around with them. But she never made any real engagements with them until she met Jim. She liked him very much and used to meet him almost every Thursday and Saturday. After she had known him a few weeks she spent the night with him, and after this did so several times. Besides, she was often with him late at night. He paid her for living with him. At first she refused to take the money, but later didn't care, because she could buy pretty things." She left home, because of constant family quarreling, and went to live with Jim. "She got tired of it after three days and would have come home, but she was afraid." She wrote home that she was pregnant and that she was going to kill herself. "I went to the Charles River to commit suicide a lot of times but didn't have the courage." She was found by her mother on the street near her home. It was discovered that she wasn't pregnant. Sent to the State industrial school, Tillie "has never been known to show the slightest interest in sex-affairs". An imaginary diary (of a fantasied alter-ego called "Bet") which she wrote in the earlier period showed, says the report, "that in her imagination she was living through, not so much sex experiences specifically, as a more general sex desire to be popular among boys or young men and to be the recipient of their attentions. It is not necessary to regard these thoughts as other than wish-fulfillment fancies centering about her newly awakened sex consciousness, with all its pressure to be a personage and to experience the power that an attractive young woman can exert." The report also comments: "The reaction to Jim is noteworthy—the quick satiation was perhaps due to Tillie's youth, for it is likely that the physical sex urge was not nearly so great as the hold of ideation that centered about sex life."

The truth is that Tillie went to live with her sailor at puberty in much the same frame of mind that girls in the patriarchal regime became brides at the same age. In the *Greek Anthology* there is a bride's farewell to her childhood:

"Timarete, before her marriage, dedicated to Artemis her tambourine and beautiful doll, the coronal that upheld her hair, and, O Lady of Limnae [Artemis], a maid to a maid, as is fitting, she gave to thee these little maids, her dolls, and the dolls' dresses. O daughter of Leto [Artemis], extend thy hand over Timareteia, and sacredly keep safe the sacred child."

The prettiness of the phrasing and the piety of the sentiments do not disguise the fact that it was a child who was thus being given in marriage according to patriarchal custom. In Rome, where by tradition and late law puberty was the minimum marriage age for girls, it was the custom for them, at the celebration made in honor of their arrival at puberty, to offer their dolls to Venus—a ceremonial renunciation of childish play and a symbolic expression of their pious expectation of the gift of a real baby from the goddess of sex.

Thus, if we ask what were the motives which led Greek and Roman girls to go willingly, as they did, from childhood to the nuptial couch, we may generally exclude adult sexual passion. Duty, of course, was a motive, but duty has to be translated into self-regarding terms before it can be an efficient cause of action. The chief motive was, as appears from classical literature, the dulness of life under the parental roof and the desire for the dignity and authority and comparative freedom of wifehood. These ancient motives still hold sway in a modern time when nuptials at puberty are necessarily illicit; girls will pick up sailors in the park, not out of adult sexual passion but as a reaction from dull or quarrelsome homes and in order to enjoy the (probably illusory) dignity and authority and freedom of sexual companionship. It is a way of being grown up all at once, which appeals strongly when the growing-up process is made to seem meaningless to a girl-child.

Another motive, once having the backing of Church and State, was anxiety lest the time of greatest sexual attractiveness to men be passed over and the chance of mating lost forever. The poet Herrick echoes the encouragements and warnings of the classical world to these pubescent girls:

"Gather ye Rose-buds while ye may,
Old Time is still a flying:
And this same flower that smiles to day,
To morrow will be dying.

"That Age is best which is the first,
When Youth and Blood are warmer;
But being spent, the worse, and worst,
Times, still succeed the former.

"Then be not coy, but use your time;
And while ye may, goe marry:
For having once but lost your prime,
Ye may for ever tarry."

These sexual anxieties do not fail to occur to girls who are just awakened to consciousness of their sexual attractiveness and are provided with no program for using it over the educational period of adolescence. The sailor in the park is real; the opportunities of marriage years hence too dim and shadowy. They are dim and shadowy because the fear of sex has prevented, as in Tillie's case, any rational dealing by her family with the subject of her sexuality. This patriarchal mode of bringing girls up in ignorance of sex was once a useful mode of making them jump at the first chance of marriage offered by the family. It is now, all unwittingly, a mode of making them jump at the first chance of illicit sexual companionship with an attractive male. But it is childish curiosity, pride and sexual anxiety—not sexual passion.

Tillie's family, when she began to show an interest in boys, had used the methods of "scolding and hollering" at her; "and all that does", said Tillie, "is to make a girl worse". Tillie has modernized her family's methods of dealing with girls, for the benefit of her younger sister, Eva, who has now been told about sexual matters. They are able to help a girl next door, too. "A few months ago when her visitor called at the home she found the mother busily engaged in baking and the girls in getting the rooms in spotless condition; they were preparing a party. 'It's my birthday,' Tillie explained. 'But really the party is for Janet. She's a girl next door who's getting into bad company. She has a stepmother and things aren't very pleasant for her at home. I remember how easy it is to go wrong. I'm planning it so that she can meet some nice boys and girls.' "

An extreme but by no means unique example of childish ignorance is that of Emily, another girl studied by the Judge Baker Foundation (Case 15). At 11 years old she ran with a crowd of boys and girls who had sexual relations with each other. "She did just what all the other girls in the crowd did * * *. Most of the boys did these things to her. * * * No grown person had ever talked to her about these things and she didn't understand just what it was. The girls talked a great deal about it, but they never said anything about babies, and that sort of thing. In fact, at that time she did not know that babies came that way. This crowd of boys and girls met at the home of one of the girls whose mother was away working."

The patriarchal mode of bringing up girls in ignorance so far as possible of sexual matters, of segregating them from boys as long as possible, and of repressing their sexual interests as completely as possible, was admirably adapted for its purpose—that is to say the purpose of turning them over as docile child-brides to the husband of the family's choice. It is now, under modern conditions, merely adapted to the purpose of turning them over to casual sexual exploitation by the first exigent males they may happen to meet. This system of girl-training assists the recruiting of prostitution and furnishes a steady supply of sexual gratification to men who do not mind exploiting ignorant girl-children. Patriarchal education meets these demands, just as in ancient times it met the demands for docile child-brides. The gangster's maxim, 'Take 'em young, tell 'em nothin', treat 'em rough' is an accurate rendition of the patriarchal theory of the proper education of girls; and by the parental method of telling 'em nothin' they are well-prepared for being taken young and treated rough in that sexual underworld in which the patriarchal code still flourishes in all its raw cruelty.

Our list also includes girls whose sexual interest in men is genuine but indiscriminate—'promiscuous' is the social workers' term. It is doubtful if real sexual promiscuity exists short of prostitution. But among the conditions which are so described is one which represents the converse of the Don Juan type among men. Don Juan has been thoroughly studied of late; and it has taken only a little study to discover the obvious fact that he is not a lover of women but a hater of women. So with Donna Juanna—she sleeps with men because, oddly enough, she despises them, and thereby demonstrates her superiority to them. We have not time at this point to go into the genesis of this emotional trait, save to note that it takes its origin in unsolved parental fixations and represents a regression and a turning aside into an emotional blind-alley along the path of sexual development. Another sort of apparent promiscuity is an overcompensation against a secret or unconscious fear of homosexuality (which sometimes finds conscious expression in the fear of not being attractive to men)—the girl demonstrates her femininity to herself again and again: but the reassurance does not allay her fear, and it must needs be demonstrated endlessly. Her fear is correct, and her behavior only proves to the expert eye that she does not yet know what heterosexuality is. In both of these instances of sexual promiscuity (hate-sexuality and reassurance-sexuality), the motives are essentially self-regarding; and where so much of the sexual interest is thus centered in the self, not enough is left over to invest any particular man with more than a transitory interest for her. This, of course, is a defect and not an excess of heterosexual passion.

Finally, not to prolong endlessly the catalogue of sexual infantalisms, there is the girl whose sexuality has been so successfully repressed by patriarchal education that it can only find expression under the influence of alcoholic stimulus, which is thus (consciously or unconsciously) indulged in for that purpose. The Chicago Vice Commission's report gives a description of the uses by young people of the sexual opportunities afforded by the lake steamers. "In the barroom there were about 20 young girls and boys sitting at tables drinking beer. In stateroom No. 28, two boys and two girls were lying in the berths, all were under the influence of liquor. In room No. 56 were found two young men and two girls; one of the girls appeared to be very drunk. Three boys visited room No. 51 during the trip."

What is sometimes called 'Puritanism' regularly seeks this infantile release from its patriarchal inhibitions. A passage in a recent novel describes a similar scene and permits its philosophic young hero to comment upon it. "He looked about him at the others, among whom they mingled at the play-places, the dancers, drinkers, spooners, gigglers. * * * He noted, as from a distance, the effort to drum up excitement, by music, drinking, dancing, loud talk and loud laughter, sheer mechanical noise; it was an artificial excitement, not the exuberance of a mood; it was a means to an end, a means of escape. * * * He suspected these youths and girls of being all oppressed with something—with fear, perhaps. They were not playing, they were working, working hard to throw off that burden for a moment, to leave it behind, to forget it. But it was so much a part of their very selves that only by some outside help, by the aid of drums, gongs, violins, whisky and beer, the rush of speed, an atmosphere of other people's excitement and other people's noise, could they hope to attain the blessed relief of forgetfulness. They were seeking a supreme moment of intoxication in which they could be their natural selves." Needless to say, this alcohol-stimulated release from inhibitions is an infantile and not an adult sexuality.

It may have seemed paradoxical when it was announced at the opening of this section that girls become sexual delinquents through a lack of heterosexual emotions, through a deficiency of passionate love for the other sex. This, however, is the end at which we have arrived. If the concept seems too novel to be at once accepted, it is because of unfamiliarity with the conclusions of modern psychology, among which none is more thoroughly established than this; and this outline may at least send the doubting reader to school to the psychologists to have the patriarchal cobwebs brushed out of his brain.

§ 3. The Effects of Patriarchal Sex-Education

The three aspects of patriarchal child-training, the results of which we have been observing, are inculcated sex-ignorance, emotionally enforced sex-repression, and physically enforced sex-segregation. These need, perhaps, more specific definition.

(1) *The inculcated sex-ignorance* of which we speak is a positive state of misinformation, not a mere absence of knowledge. The child has its own infantile theories as to how babies come, usually arrived at on the analogy of defecation. The sexual organs are, on the basis of childish experience and fantasy, regarded as having merely urinary and selfward pleasure-giving uses. These theories, which separate (as in savage theory) the uses of the sexual organs from the ideas of pregnancy, childbirth and parenthood, are in the absence of correct parental instruction retained by the child until he comes under the educational influences of a pre-adolescent gang or of a somewhat older friend or sometimes of adult servants. The information then given about sexual intercourse is assimilated to earlier disgust-repressions in connection with the urinary and anal functions, and is often received with a shock and frequently with incredulity. The idea that his parents could be addicted to such 'disgusting' practices is frequently to the child a horrifying one. Under the quasi-homosexual influences of the gang or special friend, however, the idea of auto-erotic pleasure is extended to include sexual intercourse. The idea of parenthood, if not unknown or forgotten, is emotionally irrelevant to these ideas of sex. In the childish sexual experimentation which may ensue before puberty, sex and parenthood are of course unconnected in fact; and in any case, they are dissociated in the childish ideal of sexuality. After puberty the prospect of parenthood in connec-

tion with sexual intercourse is regarded as in the nature of ill-luck; as an unpleasant idea, it is frequently repressed from consciousness. Parental warnings at this date are habitually ignored and forgotten. Kammerer's Case 21, though warned by her mother at 13, had at 15 "no fear of any consequences resulting from this [her first sexual] intimacy. She appreciated that she was doing wrong in allowing the relationship, but never worried about it". She was already pregnant, but "never associated her run-down physical condition with a possible pregnancy". Kammerer's Case 27 was ready to enter high school when she became pregnant, and the cessation of her menstrual periods had caused her "no alarm whatever". The attitude of 'never thinking at the time about consequences' is quite common, and young girls brought to the doctor by their mothers are not infrequently just as surprised as their mothers are to learn that their 'illness' is simply pregnancy.

This ignorance is not limited to any class. Isabel Davenport had submitted to her by girls who were high-school graduates and prospective teachers some 880 anonymous questions about sex, to which answers were desired; the information thus shown to be lacking covers the whole field of sexual physiology and psychology, and the questions reveal "the trends of interest, the ignorance and superstitions, the gropings for light" of ordinary girlhood. From a study of these amazing and heart-breaking questions Professor Davenport learned of "the fairly incredible lack of penetration of the viewpoint of modern science into the thoughts of girls relative to their own bodily functions as women". "Girls of the present day", she concludes, "are evidently being taught just those superstitions, and trained into just the same unwholesome attitudes, that we of the older generation were subject to in our girlhood—while in every other phase of individual and social hygiene, in the intervening years, our American world has undergone an evolution so great as to recreate our outlook on life."

This inculcated ignorance of even primary sexual physiology is inherited from a patriarchal régime in which marriage at puberty was expected to bring the wisdom of experience: 'Open your mouth and shut your eyes, and I'll give you something to make you wise.' The feminine ignorance of such dangers as those of venereal disease was convenient in a patriarchal world in which, when a wife was infected by her husband, it was good social policy to let her think her resulting ills the normal condition of being a female. But such inculcated feminine ignorance is indefensible in a world in which women are conceded to have rights to happiness.

So much for the inculcated sex-ignorance of girls. That of boys is only less extensive and less tragic.

It is an ignorance which consists to a great extent of defensive superstitions. Some of the questions handed in to Professor Isabel Davenport reveal their character: as for instance, that sexual relations are necessary for a boy after 14 to prevent consumption, and that the use of a certain device to prevent pregnancy produces consumption in the man. Another very common one is to the effect that sexual intercourse with a virgin is a cure for venereal disease. 'Gutter-education in sex' has recently been publicly recommended by some mischievous medical obscurantists, but it is of such maxims that gutter-education in sex is largely composed.

In this connection it is interesting to note some of the answers, given by several of a group of eminent psychopathologists and gynecologists, to the question in the Watson-Lashley Questionnaire on sex-education: "Is the average medical practitioner competent to give sex-instruction to children?" Dr. L. H. Bernd: "No. As there are few Hugh Youngs or Jeannette Shermans in the profession, the average medico is nearly as unintelligent as the parent, judging from the mass of misinformation some patients receive." Dr. T. H. Ames: "No. The average medical practitioner never heard the word sex mentioned in medical school and has never discussed any sex problems with any one. He is himself shocked at mention of the subject. He is not tolerant of a sex emotion as such, but he tolerates the idea of venereal disease." Dr. S. E. Jelliffe: "My experience is that he is a great prude and knows little of the psychology of sex. He has a narrow orthodoxy which is mostly false." Patriarchal sex-education of boys by ignorance, misinformation and superstition has, unfortunately, had until the present day the assistance to a great extent of the family doctor, who had himself received all of his own education on this subject in the gutter, since it was not available in medical school.

(2) *Emotionally enforced sex-repression* is a similar relic of patriarchal education. It was of value in the past in preventing

the growth of the sexual emotions to a point where they required love-choice, wooing and real matehood. The infantile state of female sexuality was more convenient for arranged marriages. The Laws of Manu sum up the patriarchal attitude in disapproving "the voluntary union of a maiden and her lover" in marriage, and in declaring that marriages in which the father gives away his daughter are "blessed". The bride might see her husband for the first time on her wedding day. It was necessary that her sexuality should be infantile and indiscriminate, ready to attach itself to the first man given her as her bedfellow. It was, to be sure, equally ready to attach itself to the next man, and the next—but that situation was met by the device of seclusion from other men. It was correctly assumed that a woman thus kept in a state of sexual infantilism would be unfaithful to her husband at every opportunity; and so she often was, in spite of guards and bolts and the danger of death if caught *in flagrante delictu.*

This emotional sexual infantilism has in women frequently a physical corollary in an inability to reach the normal climax in the sexual act. This partial frigidity is often characteristic of women who go in for multitudes of sexual affairs—they are driven to go on seeking vainly for the satisfaction of which they are deprived. Dr. Hamilton, in his study of 200 wives and husbands, found that lack of capacity for achieving this satisfaction in sexual relations was reported by 15 of the 24 women in this group who had committed adultery, though it was reported also of 31 of the 76 women who had not committed adultery. In any event, the condition does not make for happiness in marriage. On the other hand, it notoriously makes easier the career of prostitution, and more emotionally endurable the experience of being passed on from one man to another in what Miriam van Waters calls the "unbelievably tragic and unbelievably common" experiences of those girls who are run through the mill of sexual exploitation by men.

The power of the instincts is such, however, that more or less adult attitudes are achieved by girls through the process of adolescence, if a fixation at an infantile level does not occur in childhood. Sex-ignorance and sex-repression must be regarded as the barriers against which the instinctive growth processes contend.

In boys this emotionally enforced sex-repression tends to make them shun normal social contacts with girls, and tends to confine their emotional life within a boy-gang—where, except under highly organized, adult-managed, disciplined and elaborately idealized conditions, the homosexual atmosphere is conducive to anti-social feats of derring-do, and may be conducive to overt homosexuality. The heterosexual emotions tend to be held down to a primitive level of disgust, curiosity and brutal exploit; they can be educated out of this infantile sexuality only by normal social contacts with girls, contacts in which the sentiments of comradeship, respect and understanding can arise. Without such sentiments, the terms of association with respectable girls are found too difficult, and the girls themselves are likely to be regarded as both dull and alarming: dull because they are not boys, and alarming because their instinctive feminine demand for something in the nature of wooing is felt as a reproach by boys in whom the instinctive male aptitude for gallantry has been repressed. The boys are thus uncomfortable in their society, aware that something is expected of them, and not knowing how to behave. On the other hand, the boys' primitive sexual curiosity, disgust-superiority and sadistic exploit tendencies find no reproach in the sexually infantile society of prostitutes, 'tough' girls, young female morons, and neurotic boy-girls. They know how to treat these, and feel 'at home' in their society, while remaining awkward, contemptuous and timid in the presence of girls whose instinctive growth-processes have carried them to more adult levels of sexuality. In boys there is also, of course, an instinctive growth to adult levels of sexuality, but it is hampered and sometimes permanently checked by barriers of sex-ignorance and sex-repression. In any event, these constitute emotional impediments to love and trust which it takes years to surmount—years of adult life which might be devoted to adult tasks but which must be devoted to a prolonged attempt to solve adolescent problems.

(3) *Physically enforced segregation.* It is true that, except in some immigrant groups which still try to live patriarchal lives, we do not keep boys and girls apart in American life by locks and bars, guards and duennas. What we have is rather the disintegrating fragments of those old patriarchal methods—stern paternal injunctions to daughters against 'going with boys', and sour maternal refusals of hospitality to a girl's boy-friends. The stupidity of these procedures is notorious—the girls meet the boys outside, and tell their parents whatever lies are necessary. Less

tyrannical but almost equally stupid is the other half of this patriarchal method, the parental command to daughters to bring their boy-friends home for family inspection and approval. So much does this savor of the patriarchal preliminaries to marriage that the alarmed young man, having been given the once-over by the family, promptly flees; and the girl, having learned her lesson, runs no risk of losing her next boy-friend in this fashion. These patriarchal efforts, though futile as regards their purposes, of keeping the emotional life of young people under family control, nevertheless constitute an effective means of discouraging boys and girls from normal social relations in early adolescence. Professor Isabel Davenport justly complains that "conventional companionship between the sexes—which is the only means by which sympathetic understanding and wholesome love interests can be engendered—is not only not taken into account in our family and social policies below the leisured classes, but is effectively discouraged by our educational, economic and sport systems".

Even in the leisured classes, exempted in the above quotation from the charge of sex-segregation, the unwholesome fashionable practice of sex-segregated schools brings young people into a homosexual atmosphere, which delays when it does not drastically set back their psychic growth. These homosexual 'crushes' are conventionally ignored, particularly in girls' schools, because of the patriarchal tradition which has always preferred homosexuality to heterosexuality, as being more infantile and hence less dangerous to the patriarchal régime; but in modern society this attitude is a stupid anachronism. "From the psychologist's point of view," says Leta S. Hollingworth, "the problems connected with the crush are more troublesome, because less healthy, than those arising from the love of one of the opposite sex."

Even aside from such definite segregation as occurs in one-sexed schools, Professor Isabel Davenport finds that our present sex-system "is to keep girls and boys separate all along the line—not only actually in space, but in mental interests. Girls are trained to play with girls and leave the boys alone. Boys are trained to play with boys and leave the girls alone. And each side is trained into [accepting] the undesirability of intermingling. * * * Inspiring this practice is a still more dangerous spiritual outlook. The sexes are not recognized, explicitly or implicitly, as existing for each other, as actually having no meaning apart from their relation to, and life in, each other." Professor Phyllis Blanchard notes that at the International Conference of Medical Women in New York in 1919, "Dr. Constance Long (of England), Dr. Eleanor Bertine (of New York), and other leading medical women, emphasized the increasing rôle which homosexuality is coming to play in the life of the modern girl. According to their view, it is the failure to transfer the libido from a love object of the same sex to one of opposite sex, which is responsible in part for the increasing number of women celibates and divorces."

We have seen that the few aspects of contemporary adult life to which patriarchally educated young people are immediately fitted are such as are relics of the patriarchal past—whether still having a measure of social dignity and usefulness, as the Army and Navy (and on another page the Church has been named in this connection), or socially disreputable, as prostitution and criminal gangdom. It has also been noted that art represents a special mode of gaining social acceptance for infantile traits; but art has its own adult discipline and technique, and thus affords no refuge for infantilism in its raw state. There are a few further refuges for the patriarchally-trained boy or girl, requiring no further psychic growth, but they are few. A boy can run away to sea. He may become a cow-boy, wear high-heeled boots, embroidered 'chaps' and silver spurs. In either case society will accept his occasional getting drunk and staying with a harlot as a sufficient demonstration of his manliness. But the list of such refuges, though this does not pretend to exhaust it, is short.

As for girls, they may gain in some respectable circles a degree of approval for submitting to emotionally meaningless marital relations in the submissive spirit inculcated by patriarchal education—the spirit illustrated by Jessie Taft's Mary, who philosophically accepted sexual intercourse with the man in the foster home to which she was sent "as part of the day's work, something which went along with living in this foster-home which for the most part was desirable. * * * When Mary was asked how she felt about sex, she replied characteristically and cheerfully: 'Well, the world is made that way, you just have to accept it. It isn't any use to worry about it, you might as well take people as they are.'" But for the girl as well as the boy the opportunities of self-respecting use of patriarchal sex-attitudes is limited, the refuges few. Most of these boys and girls confront an adult world to the demands of which they must adjust as well as they can. This means a repudiation, to some degree, sooner or later, of all that they have learned of sexual infantilism. It means a desperate effort to be emotionally grown up, since that is (subject to the reservations already indicated) the only way of achieving any happiness or success in life. In this struggle to become adult, to learn the lessons of love and work, their instincts are fighting for them; and if their minds are capable of understanding their instinctive heterosexual wishes and of giving them conscious direction, they may succeed in spite of the most frightful misadventures on the way.

To the extent that their instincts have been too deeply poisoned by patriarchal training and by the emotional regressions into which it has led them, they will be unable to find satisfaction in the world they live in. Its incentives will be ineffectual with them, its rewards meaningless. Hurt and chagrined by continual reachings out for well-advertised apples of joy that prove to be ashes in their mouths, they will conclude that life is a cheat and a lie. They will, perhaps, keep on punching the clock or making the bed, but they will be visited by gleams of what will seem to them the True Truth, the truth beyond all our human shows and vanities; it will be, as one to whom it was familiar as "the White Logic" has described it, "the antithesis of life, cruel and bleak as interstellar space, pulseless and frozen as absolute zero, dazzling with the frost of irrefragable logic and unforgettable fact". And this terrible truth is: that life goes toward death, that with each day we approach, even as the dumb ox, nearer to the slaughter. For death is necessarily the ultimate meaning of life to those to whom its other meanings are meaningless. They feel that they have seen beyond the veils of illusion.

Yet those illusions are still warm and dear to them, because the truth is so cold and terrible. And to create these illusions—that life is worth living, that love is not a lie (not to mention the comforting illusion of sexual potency)—alcoholic encouragement is required, and may be required in such excessive quantities as to constitute chronic drunkenness.

Dr. Frankwood E. Williams, in discussing the relation of alcoholism to mental disease, remarks that fifty years ago those who found the first condition so commonly characteristic of people afflicted by the second, took for granted that it was alcohol that had wrought the mental havoc. "But, as so often happens, a more careful study of the problem has shown that the early reports are inaccurate, due to a frequent getting of the cart before the horse. The excessive drinking of alcohol, which leads to the production of what are known as the alcohol psychoses, is frequently but a symptom of a previously existing and underlying nervous and mental condition. A comparatively mild, but important, type of mental disease exists in many of these individuals before they become alcoholic, and their becoming alcoholic is, in fact, dependent largely upon this previous mental condition."

Since alcoholism is here being put among the 'effects of patriarchal sex-education', it behooves us to be careful not to overstate our claims. Feeble-mindedness bears a share of the responsibility for alcoholism; poverty is directly contributory, in creating unendurably severe conditions of life; and greed is, as always, responsible for the exploitation of human weakness. Mental conflicts, fears, anxieties, and other neurotic or psychotic incapacities for dealing adequately with life's realities must bear the rest of the burden of alcoholism, and, indeed, divide with poverty and greed their own responsibility. The origins of neurosis and psychosis have been found by modern psychology to lie in what we have here called 'psychic failures to grow up', fixations at and regressions to infantile erotic levels, with consequent maladaptations to adult standards of life. These regressions are in turn found to be due to specific environmental and social influences of childhood, and in particular to failures of the parental family to encourage or permit normal psychic growth toward adulthood. The further general origin of these family and environmental failures in patriarchal attitudes of mind, once socially useful but now mischievous in their effects, is the newest study of modern psychology and the theme of this book. It is in this exact sense that we hold patriarchal sex-education in contemporary life responsible for alcoholism and for such other results as will be immediately discussed here.

The drunkard drinks in order to feel equal to the task of living. Alcohol is the neurotic's courage. Under its influence he is not ashamed for the moment to live down to the level of the sexual infantilisms which he has been unable to outgrow, which he has been unable to satisfy in socially acceptable symbolic expression, and which he customarily hides. He can, among boon friends, exhibit his anal-eroticism, give his repressed homosexual tendencies an airing, indulge his sadistic and masochistic propensities without offense—for there is the drinker's code which rules that what is said and done by a drunken friend does not count, since nobody knows what day he himself may need this same tolerance. Thus barricaded against the fear of life that oppresses him, the drinker may even bring to light hidden generosities and sympathies and capacities for understanding human nature. He may be in certain special respects a better man drunk than sober. He is living for the moment in the old patriarchal world, and he has all the old patriarchal virtues. He is a hero in a barbaric epic. He is free from care.

"Oh I have been to Ludlow fair
And left my necktie God knows where,
And carried half way home, or near,
Pints and quarts of Ludlow beer:
Then the world seemed none so bad,
And I myself a sterling lad;
And down in lovely muck I've lain,
Happy till I woke again."

To be sure, this dream-world collapses about one's head. But for many neurotics it represents the most successful terms which they can make with life—short, of course, of the painful process of growing up. Alcohol is the first blessed refuge to the incompletely heterosexual men and women who are obliged to live in and adjust somehow to a heterosexual adult world.

But there are some to whom these periods of surcease are not enough, or who are left by alcohol the worse for coping with the realities of life. To them the narcotic drugs come with a message of consolation. "One of the effects of opium", says Dr. Lawrence Kolb of the United States Health Service, "is the obliteration of mental conflicts and of the uncomfortable pathological strivings that result from them. The tensions, both physical and mental, produced by these strivings, are relieved, and under its influence the neurotic or psychopathic patient feels free, easy and contented. The contrast with his usual state is so great in some cases that he is actually happy." True, again, that this comforter betrays. It relieves him of his anxiety, only to plunge him into anxiety's deepest abysses. "The reflex from waning narcotism accentuates the original tensions, * * * and in the end the patient is worse off." Dr. Kolb declares that the heroin-maddened criminal is a myth, though "the continued effect of the drug is to create petty thieves, because the lethargy, loss of ambition, idleness and physical depletion produced by the drugs, together with the social and legal difficulties of an addict's career, result in moral deterioration and financial embarrassment".

Of 230 drug addicts studied by Dr. Kolb, 9% represented the results of legitimate prescribed use to alleviate prolonged physical suffering ('legitimate addicts'), 5% accidental cases due to self-medication or too-liberal prescribing, while 86% "had been affected with some form of nervous instability before they became addicted". Since the 1915 Harrison Law restricting the sale of opiates, the proportion of accidental addictions has dwindled, and that of neurotic and psychopathic addiction is correspondingly larger. Dr. Kolb's studies of narcotic addiction "have shown that various unstable people get a sense of release from the use of narcotics that normal people do not experience. It is easy to see why this is true in the case of psychoneurotics, who as a class are afflicted with fears, uncertainties, feelings of inferiority, and unusual inhibitions. They meet life as a rule on a lower plane than normal people and get less satisfaction out of it. The narcotic properties of morphine and heroin remove their inhibitions and fears and bring them temporarily up to the level of normal men. Under the influence of these narcotics, they have a confidence in themselves and a sense of ease they do not usually feel * * *." The life histories of the psychopathic addicts "showed that as boys a large proportion of them had played truant from school, had been problems at home, and had had difficulties with the police, and that later on as men, before becoming addicts, many of them had been guilty of repeated drunkenness, stealing, idleness, habitual gambling, or even attempted robbery and murder.

"The psychopath, the inebriate, the psychoneurotic, and the temperamental individuals who fall easy victims to narcotics, have this in common; they are struggling with a sense of inadequacy, imagined or real, or with unconscious pathological inhibitions that narcotics temporarily remove; and the open make-up

[Dr. Kolb elsewhere defines this as meaning care-free, an apparently unrepressed and normal air] that so many of them show is not a normal expression of men at ease with the world, but a mechanism of inferiors who are striving to appear like real men." Cocaine, before its effects have passed over into anxiety and persecutory delusions, "increases sex power", and is a mental stimulant. A prostitute "said that the drug transported her to heaven". A negro with an intelligence quotient of 69 [indicating feeble-mindedness] said: "It gives me will power and makes me feel happy, good and strong."

Among the personal histories of these patients is one of a physician, aged 53, who had never been self-supporting. "The next meeting with his mother was a love-feast; he embraced her with childish happiness, and it was plain how much her blind coddling had contributed to his ruin. * * * If he had escaped narcotics, but not the influence of his mother," says Dr. Kolb, he might have been "as respectable as could be expected of a neurotic parasite". Freed from his mother, he "might now be a useful citizen". Other cases are given in which, by very discreet self-prescribing of an opiate, the previous deterioration caused by alcoholism has been stopped, thus enabling some very neurotic individuals to live useful and respectable lives—a state of affairs precariously dependent, however, upon the drug, withdrawal of which through any circumstances would probably result not merely in prolonged and intense suffering but in "economic if not physical disaster".

The inability of the alcoholic and the drug addict to face the realities of life is an inability to understand and respond to adult heterosexual incentives. It is inability to find normal satisfactions in mate-love and family life, and in the disciplined work which takes its meaning from the love and family life which it supports and promotes. This is as true of women as of men. Normal heterosexual emotions give a validity to daily tasks which is otherwise absent, and which must be sought—and can rarely be found—in egotistic self-expression. It can rarely be found in such egotistic self-expression for the reason that society rarely encourages or rewards such self-expression, except when it is manifest in terms of art, which requires not only high natural aptitudes but a special discipline of its own, not less exacting than though different from that of ordinary work. This means in effect that for the aesthetically ungifted or undisciplined, self-expression has to be secured vicariously by the process of unconscious identification, through the art products of others, by reading books, looking at pictures and listening to or playing music. Amateurism in the arts is important as increasing the degree of possible vicarious relief to be had through the appreciation of art. The love of Nature also has its solaces, to these as to all wounded spirits. The alcoholic or drug addict is thus a person who is unable to make use of or to get sufficient satisfactions from the relief which the appreciation of art or the love of Nature provide for the pains of mental conflict and repression. His maladjustment is too deep for such ministrations to be of effect. He has tried the joys of love, after his fashion, and found them hollow. He has tried work and found it a meaningless and intolerable tyranny. He characteristically prefers the excitements and even the losses of gambling, and he admires if he does not emulate the exploits of crime by which wealth is gained without the insufferable inanities of honest labor. He has tried obedience and conformity and found them to be the maxims by which the strong teach self-slavery to the weak. He is not, however, a reformer or a revolutionist, for he lacks any conception of or loyalty to a different and presumably superior social order, even that of 'Nature', nor could he join effectively with others in attempting to bring such a different social order into existence—indeed, he characteristically regards social reformers and revolutionists as pathetic fools. He believes in the earthly permanence of the conditions to which he cannot successfully adjust; he is not even a rebel, being without hope. He is, to his view, a round peg in a universe of square holes, or a pot which the Potter has cast awry. He may be the happier, in his fashion, if his maladjustment takes definite form in criminality, for there his misery will find company; and so also sometimes if he is led to interpret his maladjustments to normal life as being the characteristics of a 'third sex' of 'Uranians' or what not, which has the dignity of a cult and some of the honors of persecution. He is unhappiest when most earnestly striving, by misdirected efforts, to conform to a world which he secretly hates and despises and fears. His shifts from heroic defiance to timid submission are beautifully portrayed by the poet par excellence of youth's morbidities, Housman, who has so nobly exercised in behalf of such emotional conflicts the religious function of interpretation and absolution:

"The laws of God, the laws of man
He may keep that will and can;
Not I: let God and man decree
Laws for themselves and not for me;
And if my ways are not as theirs
Let them mind their own affairs.
Their ways I judge and much condemn,
Yet when did I make laws for them?
Please yourselves, say I, and they
Need only look the other way.
But no, they will not; they must still
Wrest their neighbor to their will,
And make me dance as they desire
With jail and gallows and hell-fire.
And how am I to face the odds
Of man's bedevilment and God's?
I, a stranger and afraid
In a world I never made.
They will be master, right or wrong;
Though both are foolish, both are strong.
And since, my soul, we cannot fly
To Saturn nor to Mercury,
Keep we must, if keep we can,
These foreign laws of God and man."

In all except the happiest lives, nurtured under the most favorable circumstances, the period of adolescence in our transition era is a time of trial. So powerful have been the effects of patriarchal education that, as manhood or womanhood comes in sight, youth feels acutely its inadequacies for the rôle of responsibility so soon to be thrust upon it—and retreats in alarm back into something like childhood. Lingering there, as in an enchanted garden, it marshals all its emotional protests against adult life. And it may go on into adult life enriched by that delay, knowing more of the infinite possibilities of our human nature, lessoned in tolerance, and more able to help others through that difficult period. But this enchanted garden of adolescence has its jungles and its abysses, into which youth gazes with a fascinated curiosity, before—all too unencouraged and unhelped—it accepts the efforts and responsibilities of adult life.

Let us peer into those jungles and abysses.

CHAPTER XII

THE FOUR PATHS OF YOUTH

§ 1. The Path Toward the Abyss of Double Personality

There are four ways of dealing with mental conflict. We may think of them as four paths open to the feet of youth. One of them, though difficult to characterize in this metaphorical manner, may be said to skirt the edge of an abyss before finally, if followed to the end, it goes over and down. The second leads away toward the caves of dream, the caverns of living death. The third winds endlessly through the jungle of neurotic suffering. The fourth—and any of these three may debouch upon it—is the way out of the jungle, the path toward adulthood.

The first method of dealing with mental conflict is to repress the forbidden wishes wholesale into the unconscious mind, deny and forget them, and leave them to constitute an interior and different personality, unknown to the conscious mind and for the most part kept effectually in chains—but, when it becomes too powerful, likely to break out and act and speak for itself in ways alien to the conscious mind. This in its extreme forms constitutes the 'demoniac possession' of ancient and medieval times and the 'double personality' of modern times, the Dr. Jekyll-and-Mr. Hyde phenomenon, in which two (or even more) selves share by turns the possession of the same bodily faculties. We are only interested here in these extremes of psychic disorder for the light which they throw upon the less extreme and very familiar traits of 'split personality' in ordinary life. The beginning of the path to 'double personality' is in what is sometimes incorrectly called by observers 'hypocrisy'; and again, quite accurately, 'fooling yourself'. It is mistaken for hypocrisy because it seems as though the person could not fool himself so well—as if he *must* know that his deeds of last night belie his words this morning, week in and week out. But it is really a case of fooling himself; for his behavior of last night is so abhorrent to the conscious mind that by this time it is successfully forgotten and may without deliberate or conscious insincerity be denied. The arrangement is a very convenient one, for the forbidden wishes thus have assurance of having full charge of his personality every now and again if they will allow themselves to be utterly repudiated during the intervals. The repressed part of the self, all compact of forbidden wishes and the practical knowledge of how to achieve them, was once called 'the Devil', and is still thought of as a force wholly alien to the true self. This is already a split personality. When carried some steps further it becomes the phenomenon of the innocent Dr. Jekyll and the criminal Mr. Hyde sharing the same body by turns. That kind of extreme 'demoniac' possession is not here held up as a practical warning against fooling oneself, since fooling oneself may go on very long and extensively without reaching the point of double personality. But it is important to know what lies at the end of the path if it is pursued to the end.

The forbidden wishes in these cases are technically construed as sexual by modern (and especially Freudian) psychology, though they may take form as the symbolic substitute-actions of theft or murder. The abhorrence with which they are originally felt is because they concern the parents. They represent the first shocked apprehensions of sexual feelings toward the parent of opposite sex, and the jealous death-wishes felt toward the other parent. This situation is one which arises in human life because of the necessity of prolonging parental care beyond infancy; that is, the emergence of childish sexual feelings toward the parents is a specifically human problem. Were those wishes to be fulfilled in reality in post-pubertal filial life, the family as a social institution could not exist. The incest-taboos by which they are repressed are the earliest, apparently, of all human institutions, the foundations of human society. In savage society, however, the sexual impulses thus repressed within the family circle are encouraged to precocious expression outside—an expression too precocious to fit in with the longer period of childhood and education required by civilized life. The sexual emotions, however, are normally detached from the parents by the processes of psychic growth toward adulthood, which gradually attach them to others, first parent-substitutes and then possible mates.

This normal process of psychic growth is hindered by anything which on the one hand discourages the extension of love emotions beyond the family, and on the other hand increases the feeling of guilt in connection with sexual feelings. There is thus created an impossible situation in which childish love is confined within a domestic realm in which it is felt (because of its sexual wishes and jealous death-wishes) as frightfully criminal. The conscious mind must not merely repudiate, forget and deny the childish sexual wishes concerning the parents, but it has to keep on repudiating, forgetting and denying the further polymorphous-perverse elaborations of those wishes, the homosexual, sadistic, and masochistic fantasies which in lieu of development toward adulthood represent the field of psychic interest. That is to say, the patriarchal mode of discouraging young people from growing up, lest they choose their own mates and their own work, and of promoting an excessive piety and obedience toward their parents, created a situation in which split personality was one of the inevitable results. This, however, was recognized by the ancients, who took over certain sex-orgies of a religious nature from savage life, and used them as periods of license in which all the forbidden impulses could be indulged, either directly or in emotionally satisfying symbolic forms, as in the wild Thracian rites celebrated by Euripides in his Bacchae, the 'blood feasts of the Bassarid' and the 'Maenad revels' and the more vulgar Roman Saturnalia. These Saturnalian holidays have some lingering modern analogues, as in the traditional 'Quatz Arts' ball in Paris, in which there is a sanctioned expression of all the polymorphous-perverse sexual infantilisms. But because of the connection of these periods of license with pagan religions, they were prohibited by the Christian Church, though they reappeared in the late medieval recrudescence of the savage witch-cult in Europe, and were regularly associated (at least in orthodox accusations) with the heretical cults, and indeed continued an only slightly disguised existence in the Christian festivals that superseded them.

They were in turn stamped out in that form by Puritanism. But Puritanism, which took away that species of permitted relief for repressed sexual infantilism, exacerbated the feelings of guilt in connection with sex; and it not only produced its own huge crop of demoniac-possession cases, but short of these, it instituted as a common middle-class trait, mocked at by the aristocracy as mere 'hypocrisy', a split-personality habit of forgetting and denying its occasional outbursts of infantilistic sexual gratification. The Victorian teaching of 'purity' to young people, *i. e.*, the teaching of the idea that nice young people were totally devoid of sexual impulses, promoted the tendency toward split personality by making boys and girls repudiate the facts of their emotional lives. The ascetic reformer or cleric who professes complete sexual holiness, and occasionally is guilty of homosexual practices which he promptly crosses off his record as 'not counting' since he is 'not really that kind of person'; the conventional girl who professes complete chastity, and is able to forget and deny her occasional lapses when under the sudden and overwhelming domination of her repressed sexuality—these are familiar examples of split personality. Even when the tendency does not carry the individual to its ultimate result in loss of power to control personal behavior, through periodic anarchic upheavals of the repressed impulses, even when it is near enough to the hypocrisy that it looks like to maintain a dim awareness of the existence of the prisoner chained in the cellar—even when it represents a kind of shrewd working arrangement with him by which he is given his holidays and then locked up and forgotten for the time—it still represents a loss of integrity of character in the literal sense of oneness. It achieves only a false accommodation to adult social and sexual standards of life on terms of occasional lapses into infantilism. It is not the path to adulthood.

We may think of these four paths, not as leading away in entirely separate directions, but as winding about and crossing each other at intervals—which is what happens in the actual behavior of the individual. It is possible for one to step from one path to another at almost any moment. This path, it has been said, skirts the edge of the abyss of double personality before it goes over and down. But it may cross and thus lead into the second path, which goes off toward the caves of dream.

§ 2. The Path Toward the Caves of Dream

The second path represents a different mode of dealing with forbidden impulses, so as to avoid the psychic pain of their conflict with the social wish for approval. Ultimately dangerous, it is in its less extreme manifestations a very common and apparently harmless psychic dodge. Here, again, we will go to the end of the path, peer into the dark caverns, and in view of that destination interpret the significance of its beginnings.

In ordinary life and in its least morbid form, the trait we are here considering leads us to blame anything and everyone but ourselves for our mistakes and failures. It is a childish and also a savage trait. If we stumble headlong over a footstool, it is not our own heedlessness that is at fault but the perversity or negligence of the person who left it there. It is not pleasant to blame ourselves for anything, and it is always easy to blame the outside world of people and things. This ascription of blame can easily be justified by argument. It is easy for the savage to prove to his own satisfaction that an enemy must have bewitched the animal he is hunting, so that it was unhurt by his arrows; or the girl he loves, so that she remains indifferent to him. It is just as easy for a boy to prove that he is really a blameless victim of the machinations of others in any transgression; just as easy for a man to prove that it is not his fault that he lost his job or his sweetheart; just as easy for a girl to prove that she was the unwilling victim of a wicked seducer—all to their own satisfaction. 'Passing the buck' is the popular phrase for it. 'Projection' is the scientific term. In matters of sex, which bear so heavy a burden of guilt-feelings as a result of patriarchal education, it is inevitable that the buck should be habitually passed to other people, that the forbidden emotions should be projected into the outer world.

Again it may be protested that it is not as a warning of an imminent danger to buck-passers that we follow this tendency to its psychotic conclusions, since buck-passing can be indulged in to a very considerable extent without necessarily leading to such mentally disastrous results. Nevertheless, when the psychosis is actually reached, the path which led to it is unmistakably the one of buck-passing. Now let us consider an extreme case, and its explanation, as set forth by Dr. Bernard Hart in a passage which is a model of lucid psychological exposition:

"In 'Old Maids' Insanity', for instance, an unmarried lady of considerable age, and of blameless reputation, begins to complain of the undesirable attentions to which she is subjected by some male acquaintance. She explains that the man is obviously anxious to marry her, and persistently follows her about. Finally certain trifling incidents lead her to believe that he is scheming to abduct her by force, and on the strength of this she perhaps writes him an indignant letter, or lodges a complaint with the police. Investigation follows, and it is found that the man is not only entirely innocent of the charges levelled against him, but that he has never expressed the least interest in the lady, and is probably hardly aware of her existence. * * *

"This by no means uncommon sequence of events can be easily explained with the aid of the psychological laws now at our disposal. The patient's sex instincts have been allowed no normal outlet, and have finally become sternly repressed, generally with an exaggerated development in consciousness of the opposite quality. This latter, of course, constitutes the prudery so frequently observed in such cases * * *. The repressed instincts gain an indirect expression, however, by the mechanism of projection. The desires originating therefrom are roused to activity by the man in question, and the real state of affairs is that the lady is in love with the man but, owing to the repression, the mind will not acknowledge that these ideas and emotions are a part of itself, and finds a solution of the conflict by reversing the significance of the desires and projecting them upon their own object."

Self-reproaches are sometimes thus literally projected upon the outside social world, these constituting the "delusions of reference". "The patient", as Dr. Hart describes him, "is intensely suspicious; if two or three of his fellows converse together he imagines that he forms the subject of their remarks, the casual stranger becomes a designing enemy, until finally every trivial event is welded into one vast conspiracy to destroy him. In patients of this kind, the development of hallucinations is extremely common. The reproaches are not merely construed into the actions of those about them, they are handed over to altogether imaginary persecutors. The portion of his mind which the personality has cut off and declined to acknowledge makes its reappearance as an hallucinatory voice. Thus one patient, whose mode of life had wrecked both himself and his family, discussed his former experiences with revolting complacency. He complained bitterly, however, of the system of persecution to which he was subjected; people concealed themselves in the ceiling and under his bed, and poured upon him a flood of abuse and threats, which rendered existence almost insupportable. Hallucinations of this kind may be regarded as literal examples of the 'small voice of conscience', distorted by repression. It will be observed that such a patient has successfully avoided the sting of remorse, but he has exchanged Scylla for Charybdis, and has sacrificed his mental integrity to obtain the hardly more desirable alternative of a constant persecution."

The 'projection' mechanism, the device of passing the buck to the outside world, thus effects its aim of avoiding the pain of mental conflict only at a price. Like an opiate drug, its use tends to be increased continually, since the pain of self-reproach is all the more unendurable after the relief that it has afforded. More and more the ego is 'purified' of its sexual impulses, its sadistic wishes, its anal propensities, its hate and murder thoughts—but the result is that the 'purified' individual now lives in a universe inflamed with sex, brutal with sadism, besmeared with filth, and hot with murderous hate, all directed toward the one spotless individual. At this point the complaints of the spotless one against attempted rapes and murders and gigantic world-wide conspiracies are recognized as 'delusions of persecution'. Or his elaborate effort to avoid contamination from the universal dirt or disease of the rest of the world is recognized as a 'washing-mania' or as 'agoraphobia'. Thus Miss R., whose narrative of her sufferings has been published and interpreted by Alfred Adler, writes: "I thought that the people who accidentally trod in the footsteps of a lupus sufferer [lupus is a skin disease] would spread the germs over the whole city. 'Where,' I asked myself, 'is there a place on earth where there is no lupus? Where is there a spot where no lupus sufferer has left bacteria behind him?' The whole world appeared to me infected. I felt as if I were surrounded by bars through which there was no way out. At the same time I felt I hated and loathed the lupus sufferers. Father's objection that all other people existed without such fear was of no avail. It seemed to me as if lupus was there for me alone. A punishment for me alone. Like a horrible, gigantic spider the dread of the devouring disease crawled through me. If I had known of some way by which I could have killed myself quickly I would have done it. But I knew none. Miserable to the point of being almost feelingless, I commenced washing my hands and face with potassium permanganate. I rinsed my mouth thoroughly with Lina's antiseptic. I would not wear my coat again. I imagined that I had infected it by wearing it when I passed the lupus hospital. I wore gloves when I took my shoes off, and was careful never to let the shoelaces touch the soles of the shoes, which part I regarded as particularly badly infected. * * * One day a piece of lace slipped out of my hand to the floor. Mother had to give it away. I did not want to touch even mother any more, since she had to come into contact with the floor when she washed and cleaned. * * * Then I got the idea that one could never know whether money had been touched by a lupus sufferer or not. So I did not touch it any more unless I first covered my hand with a piece of paper. * * * Finally I did not touch anything any more without paper." Her own family becomes taboo. "And when some one touched me by accident I raved and stormed, had crying spells and threatened to kill myself. * * * I used only one and the same chair and no one else was allowed to sit in it. I also selected my own knives, forks and spoons, which were put in a certain place to be protected from infection by the rest of the furniture. I took strict care of my things. Woe if mother happened to put a wrong fork on my special plate. One day, during house-cleaning, my water glass with my toothbrush in it was accidentally put on the table. When I saw that, I grew furious, swore at my mother in vile language, menaced her, threatened to kill her—I don't know what else I did in my rage. * * * The thought especially that a lupus sufferer might kiss me made me shiver with fright. Finally I fancied that the mere thought of contact with lupus might produce the disease, that the thought might be as much as the act. * * * I also often thought—we lived on the ground floor—how easily some one could climb in at the window—and what is more, it might be a lupus sufferer." All this is still in the realm of neurosis, but is dangerously close to a psychosis.

It is not, however, too late even here for a climb back to adult normality. Adler remarks that in order to free her from these compulsive activities, she "would have to learn to recognize what the purpose of her symptoms is and what she achieves thereby; that she wants unconsciously to detach herself by [means of her neurotic] compulsion from the [adult] compulsion of communal demands; that she has built a secondary battlefield in her intense desire to avoid the principal battlefields of life [*i.e.*, work and love]; that she wants to fritter away her time so as to have none left for the accomplishment of her daily tasks; that she intends to evade life's demands with excuses, curses, alibis or ostensibly good reasons". Life itself, when Miss R.'s story breaks off, is apparently teaching her these lessons, and enabling her to grow up, through self-understanding. For "when one has done a right-about-face and set foot on the road to normal conduct," says Adler, "one progresses along this road in the right direction as quickly as one retrogressed before in the wrong direction. Just as every step in a neurosis inevitably destroys courage, every step out of a neurosis builds up courage and with it strength and social feeling."

But struggle is painful, particularly unaided struggle. In such struggles, moreover, even the wish for health may be slyly used by the unconscious mind to aid in elaborating pseudo-adult modes of behavior in which the infantile wishes can disguise themselves. From too prolonged and unendurable struggles, which do not succeed in finding the true way out of mental conflict, the extreme uses of the projection-mechanism offer an all-too successful escape, into paranoiac 'persecuted innocence'.

It is not our intention here to catalogue the morbid depressions, emotional dementias, delusions, obsessions, manias and phobias, the various measures by which the mind so dangerously protects itself against the pain of internal conflict. It is enough to note that they are the antechambers of the ultimate caves of dream. As these tormented souls go into the shadows, the realities of life grow dim and the struggles of adjustment to which others devote their lives are matters 'unworthy of the expenditure of any mental energy'. Their mental energy goes unweariedly to the weaving of the dream-curtains which shut out the world.

Yet these self-imprisoned victims were once as eagerly active in the world of realities as any of us. It was a definite series of psychic wounds which made them flinch and at last turn away from reality—and behind those wounds, a series of predisposing influences unwittingly calculated to rob them of the robustness necessary for the give and take of life, including its failures, its griefs and its humiliations.

The earliest schooling for life is that of childhood, the parental home; and whatever influences in that early school tend to make the child unable to cope with reality, whatever training makes him fear to face the truth about himself, whatever encourages him in the prolonged use of the infantile 'projection'-device as a habit of mind, whatever robs him of the natural incentives of growth toward independent adulthood, whatever keeps him too long a child under the maternal wing or the paternal shadow, must bear the responsibility for the adult weaknesses which cannot bear the truth and struggle of life and which weave about his mind their fatal cocoon of self-protective dreams.

We have seen that the patriarchal system of education was appropriate to its times; yet this education, with all its buttresses of patriarchal philosophy and religion, was confessedly an inadequate preparation for the hurts of life. Men and women went mad in patriarchal times, or drooped into 'melancholy', as it was called, from thwarted love, or grief, or fear of the devil. Robert Burton, in the 17th century, himself a melancholiac, has left us an impressive compendium of classical, medieval and renaissance medical and literary lore and anecdote, a kind of pre-scientific precursor of our Freudian literature of neurosis and psychosis, in his *Anatomy of Melancholy.* There, as in Dante's vision, we can see these 'souls on fire', laughing and weeping and arguing in their private hells. We have but inherited the inevitable failures of the patriarchal mode of education-for-life, while at the same time by our new adult standards of behavior increasing the difficulty of the struggle and yielding fewer places of refuge. The medieval monasteries and nunneries were complex institutions with a multitude of functions; they were schools, they were workshops, they were adjuncts of the governing power; but among all their other uses they were refuges for two groups who now have to meet the outside world on harsher terms—the feeble-minded, who were there disciplined and made useful, and the neurotics, who were given unusual opportunities to sublimate their mental conflicts in faith and good works. Modern life has swept these refuges almost out of existence, and yet has retained the patri archal education-for-life which produces in immense numbers those who are unable to adapt successfully to adult heterosexual standards of life.

Dr. Frankwood E. Williams has drawn an impressive picture of the situation upon the basis of recognized yearly statistical expectations of mental breakdown. He bids us see the army of American men and women marching along the path of life. "From this army of Americans, 50,000 dropped out last year after a long period of struggle—an exquisitely brave struggle for many of them—these 50,000 finally gave up. They were admitted as new patients to the hospitals in the country maintained for the insane. There are 50,000 each year who are new patients." This does not include the mentally defective and the epileptic, nor those suffering from neurotic incapacities. Nor does it include all of the mentally diseased—"only those whose conduct was so unusual or bizarre" that a "lay judge" has been impressed with the desirability of locking them up. "In some communities the figure includes only those of whom the community is afraid"—for the concept of insanity as a sickness to be treated and if possible cured is still new in our civilization. "At any rate, there were 50,000 last year and before this time next year there will be 50,000 more. We can be quite sure of this; the number increases a little each year.

"As the world is at present, this number will not be decreased for a very long time, and we are perfectly safe, therefore, in using it as the basis of a few computations.

"There are in the country, then, 250,000 people within five years of the state hospitals. Some of these are very close—a week, a month, six months, a year—but every one—man, woman, and child—before five years. Nothing but a miracle will stop it and there will be no miracle. * * *

"It is not a strange army of phantom people * * *. They are mothers and fathers and boys and girls. They are counting their Christmas money and checking gift lists just now; they know the rush-hour crush at Times Square; they have been thrilled as the subway train has dashed out of its tube onto the Charles River Bridge towards Cambridge; they know their way about the 'Loop'; they wait for the Oakland ferry; they hurry to Washington and Illinois streets for their car home. They are very real; and there are 250,000 of them."

About half of them "are now in the twenties or younger—young men and young women at the beginning of things; with school but recently finished or more ambitious school plans just undertaken; experiencing the new thrills of business; giving pledges and making new homes. Plans, plans, plans they have—but there is only one plan. Really, the gods might laugh. The dreams they have! The things they are going to do! But there is one plan. Year by year they will move steadily in one direction—towards the hospital." Some of them are boys and girls in high school, many of them "already beginning, in their oddities and idiosyncrasies of behavior, to give evidence of difficulty in adjustment." Some will go to college, "where, on entrance, they will be given a physical examination (with exercises prescribed to straighten out their shoulders) and a psychological examination (I. Q. found unusually high—undoubtedly a future intellectual leader) * * *." Some will finish "with honors and keys and the blessings of faculties who have daily nurtured them for four years but who have never for an hour understood them." And all of them doomed, not by heredity, not by anything in human nature, but by preventable causes in their emotional training, to be "gathered to * * * the hospitals for the insane."

It may seem to be an undue simplification of this tragic problem to say that patriarchal education by sex-ignorance, sex-repression and sex-segregation is ultimately responsible for this ending of a gallant struggle. But these are the social-historical terms by which we seek to generalize the actual findings of the experts who deal with the individual cases. It is well known that the psychoses involve regressions to an infantile level of sexual interest, often sadistic-homosexual, or self- and anal-centered. It is well known that these psychic regressions are correlated with family conditions of extreme parental severity or indulgence or both, with parental alcoholism or prostitution, with broken homes, stepfatherhood or stepmotherhood, with illegitimacy and a consequent lack of normal parental care, and in general with early home influences which discourage or prevent emotional growth toward adulthood. We deliberately call these various conditions 'patriarchal education' to emphasize the qualities of emotional repression which they all have in common with, and which they derive from, the principles of child-training under the patriarchal régime.

It is important here to be able to see the essential likenesses which exist under superficial differences. Thus we have noted that extremes of parental coddling, severity, and neglect all have the same effect of hindering the child's psychic growth, being equally effective as discouragements of the instinctive tendencies toward adulthood; they are commonly intermingled or alternated in patriarchal training, and it is only by superficial manners that they are to be distinguished, for coddling is only a pseudo-kindly way of robbing the child of his independence, severity is a brutal form of coddling, and both constitute a complete neglect of the child's real needs: toy, slave or foundling, the child is unhelped to grow up. And again, we need not hesitate to describe the most extensive sex-'knowledge', which omits everything of adult emotional importance in the sexual relationship, as 'sex-ignorance'; nor should we hesitate to class the sexual exploitation of girls by men, or the sexual association of boys or men with prostitutes to the exclusion of normal social, affectionate and romantic relations with girls, as 'sex-segregation', however paradoxical that might sound; exactly as we are obliged to class a variety of morbid 'expressions' of sexual emotion as the symptoms of 'sex-repression'. Upon this understanding, the ascription of psychotic results to the influence of these three patriarchal factors becomes, except for the use of the historical term 'patriarchal' to describe them, a commonplace of modern psychopathology.

We will quote here from a psychoanalytic study by Lucile Dooley some details of a case of manic-depressive psychosis which illustrate the regression of the sexual interest by degrees to the lowest level and its subsequent climb back to normality. "The first regression of the libido was to a stage in which she evinced the hysterical desire of attention, and was expressed in tearing up the blankets on her bed to obtain the bright-colored strips for ribbons; by the invention of all sorts of symbolic games which expressed the repressed fixations on the father; in dramatic representations and the creation of poems which embodied her erotic fantasies. Then she sank to an infantile level, where she loved to be commanded, dramatized Hugo's *The Orders of the King* [which would furnish materials for masochistic rape-fantasies], and fancied herself a prisoner in the Kaiser's palace. In this stage her father was * * * the one who must be obeyed, and as such was variously depicted as the Kaiser, king, Harry Thaw, villain in the play, etc. Narcissistic impulses also developed, and finally, sinking below the infantile to the prenatal level of dementia praecox in its lowest stages, she became not only auto-erotic but a 'smearer'."

At this point we will interrupt the story to give an outside picture of a similar case, treated without scientific understanding in the medieval manner which still lingers on into our times: "No one comes to see her. She has been in the Elgin State Hospital for many years. Her deterioration has dragged her below the level of the animal. She has torn into bits every blanket and every particle of clothing that has been given to her. Her room contains nothing but a bare bed. She has slept nude upon the springs. A strap about her waist has held her to it. The demands of nature have been acceded to as they manifest themselves. Attendants, nurses, and doctors fear her." She was 25 when she entered the hospital—fourteen years ago. It is to this ending that her bright drama of childishness has come. She was afraid to grow up—afraid of life, and without help or understanding in her weakness, encouraged by her early environment to evade the responsibilities of reality and take comfort in self-protective fantasies of childish power. Her wish has come true—she is a child, but how!

We go back to our other and more fortunate patient: "The interesting part of this case is * * * the complete cure which the analysis effected. As the girl began to recover, she retraced all the steps by which she had sunken to this lowest level. The first indication that she was coming up from the pre-natal plane was a desire to scrub the floor and walls of her room, which she had made utterly filthy in her archaic state. Then came a strange case of infantile foot-fetishism, and finally the adolescent level of hysteria was reached, which clung a long time with its color symbols and other delusions. Finally she retained of her insanity only one symptom,—a recurrent dream, in which she was combing the snarls out of her hair. When a lock was pulled out it turned into a snake, which she burned. When the last lock was pulled out and burned, the dream did not return again, and as her complexes,—the abnormal love of her father and hatred of her sister,—had been smoothed out earlier in the treatment, she became a normal adolescent, with no tendency to lapse into the old neuroticism."

§ 3. The Path Winding Through the Jungle of the Neuroses

The psychotic tends to repudiate everything in himself that he does not approve—and before he has finished he has 'projected' so much of his ego out into the cosmos that there is little left to call a self at all. But the neurotic, on the other hand, so thoroughly identifies the outer world with himself, finds in it so many symbolic analogues to his own wishes, expands his personality to include so many people and things, that he has been described as 'introjecting' the cosmos into his ego. This, too, is a natural childish and primitive human trait. It is manifest in the savage's identification of himself with his totem, the patriot's identification of himself with his country, the lover's identification of himself with his beloved. This expansion of personality brings its joys but also its pains. The housewife who magnifies her ego by taking pride in her house must pay for her satisfaction by the deeper because more 'personal' hurt which she feels at any criticism of its arrangements or cleanliness. If your personality has taken a political party or a religious sect into itself, then you will find frank discussion of its shortcomings as offensive as if it were your wife or child that were under discussion; and people who know that you are 'touchy' about certain things will try to avoid those topics in your presence, so as not to arouse some immoderate outburst of personal resentment. The more expanded the ego, the more subject its feelings are to hurts.

Now this mental trait of ego-expansion is commonly made use of in an effort to diminish the pain of mental conflicts. There is nothing cowardly about it, and at its best it is a healing process. Thus an identification of oneself with Nature is an immemorial way of finding comfort for the griefs of love and the hurts of pride; and a special form of this identification constitutes the profound psychic satisfactions of art. Ferenczi, to whom the term 'introjection' is due, describes its use by the neurotic as "a kind of diluting process, by which he tries to mitigate the poignancy of free-floating, unsatisfied, and unsatisfiable, unconscious wish impulses". It must be added that it sometimes succeeds admirably in performing this function, whereupon it is called 'sublimation'. It is its failures, which are perhaps not more frequent than its successes, which cause it to be regarded as a symptom of neurosis. The difference between a neurotic symptom and a sublimation, though very real, is often originally a matter of social circumstances which determine whether the behavior in question is to be regarded as useless and mischievous or as useful and rewardable: if the latter, then the behavior, whatever it may be, constitutes a bond instead of a barrier between the individual and society, and he finds it possible to achieve miracles of self-discipline. Thus the duck-hunting in the garret indulged in by Hjalmar and Old Ekdal in Ibsen's *Wild Duck* was a neurotic symptom of their wish to escape from the serious responsibilities of life; but if, somehow, duck-hunting in garrets had become a popular sport, and people had come to them to pay for lessons, they would have been transformed by that accident into 'artists' of a sort. At least no artist can see that drama without thanking his lucky stars for the social setting which has conceded to his own boyish day-dreaming the privilege of being disciplined into an art and made the means of achieving public approval, when it might quite as easily have been contemptuously rejected as a mere waste of valuable time! Who knows, perhaps stubborn little vagabond Tom, who wouldn't go to school and would follow circuses and parades (see Chapter XI, §1) and whose maxim was 'Come on, fellers, let's have a song and dance!'—perhaps he has found a happy destiny in singing mammie-songs for the talkies, and now dictates letters to his boy and girl fans telling them that industry and conscientiousness are the keys to success. Anybody—almost anybody—can be industrious and conscientious in doing what he wants to do; and, though it is probably immoral and misleading to say so out loud, the stone rejected by the builders sometimes becomes the cornerstone, the most childish and absurd ways of wasting time are sometimes the beginnings of publicly adored careers, not only in art but in science.

The world, however, being what it is, only certain forms of identification-behavior lend themselves to cultivation as arts; and many others are inevitably regarded by the world as nuisances. We approve the identification-behavior which makes a man spring passionately to the defense of a relative or a friend who is spoken ill of; but similar behavior with regard to, say, the climate of a given region, is tiresome and, we feel, uncalled for. "When introjection of the environment is carried to excess," says Ernest Jones, "it greatly increases the sensitiveness of the person in question * * *. As is well known, the sensitiveness of some patients with advanced nervous invalidism is quite appalling; every trivial occurrence affects them in a personal way, and they are deeply moved by the most transient impressions", and "exacerbations of suffering may be brought about by slight happenings * * *". In the case of Miss R., above, along with her near-psychotic projection of her own sexual desires and unconscious guilt upon the outer world, there was at work also the counter-mechanism of neurotic identification of herself with outer objects; thus it was not merely her toothbrush glass that had been put in the wrong place, but her sacred suffering 'self' that had been insulted and injured. Such neurotic patients, as Jones says, "suck the very life-blood out of all about them in their insistence that these should constantly make the finest adjustments in their environment. * * * The most interesting manifestations of introjection are those relating to the persons in the patient's emotional attitude." He cannot be impersonal or objective about people. "He transfers on to them various affects [*i.e.*, emotional attitudes]—love, hate, and so on, that arose, perhaps years previously, in connection with quite other people, just as a child who has once been hurt by a doctor is for some time afterward fearful of every doctor he encounters. For this to happen there has only to be instituted the slightest resemblance between the original person and the present one; such a patient, having once intensely hated some one with a given characteristic, say red hair, will be ready to hate any one he may later meet who has the same characteristic. * * * Every physician who has had much experience with psychoneurotic patients knows how variable, unreliable, and changeable is their attitude to him; in fact, their 'capriciousness' is generally notorious. On a slight change in his manner or in his treatment of them, and often quite spontaneously, their attitude alters, trust is replaced by suspicion, resentment by gratitude, and so on, the extent of the alteration being quite out of proportion to the exciting cause * * *. This puzzling behaviour, however, becomes at once comprehensible as soon as one realizes that it is determined, not by the external occasion, to which it is so disproportionate and abnormal a response, but by previously existing and usually unconscious emotions which the occasion merely evokes. * * * A word or tone used by the physician unconsciously reminds them of some forgotten experience, and it is to this past experience that they are reacting * * * "

It is easy to realize how these neurotic emotional instabilities affect love and work. The employee who sulks or 'flies off the handle' at trivial matters, whose promising abilities are mysteriously diminished by unknown causes, who 'cannot be depended upon' or who 'cannot get along with people', becomes increasingly unemployable; unfortunately the same cannot be said in many industries for the employers, or even the foremen and foreladies, who by lingering patriarchal tradition too often have full social consent to take out their sadistic impulses, inferiority feelings and unconscious grudges vicariously upon the unfortunate work-people under their charge—though in the long run their neuroses, however socially protected, injure their chances of economic success.

Dr. V. V. Anderson, director of the medical research bureau of R. H. Macy & Co., in New York, has published a valuable study of the psychic problems of employees and the way in which these affect their industrial usefulness. "About 20 per cent of the employees of mercantile establishments—and this is probably true of other business and industrial organizations—are what may be called 'problem' individuals," says Dr. Anderson. "That is, as personnel material they are either liabilities or unconscious liabilities to the business man. It is from this group that are drawn the repeated transfers from job to job, or resignations, or lay-offs. These are the work-failures that in the majority of cases are a drag on the organization.

"As the employer sees these individuals they are production problems, or chronic health problems, or chronic attendance problems, or marked disciplinary cases, or the like, and from his viewpoint he is better off without them.

"As the psychiatrist sees them they all present distinguishing physical and mental characteristics that underlie and explain not only their job maladjustments, but faulty adjustive efforts and failures in other life situations." Besides faulty physical conditions and specialized job disabilities, the chief outstanding cause of work failure is found to be 'maladjusted personality'. Dr. Anderson shows how "many of these individuals may, through proper study and treatment, be adjusted and become assets to the employer, thus cutting down turn-over among employees and increasing production efficiency".

One aspect of the employment situation, with which Dr. Anderson does not deal, perhaps because it is so obvious, is the unconscious identification by employee of his employer with his own father, and the carrying over into the job of infantile filial attitudes, which are often in the nature of an unbounded awe and trust, followed by profound disillusionment, hurt, and sulkiness when it is discovered that he does not live up to these exaggerated standards of God-like justice, sympathy and power. Or, as in schools and colleges, the habitual attitude of filial defiance, of deceit or of unenterprising dependence, is brought into the employee-employer relationship. The industrial realm as a whole, however, is barely beginning to emerge from patriarchal ideals of whimsically autocratic management, and the neuroses of employers want study quite as much as those of employees. Mary C. Jarrett, an expert in the use of mental hygiene in industry, does mention two instances in which the neuroses of minor bosses was recognized by their employers as a problem: "Foreman, a high-strung man, in whose department all the employees seem tense and irritable." "Superintendent who has no use for women. Carries this to such an extent that women employees cannot consult him." But the inquiry reaches no higher. Studies of a more far-reaching sort may have to wait until some body of workers has the money and the political power to promote psychiatric investigations of the kinds of men who are our typical captains and lieutenants of industry.

In the realm of love, the 'efficiency' and 'employability' of individuals is even more seriously hampered by neurotic traits; but patriarchal conditions have accustomed us to these defects, and patriarchal philosophy has sought to reconcile us to them as 'inevitable' aspects of 'human nature'. The picture presented above by Dr. Ernest Jones of the neurotic might almost stand unchanged as the patriarchal idea of the lover or husband. It may here be paraphrased as follows: Every woman who has had much experience with lovers (and every man who has had much experience with sweethearts) knows how variable, unreliable, and changeable is the attitude of many of them—in fact the 'capriciousness' of men in love (and of women in love) is notorious. On a slight change of the loved one's treatment of them, and often quite spontaneously, their attitude alters, trust is replaced by suspicion, resentment by gratitude, and so on, the extent of the alteration being quite out of proportion to the trivial slight unwittingly inflicted or the small favor carelessly granted. This puzzling behavior, however, becomes at once comprehensible when one realizes that it is a response not to the behavior of the actual loved person, but to unconscious memories of similar behavior by a beloved parent, with whom the loved one is unconsciously identified. The lover is not enraged at his sweetheart so much as at his mother; nor is it she herself at whose tenderness he bursts into tears, but the tantalizing ghost of his mother, which has embodied itself temporarily in her form. The frigid wife is troubled, not at the intimate embraces of her actual husband, but at those of the father with whom she has unconsciously identified him. The truth is that these lovers are not dealing with realities but with phantoms of their childhood. Nor, as long as this is true, can any real person hope to satisfy them in love. Their emotions go beyond the living world into the realm of shadows; they are haunted by the past. They are paradoxically in the pitiful situation symbolically expressed for them by the sick poet Ernest Dowson; for however conventional and legal may be their love-relations, these are, all unconsciously, as much substitutes for the real love-object as was Dowson's prostitute—and 'Cynara' may stand for the intruding parental image:

> "Last night, ah, yesternight, betwixt her lips and mine
> There fell thy shadow, Cynara! thy breath was shed
> Upon my soul between the kisses and the wine;
> And I was desolate and sick of an old passion,
> Yea, I was desolate and bowed my head.
> I have been faithful to thee, Cynara, in my fashion."

The realm of love is cluttered up with men and women who have never grown up to psychic adulthood, who are incapable of any but the physical forms of love and matehood, and who are still being faithful in their neurotic fashion to a childhood image of a beloved parent. These are the intolerably 'capricious' lovers and sweethearts who are plunged from heaven to hell over nothing at all, who turn in an instant from utter trust to the vilest suspicions, whose moods are incomprehensible to their loved ones and even to themselves, and who make of love a hell of torment for both. But, as with many work-failures, many of these love-failures are not hopeless; "many of these individuals may, through proper study and treatment, be adjusted and become assets" in the realm of love and family life, "thus cutting down turnover" (or divorce) in marriage "and increasing efficiency" in marital and family happiness. It is to be hoped that this application of industrial-efficiency phraseology to love will not seem vulgar. If it does, we must plead that the cost-price to society of love-failure is now beginning to be reckoned in terms of the public money required for repairing the social consequences of broken homes; and that individual psychic disabilities, like physical ones, represent problems with which society in its own interest must increasingly deal: a man and woman who are failures in love are frequently, together with their children, 'on the county' just as much as if they were cripples being supported in institutions. Modern society has found itself obliged to minimize, by a variety of protective measures, the creation of physical helplessness; and quite as surely it has to turn its attention to measures which will diminish the number of psychic cripples, of men and women incapable of those love-emotions which are requisite for stable family relationships. As for the neurotic individuals, their very suffering testifies to their wish for psychic health; their desperate misadventures, their idealistic over-compensations to ensure self-respect, and their rash commitments to adult responsibilities too heavy for them to bear, are indicative of the mental conflicts in which they are endlessly engaged. They are neurotic because they are striving, in inadequate ways, to achieve psychic health. If they did not struggle—(the feeble-minded do not struggle)—they would not be neurotic.

§ 4. The Need of a Path of Knowledge Toward Psychic Health

There may be very real social values in the propensity to take the cosmos into one's ego. The intellectual or the artist may fight out his internal battles in theories or fantasies which involve the destinies of the world; and it does not detract from the aesthetic value of his theories or his poems if we discover from his biography after his death that he had to invoke the protection of a vision of freedom for all mankind from hateful laws, and thus implicate the whole human race in his domestic problem, in order to feel free to make illicit love to his favorite pupil or the red-headed girl next door. It is a tribute also, no doubt, to the sensitiveness of his conscience that he could not simply make love to her, but had first to assure himself of the sociological correctness of the proceeding and secure the blessings of the Pagan Past or the Utopian Future—of everybody, as it were, except his wife—upon their embraces. It may be a somewhat comic procedure, but it is less cowardly-convenient than gratifying his wish on the one hand and morally repudiating it on the other by the 'split-personality' device. It is decidedly less morbid than attributing to the young lady frightfully sinful designs upon his own Galahad-like self, by the mechanism of 'projection'. Identification of his own unhappy predicament with that of others of the world about him may make him a poet, one of

> "those to whom the miseries of the world
> Are misery, and will not let them rest."

But, though all this may be so important to the world that the mere solution of their personal problems does not matter, though we should upon due consideration be content to let them 'learn in suffering what they teach in song', the fact remains that in conducing to the world's education or delight they have not solved their own personal problems. And in young people who are not destined to be artists, where there is no future poem or symphony or painting or novel to throw into the balance, this solution of personal problems becomes a major concern affecting their education, their jobs, their capacities for good citizenship, perhaps their ultimate sanity and certainly their happiness in love and marriage. For at least all but those with the artist's profound resources it is true that "life is not made richer by these emotional conflicts. Only those can think so", says Dr. Frankwood E. Williams, "who love to hug their troubles to themselves in sweet melancholy. Moral stature is not increased thereby; rather it is stunted, or warped, or twisted. Strong prejudices, unreasonable likes and dislikes, loves and hates, gusts of blind emotions that surge through us at critical moments and upset our carefully thought-out judgments and plans of conduct—these are the rewards of our early blind combats." By these unsolved conflicts, says Dr. Williams, "something is made, surely; one may call it character if one likes. So one might make a road by throwing onto a path across a field some sand and cinders, ashes and garbage—in fifteen years it will be something; one may call it a road if one likes."

No, it is not so likely that they will be 'cradled into poetry by wrong'. "Probably", says Dr. Williams, "the greatest number of these children, left alone to devise methods of warding off inroads upon their personalities, will curl up within themselves and thenceforth look out timidly upon the world. They will drift into quietly rebellious, dispirited, unhappy mediocrity—and a mediocrity that is man-made, not god-made; a mediocrity that is not expressive of any inherent lack of capacity * * *. Excellent intellects there will be among them, but intellects that cannot be freely used because of the imposed emotional handicaps. Among this group, too, there will be those who will meet similar problems with an opposite type of reaction; instead of timidity, with boldness. But a boldness that is not courage but is fear. Fifteen years from now they will be the 'hard-boiled', and become the bullies in the market place, or on court benches * * *." Among them will also be the delinquents, some of whose careers have been considered earlier. There will be others who, starting out hopefully, will not "long remain efficient in the home, the shop and the office. It is odd, too, because they had been told not to worry about things, to control their tempers, always to be cheerful and to smile in spite of everything, to be brave and courageous and to believe in success and to keep themselves pure." They will fail in life because they are following the examples set for them by their parents, who, along with all these fine words, have really been teaching them the trick of "suffering (and making others suffer) and failing in their responsibilities (and hindering or causing others to fail through carrying more than their load)"—the whole bag of neurotic tricks, including "hysteria, neurasthenia, 'nervous prostration', morbid fears and anxieties, nervous stomachs, headaches and backaches and a variety of other 'nervous' aches"—by which adult life may be avoided without any self-reproach.

Yet frequently enough the slightest expert help serves to set them upon the right path. We will later note the organized social efforts to provide such help, in kindergartens, public and private schools, colleges, shops and offices. Here we will note the character of the help given. It goes hand in hand with the effort to promote physical health, by curing and preventing disease and removing or mitigating physical handicaps; and with the other effort, all too inadequate in our transition era, to mitigate the effects of harsh and inequitable economic arrangements, by securing to children opportunities of education and work beyond that which their parents may be able to provide, and by lightening when necessary and encouraging people to bear when possible the economic burdens under which they sink by the wayside. Allied with these efforts, and often essentially requisite to their success, is the effort to promote psychic health. Let us first consider and then interpret this effort. The Division on Prevention of Delinquency, of the National Committee for Mental Hygiene, has prepared an outline showing the methods used in child-guidance clinics in the "Psychiatric Examination of a Child", from which we quote:

"In questioning the youngster he [the psychiatrist] * * * should first study the social history and in the light of that explore the child's attitude toward himself and his various reactions to the described family, school and street situations. It is important to know how conscious the child is of his difficulties, what he considers to be his main troubles, where he puts responsibility, how he feels about his special weaknesses and failures, and what needs he is trying to satisfy by his unwholesome behavior. * * *

"One of the most important lines of inquiry is that into family relationships. The social history will have revealed some of the possible sore spots—a divided household involving a conflict in the child's loyalties; a step-parent of whose existence he is jealous or whose discipline he resents; a mother whose death or absence he cannot resign himself to; a parent whose severity makes the child feel that he is not loved; parents of whose bad habits or unethical behavior he may secretly be ashamed; brothers and sisters who are better adjusted or more popular than he; a younger child who has supplanted him; an older child who disciplines him; and so forth. Often there is no definite indication in the history of an emotional involvement, and only the existence of a provocative situation will give the psychiatrist a clue to the central difficulty with which the child is unsuccessfully coping. The psychiatrist, even in the course of examination of these family entanglements, is helping the child to see objectively relationships which he may never have discussed before, and thus giving him a chance to express his feelings and to grasp the point of view of others in the family. The mental examination should reveal to the psychiatrist not only the distortions in the child's point of view which must be corrected, but also the harmful attitudes and exactions of the family which can be regarded as avoidable causes of the child's maladjustments. In this connection the psychiatrist should let the child feel that as much attention will be given to his side of the story as has been given that of the adults.

"School relationships are a second important field of study. Examination should touch all the subjective aspects of the child's school reactions—whether he likes school, when and for what reason he began to dislike it, what subjects he likes or dislikes, whether he likes or dislikes his teachers, whether he feels he is being fairly treated, whether he feels he is responsible for his difficulties or blames his teachers and schoolmates, whether he appreciates his mental abilities or deficiencies, whether he is ashamed of his intellectual disabilities, whether he gets along with other children or feels insignificant, inferior, or an outcast. If his attitudes are later to be corrected, it is important, in going over these points with him, to find out just how much insight he has, on what sensitive spots pressure could readily be relieved, and in what respects he is most accessible to readjustment. An incidental function of the examination is to help him to see his school situation realistically, to get him to face the necessities of school adjustment, and to supply him with some notion of the reasons for demanding this adjustment of him.

"In covering the routine topic of habits the psychiatrist should take the precaution of finding out whether the child has been shamed or frightened by adults anxious to cure him of enuresis, masturbation, or the like. It is worth while, when there is a history of such habits, to present casually to the child a point of view free from moral condemnation and medical threats.

"Inquiries should be made into the child's dream life, as his dreams often give us an insight into his desires, his fears, or his conflicts. The child's fear attitudes are important as well as his other emotional responses, whether of concrete punishing forces or such things as ghosts, and so forth.

"The social history should again furnish the psychiatrist with an economical guide for investigating the child's interests and discovering what satisfactions they give him. This inquiry should throw light on the amount of recreation actually provided for him as well as the substitute satisfactions he has found for the lacks in his environment. His vocational ambitions are a related subject of great importance since they reveal not only the trend of his interests, but his estimate of himself and his possible ignorance of the realities.

"The child's social relationships, his needs, abilities, and aspirations are another important phase of his problem which are best approached in a discussion of the social activities and companions described in the history. Is the child a leader or one of the led; does he feel inferior because he is physically weak, colored, Jewish, Italian (etc.), cowardly, poorly dressed, awkward, redheaded, or retarded? Is he called uncomplimentary nicknames and does he feel 'picked on'? Does he feel unpopular and what makes him feel so? In this concrete connection some of his personality difficulties may be mentioned—his bad temper, failure in team play, love of limelight, habit of teasing or tormenting others—qualities revealed in the history and examination, but of whose existence he may not be aware in terms of their detrimental social effects.

"The child's attitude toward the opposite sex and his sex knowledge and practices should be delicately investigated lest his interest be excited or his possible conflict deepened. Perhaps an approach to sex topics might be made while discussing the child's companions. He is often more willing to repeat 'bad' words he has heard used, or to describe things he has seen others do or heard them tell about, than he is to discuss his own personal experiences. His manner and definiteness in reporting concerning his friends will give some indication as to how far his own knowledge and experience extend. What does the boy think of his sisters, of girls in general, and so forth? When the child has engaged in sex activities or delinquencies, it is important to discover whether he has any emotional conflicts and whether he is aware of the social significance of his behavior.

"In the case of other delinquencies, the psychiatrist's main effort should be directed toward keeping the child's confidence and of not allowing him to connect the psychiatrist with any fears of punishment. The child should realize that confession is not the chief objective of the examiner; that the latter already is fairly well acquainted with the facts and that his principal interest is a sympathetic inquiry into motives and provocations. However, if, according to the social history, the child will not admit his responsibility for the delinquencies under discussion, the psychiatrist should take care not to take any moot points for granted, but to receive information with judicial friendliness. The child's motives in the delinquency, his appreciation of its seriousness, his sense of responsibility, his possible shame or daredevil pride, the physical and psychic needs he satisfies should be the important questions in the mind of the examiner.

"In his summary, the psychiatrist can give briefly a tentative estimate of the child's motivating mechanisms, the degree of his insight, his resources for adjustment, and remediable difficulties in the environment."

Now the generalization which we propose to make upon this account of an expert psychiatric investigation of children may be surprising and will to some readers be rather appalling; it might as well be put forward without preamble, and afterward explained and justified. It is this:

In such a conference as this between the psychiatrist and the child we have a kind of artificial laboratory model of the natural and correct relations between the older and the younger generation, and in particular a picture of the modern educational relations between parent and child, displacing the patriarchal parent-child educational relationship completely.

It is a true model, except that necessarily it artificially concentrates into a few hours the educational relationship which in life would extend naturally over the whole of the growing-up period. It is an exact model, insofar as attitude is concerned—the replacing of threats or coaxing by an objective and realistic friendliness. It is an exaggerated model, in the amount of expert knowledge that it suggests. It is not necessary that a modern parent should know *all* about mental diseases, any more than it is necessary that he should know *all* about physical diseases. But it is desirable that he should know that they exist, just as he knows that diphtheria and typhoid fever exist—and he may reasonably be expected to recognize some of the symptoms of mental ill-health, just as he recognizes those of physical ill-health. The symptoms are as obvious in one sickness as in the other. A parent does not have to be an expert in either physiology or medicine in order to recognize a child's chronic stomach-aches as a symptom pointing to something wrong in its regimen; and no more need a parent be an expert in morbid psychology to recognize that chronic ill-temper, lying, excuses, unpopularity, bragging, self-pity, inattentive day-dreaming, fears, clinging attitudes, and so on, are symptoms of something wrong in his psychic life. We have experts to diagnose and advise and treat both these cases when and if family remedies fail. As a matter of fact these childish traits are not ignored by parents; there is a traditional parental lore concerning their treatment, dating from patriarchal days—only most of it is wrong. Certain childish traits are mistakenly encouraged in accordance with patriarchal lore, and others receive an immense amount of repressive attention in the way of scolding, threatening, whipping, pleading, etc. *It is not true that parents are too busy to deal with these psychic problems; they lie awake nights worrying and weeping about them, they expend an amount of energy in wrong directions sufficient if properly directed to deal with ten times as many children.* It is not so much that they are merely ignorant as that they are too expert in patriarchal methods which do not work under modern conditions. They know an immense amount about bringing up children, and it is practically all useless or mischievous.

The situation is like that of agriculture in patriarchal countries where scientific methods are just being introduced. The peasants know all about farming; have they not the methods handed down from their fathers and grandfathers through the centuries? In Russia they know, for example, that the proper way to save the crops from the ravages of insects is to have the priest lead a procession of the villagers with banners and ikons and holy water through the fields, and repeat the sacred and powerful adjuration of St. Tryphon:

> "Worms and grasshoppers!
> Mice and rats!
> Ants, moles and reptiles!
> Flies and horseflies and hornets!
> And all flying things that wreak destruction. . . .
>
> "I forbid you in the name of the Savior come upon earth to suffer for man.
>
> "I forbid you in the name of the all-seeing cherubim and seraphim who fly around the heavenly throne.

"I forbid you in the name of the angels and the millions of heavenly spirits standing in the glory of God.

"I forbid you to touch any tree, fruitful or unfruitful, or leaf or plant or flower.

"I forbid you to bring any woe upon the fields of these people!"

And the American observer, Albert Rhys Williams, comments: "Surely, if there were any pity or poetry in the soul of a worm, it could not spoil the fields of these poor folks, standing devoutly with bowed heads, trusting in the magic of these words come down through the ages." He discusses the subject with one of the village elders. In America, he says, "we raise crops, not by processions but by plows, deep cutting plows and irrigation and chemical protection against insects". "Quite so," is the conciliating answer; "maybe we ought to do more of that. That is what Fedosiev [the village Communist peasant leader] all the time is telling us. But he talks too much. Besides, he doesn't go to church any more." But, the village elder is asked, does the procession really save the harvest? It used to, he says. "If this fails today, it is because we fail. It is our lack of faith, God punishes us for our sins. Our village has grown indifferent and pleasure-loving."

The same situation exists with regard to medicine in patriarchal countries where modern science is an alien intruder. Ophthalmia has always been very prevalent in Egypt, and early in the last century the English traveler Lane found there the following modes of treatment: "Some, for this purpose, take a piece of dried mud, from the bank of the Nile at or near Boolak, the principal port of Cairo, and, crossing the river, deposit it on the opposite bank, at Imbabeh. This is considered sufficient to effect a cure.—Others, with the same view, hang to the head-dress, over the forehead, or over the diseased eye, a Venetian sequin; but it must be one of a particular description, in which the figures on each side correspond, head to head, and feet to feet." A person afflicted with a sty "goes to any seven women of the name of Fat'meh, in seven different houses, and begs from each of them a morsel of bread: these seven morsels constitute the remedy. * * * Another supposed mode of cure in a case of the same kind is, to bind a piece of cotton on the end of a stick; then to dip it in one of the troughs out of which the dogs drink in the streets of Cairo, and to wipe the eye with it."

These patriarchal practices in agriculture and medicine are magical rites; and much of patriarchal child-training is of precisely the same sort: words and gestures, solemn adjurations and beatings, intended to scare or knock the Devil out of children, and serving (as magical practices do) to relieve the anxieties which they, the parents, feel—giving them respite from their fears and an emotional assurance of the future fulfillment of their wishes—but having no realistic results of the sort expected in the behavior of the children themselves.

There is another respect, however, in which these patriarchal rites do not fail but succeed in their purpose—the fundamental purpose of patriarchal education, which is not to promote the well-being or least of all the happiness of children, but to keep them in a state of emotional subservience. Not long ago it was a respectable parental practice for parents to assure their children that the fairly universal childish habit of masturbation would inevitably result in insanity. They knew better, if they had not entirely forgotten their own childhood. But even when they knew it to be a lie, they regarded it as the proper lie for children to be told. It was not simply a mistake about a scientific fact, but a pseudo-scientific version of the horrible bogeys with which children have always been threatened in patriarchal households. It was a part of the patriarchal method of governing children by fear, of darkening the ways of life for them, so that they would walk fearfully among gibbering fantasms. Patriarchal child-training lore is full of these hobgoblins, intended to frighten children out of their courage, independence, and curiosity about life; intended to make them docile in all things, and particularly in sex.

The learned brothers Grimm, at the beginning of the last century, made a collection of stories told to children which they had collected from the nurseries and firesides of Germany.

Many of these are charming magic-fantasies, which serve now, as of old, the purpose of imaginatively fulfilling the child's wish for power. Some of them, however, betray a didactic purpose of frightening the child into obedience. *The Frog Prince,* for example, is a tale obviously useful in reconciling young girls to their destiny of arranged marriage with a man of their parents' choice. He may seem as repulsive as a frog at first, but he will turn into a handsome young prince after he had slept in her bed for three nights. *The Robber Bridegroom,* in the form in which it comes to us, does not draw the proper patriarchal moral, since it is the man of the father's choice who turns out to be a horrible ogre; and the girl's repulsion against her affianced bridegroom is justified. Possibly it was originally a warning to girls against falling in love with men of their own choice, and going to visit them without parental permission. However this may be, see what happened to the miller's daughter! The affianced bridegroom is not at home, but an old woman is there in the cellar, and says: "Ah, you poor child, what a place for you to come to! This is a murderers' den. You think yourself a promised bride, and that your marriage will soon take place, but it is with death that you will keep your marriage feast. Look, do you see that large cauldron of water which I am obliged to keep on the fire! As soon as they have you in their power they will kill you without mercy, and cook and eat you, for they are eaters of men." Hidden behind a cask in the cellar, the girl waits. "The godless crew returned, dragging another young girl along with them. They were all drunk, and paid no heed to her cries and lamentations. They gave her wine to drink, three glasses full, one of white wine, one of red, and one of yellow, and with that her heart gave way and she died. Then they tore off her dainty clothing, laid her on a table, and cut her beautiful body into pieces, and sprinkled salt upon it." If these sadistic details seem unduly gruesome, reflect that they are quoted from a book still put unedited into the hands of children, since what was good for children in patriarchal times is presumably still good for our children. It served, however, in patriarchal times, or so we may conjecture, as a warning to child-brides; what purpose it serves now we may leave the publishers to explain. "The poor betrothed girl crouched trembling and shuddering behind the cask, for she saw what a terrible fate had been intended for her by the robbers. One of them now noticed a gold ring still remaining on the little finger of the murdered girl, and as he could not draw it off easily, he took a hatchet and cut off the finger; but the finger sprang into the air, and fell behind the cask into the lap of the girl who was hiding there. The robber took a light and began looking for it, but he could not find it. 'Have you looked behind the large cask,' said one of the others." So near was the poor girl to death before her escape. With this we may leave the fear-ridden story-lore of patriarchal childhood, which characteristically presents sex to the young imagination as a realm full of fiends and devils, incubi and succubi, furies and harpies, gnomes and trolls, sirens and satyrs, 'ghoolies and ghoosties, and things that go bump in the night', from which good children learn to pray, 'Lord, deliver us!'

The aim of scientific agriculture does not rest content with the possession of modern knowledge by an expert few—it envisages a time when all farmers will know how to raise crops; and it does not hesitate to thrust upon them strange new doctrines of spraying against insects and of encouragement of the nitrogen-fixing bacteria of the soil. The aim of scientific medicine is not merely to cure diseases after they have been ignorantly incurred, but it is ultimately to prevent disease by teaching people how to keep well; and it does not hesitate to thrust upon the ignorant and the careless strange doctrines of invisible germs and inoculation by the very diseases which are thus sought to be prevented. Both sciences look forward necessarily to a general public acceptance, understanding and use of modern scientific knowledge, which will leave the expert in the background to solve new questions as they arise and give advice at points where the best ordinary lay knowledge and practice may be inadequate. In the meantime the public is being taught; and the unflinching assumption of science is that the public can learn. However slowly, people will eventually displace their elaborate but useless or mischievous patriarchal lore with the no-more-elaborate but useful lore of modern science. Patriarchal agriculture, with its inevitable periods of famine, will not serve the purposes of our times. The patriarchal mode of dealing with disease, which brings its inevitable plagues and epidemics, will not serve the purposes of modern times. And so with patriarchal child-training lore. The aim of modern psychology is to keep people mentally healthy, and since that process must needs begin in childhood it assumes that parents can learn how to bring up children. If we are to check the flood of neurotic individuals who are unable to face the difficulties of life except on terms ranging finally from insanity and crime down to timidity and dependence, parents must learn their job.

In the light of this, let us return to the expert 'psychiatric examination of a child' and see whether the knowledge of the child's situation there intensively gained by the psychiatrist in a few hours is such as could not be gained by ordinary intelligent parents in the daily association of normal family life:

"OUTLINE FOR THE PSYCHIATRIC EXAMINATION OF A CHILD

"*Introductory statement:*

"The chief purpose of the psychiatric study is to obtain as intimate an understanding as possible of the child's own thoughts and feelings about himself and the various situations with which he is confronted. The aim should be to *grasp his point of view, to understand his attitudes.* The cues for discussion should be obtained from the social history, and the problems entered into in a friendly and sympathetic manner, with no indication of reproof. Embarrassment or reticence concerning any subject should be met by a matter-of-fact tone and manner on the part of the examiner. The following suggestions *will serve as a guide* for further questioning and study.

"*Play life and other interests:*

"Does he prefer to play by himself or with other children?

"What type of play—active or passive games? Give details.

"What other interests has he in addition to those usually considered play?

"Is he a leader among his playmates?

"Does he earn any money and what does he do with it?

"What work does he do at home?

"*Dream life:*

"Of what does he dream? Tell dreams in detail, especially of home, school, fear, or other nature?

"Does his dream life suggest dominance by emotional conflict or disturbance of any kind?

"Does he daydream? What about? Any nightmares or sleep walking?

"*Fears and emotional conflicts:*

"Of what things is he afraid? Describe in detail origin, character, etc.

"What is his attitude toward sex matters? Any repressions or conflicts associated with this field?

"Are there indications of any feeling of inferiority with compensating mechanisms?

"Attitude towards situations or persons, and enuresis, masturbation, stuttering, etc., if present?

"Attitude toward body:

"Any complaints? What? How long?

"Ever faint or feel dizzy?

"What is his attitude or interests towards his bodily functions and personal hygiene?

"What are his habits in eating, sleeping, etc.?

"Attitude toward school:

"Does he believe that he gets along well or poorly in school and why?

"Does this compare with the reports from the teacher?

"Does he like school? If not, why?

"What is his feeling toward his teachers? Classmates?

"What are his scholastic ambitions?

"Attitude toward companions:

"Is he a 'good scrapper'? How does he get along with companions?

"Does he get angry with them? Does he feel that they tease him too much?

"What does he think about his companions—that they are good or bad?

"Has he learned bad words or bad habits from them?

"Does he prefer companions of the same or opposite sex, and why?

"What special chums? What do they talk about?

"Attitude toward family situation:

"Is he punished or teased much at home? Does he deserve it?

"Does he like best his father or mother and why? Who is his favorite in family and why?

"Does he feel that he or another child is the favorite?

"What are his feelings towards his brothers and sisters?

"Are there other relatives whom he particularly likes or dislikes?

"Attitude toward misconduct or bad habits:

"What has he to say about his difficulties?

"Try to get him to work out the beginnings of his offenses,

habits, etc., and give details as to his first experiences in lying, stealing, or sex experiences.

"Is there anything in his life which serves to explain his bad conduct?

"Is he defensive, honest, etc.?

"*Attitude during interview:*

"What special attitude or reactions during examinations?

"Attitude toward examiner?

"Is he self-conscious, ill at ease, restless, flighty?

"Does he flush easily?

"Is he boastful, 'smart Alec,' etc.?

"Is he indifferent or apathetic?

"Does he enter into the spirit of the occasion?

"*Note:*

"Certain cases will call for special inquiry into memory fields, orientation, etc., especially when related to organic processes and also where the question of consciousness is involved.

"Peculiar ideas, delusional trends, phobias, and other unusual manifestations found as a result of social history or observation should be carefully followed up."

Such knowledge of a child as this, it will be perceived, *can readily be gained by any intelligent parent, without any special diversion of energies from the other tasks of ordinary life;* all that is required is the contact afforded by family association—and the cultivation of a friendly objectivity which will make the child trust his parents instead of hiding his emotional life from them. It is this latter maxim which is difficult for patriarchally trained parents to construe aright; for it does not mean—as some have wishfully thought it meant—that they are to pry and snoop into a child's emotions. It does *not* mean that 'mother is your best friend—tell everything to mother!' It does not mean that mother is to lie awake and wait for her little boy of 18 or 22 to come home, and make him sit on her bedside and tell her everything that happened at the party, and what girl's hand he held, if any. That is only a pseudo-modern version of the old patriarchal trick of keeping children from growing up, of infantilizing and homosexualizing them.

So that, beyond the details of modern child-training—which can be twisted to the most preposterous and poisonous uses, and frequently are—we must look to the purpose of this training. It is to help children grow up to emotional independence of their parents, to grow up to the full capacities of heterosexual love.

If this modern child-training is not to be misconceived and misused, emphasis has to be put upon these two things, which are the negative and positive aspects of the same thing—emancipation from the home, and the achievement of heterosexuality. This is the touchstone by which it may be determined whether a child, an adolescent (or even as things are, an adult—even a husband, a wife, a parent!) is growing up: is he—or she—becoming more emancipated from the parental home? is he—or she—becoming more fully (and not in pseudomorphic exaggerated pretense) heterosexual? This is the test of the home, and of parents: do they encourage children toward independence of parental love and care, by enabling them to dispense with it gradually and in due order? do they encourage children to develop their full capacities for heterosexual love?

The choice is plain. The old militaristic-homosexual education, however disguised in polite or idealistic phraseology, still grinds out young people more fitted (by sexual regression into infantilism) for irresponsible 'love' without marriage and for dutiful marriage without love than for modern adult relationships. If we are to emerge from the consequent welter of neuroticism, *we must accept the full and passionate love of the other sex as the normal goal of youth* and use the educational period of adolescence as a normal approach to mating.

CHAPTER XIII

Adolescence and Heterosexuality

§ 1. Heterosexual Development in Adolescence

The idea of full heterosexuality, or the complete capacity for the love of the other sex, as requiring some years after puberty for its attainment, is one which contradicts some patriarchal assumptions and requires to be justified at some length.

We are accustomed to speak of boys and girls of 15, 16, 17 and even later as children; but in part this nomenclature represents an effort to *keep* them children—to forget, and to induce them to forget, as it were, the inconvenient fact of their biologically adult capacity for begetting and bearing children of their own. Underneath our formal attitude, which treats these biological capacities as if they were in early adolescence non-existent, there lurks a very real fear of these biological capacities. That is, the older generation is afraid that the boys and girls will produce babies before they are able to support them. As this burden would have to be borne by the older generation, it is thought necessary to repress the heterosexual impulses until a later age when these young people are in a position to assume the social burden of parenthood themselves.

The repression of heterosexual impulses, however, cannot—except in its extremest forms, by bringing about a homosexual aversion from the other sex—prevent the sexual act from occurring: what this repression of heterosexuality does is to prevent the sexual act from having its normal emotional significance as a part of the sexual cycle that leads from courtship to love-choice, mating, parenthood and family life. Discouragement of the heterosexual impulses cannot (except as noted above, by creating homosexual aversion) destroy the physical urge toward coition; all that repression can do, and what it does do, is to destroy the normal sexual emotions which provide a correct biological setting for the sexual act, by preliminary search for a mate, and by the tests and delays of courtship. The normal human sexual impulses in their entirety do not lead females to have casual sexual intercourse with any attractive male at the drop of a hat, nor lead a male to have casual sexual intercourse with every attractive female as chance may offer. This behavior represents the repression of the hetero-sexual impulses toward courtship and love-choice, toward mate-hood and family life, leaving only the coition-impulse divested of all its normal emotional significance and free to operate out of its setting. The repression of heterosexual impulses, therefore, is no effective guarantee against sexual intercourse, but it is a pretty good guarantee that when it does occur it will occur without courtship and love choice, and that it will occur quite irrelevantly of opportunity for matehood and family life. Repression does not repress sexual intercourse, it represses only the sense of sexual responsibility. Repression therefore incidentally promotes premature, accidental, irresponsible and illegitimate parenthood.

This is not a paradox; it is one of the most soundly established conclusions of modern psychological science. Its validity may be illustrated by reference to the facts of illegitimacy. Some of the facts of illegitimacy belong to another category, representing as they do the old rural and pagan custom of sexual betrothal (see pp. 145-147 above) and of not marrying until after children are born and family life established; and other facts of illegitimacy represent a conflict of mores in which men trained in patriarchal irresponsibility take advantage of this pagan custom by deceit or desertion. Excluding these, we find that illegitimacy cases involve invariably the psychological factor of deficient heterosexuality.

In a very large group of illegitimate mothers, and of illegitimate fathers so far as these have been found and studied, the deficiency in heterosexuality is one of the aspects of feeblemindedness; inherent mental incapacity has made it impossible for them to grow up emotionally, and the exercise of their physically adult sexual functions on an infantile emotional level has casually brought about a parenthood the emotional responsibilities of which they are of course unable to sustain.

In a smaller but by no means inconsiderable group of girls, a socially inculcated ignorance of sex, sometimes as to its very facts, and quite generally as to its significance, has resulted in an emotionally childish complaisance with the sexual demands of men out of desire for attention and companionship, out of the wish to please, or out of the fear of displeasing, say an employer, or any other male person who is in a position to punish them or give them favors—not excluding immediate male relatives. These girls can grow up emotionally. They are capable of learning and living up to their immediate maternal responsibilities and at a later age (if they are not wrecked in the meantime by the social consequences or punishments of illegitimacy) they are capable of healthy courtship, love-choice and matehood. With this group of girls may be classed a similar group of boys and young men, who, if less technically ignorant than the girls of the facts of sex, are as much surprised as the girls or even more so at the intrusion of the reality of a baby into the play-world of sex; but who are capable of assuming or learning the emotional responsibilities of parenthood, and, if there is any basis for it in the situation, of construing the casual sexual adventure as a mode of courtship and accepting the girl as a wife and mate. To distinguish illegitimate parents of this group from that of the first and third groups is one of the practical tasks of the social agencies which deal with illegitimacy cases.

The third group of illegitimate parents is a large one. It includes boys psychically attuned to quasi-homosexual gang friendships, to whom sexual relations with girls are no more than an exploit to boast about to the other fellows, like jumping freight trains or stealing; and girls of such emotional immaturity that they are willing to accept companionship with boys upon these terms, usually under the influence of a quasi-homosexual crush on a girl friend who must be followed and emulated in everything. With regard to both boys and girls, these irresponsible physical relations with the other sex, unaccompanied by personal emotions, not led up to by comradeship and courtship, and committing them to no emotional responsibilities, it is clear—though this may be to some a hard saying—that these are mere substitutes for the homosexual relationships which are unconsciously desired. They are not except in physical form heterosexual; they take their unbiological character of irresponsibility from their psychological content of unconscious homosexuality. Not merely does the illegitimate father usually despise his casual partner, but she frequently despises him, and wishes never to see him again. This then, is obviously not heterosexual passion but a regression to an infantile-homosexual level of emotion.

Thus, contrary to the ordinary supposition, society is not protected against the burdens of premature, accidental, irresponsible and illegitimate children by the social repression of heterosexual passion. It is, rather, a deficiency of the normal beginnings of heterosexual passion in young people which leads them to become parents at an age when or under circumstances such that they are incapable of assuming the economic burden of parenthood.

If this is true, then it would seem that the converse must be true—that the normal growth of heterosexual passion in young people is an insurance against illegitimate or premature parenthood. Preposterous as this would appear to the fear-ridden patriarchal mind, it also is true. The normal development of genuine love between young people of opposite sex is accompanied by a development of emotional attitudes of responsibility which eliminate at once the recklessness and indifference which are responsible for most of the illegitimacy problem. In love, as distinguished from childish and quasi-homosexual exploit, curiosity and sport, sexual relations are a serious matter, not to be entered into lightly and casually.

Our reproductive instincts have their own methods of securing nurture for the child that is to be born. These instincts normally, if permitted to do so, protect the future child from neglect by an elaborate series of compulsions. One of these instinctive compulsions brings about a raising of the threshold to sexual intimacy, at the same time that desire for sexual intimacy is heightened by the glandular processes of puberty. That is to say, the normal sexuality of the adolescent has first of all its aspect of sexual shyness. It is not the artificial quasi-homosexual hostility and contempt brought about by ignorance, fear and sex-segregation. It is a shyness which subserves the selective purposes of the reproductive instincts by diffusing sexual emotions through the whole field of social relations which they are destined to occupy in adult matehood, thus strengthening the power of the sexual bond. Thus instead of the boy and girl being brought together for a brief, physically inept and emotionally inconsequent sexual act, they are brought together in play and friendship and the beginnings of love.

A psychologically correct though perhaps verbally over-sentimentalized description of this sexual shyness of adolescence is given by the poet Stevenson; in spite of some Victorian touches in the style of utterance—and of suggestions of a special sex-consciousness about female legs, to the exhibition of which youth is now accustomed—the account remains essentially true for our so-called 'flappers' and 'sheiks':

"The brooding boy, the sighing maid,
Wholly fain and half afraid,
Now meet along the hazel'd brook
To pass and linger, pause and look.

"A year ago, and blithely paired,
Their rough-and-tumble play they shared;
They kissed and quarrelled, laughed and cried,
A year ago at Eastertide.

"With bursting heart, with fiery face,
She strove against him in the race;
He unabashed her garter saw,
That now would touch her skirts with awe.

"Now by the stile ablaze she stops,
And his demurer eyes he drops;
Now they exchange averted sighs
Or stand and marry silent eyes."

As to what follows we should perhaps nowadays prefer a more jocose or patronizing account, such as is admirably given in Booth Tarkington's stories of young Penrod; but if Penrod could speak for himself, he would speak at least in certain moods with the tongue of the Victorian poet:

"And he to her a hero is
And sweeter she than primroses;
Their common silence dearer far
Than nightingale or mavis are.

"Now when they sever wedded hands,
Joy trembles in their bosom-strands,
And lovely laughter leaps and falls
Upon their lips in madrigals."

Our point is that shyness is a function of sex, with an important biological purpose. Our argument is that a healthy and unrepressed adolescent sexuality carries this protective shyness with it. The word 'protective' here should not be misunderstood; the sexual instincts are not protecting maidenly and boyish 'purity,' they are protecting the child that is to be born, by a selective process which is to test the emotional capacity for matehood of each of these individuals with a number of other individuals, and which now in its early stages is cultivating that capacity by symbolic tests which are an emotional education.

The instincts, of whose prevision for the care of the next generation we have heard such wonders in the kingdom of the wasps, need not astonish us if in human beings they work with similar prevision through emotional media; nor, after marvelling at the uncanny wisdom of instinctive sexual behavior among insects, should we attribute only the most preposterous recklessness and folly to our human sexual instincts.

The human sexual instincts may be said to have an advanced and a reserve line of operation. The advanced line takes account of the need for prolonged nurture of the human infant, and uses the delays and tensions of courtship to effect a selection of mates and to cultivate in them an emotional fixation upon each other which will serve the purposes of prolonged parental care. When this advanced line of instinctive operation is destroyed, as it is in individual lives through the pressure of hunger or danger, and in large groups through social cataclysms such as famine and war—when these refinements of biological purpose can find no emotional field in which to work—then the reproductive instinct falls back upon its reserve line of operation, its unshakable Hindenburg line. Then it bids life be renewed without care of what may happen. Then it depends upon mere numbers, as down in its lowest scale of activity, where multitudes are blindly spawned to die by the millions to maintain the species-life.

In idiots and imbeciles there is no higher emotional field, and in the feeble-minded but a slight one, through which these advanced instinctive purposes of child-nurture could operate. In all other adult human beings there is potentially such a field of personal and responsible sexual emotions, though the full development and exercise of these emotions is sometimes systematically interfered with: in prehistoric life, as we have seen, by acute food-anxieties which spasmodically repressed the sexual emotions to an infantile and impersonal (and, apparently, if we may judge by the survivals in the later witchcraft cult, polymorphous-perverse and sadistic) level at which they were used for magical anxiety-relief purposes; and in the patriarchal régime by chronic property-anxieties which habitually repressed them to an infantile and homosexual level at which they could be used for the purposes of family security. Modern machinery, by setting mankind free to the extent that it has from these psychically devastating anxieties, enlarges correspondingly the extent to which these adult sexual impulses of delay and choice can be given general social encouragement in their development and expression.

The beginnings of adult sexuality in adolescent shyness is marked not only in civilized lands but in savage cultures in which there is customarily no long delay before the sexual life is overtly begun. Early in Samoan adolescence, says Margaret Mead, "Girls have lost all their nonchalance. They giggle, blush, bridle, run away. Boys become shy, embarrased, taciturn, and avoid the society of girls in the daytime and on the brilliant moonlit nights for which they accuse the girls of having an exhibitionistic preference."

This early adolescent sexuality does not appear in itself to call for expression in the sexual act; let alone, as it is by intelligent modern parents in Western civilization, this early adolescent sexuality moves toward its own ends through a characteristic course of development. The adolescent boy and girl have entered upon a new world, in which it is some time before they can be at ease. What was before puberty an interest scarcely differentiated from and not outranking their affectionate friendships with companions of their own sex, becomes now a troubled but fascinating series of contacts with a special emotional quality of their own. Their new heterosexual companionships are often at first quite clumsy and self-conscious on both sides, because of the access of contradictory feelings—the heightened physical attraction felt to members of the other sex, and the strange new shyness in their presence. A kind of extravagant showing off may alternate with periods of tongue-tied misery.

The truth is that they are at this point still as much afraid of as attracted to each other; this is the case for a very definite reason—that their love-capacity has not yet become sufficiently detached from the family group, from the parents and the older persons of the opposite sex who are the parental surrogates. If these young people are to begin overtly sexual relationships at this stage, it will most likely not be with each other at all but with older men and women who find opportunities for easy conquests in the unformed and still half-filial love-psychology of these youngsters. So it is in Samoa, where in spite of social encouragement the boys are timid in their courtship, requiring elaborate John-Aldenish go-between assistance from boon companions, and where "more frequently still an older man, a widower or a divorced man, will be a girl's first lover. * * * The older man is neither shy nor frightened". In Samoa, as in Western civilization, "the amorous excursions of the older men among the young girls of the village", and the seduction of young boys by older women, are socially reprobated: "But both of these are exceedingly frequent occurrences".

That is to say, this shy adolescent sexuality does not of itself require expression in the sexual act. Outside forces are required. In patriachal life, throughout the Mediterranean-Oriental civilizations, girls at this early adolescent age were hustled into marriage with middle-aged strangers, or put to bed with frightened boy husbands while the wedding-guests got merrily drunk and shouted jesting encouragements to them through the bed-curtains.

The Renaissance poet Herrick, whose mind was steeped in classical sex-idealism, wrote an 'epithalamie' to Sir Thomas Southwell and his Ladie, in which the old patriarchal consolations and encouragements are administered to "the bashfull Bride", whose sexual immaturity and docility are alike taken for granted, and to the Bridegroom, who obviously needs all the encouragement he can get:

"O *Venus*! thou, to whom 'tis known
The best way how to loose the Zone
Of Virgins! Tell the Maid,
She need not be afraid:
And bid the youth apply
Close kisses, if she cry:
And charge, he not forbears
Her, though she wooe with teares."

In Western civilization, as in Samoa, the immature sexuality of early adolescence is frequently taken advantage of by older men and women, who exploit the as yet unbroken filial pattern of affectionate obedience for their own purposes of pleasure and to give themselves the egoistic satisfactions of conquest not so easily to be had from sexually mature persons. Many of Casanova's sexual exploits fall into this category of pseudo-paternal exploitation of little girls. These exploits might not even have required a Casanova—in view of such incidents as those related by Commenge, of the little girl of 14 who "sacrificed her virginity at a fair in return for a glass of beer", and of "another girl of the same age, at a local fête, [who] wishing to go round on the hobby-horse, spontaneously offered herself to the man directing the machinery for the pleasure of a ride".

Again, in some social milieus of Western civilization, as in Samoa, the youthful mores, the current standards of masculine enterprise and feminine attractiveness, may require that the sexual act be performed, if only to boast about, if only to prevent a feeling of inferiority to others in the same age class. Little 12-year-old Douglas, one of the juvenile-delinquency cases back in Chapter X, had become neurotic out of a sense of inferiority to the other boys at school, because he thought they all had sexual relations with the girls; he had taken to stealing, as a substitute form of manliness. Others of these juvenile cases illustrate the social pressure of parental examples of illicit sexuality; and still others the social pressure of poverty, which may leave sexual activity as the only adolescent resource in the desperate quest for affection, sympathy, or amusement.

Even so, adolescent sexual shyness is hard to break down, and in Western civilization it frequently requires the assistance of alcohol. In degraded slum environments the sexual initiation of the young girl is frequently recorded as accomplished by rape as a matter of course, the preliminary wooing consisting of a blow from the fist in the stomach to knock her helpless. In politer environments there is frequently a prolonged neurotic conflict in a boy's mind before he can overcome sexual shyness. Moral literature has recorded many examples of heroic struggle with sexual temptation, but it has neglected the field of those heroic struggles undergone by the shy youth before he can do what he believes to be his duty, and reassure himself as to his 'manliness', for instance in visiting a house of prostitution; or, now that that is less fashionable, in effecting a sexual relationship with his girl-friend. The girl-friend, also, may be heroically doing what she feels the Younger Generation expects of a modern girl.

Stendhal has given us an admirable account of such an incident in an 1830 setting—an incident, that is to say, in which sex ministers to adolescent neurotic egotism. Mlle. Mathilde de la Mole has granted a rendezvous in her bedchamber to Julian Sorel, her father's secretary. "Julien was in a quandary; he knew not what to say or how to behave; he did not feel the least particle of love. In his embarrassment he decided that his best course was to be enterprising, and offered to salute the fair Mathilde's lips.

"'For shame!' she said, pushing him away.

"Well pleased with his repulse, he hastened to make a survey of his surroundings." They talk, the girl making "an ineffectual attempt to impart to her words an easy conversational tone. * * * Then their embarrassment returned and settled on them again, deep and painful on either side." Julien at last "plucked up courage and ventured to clasp to his bosom the beautiful girl", and "encountered no resistance worth mentioning. * * * They discussed plans for meeting in the future." The girl miserably wishes he were not there. " 'I must say something to him, however,' she finally told herself; 'it is expected of me; every girl converses with her lover.' * * * But never were matters of such a tender nature discussed in such a tone of freezing politeness. Up to that point the temperature of the assignation was below zero. It was enough to make one loathe the very name of love." After a long period of irresolution, which "might have appeared to a superficial observer the result of the most deep-seated hatred"—so stubborn was the conflict between her feelings and her determined will—"Mathilde yielded and became his mistress. But, if the truth must be told, her transports were not genuine. Passionate love was not there, only its counterfeit presentment.

"Mlle. de la Mole believed that she was fulfilling a duty toward herself and her lover."

Malinowski had described in detail the magic of love and beauty employed in the Trobriand Islands, the spells which promise "so to increase personal attractiveness that the performer may become erotically irresistible to some one member of the opposite sex". That such magic is being made is always known by the person who is to be charmed, and so it is almost invariably effective. In Western civilization, in certain social milieus, there are, or used to be, traditional pieces of secret (and wholly false) information, passed down in all good faith from an older to a younger age-group of adolescent boys, to the effect that certain popular non-alcoholic drinks, of specific flavors, or certain specific kinds of candy, are aphrodisiacs; and shy youths neurotically obsessed with the necessity of proving their manhood by effecting an actual sexual relationship, have with deep Machiavellian cunning persuaded their girl-friends to drink such a potion; and, thus emboldened by the promise of success afforded by that extraneous aid, have proceeded to make sexual advances, which, so the account always runs, are crowned with success. Other accounts, from women, dovetail interestingly into these masculine accounts —being to the effect that this boys' secret was widely known among girls also; that it was sometimes regarded by them as an irresistible masculine maneuver, since it was impossible for a girl to decline such a supposedly harmless drink without betraying the possession of knowledge that no nice girl should have (and the offer might only be intended as a test of their niceness); but that the love-potion, when helplessly imbibed in this predicament, gave them the comforting assurance that whatever subsequently happened woud not be their fault.

However it may be in the Trobriand Islands, it seems clear that heterosexual passion does not require the reassurance which the use of supposedly irresistible aphrodisiacs may offer, and that these usages among civilized adolescents are not merely for the purpose of overcoming social inhibitions but for the purpose of bolstering up a neurotic and egotistic determination to a point where it can overcome sexual shyness. The imaginary aphrodisiac is required, not to assist the sexual impulses, but to conquer them—the natural sexual impulses, that is to say, toward delay, tension and love-choice.

We have seen adolescent sexuality pushed into pseudo-adult sexual acts which are emotionally barren of significance (save as they may have egotistic significance)—pushed by a variety of outside social influences ranging from pride to poverty, from a glass of beer or a ride on the merry-go-round to a blow of the fist, from the sanctities of patriarchal marriage to the campaigns of a Casanova, from the desperate need of sympathy, of companionship, of amusement, from fear, from obedience, from custom, from duty, from piety, from pity, from everything except sexual passion.

So let us go back to sexual passion, or to its normal adolescent beginnings, and see how it expresses itself in civilized life when let alone. We left these boys and girls at the giggling stage, profoundly allured by and strangely afraid of each other. Striving earnestly to conceal their helplessness, they succeed in finding things to talk about and to do in each other's company, so that they gain gradually the reassurance of familiar friendships. It is as friendships that they prefer to construe these relationships, though into them there come hints of new and unknown depths of emotion, like sudden breaths of overpowering fragrance—premonitory gusts of sweetness, awe, melancholy, sadness, tragedy. They seem to be living instruments upon which Life is beginning to play a strange new music. For a while very disturbing, these emotions presently become fascinating to them, and their experimental cultivation becomes a secret and absorbing preoccupation. They discover, too, the emotional power which they possess over the other sex, and exercise it with what might seem callousness or cruelty except that their victims are usually playing the same game. They are finding out what they are like—a highly interesting and very instructive but still very egotistic occupation. It would appear that they are still far from the mating crisis. It would appear that they have still a considerable way to go before they reach that goal.

All this intense experimental exploration of the rich field of emotional response to and power over the other sex goes on as a kind of second or inward life, sheltered behind the outer one of study, play, and family existence. These other sides of life have much in them to minister to their animal and social wants, their pride, their appetite for affection, so that there is no emotional need for them, as there may very well be for those whose lives are more barren or embittered, to seek to realize at once upon the mysterious promises of sex by hurrying into adult sexual activities. Their activities are, however, in an emotional sense, deeply sexual all the time. It has been an egotistic and experimental sexuality, for the most part; yet it has not been conducted without learning a great many lessons in sexual tact and sexual adjustment, nor without unconsciously making and storing up a great many sexual observations and judgments. At the same time, the affectional bonds which have held them to the home have been insensibly relaxed day by day. They are no longer centered emotionally in the parent-ruled realm. Their admiration for other older people, their hero-worship of this or that man or woman in the adult world, wanes too. They are setting free from its infantile moorings their emotional capacity for love. In the very midst of what was perhaps intended as another egotistic triumph, the gaining of the attention of some attractive fellow-adolescent of the other sex, they find themselves hard hit by something unexpectedly painful and humbling, something very 'real', which is first love.

We need not pursue these adolescent love-experiences in detail. They are beautiful and tragic from within, though from without they may seem absurd or comic in their exaggeration of emotion and in their quick recoveries and abrupt shifts. As Friar Lawrence said to Romeo:

> "Holy St. Francis! what a change is here;
> Is Rosaline, whom thou didst love so dear,
> So soon forsaken? Young men's love then lies
> Not truly in their hearts, but in their eyes.
> Jesu Maria! what a deal of brine
> Hath washed thy sallow cheeks for Rosaline;
> How much salt water thrown away in waste,
> To season love, that of it doth not taste!
> The sun not yet thy sighs from heaven clears,
> Thy old groans ring yet in my ancient ears;
> Lo! here upon thy cheek the stain doth sit
> Of an old tear that is not washed off yet.
> If e'er thou wast thyself and these woes thine,
> Thou and these woes were all for Rosaline:
> And art thou changed?"

But more important than the comic aspect which these experiences may have from the outside is the instinctive sexual purpose which they serve, the purpose to which they contribute by their beauty and what seems for the time their tragedy, by enriching and bracing the emotions for what is presently to be their test. The sexual instinct has been moving along its own slow and circuitous route toward mature love-choice, gathering emotional strength and emotional wisdom along its path. It is moving by these stages of its own toward the sexual act, but toward a sexual act which will be a ratification of a mutual love-choice, and not an accident or an experiment.

Some aspects, however, of this process, before it reaches or seems to reach its goal, require comment. From an early stage of adolescence every social contact in which a boy and a girl who are experimentally interested in each other do things together, whether it is making candy in the kitchen or driving in a car or sailing a boat together, every mutually shared activity, becomes secretly for each a symbol of the deeper sharing of life together in marriage; and every physical contact, in games, in what the poet Stevenson calls so appropriately the 'wedding' of their hands, or the conventional forms of 'petting', or dancing, becomes a symbol of marriage in its intimately physical aspects—usually an unconscious symbol, and all the more profoundly sexual for being so unconscious: all these being 'trial-marriage' fantasies, as it were, which can be savored and judged without committing them to any responsibility. And at some stage of adolescence, depending upon temperament and social custom, a great deal of the experimental and symbolic physical intimacy of petting will normally be indulged in.

Now the Trobriand boys and girls are making use of sexual relations for the same experimental and symbolic purposes. In these sexual relationships they proceed slowly along the same path from egotism toward adult love-capacity. Personal preference comes gradually into play, says Malinowski, "and with it a tendency toward a greater permanence in intrigue. The boy develops a desire to retain the fidelity and exclusive devotion of the loved one, at least for a time. But this tendency is not associated so far with any idea of settling down to one exclusive relationship, nor do adolescents yet begin to think of marriage. A boy or girl wishes to pass through many more experiences; he or she still enjoys the prospect of complete freedom and has no desire to accept obligations. Though pleased to imagine that his partner is faithful, the youthful lover does not feel obliged to reciprocate this fidelity."

So far are these savage experimental relationships from constituting the mating toward which they lead so gradually, so definitely are they as yet only the prefiguring symbols of it, that *something is held back*—in order that they may savor and judge these imaginary marriages without committing themselves to any responsibility. *They do not eat together.* "To take a girl out to dinner without previously having married her—a thing permitted in Europe—would be to disgrace her in the eyes of a Trobriander", says Malinowski. "We object to an unmarried girl sharing a man's bed—the Trobriander would object just as strongly to her sharing his meal."

In our society, however, a psychologically similar situation is frequently to be found. 'Calling' upon a girl still retains in some milieus its patriarchal significance of formal courtship. Sometimes the parents of an adolescent girl will forbid her to have boys calling on her, because they cannot think of it except as a mode of formal courtship, leading immediately to marriage, for which she is still too young. Or if she is at an age however young when marriage by patriarchal standards is possible for a girl, the parents may take an interest in a girl's boy-friends, making the correct patriarchal inquiries of each to elicit information about his family and his social and financial status or prospects. All this is not merely embarrassing to the youth, who is frequently enough far from being in a position to marry at the time, and annoying to the girl, who does not want her boy-friends frightened away—but it also involves a parental misconception of the purpose of their relationship. Thus the girl may frantically and quite sincerely declare to her parents that she *doesn't want to get married,* at this time, to this or any other boy she knows. And the converse will represent the youth's feelings. Nevertheless they do want not only each other's companionship and affection, but also the experimental and emotionally educative physical intimacies of 'petting'. So that, while indulging in a physical relationship which yields at least symbolically some of the satisfactions of a sexual union, they avoid the social forms of relationship which could be construed as meaning that they wanted to be married to each other. They meet and pursue their mid-adolescent emotional experiences outside the girl's home.

All this goes to imply that the 'petting' stage of adolescent sexuality is normal and does not represent an artificial social frustration of the mating impulse. It implies, moreover, that the young savages whom we have brought in for comparison are also at the 'petting' stage of sexuality and not at the mating stage—and that their literal sexual affairs are simply the savage version of our conventional adolescent 'petting parties'. The latter would doubtless be intolerable to savage boys and girls because they are not accustomed to the endurance of any but the slightest sexual tension. Their savage culture, moreover, can with the aid of its magical-religious consolations more readily accept the hazards of pain, danger, sterility and death from abortion than ours; and it runs no mental hazards, since these sexual affairs of youth have full social approval. Savage society can therefore use the sexual relationship for the emotionally educative purposes which tend to be fulfilled by 'petting' in modern civilized society.

The sexual behavior of our times has previously been discussed in terms of a transition from patriarchal to modern usages. The savage customs which we have here brought in for comparison exhibit analogues to modern customs, in certain respects in which both differ from patriarchal conventions. In both savage and modern life the young men and girls who are to marry one another have in adolescence a socially encouraged period for mutual acquaintance, play and courtship; and though all these tend to be conducted on different planes in savage and in modern life, they nevertheless can be classed together as opposite in intention and method from the patriarchal segregation during this period of the young men and girls who are to marry one another. Courtship in savage and in modern life alike is a personal matter between the young people themselves, and not (though savage life exhibits the beginnings of this) a politico-economic negotiation between two families with the prospective bride and bridegroom as pawns. In both savage and modern life there tends to be no special class of degraded women set aside (as in patriarchal society) for masculine youth to play with, but the girls in whose society the youths learn their lessons of love are of the same social class with themselves. In both savage and modern life the sexual experiences (using that term in the broadest sense, to cover the accepted conventions of both cultures) by which girls learn their lessons of love are not regarded as unfitting them for marriage, but the contrary; in this respect again they are in contrast with the patriarchal conventions, by which the modern 'petting' experiences of a normal girl would have been regarded as at least brushing the bloom from the fruit if not of destroying utterly her values for respectable marriage.

The likenesses between savage and modern conventions and their contrasts with patriarchal conventions of youth and sex might be pursued still further. But these analogues may possibly have raised the questions: 'Does not at least a good deal of the modern sexual behavior of young people conform quite literally to savage custom? And (if this is true) does not this matter-of-fact sexuality of young moderns fulfil, even more healthily than the restricted civilized behavior described above, the purposes of emotional education for marriage?' These questions have already been discussed very elaborately under the heading 'Sex as Amusement' (Chapter IX, § 1). The answer there arrived at is, briefly, 'No,' to both questions. This answer was based upon two grounds, psychological and physical. The former asserted that sexual intercourse was irrelevant to acquaintance and emotional education, which could be achieved in adolescence either with its aid (as in savagery) or without it (as in civilized life). The latter asserted that the adolescent practice of sexual intercourse involved the waste of abortion, which is increasingly repugnant to the modern mind, however it may be taken for granted in savage life. It was pointed out that the best means of avoiding abortion are not readily available to adolescents, nor adolescent psychology apt to the care which they require. The question was not posed, however, of what would be the 'modern attitude' toward the use in this adolescent period of some as yet uninvented means of contraception which would be fool-proof and available to all. It will therefore be answered here.

The modern attitude (if this book can presume to interpret it) would be one of frank relief at the freeing of feeble-minded and neurotically reckless adolescents from the burdens of illegitimacy, abortions, blood-poisoning, etc. That an increase in adolescent sex-relations among these groups would result from the availability of such immunity is, indeed, quite possible—though among some of them there can scarcely be any increase, since these activities already occupy all their available leisure, and though mere fear of consequences has never been shown to be a practical deterrent in the realm of sex, nor removal of fear an incentive. As to psychically normal and healthy adolescents, there would be no expectation of any overwhelming increase in sex-relations as a result of the availability of immunity.

One reason for this view—which will seem merely foolish to the patriarchal mind—is that adolescents *now* believe quite generally that such a fool-proof means of immunity already exists and is available at every drug-store; yet nevertheless there is among them only a negligible minimum of experimental-curiosity use of such means, since these boys and girls generally (and not for patriarchal 'moral' reasons) prefer instinctively the preliminary excitements of play, companionship and selective courtship, until they feel that they are adult and have made what seems to be a permanent love-choice, in marriage or out of it, such as calls for sexual union. To doubt that this inner motivation could exist, is to assert that only fear can control the sexuality of youth—a patriarchal maxim which modern psychology has repudiated. There is reason to believe that it is the obstructions to the development of heterosexuality, and to adult mating, which encourage pre-adult sexual relations. And there is equal reason to believe that young people who are permitted to develop normally to heterosexual adulthood, and who can look forward over a clear path to a mating in early adult life, will prefer to enjoy all the preliminaries of courtship and love-choice which lead to matehood—not necessarily a final matehood but one which will seem emotionally final and may be so in fact—before they commit themselves in a mutual act, which may have been in savage and patriarchal psychology an irresponsible one of mere amusement, but which in modern life tends to regain all its instinctive significance as the seal of tension-tried and enduring love.

§ 2. Obstacles to Heterosexual Development

Our argument is that the social discouragements of heterosexual emotional development in adolescence are all relics of the patriarchal régime: (1) that these social discouragements have as their motives—motives of which individual parents may be consciously unaware or which they may consciously repudiate—(a) the old patriarchal fear of the personal and selective powers of normal love, and (b) the old patriarchal wish to exploit the younger generation's sexual life for economic purposes; also (2) that the infantile or undeveloped sexuality which results from these repressions is (a) not adapted to meet the requirements of modern adult life in regard to either work or love, but (b) tends according to circumstances to find refuge in (x) prostitution and crime, (y) to require the deceptive solaces of alcohol and drugs to reconcile the individual to the struggle to meet these adult requirements, and (z) in any event to waste years of supposedly adult life in neurotic mental conflict over the problems of adjustment which should be settled in adolescence.

We will now discuss, first the lingering patriarchal social institutions and ideals which have these repressive effects upon adolescent heterosexual development; and second, the situations in contemporary family life which give special opportunity for these repressive influences to operate.

Some of these patriarchal relics of custom and ideals are unfortunately to a considerable extent embedded in traditional Christian theory and practice. The Christian Church, however, has always shown a disposition to struggle with the patriarchal conventions in which it has become mired. Its original repudiation of patriarchal (and savage) sex-infantilism, though taking (for the reasons earlier shown, in Chapter VIII, § 3) the character of ascetic sublimation of these infantilisms, was informed by a spirit of sexual democracy and sexual responsibility which are identical in aim though not in method with the adult standards of modern life. It was thus on its own plane of sublimation an anticipation of the later middle-class revolt on a realistic plane against the cruel tyranny and abject folly of patriarchal sex-custom. Not only that, but in its subsequent compromises with patriarchal custom and ideals, which have made the Church in many respects the upholder of a dying patriarchalism and the preserver of the very cruelties and follies against which it fought, it has always retained sufficient of its original impulse to remain, through some of its tendencies, representatives and activities, the protagonist of sexual democracy and sexual responsibility. Some of its representatives, for example, even in the acid test provided by the birth-control controversy, have shown themselves not incapable of interpreting the needs of marriage in the light of the living spirit of the Christian dogma of sexual democracy and responsibility, rather than according to the obselete letter of an impracticable asceticism; in this respect comparing favorably with the representatives of the medical profession, too few of whom have shown the courage or even the knowledge which might be expected of them as presumed representatives of science. This may seem a too-favorable view to take of the Church; it amounts, however, to saying that the rôle of the Church is, as it has always been, a contradictory one, mediating between the childish patriarchal society of which it became the guardian and the democratic and responsible City of God of which it has never quite lost sight or hope. Indeed, the influences of the Church most unfavorable to sexual adulthood are not in its praises of asceticism so much as in the sanctions it has given to respectable hypocrisy—its contentment with covering up and putting out of sight the actual sexual misbehavior of which it theoretically disapproves. To the extent that it has accepted the late patriarchal compromise of asserting on Sunday extreme virtues which are not even attempted on week-days, and of not letting the Christian right hand know what the frail human left hand doeth in matters of sex, it has made itself in modern life the sponsor of the neurotic mental device of dissociation, by which psychic integrity is lost. The early Christian psychic purge afforded by public confession and repentance has degenerated into a more convenient and cowardly private 'repentance' and private 'making of good resolutions'—which is merely a way of saying to oneself that the incident 'doesn't count', a way of repudiating, forgetting and repressing into the unconscious the infantile-sexual aspects of one's personality. The Devil has in fact in popular Christian theology increasingly replaced Jesus as the one upon whom the burden of sin is laid; the theological concept of spiritual integrity attained through identification with a Savior who by bearing one's sins enables oneself at once to acknowledge and to be freed of them, has become increasingly meaningless to people who preferred the easier way of blaming the Devil for everything they did not approve in themselves. The doctrine of Original Sin would appear to have had important psychological values of a realistic and indeed of a comforting sort in early Christian theology. It is of this aspect of the doctrine that Chesterton speaks when he calls it "the one grand and logical base of all optimism"; the idealist, he says, tends to regard all his personal faults as "frightful secret malformations", until he "becomes conscious of that large and beautiful and benignant explanation that the heart of man is deceitful above all things and desperately wicked"—that, in fact, to put the matter into Freudian terms, everybody else is engaged in seeking to repress or sublimate just the same polymorphous-perverse sexual infantilism. If this really was the function of the doctrine (and there is interesting evidence, in the plays of the 10th century nun Roswitha, of its use for comfort and encouragement), it has since tended to become displaced by something like a doctrine of Original Purity. Not only the Protestant but the Catholic branch of the Church also, though formally retaining the doctrine, has fallen headlong into what according to its own teachings is the Manichaean heresy of dualism, and into what is certainly the psychically poisonous practice of inculcating in young people a sense of shame concerning sex.

The writings of James Joyce are a testimonial to the unedifying results of repressing adolescent sexuality to an infantile level and then threatening young sinners with hell-fire. What in theory is a common denominator of human nature has become a special and to the sinner a unique transgression. "Had it been any terrible crime but that one sin!" thinks young Stephen Dedalus, waiting to confess. "Had it been murder! Little fiery flakes fell and touched him at all points, shameful thoughts, shameful words, shameful acts. Shame covered him wholly like fine glowing ashes falling continually. To say it in words!" The point of the doctrine has been lost, 'sin' has been turned from something to which human nature is prone into an incomprehensible affront to Heavenly purity. Stephen's silly and ugly little sexual infantilities ("The sootcoated packet of pictures which he had hidden in the flue of the fireplace and in the presence of whose shameless or bashful wantonness he lay for hours sinning in thought and deed; his monstrous dreams, peopled by apelike creatures and by harlots with gleaming jewel eyes; the foul long letters he had written in the joy of guilty confession and carried secretly for days and days only to throw them under cover of night among the grass in the corner of a field or beneath some hingeless door or in some niche in the hedges where a girl might come upon them as she walked by and read them secretly") become offenses so monstrous that it is incredible that they could ever be forgiven! The fact is that to place such a stupendous moral emphasis upon such matters is to make them psychologically and permanently 'unforgiveable' by any powers of any religion: 'sin' has been made to appear more infinite than the grace of God, so that one might as well go to the Devil and be done with it. At present this kind of Puritanism in its most virulent form, in which such homage of exaggerated denunciatory respect is rendered to the 'powers of evil' as to come within an acre of Satan-worship, appears far more characteristic of the Roman than of the Protestant branch of the Church in America.

What we may understand from all this is that although the Church in all its branches is likely to be found on the one hand feebly tolerating the most unsavory patriarchal sex-compromises in adults and meekly accepting adult sexual hypocrisy as the next best thing to 'virtue', and on the other hand nourishing adolescent neuroticism by the compensatory bursts of hell-fire eloquence with which it maintains its dignity in its own eyes—as if it sought to make up for its necessitous practice of taking 'sinners' knowingly to its bosom, by scaring impressionable and ignorant children into psychic fits—these disgraceful traits are bound up with its social and political functions in a decaying patriarchal society; and in the Christian attitude, insofar as it is not thus overborne by alien influences, there is nothing essentially hostile to the modern requirements of adulthood. Christianity as the handmaid of a dying social order may stand as the enemy of enlightenment in sex as in everything else; but Christianity as a religious force is not condemned to such a rôle, and shows many indications of accepting a rôle more consonant with the requirements of the new social order. A religious asceticism in which adults in general do not pretend to believe is not the worst obstacle to the development of a healthy heterosexuality in adolescence; but a hypocrisy which adults generally do practice is a serious obstacle.

It is, then, in social and not in specifically religious influences that we are to seek for these obstacles. One of the greatest of all is the social custom of sex-segregation. In modern life this can only be effectively accomplished in schools. It is characteristic that the democratic movement which established universal free public education in the United States proceeded without hesitation to make it co-educational. The state colleges are also co-educational. It is the private educational institutions with aristocratic or pseudo-aristocratic class-aims which have harked back to the patriarchal mode of sex-segregation.

The purpose of sex-segregation in schools is—so far as it is not a meaningless aping of aristocratic Latin-European customs—a definitely patriarchal one: it is intended thereby to keep the control of mating in parental hands. Girls sent to fashionable boarding schools are intended to be kept from having opportunities for falling in love with and making rash marriages with boys. The difficulty is that they fall in love with each other and form psychological patterns if not overt habits of homosexuality. They are perhaps, as a result, more amenable to parental dictation in marriage, and they represent the last remnant of dutiful daughterly acceptance of patriarchally arranged marriage now to be found; but these fashionable arranged marriages are under modern conditions highly unstable. When this sex-segregation and this homosexual and quasi-homosexual atmosphere is prolonged by college education in a segregated woman's institution, the results are to be seen in the comparative statistics which show a smaller number of marriages among such graduates than among women who have attended co-educational colleges or among women at large. A certain proportion have graduated either into life-long homosexuality or into permanent lay nunship. In sex-segregated boys' schools there is the same homosexual and quasi-homosexual atmosphere, not very successfully sublimated by military and other idealistic patterns, but with a tendency toward sexual exploitation of socially inferior girls, the latter tendency more than the former constituting the men's college sex-pattern.

The economic situation has, of course, a direct bearing upon this use of sex segregation to promote sex-infantilism. The object is frequently to delay mating for economic reasons—reasons not of necessity, but of parental preference for an avoidance of early hardships and struggle such as would come with early marriage. The sons particularly, but also the daughters, are being 'protected' from the responsibilities, frequently grave enough, which mate-love will bring. But the young people are not permitted to protect themselves—it must be done for them in the old patriarchal fashion, by keeping them away from the other sex as much as possible in adolescence. This form of parental authority, whether it be construed as severity or coddling (and is it always difficult to tell one from the other, since they are merely the obverse and reverse aspects of traditional patriarchal parental rule) is in itself an attempt at a rationalization of a neurotic parental attitude.

One more feature of the educational situation must be commented upon. When higher education for women was proposed, it was regarded as an invasion of a field belonging (as it did in fact belong, in the patriarchal régime) to men. It was said, among other things, that it would cause the young men to fall in love with the girl students and that the college would become a matchmaking institution. That is, it would introduce the radical innovation of bringing about love affairs between young people of the same social class, who might one day be married, instead of sex-affairs between the young men and 'town-girls', who were socially regarded as inferior and ineligible for marriage. The movement for higher education of women, like that for increased professional opportunities for women, was being promoted under idealistic auspices which ignored or denied on behalf of women their possession of sexual aims of any sort, including marriage. So that it could not be frankly admitted that the association of young men and young women in higher education was desirable precisely for the reasons adduced against it, that it would promote marriages between the young men and young women students. It could not be asked pointedly why a college should not be a matchmaking institution, instead of being so far as sex was concerned an adjunct to a brothel, or a monastery or nunnery, or a hotbed of homosexuality. It had to be assumed that education existed in and for itself in a way irrelevant to the purposes of life and especially irrelevant to its mating purposes.

The reason for this attitude lay in the fact that according to the patriarchal theory women past childhood had *only* sexual purposes to subserve, as wives or prostitutes, unless they were formally withdrawn from the sexual realm as nuns. Thus, under the terms of this patriarchal concept of woman, a girl's rights as an individual had been encroached upon by her sexual status, and these human rights could only be recovered by a formal denial of her sexual uses. Somewhat as in the Middle Ages, when a girl's only chance for a higher education was (ordinarily) in becoming a nun, so now a kind of nunship had to be attributed to her for at least the time being in order to gain for her these educational privileges. Women's education in colleges of their own had been a kind of old maids' privilege. If there was to be co-education, it was felt that the girl should guarantee, or that it should be guaranteed on her behalf, that she really wanted to learn Latin and Greek and not just to have an opportunity to use her sexual wiles in securing a husband.

And it was for this reason that the whole medieval gentlemen's-sons' curriculum had in women's colleges been taken as the standard of their own higher education—since if the question of its suitability to them as women had once been conceded to be valid, these girls would have been fobbed off with lessons in cooking, dish-washing, clothes-making and servant-managing. The idea that girl students were after all (not to say, in the first place!) girls, had to be denied as one dangerous to all their educational prospects. So long as the sexuality of girls had to be construed in the patriarchal sense, as a limitation of their human rights, the time was inopportune for any realistic discussion of their needs. Only an enemy of the sex, only one who wished to relegate them to an inferior position, would suggest that girls had any sexual intentions, wishes or purposes. Their potential motherhood, and their instinctive need to select the fathers of their children, were matters to be hushed up in the interests of the girls themselves.

And so recently have we emerged from this state of affairs that many champions of the human rights of women still bitterly resent any such emphasis as we are laying now upon sex. 'Why bring *that* up?' they ask, feeling the shadow of the patriarchate in such an emphasis. But these girls who go off to college have not broken out of the patriarchal home in order to wander forever in mateless and childless 'freedom'. They are in fact using the educational period as a courtship and mating period. This is taken for granted in co-educational institutions. And it is interesting to note that even in sex-segregated girls' colleges there is now a student tradition which makes a certain amount of 'dating' with men more or less socially obligatory—a tradition now cautiously encouraged by administrative authorities, though still with one eye cocked toward the theory of student nunship and the other eye half-closed against the psychological implications of the inevitable 'crushes' among the girls. Despite such healthy corrective efforts it remains true that the girls in these sex-segregated institutions do *not* have the opportunity (to use in reverse some descriptive remarks of Professor Leta Hollingworth concerning those in co-educational secondary schools and colleges) "to know and know very well" *during these eight important years* "literally hundreds of youths of opposite sex during the years when heterosexual impulses are" *or should be* "developing. They have" *not* "had a genuine opportunity to make a real choice in mating". *To the girls in these sex-segregated schools,* "members of the opposite sex are" *not* "seen and known for what they are. They are"—*quite characteristically*—"thought of as impossibly gallant heroes, horrible ogres, glittering knights, golden-haired angels, and the like, as pictured by romanticism uncorrected by actual experience"

We are thus reduced to reversing the descriptions of co-educational psychology in order to describe sex-segregated school psychology, because the latter is so touchy a subject as to be usually treated by indirection. Pfister, the pastor-psychoanalyst, it is true, remarks: "It is certainly right and proper that boys and girls should be educated together. When boys know only the company of other boys, and girls only that of girls, healthy moral training becomes very difficult. Homosexuality is far commoner than is usually believed. Even in the best regulated boarding schools such practices are only too common. I have known young men who have suffered terribly from the consequences of many years' 'married relationships' (as they called it) with comrades at school who shared the same bedroom." Our concern, however, is not with these incidents, which everybody deplores, but rather with the fact that sex-segregated education promotes a more general and earlier baulking of heterosexual development, of which almost everybody approves. We are not here concerned, that is to say, with the occasional arrival at an overt homosexuality which can be unmistakably recognized as such; we are concerned with the widespread unconscious homosexuality which neither the individual nor society at large recognizes as such. This unconscious homosexuality is ordinarily described by both the individual and society at large as 'prudishness' and 'stiffness', or more favorably as 'unapproachable purity' or 'high ideals', or even as 'ambition and application to work which leaves no room for interest in the other sex'. Being thus disguised from both the individual and society at large, it is free to operate in its own fashion both to make mating so difficult as to be almost impossible, and to make matings unsatisfactory and unstable when they are formally achieved. If these cases are to be dealt with, and if the patriarchal custom of sex-segregation which promotes them is to be reprehended and abandoned, they have to be recognized as being what they are.

It comes down to a choice between heterosexuality and homosexuality as a goal. Clearly our modern society repudiates overt homosexuality; but the unconscious homosexuality which tends toward that goal and becomes involved in endless and agonizing struggles in the necessary post-adolescent attempt at readjustment to the heterosexual ideal now set before it—this, modern society still permits out of a false respect for patriarchal custom.

It is nevertheless true that young people may endure the influences of a sex-segregated adolescence without being psychically warped by them. The reason is that these young people have as children been encouraged by their home environment toward adulthood and healthy sexuality. The homosexualizing influences thus come too late to do them any harm. In fact it is only by reason of the previous preparation for such influences by early repressions that they are enabled to do harm. The childhood and parental influences are thus the most important of all.

Assisted, then, by mistaken churchly and educational surrenders to patriarchal sex-segregation in adolescence, *the greatest barrier to adolescent heterosexual development is provided by the parents themselves.* In an eloquent address which might serve as the text of our present inquiry, Dr. Frankwood E. Williams says of emancipation from the home and the establishment of heterosexuality: "In spite of the absolute, fundamental, and primary importance of these two things, the home, the school, and our social life generally seem to be almost entirely banded together to defeat, in so far as they can, the establishment of these two things." And specifically as to the second, he goes on to say, describing these same relics of patriarchal idealism: "Over this matter of sex we are greatly concerned. Our anxiety, however, is very badly placed: it is not fear that the child may fail in accomplishing a healthy development, thereby crippling himself in a very serious and fundamental way, but fear that in the process unpleasant things may happen, things perhaps of importance in themselves, but certainly of secondary importance to the success of the process itself. With the failure of the latter [*i.e.*, the failure to establish heterosexuality], the consequences for the child (and society) are inevitable and permanent; with the former [*e.g.*, the accidental infringements of our sex-mores] the permanence and importance are entirely as we choose to make them. So greatly", he repeats, "have we magnified the importance of some of these secondary matters that the home, the church, the school and society generally would seem to be banded together to defeat the child in attaining a healthy hetero-sexuality."

We cannot do better than quote further from Dr. Williams. "If hetero-sexuality is not accomplished in these four or five years [of later adolescence] it never will be accomplished in a normal way. It may be accomplished later by some technical [*i.e.*, psychotherapeutic] interference, but then only after much conflict, failure, and [mental] illness. These four or five years hold the only chance the average boy and girl will have to establish their hetero-sexuality. Once prevented, it can never come naturally and normally again. * * *

"We tried for a time to protect ourselves and our children (it really amounted to an attempt to defeat the effort of the child to establish hetero-sexuality) by keeping them completely ignorant of all sex matters. The tragic results of this no one knows quite so well as the psychiatrist. Even people generally are now awake to the consequences that have followed, and efforts are not now so commonly made to keep individuals in ignorance until the night they are married.

"But there are bars we still do put up. Hetero-sexuality cannot be attained in a vacuum. It cannot be attained by itself. It does not just happen; it is a development and growth that is nourished and continued by what it feeds upon. Hetero-sexuality will be established through contact and experience with the opposite sex. Anything, no matter for what purpose, that tends to make this contact too difficult, is not in the interests of the child or the parents or society.

"Yet an effort is made, when signs first begin to appear that boys and girls are becoming interested in each other, to keep them apart. We are so fearful that something is going to happen. Nothing—nothing so tragic could happen as that they should fail to accomplish this objective [*i.e.*, the establishment of hetero-sexuality]. Nothing! But we are so fearful. We lose sight of the importance and the necessity of the thing the child is attempting to do * * *.

"Parents attempt to keep girls away from this boy, or boys away from this girl. If unsuccessful, they then attempt very carefully to select the boy or the girl with whom their child may have contact. If done with real insight and understanding, this may be well, but, on the other hand, it would be well to let the boy or the girl do a little of the choosing, for after all it is their psychology that has to be handled, not the parents' psychology.

"The girl or the boy who may satisfy the parents' emotional needs may be entirely unsatisfactory for the needs of the boy or girl. While we may well be careful here, a great deal of latitude is wise." In unsupervised contacts of his own choice he may learn more that will be helpful to him "than he did at the very nicely supervised dance that was given the week before"

Dr. Williams then refers to the "unhealthy ideals" that are forced upon young people by their parents. "One of the worst is this—the idealization of women themselves, the placing of women upon pedestals as something too fine, too sacred, too fragile to be handled in any but the most genteel, considerate way." He remarks that "nobody knows as does the psychiatrist how devastating the damage has been to thousands of men and women, through this utterly false ideal". This false purity-ideal, he says, "is one of the chief causes for the failure of the establishment of heterosexuality on the part of the boy, which later interferes with his married life, which drives him to prostitution, which drives him to abnormal sex expression, and to those twists and quirks of personality and character that go deep in his life and fundamentally change and frequently ruin it.

"Equally unhealthy ideas", says Dr. Williams, "are foisted upon girls in regard to the depravity of men, and the great care that they must use, therefore, in protecting themselves from the sexual attacks of men. In order to 'protect' them, they are so filled with fears that they are seriously handicapped even in everyday social relations; and their hetero-sexual development, necessary in happy marital relations, successful motherhood, and all adult social contacts, is defeated."

It remains to be explained why so many parents adopt these patriarchal attitudes. It is not entirely out of reverence for the past, or because of ignorance of the needs of children. It is essentially because these attitudes fulfil a neurotic wish cherished by the parents themselves. It is because they (often unconsciously) wish to keep their children from growing up.

Our modern culture has formally broken with the patriarchal past and adopted as its maxim a saying handed down from pre-patriarchal barbarism: "a man shall leave his father and his mother, and shall cleave unto his wife." It is no longer socially proper for parents to hold sons and daughters in permanent bondage, as they might in patriarchal times. The wish to do so must disguise its final intent and clothe itself in apparent unselfishness. The disguised nature of the wish, its inappropriateness to modern life and its results in the unhappiness and uselessness not only of the child-victims but of their parent-exploiters, constitutes it a neurosis. What, then, are the circumstances under which it arises?

When a man is in the lingering patriarchal situation of being married to a woman whom he did not choose and does not love, i.e., who does not represent an adult love-choice on his part, because of an unconscious fixation upon a parent, he is sexually impaired, and is not unlikely to become psychosexually impotent to some degree. Whether short of that or not, he typically struggles to establish his masculine authority in a variety of symbolic and dramatic ways, within and without the home. He is one of 'the bullies of the market place' and the judge's bench, to whom reference has been earlier made. The home, however, traditionally affords him a sphere of lordship of which he takes advantage. He can give himself the needful illusion of power by ordering his children about, the illusion of indispensability by making all their actions hang upon his decision or permission. He is secretly moved, moreover, by a jealousy of his sons; and he can always find the most 'moral' excuses for what is in effect his effort to castrate them emotionally. He is in the same way secretly jealous of the younger men, one of whom might come to possess some daughter of his, and he undertakes both to drive them away and to bind her to him in the most dutiful obedience or the most tender affection—or perhaps he persuades her that she is an invalid, like Elizabeth Barrett's father, from whose tyrannical and morbid care Robert Browning had to snatch his bride away.

There is the answer, baldly and brutally put, and in terms of a fairly extreme case. But the value of extreme cases in neurosis and psychosis is that they enable us to understand the significance of the less obvious symptoms in less extreme and more thoroughly disguised cases. This case represents the regression to an infantile power-level of a male sexuality which has never become adult, has been incapable of instinctive love-choice, and seeks to reassure itself against conscious or unconscious impotence-fears by the neurotic exercise of parental power and the neurotic sexual victimization of children—which according to patriarchal tradition is permissible so long as it stops short of overt incest.

There are, to be sure, modes of 'sublimating' these impulses, but they are difficult to find and use and are seldom more than partly successful in relieving such a man's children of his overpowering tyrannies or his overpowering kindnesses.

So much, in extreme terms, of the man. When a woman is in the same lingering patriarchal situation of being married to a man she cannot love because of unconscious fixation on a parent, she frequently enough is psychosexually frigid to some degree. If she has children, she regresses to a little-girl-with-dolls stage of power-sexuality which she calls being maternal. She exploits her children, tyrannizes jealously over her growing daughters and seeks to make her son her beau. These tyrannies and victimizations are easy to dress up in moral robes as duty and maternal devotion. She keeps her sons from marrying if possible, and tries to make her daughters devote their lives to waiting on her. Again the case is put in fairly extreme terms, so as to shed light on less extreme and less obvious cases.

If a sexually adult person is married to such a neurotic, he or she escapes sooner or later and makes a real mating, legally if possible. But the children may not be able to escape for years. If two such persons are married, they may compete childishly for the children's love.

Normal parents, in love with one another, not only leave their children free to become adults but encourage them in growing up; if in no other way, yet in the very significant way of furnishing them normal models of manhood and womanhood which are incentives in their own achievement of adulthood. Infantile parents may, as above, set them a discouraging model of domestic quarrels and jealousy. If one or both parents, incapable of a real mating, should seek solace in irresponsible adulteries, there will be an added element of childish humiliation and shame on behalf of the parent, to further discourage the growing child. If one or both of the parents should seek solace in drink, there will be the further discouragement of neglect. The complete neglect of abandonment, which is in itself indicative of sexual infantilism, is a terrible discouragement to a child.

It very often happens that one such sexually infantile parent is left with children by the desertion, divorce or death of the marital partner. Then, in the first and second instances (desertion and divorce), the situation can be interpreted in such self-pitying terms of difficult economic struggle and heartbreak as to distract attention from the ruthless emotional exploitation of the children—which would have gone on in any event but which is seldom improved by the absence of the other parent and never by the inculcation of shame by the remaining parent in regard to the absent one's derelictions. This used to pass in social service work as an example of the harm done to children by 'broken homes'; but it is increasingly recognized that these homes had not the basis of adult sexual love between the parents to keep them unbroken. In the last case, that of the death of the other parent, grief is the excuse for the emotional exploitation of the children by the survivor. Normal women, however, can be widows without ruining their children's lives. If they truly cherished an adult love for the lost husband, they will not need to regress in widowhood to the stage of making Little Lord Fauntleroys out of their sons. The same considerations apply to widowers and to both men and women after divorce. In these situations divorce is a symptom of sexual infantility on one side or the other if not both. This is not a condemnation, however, of divorce; the difficulty lies in the original marriage as not representing an adult love-choice—the divorce is merely the confession of that fact, and affords an opportunity for what may or may not be a more mature choice and a more stable marriage.

These excuses, however, which parents present to themselves and the world for their emotional exploitation and enslaving of their children, these interpretations of their viciousness in terms of nobility, are valid only so long as people accept them. They are valid only so long as the repute of the patriarchal tradition lends them weight They are disguises only so long as they disguise the truth. When people no longer are fooled by these disguises, when they no longer admire as 'maternal devotion' and 'paternal discipline' the morbid possessiveness of parents, then parents are unable to 'get away with' such behavior. For they are unwilling, except in desperate cases, to *seem* bad parents; they will go on being bad parents only as long as everybody tells them what fine parents they are, so that they can believe it themselves. When these patriarchal rags are stripped from such parental cruelties by psychiatrists and teachers, doctors and social workers, friends and relatives, the jig is up. They cannot go on *knowingly* spoiling their children's lives. They turn, pathetically or earnestly, for guidance in honest parenthood to those who have unmasked them; they begin the slow and difficult task of growing up themselves, if only for the sake of their children.

We may hope, therefore, that an exposure such as this book attempts of the true significance of these patriarchal ideals and their inappropriateness to modern life, will help to rob neurotics of their last defences against self-realization and make easier the task of their re-education—which is necessary if the fatal chain of neurotic-parent-and-neurotic-child is ever to be broken.

CHAPTER XIV

THE MATING AGE

§ 1. Coming of Age

It is frequently assumed in sociological generalizations that savage boys and girls of 15 or 16 years of age are already 'mated' and probably have been since puberty. This, we have seen, is not the fact in the savage societies which we have considered. At 15 or 16 the Trobriand youths are still slowly approaching the mating age, the girls not yet necessarily arrived there. "As time goes on, and the boys and girls grow older," says Malinowski, "their intrigues last longer, and their mutual ties tend to become stronger and more permanent. A personal preference as a rule develops and begins definitely to outshadow all other love affairs." The adolescent Samoan girl, Miss Mead tells us, though looking forward to marriage in due time, wishes meanwhile to "live as a girl with as many lovers as possible"; and to the idea of taking on the adult responsibilities of marriage she replies deprecatingly, "Laititi a'u" ("I am but young"). At the age of about 25 or 30, we learn, the Trobriand young man begins to want children and a house of his own, and seriously considers marriage. This marriage, however, is in a sense—though it brings new privileges—only the public ratification of an already established mating. "In the ordinary course of events," says Malinowski, "every marriage is preceded by a more or less protracted period of sexual life in common. This is generally known and spoken of, and is regarded as a public intimation of the matrimonial projects of the pair. It also serves as a test of the strength of their attachment and extent of their mutual compatibility. A trial period also gives time for the prospective bridegroom and for the woman's family to prepare economically for the event." This is similar to the pre-patriarchal form of 'sexual betrothal' previously discussed as a rural custom of northern Europe, and from thence introduced into America, where its influence persists despite culture-clashes with the patriarchal traditions of male sexual irresponsibility. The custom is also found increasingly in urban centers. And it bears, moreover, an analogy to the conventional engagement period.

The mating age is everywhere partly dependent upon economic and social factors. The marriage age may be wholly dependent upon them; pre-adolescent girls and boys may be married as in Brahmin India, or marriage may be postponed for men until 35 or 40 as in classical Greece: but this can scarcely pretend to be 'mating'. The economic and social opportunities, however, do hurry or delay the mating age—by which is meant the age at which young people are physically and psychically able to assume the burdens of marriage and parenthood. The pioneer or free-land period in America, lasting into the 19th century, lowered the marriage age and undoubtedly in a great many instances inducted into the matrimonial state people who were emotionally still children and physically far from adult size and strength. "According to report," says Arthur W. Calhoun, "the girls of North Carolina married so early that grandmothers of 27 years of age were frequently found"—which means conception at 12 years 9 months. "Instances are recorded of the marriage of * * * girls in the early teens and even younger. * * * Early marriages were usual in all the States. Even girls of the 'higher' classes often married at 13." And as late as the decade following the Oregon free-land law of 1850, it was there "not uncommon to see brides of 14. * * * Some persons tell of having found married women in the woods of the Columbia [river] playing with their dolls."

This is a reversion to the patriarchal exploitation of girl-children in marriage, against which Aristotle protested on eugenic grounds, pointing out that: "The union of male and female when too young is bad for the procreation of children; in all other animals the offspring of the young are small and ill-developed, and generally of the female sex: and therefore also in man, as is proved by the fact that in those cities in which men and women are accustomed to marry young, the people are small and weak; in childbirth also younger women suffer more, and more of them die; some persons say that this was the meaning of the response once given to the Troezenians ['Shear not the young field']—the oracle really meant that many died because they married too young; it had nothing to do with the ingathering of the harvest." He recommended 18 as the proper age for women to marry.

Free land does not automatically make adult women out of little girls, though it may make wives and mothers out of them. On the other hand, there is no doubt that upon the whole the conditions of pioneer life were such as to promote adult emotional capacity at an age earlier than in a more sheltered life. The agricultural requirements for adulthood were fairly simple. "A German-American writing in 1826", Professor Calhoun reports, "said that in the country as soon as a young fellow had gathered a few dollars, seldom over one hundred, he thought of marriage. The wedding gift to a son consisted of a horse, farm implements, and seed; a girl received a bed, a cow, kitchen utensils, and maybe a clothes chest, tables, and chairs. The young man procured a hundred acres of forest; relatives put up a house and stable; and in two or three years he was tolerably well-fixed, for the pair were used to work." Our grandfathers or great-grandfathers who married at 17 or 18 were thus more economically adult than their descendants are likely to be five years later; and the same may be said of our grandmothers or great-grandmothers.

Mrs. Trollope in 1828 saw such a pioneer family near Cincinnati, living in a farm-clearing "in the very heart of the forest", with its cows, pigs and chickens, corn fields and potato-garden, and two-room log hut with a lean-to kitchen. "The farmer's wife, and a young woman who looked like her sister, were spinning, and three children were playing about. The woman told me that they spun and wove all the cotton and woollen garments of the family, and knit all the stockings; her husband, though not a shoemaker by trade, made all the shoes. She manufactured all the soap and candles they used, and prepared her sugar from sugar trees on the farm. All she wanted with money, she said, was to buy coffee, tea, and whiskey; and she could 'get enough any day by sending a batch of butter and chicken to market'. * * * She did not look in health, and said they all had ague in 'the fall'; but she seemed contented and proud of her independence; though it was in somewhat a mournful accent that she said: ' 'Tis strange to us to see company. I expect the sun may rise and set a hundred times, before I shall see another *human* that does not belong to the family.' "

Our grandmothers or great-grandmothers may or may not have been, at 17 or 18, adequate to immediate maternity. There is some medical dispute about the physiological as well as the eugenic disadvantages or advantages of maternity at such ages, and the subject has not been thoroughly investigated. There is no doubt that the constant childbearing which was one of their important economic functions in this peasant régime was very hard on them, but again we do not know whether their youth aggravated or mitigated that hardship. We are to-day prejudiced against early childbearing on social grounds, for it does not fit in with the tendencies of our economy and culture; the surviving peasant custom of early and constant childbearing which we can see in the Southern mountain districts to-day does not commend it to our admiration. But there is reason to believe that, with marriage in sight from an earlier age and with the rural freedom of courtship, girls were emotionally more adult at these ages than their granddaughters or great-granddaughters are likely to be until several years later.

The prime social-economic circumstance affecting the mating age of the modern youth and girl is the entrance of the latter into the general fields of work and higher education previously restricted to men. This means for her a longer period of sexual selection, a larger field of sexual choice, and activities of sufficient interest to make the delay not too onerous.

The marriage age for girls in America has been gradually raised in law, from the puberty-level which we inherit from the Roman system, to 16 or 18; and it tends to be raised in fact above that level. At the same time various economic factors have in America contributed to lower the marriage age for men in practice far below the classical level. The U. S. statistics bearing on this point are not susceptible of answering the questions of fact which it would be most useful to know—they do not reveal the ages at which people *get* married—but the Groves and Ogburn tables show that of 18-year-old girls only about one-fifth are already married; and that of 26-year-old men over half are already married. They also show that of the increase in marriage between 1910 and 1920 the proportion was greatest for young men of 20 to 30. The increase in the number of wives found among girls of 18 was no greater than that found among young women of 24, while the increase in the number of wives in the 17-year-old group was less than that in the 30-year-old group. These statistics merely confirm the observation that the marriage age for men is being lowered, that of girls raised.

Thus for both young men and girls the period of education and of early adjustments to the world of work represents a time of serious sexual selection through courtship. It is also unquestionably the time of physical and emotional coming-of-age, so that these courtships, for normal young people, will be emotionally decisive. They may still be in fact experimental, through lack of sufficient experience. But emotionally they will be final and will demand ratification. This period of normal maturity, which differs in individuals and in social environments, may roughly be set in our contemporary American life at 18− to 21+, with the understanding that it typically occurs earlier in girls than in boys.

These figures are intended as suggestive, and they are necessarily vague at both margins. They are set down after a vain attempt to find figures which better reflect the considerations involved in coming of age. These considerations, which may be listed as (1) tendencies in marriage legislation, (2) educational opportunities, (3) economic tendencies, and the facts of (4) physical and (5) psychic development, are briefly as follows.

(1) The respective ages at which girls and youths may marry without parental consent are generally 18 and 21; the minimum ages of marriage tend to be raised from puberty in both cases to 16 for girls and 18 for boys. Richmond and Hall, representing the expert social-service point of view, describe the marriage of a girl between 16 and 18 as a 'youthful marriage' and that of a girl under 16 as a 'child marriage'.

(2) Compulsory education is at least nominally undertaken by all the States; it is correlated with child-labor laws which do not generally extend protection beyond the age of 14, but despite setbacks (such as the failure of the States to ratify the child-labor amendment to the Constitution, and the degradation of the South under mill-owners' rule) the tendency is upward toward 16 and even 18. The public high-school enrollment doubled from 1908 to 1918, and doubled again in the next five years;

approximately half of our total age-group of 14–17 years is now in secondary schools.

(3) The economic influences are complicated and diverse in their effects upon coming-of-age. They include chiefly the decay of the apprenticeship system, the restriction of immigration, and the entrance of women into industry.

(4) The age-definitions of maturity (or of the end of adolescence) are contradictory and in so far as they pretend to be based on physiological data, vague or irrelevant. When examined they turn out really to embody traditional Graeco-Roman conceptions of social, political and legal status as determined by age. Nothing of physiological significance marks any of the particular ages of 18, 20, 21, 22, or 25—the various end-terms of adolescence found in the different definitions. As a whole they do practically represent the usual limits of growth.

(5) Aside from other psychological considerations, conceptions of status—that is to say, social expectations—still largely determine adulthood. It appears to be reached in social status not at a single bound but by degrees. Graduation from high school and college and going to work, however, are important status achievements in contemporary life and they suggest 18 and 22 as significant years in both society's and youth's own notions of adulthood. The age of male economic power to marry or support a family is too accidental and uncertain to have any psychological significance for either society or the individual as determining adulthood. Marriage is something that happens after people are adults, not (save to a swiftly decreasing extent for girls) the gateway to adult life.

These considerations obviously bar any false precision in the definition of adulthood. In human society, however, in which parental nurture must be prolonged beyond puberty, not only does puberty not constitute adulthood, but sufficient time must elapse and sufficient experiences must be gained for the love-emotions to detach themselves from the parental image and from their filial pattern of expression, and for them to develop along the new track of heterosexuality to a new kind of emotional fixation. This psychological process constitutes adolescence, and its end is reached when these psychic processes—emotional graduation from the home, and achievement of the capacity for heterosexual love-fixation—are completed. This happens (if it does happen) more or less concurrently with the achievement of full size and strength, and with the beginning of work or the end of formal education. Of a great many boys and girls we must grant that they are young men and young women at 18 years of age. Of others we may say that the concatenation of adultifying processes in psychology and circumstance is producing a satisfactory but slower arrival at adulthood at some age between 21 and 25. Of still others it can be said that they are not in process of becoming adults at all; or that their emotional coming-of-age is being seriously halted by repressive influences (which include coddling); or that they are violently over-compensating against their delay along the path to adulthood by a symbolic and fictitious grown-upness. In this chapter, however, we are attempting to trace the path of normal heterosexual development—not of an ideal normality in a Utopia nor again in a world of decaying patriarchal attitudes, but in what seem to us the most characteristically modern aspects of contemporary life.

A healthy and easy emotional graduation from the parental home is presumed to have occurred. The term 'graduation' is here deliberately used instead of 'emancipation', as being perhaps less suggestive of what it is not; and perhaps it will not be superfluous to pause here and say that the emancipation in question is not necessarily achieved through 'leaving home', though it does ultimately imply that.

Emancipation from the home refers to freedom from the emotional need for parental care, including both parental tenderness and parental authority. But it does not mean a rebellion against parental authority nor a repudiation of parental tenderness. These represent a false and not a real emancipation. Nor does it imply immediate ability to get along without economic aid from the parents, though it prepares for that. It means being emotionally oriented to the larger world outside the home. And all of this has a much more direct bearing upon the development of heterosexuality than might appear. Joanna Colcord tells of a mother who could not understand why her son should have become a wife-deserter: "He ought to be a good boy," she complained; "I carried him up to bed myself every night till he was eleven years old."

The two ways of preventing emancipation from the home were well set forth by the wise old Inca Viracocha (or perhaps by the shrewd Garcilaso, retailing his own observations under that more illustrious name) as follows: "Parents are oftentimes the cause of ruin to their children, when either they educate them with such fondness that they never cross them in their wills or desires, but suffer them to act and do whatever they please, whereby they become so corrupt in the manners of their infancy that vice grows ripe with them at the years of manhood. Others, on the contrary, are so severe and cruel to their children that they break the tenderness of their spirits and affright them from learning, discouraging them in that manner by menaces and lectures of a supercilious pedant, that their wits are abased, and despair of attaining to knowledge and virtue. The way is to keep an indifferent mean between both, by which youth becomes valiant and hardy in war, and wise and political in times of peace."

The 'achievement of heterosexuality' may similarly profit by being defined in negative terms before we proceed. It is not a state of continual and impersonal erotic inflammability by the other sex; that is a symptom of feeble-mindedness or of senile decay. The heterosexual impulses in their normal human development are progressively selective; and equal erotic responsiveness to the attractions of all good-looking persons of the opposite sex represents a failure to achieve or a regression back from the characteristics of adult heterosexuality. Heterosexuality does not mean that attitude toward the other sex which places value only upon its individuals as possible contributors to one's own sexual pleasure; that is infantile auto-eroticism. Heterosexuality does not mean inability to deal with women upon any but restrictedly sexual terms or terms implying the traditional subservience or inferiority of women; that is an overcompensation against an unconscious (and well-grounded) fear of homosexuality. Heterosexuality does not mean being a 'cave-man', or any of the other exaggerated and dramatic poses by which sexual infantilisms are disguised or sought to be escaped.

Heterosexuality does mean erotic responsiveness to the other sex in general, but of an increasingly selective and increasingly personal sort. Heterosexuality in its normal development is subject, of course, when defeated of its aim, to the reaction of falling back temporarily to a more infantile, less selective and more impersonal level; this happens or tends to happen so regularly in the defeats and losses and baulkings of love, that the career of the individual is (usually and perhaps always in emotion, if not in actual behavior) a series of ups and downs and not a uniform progression; and these temporary regressions (which have ego-reassurance values) do not mean lack of progress in emotional development or prognosticate failure in achieving full adult heterosexuality, unless the individual has been so emotionally injured by early severity or coddling that these regressions become permanent. The progression is toward capacity for both intensity and diffusion of love; for its diffusion in social (work and play) interests not only outside the selected and intense love-relationship but also within that relationship, so as to make it a more resistant, flexible, and enduring mutual bond, and hence more serviceable for the parental-family relationship which is its final use and instinctive aim. These final purposes, however, being instinctive, may remain unconscious; the heterosexual development, seen at the point of conscious feeling, is simply one of progress in what may seem the three separate realms of love and work and social life—of greater seriousness in love, greater ambition in work, and greater ease and adaptability in social life.

We have taken for granted (since this section is a sketch of normal and successful development) an absence of repressive influences in childhood and a healthy social environment in adolescence, affording full encouragement to the growth of the heterosexual emotions. We have carried our adolescents through the formal education and the informal unsegregated companionships which gradually detach them from their childhood homes and attach them to the larger world of work, general social relations, and mate-love. At the same time they have reached approximately their full development in size and strength. They are no longer adolescent children. They have finished high-school, and they are already at work, or they are in or leaving college. At whatever point their environment gives them the feeling of being young men and young women, by laying upon them increasingly adult tasks and responsibilities—and in despite of their lack of complete economic independence—they have 'come of age' and are adults. Young adults, to be sure, but adults none the less. And one of the necessities of being adult is a facing and solving of the mating-problem.

The mating situation becomes a problem to be consciously solved for various reasons. For some of them it will be a problem only in terms of personal choice. That is, for some of these young people the arrival at the adult age of 18 or 21, or whatever it may be, will be an arrival at opportunities for marriage. No economic or social obstacles will prevent their taking the final step toward which the heterosexual impulse, after its adolescent delays, will imperatively urge them. But because it is a final step, and because it must be faced by the conscious mind, it will constitute a problem.

Even the Trobriand youths and girls, who, by the simple process of sleeping for a while with everybody they fancied, have drifted into a particular association which has stood the test of time, must sooner or later consciously face the problem of whether that association is to become a marriage. Divorce among the Trobrianders is easy, and yet marriage remains a step to be seriously considered. A pre-marital association can be broken off with no more trouble than their private griefs may bring. But a marital association is a public matter, having about it an air of final choice. This emotional finality, which ease of divorce does not in the least remove, is due to the fact that the marital association implies children. Loves may come and loves may go, leaving nothing but a memory, but children remain and have to be brought up. The marital choice is thus a permanent one in the respect that divorce does not abolish the children. This is true even though in the Trobriands the accepted dogma of 'no paternity' requires them to believe that the children are only the mother's. In Trobriand terms, the woman's marital choice determines into whose hands these reincarnated beings shall be placed, whom they will (in spite of the assumed lack of relationship) resemble, whom they will have as a protector, guide, model (if a boy), and friend, in their early years. The possibility of subsequent divorce does not diminish the emotional (and in some respects the actual) finality of the marital choice. The question of marriage has thus not been solved by sleeping together; it still has to be dealt with by the mind, in the light of such knowledge as it can muster; and young men who were found sufficiently agreeable as bedfellows have been refused as husbands by Trobriand girls on account of their being, after all, 'lazy good-for-nothings' in all other respects. A healthy heterosexual impulse takes what we call 'character' very seriously into consideration when it is a question of marriage and hence of the nurture to be expected for children.

In our conventional civilized life, precisely the same motives will be found to operate. Our young woman just arrived at adulthood and (in this instance) able to get married at once if she wishes to do so, will nevertheless find that her sexual impulses, now that it is a question of mating, will use for their purposes her social intelligence—and will seek to prolong the delay before the final act of mating, until the instinctive selective process, which has thus far proceeded along emotional lines almost exclusively, can be brought into the realm of social judgment. That is to say, the emotional selection which has been the normal adolescent mode of feminine choice, has been influenced by all the symbolic evidences of masculinity, everything which indicates power, physical or social. When the filial pattern is broken up, so that the girl is no longer in love with clergymen, schoolmasters, outstanding political figures, and other embodiments of parental power—when her heterosexuality becomes first emancipated from the home and free to express itself in conscious erotic attractions—she will normally fall headlong in love (according to her tastes) with (1) football heroes, (2) young men of wealth or superior social station, (3) actors, poets, or artists of some sort, or (4) especially gifted young intellectuals. All of these, in their different ways, manifest or embody power of a traditionally masculine sort, of which female heterosexuality must take cognizance, to which it must (according to its tastes) respond. Her physical heroes speak to her unconscious mind, seeming to offer her their strength and courage to defend and protect her and her children. Her social heroes seem to offer her a different but not less real protection. Her artist heroes have for her a complicated charm, partly due to their uncanny knowledge of all the hidden secrets of her nature, and partly due to their helplessness; but in addition to these godlike and infantile attractions, they have also a reputation for being 'successful with women', which seems to promise her skilful initiation into all the mysteries and delights of sexual love. And even the lonely intellectual, however socially awkward and however socially reprehended for his lack of interest in the ordinary fields of masculine achievement, may be to her a hero, a future leader of successful revolt in the world of thought or politics, with in any event a distinction in his ability to go against the currents of life, which is one of the highest masculine attributes, and seems to promise her a dangerous but glorious adventure in mateship. All these considerations (if they are felt by the girl herself, not merely urged upon her egotism by outside social influences) are not matters alien from sexual preference but a part of it. An adolescent girl ordinarily tests her sexual temperament by experimentally indulging in several of these varieties of love-affairs—usually at a sufficiently safe distance. Such a 'love affair' is for her none the less real and important if, as often happens in early adolescence, the loved one remains wholly unaware of it. The processes of adolescent emotional development tend to swing back and forth between sentiment and sensuality, never at first uniting them in the same experience. There will have been, after these sentimental episodes, others representing an eager but less highly personal exploration of the possibilities of erotic response to the other sex. But when the sentimental and the erotic emotions have finally been united in the love of an individual, there still remains for the girl a final act of choice, which normally brings her love-affair into the penultimate arena of social judgment. Her soul as it were and her senses have both ratified her love-choice, and are reluctant to submit the decision to any further authority—but her sexual instinct urges the completion of the selective process.

'Social judgment' is not what papa and mama may think of the young man, though that may enter into the matter significantly. Nor is it what her social circle may think of him, though that too may be important. It is not a question of their judgment upon him, but of hers—of hers, not in the secret cave of mid-courtship, where he is free from competition and comparison, but in the full light of daily existence where he is a man among other men. If she happens to have already mated sexually with her lover, this test still has to be endured—and it may be a disillusioning one. He has, in the earliest stage of the courtship, run to her satisfaction the gauntlet of certain tests of comparison—but though they were symbolically serious and important, they were not socially so. The ability to win a game and knock a rival down, to order a dinner and pay a compliment, to read poetry and make love with expertise, to think strange and rare thoughts and tell the world to go to hell, are all important symbolic attributes of masculinity; but how 'real' are they? How far do they imply masculine character in fundamental things? These questions are only to be answered by looking at him again as he goes through the world of people. Their reactions to him are significant; for they are not all soul-sick and sense-hungry for him, and their tones, their glances, their attitudes reveal a judgment which the girl's mind must either accept or reject. But, aside from their reactions, she can see him for herself—how he behaves in work and play and study, in victory and defeat, in meeting the demands of life.

A great deal depends upon her judgment and decision. Marriage is a serious matter, divorce something not lightly to be undertaken. But these are legal considerations, and we are concerned with psychological states. Let us then, for the moment, abolish legal forms. Let us say that this young woman believes in freedom, and that the community in which she lives is sufficiently tolerant or helpless, so that a free union will be accepted. She is free to walk out on her mate at any moment. But she happens to be very much in love with this young man. She is not looking forward to walking out on him, ever; nor does she expect him to walk out on her. She is committing herself wholly—when she does commit herself. If he seems afterward to be turning out to be a liar or a brute or a weakling, if he appears to have no real qualities behind his charms, she will be not merely hurt but incredulous. It will be long before she accepts the truth and admits herself a fool in her love-choice. She will try to prove herself wrong, try to persuade herself that she is asking too much of him; and then try to prove that he can measure up to at least her minimum demands. How many years of her youth will she give to these efforts before she actually walks out on him? How much of discouragement will she suffer for her failure?

But she has not yet made her love-choice. This may have been an infatuation, natural enough and instructive in its way—nothing to regret when her private grief is over, if only she does not make the foolish mistake of taking it too seriously *now*, and regarding it as mate-love. To be sure, she does not commit the disloyalty of thinking these things consciously. She is proud of him, she is showing him off—but her unconscious mind is taking note of whether he really is some one to be proud of. The world may be fooled, papa and mama may be taken in by him, but her unconscious mind, sharpened to its keenest distrust, is not so easily deceived. Her instincts are fighting on her behalf for the nurture of her future children. The safety of the species is at stake.

It may appear, indeed, to be slightly less at stake when legal marriage is, as is usually the case, what is in question—since legal marriage offers formal guarantees of security. But everyone knows of how little worth are these formal guarantees. If she has chosen for herself a good mate, they are not needed; if she has chosen a neurotic wastrel or drunkard, the formal guarantees of security are a hollow mockery. The success of her marriage depends upon her choice. It will depend also on other things later, but at this moment success and failure lie in her hands. Naturally it is a time of delay, not a time of rushing blindly ahead. The delay, it is hoped, will be one of triumphal progress. She has not been a fool. This is her mate, and what she feels for him is mate-love.

So far has her sexual instinct carried her—through a series of delays and experiences and half-matings to its immediate goal of love-choice and sexual union—not stumbling into it by accident nor trying it in casual experiment, but leading up to it as an emotional finality.

There is, however, an end to this instinctive procrastination. The sexual instinct provides its own delays to be endured and its own trials to be undergone, it carries youth and girl through the epic drama of sexual selection according to the higher mammalian mating pattern, with some human refinements of its own to induce between the two who choose each other an emotional fixation which should serve the purposes of prolonged parental care. The sexual instinct will even accept and use as its own selective devices the social hurdles of education and jobs. Its aim, no less than that of society, is security—security for the unborn. But it goes toward sexual union, and when its conditions are fulfilled it demands ratification. This goal has not been reached for nothing. The sexual instinct has not come so far only to be fobbed off with fine words. If there is any further delay before sexual union, it is over the protest of the sexual instincts and against all its powerful compulsions to the contrary.

Any such further delays will depend upon the force majeure of fate or society or individual purpose—accidental absence or violent separation or wilful self-denial. We may here ignore the first two; as for self-denial, it requires the consent of the mind. The mind's consent to further delay was formerly won by prolonged subjection to social distortion; but that is not now to be counted upon, and where it exists must be reckoned a neurotic weakness. Not superstitious fear, then, but only such reasons as the mind can wholly approve will account for further delay in despite of the instinctive urge.

§ 2. Obstacles to Mating

Reasons for further delay in mating may exist, or appear to exist; and delay, if it is not too long, can be accepted, with however ill a grace, by the sexual instincts. Such a wilful delay, for example, as that represented by the few months which may be still necessary to complete a period of schooling, or any other obvious and socially more or less imperative task, is endurable by normal sexual instincts. But several years' delay means a cheating and defeating of the instincts, which, it may be said dogmatically and in spite of romantic instances to the contrary, are not geared to endure such prolonged tension. Under prolonged delay, as in the preposterous 'engagements' of several years' length, if there ever were any adult sexual wish, it becomes weakened, and 'gleam by gleam, the glory drops from their youth and love'. What is thus supposed to be merely postponed is in all truth given up forever; no final marriage can ever be the union so long ago desired. In fact, as Paul Popenoe brusquely remarks, "a long engagement commonly shows lack of real interest on the part of one or both of the partners. Such engagements are usually broken off once or twice and renewed again later on; all of which indicates that something is wrong". He enunciates the common-sense modern rule "that if a man and woman are deeply in love, and if they had any right to become betrothed, they should and will marry without dragging things out indefinitely".

The social and economic conditions and traditions of modern society are, however, still so lingeringly patriarchal at this juncture that it is customary for a vast number of genuinely adult love-matings to be baulked, on the theory that the people concerned are 'too young'. And we must now consider the more complicated psychology of those young adults for whom marriage is indefinitely postponed. They are usually a year or two older than their grandfathers and grandmothers were when they were married; they are old enough physically, mentally and emotionally to be as capable of bearing the responsibilities of matehood as they ever will be: so that what is meant is that the young man is not at present capable of supporting a wife in idleness or children at all.

This, as we will undertake to show, is a patriarchal and not a modern condition of marriage, and represents a false ideal of economic adulthood. We are now immediately concerned with its psychic results.

The results of customarily setting marriage outside of and beyond the educational period may be to extend for young people the period of selective association and in general the normal behavior of adolescence to a year or two beyond what would have been and tends to be their mating-age. In so far as this is successfully done, it may be regarded as one of the special accomplishments of modern culture. But modern culture cannot work psychic miracles. It cannot and does not successfully extend adolescent psychology over the whole term of college life. That is, it can and does extend boyish and girlish dependence, irresponsibility and silliness far up into early adulthood—much to the detriment of the early adult educational tasks which they are supposed to be pursuing. But it cannot and does not delay the mating age so indefinitely without emotional stultification of the individuals.

This stultification ordinarily occurs in the effort to construe early adult mating choices as irresponsible play, in obedience to the social theory which prohibits the young people concerned from regarding love-choice as a responsible action preliminary to matehood. But if love-choice is not a responsible action, neither is sexual union. It too may be regarded as an inconsequent and trivial matter. That is the logic of the situation. Young adults who are barred by social rules from matehood cannot continue to take sexual relations seriously.

Romantic literature, it is true, may serve in adolescence to disguise the situation. It leads them to look forward eagerly to love-choice, as though the love-choice of young adults really mattered. It does not reveal to them that according to our social rules the love-choice of such young and economically helpless lovers is worthless. Over that painful social fact it draws the veils of illusion. So that for young people whose instinctive respect for love is encouraged by romantic fiction there is bound to come a rude awakening.

Sometimes, afterward, they blame romantic fiction for deceiving them. They remember bitterly their trustful belief in the fairy-tales of young love triumphing over social obstacles. They feel ashamed that they should have been so gullible. But romantic fiction is scarcely to blame. Its happy fantasies are true to their instinctive wishes, and in fulfilling those wishes it must ignore or deny the hateful contrary facts of our social life. But it is true that their awakening from their wish-dream to the commonplace and universally accepted fact of the social inconsequence of young love comes as a shock.

Their disillusionment inevitably goes to extremes. They are faced abruptly with the necessity of adjustment to the actualities of life. And in order to make this adjustment, they must alter their instinctive set of valuations. Romantic literature has proved a false guide, and all its counsels are rejected. Romantic literature has told them that young love-choice is sacred; and it lied, for nobody regards young love-choice as of the slightest importance. Romantic literature also proclaims sexual union sacred, as the seal of the finality of love-choice; evidently that too is a lie. Youth's disillusionment extends throughout the sexual realm, and involves a necessary revaluation of the sexual act in the light of practical facts. And in the light of practical facts its value—formerly put at the highest instinctive level—now appears to be very slight indeed. In the effort to clear their minds of romantic illusions, young people tend—not without pain—to accept the most trivial valuation of the sexual act.

The disillusionment takes place not only in the minds of individuals by themselves, from observation of the world, but also as a typical campaign of early adult seduction between a youth and a girl. Either the youth or the girl may be the already disillusioned one, urging upon the other the practical unimportance of the sexual act, so that it may be immediately shared as amusement. But though the case of the disillusioned girl seducing the idealistic youth is newer and properly occupies the attention of fiction and drama, the case of the disillusioned youth and the idealistic girl is still the more typical one and will be used here in illustration.

The commonest example is that of the young man with previous casual sexual experience who is going with a sexually inexperienced girl; he is impatient of her unwillingness to go beyond the bounds of adolescent petting, and delivers in effect and frequently in so many words an ultimatum: unless she will have sex-relations with him he will stop going with her. It is not a matter of refusal of marriage, since marriage is already understood by both to be out of the question. The young man's attitude is usually established by himself and others on physiological grounds: having had sexual experience, he finds intolerable the unrelieved excitation of prolonged adolescent petting which is all the girl is prepared to give him. But this intolerability of prolonged sexual tension is to be interpreted in terms of its indefiniteness of extension through time. If it were to be endured merely for a few months preliminary to a real mating, it would not be found so intolerable in fact. But there is no real mating to be looked forward to in this case, and so the idea of waiting is robbed of biological meaning. 'Waiting'—for what? One can wait for something, but one cannot wait for nothing; and one doesn't. It is then the *meaninglessness* of the prolonged sexual tension which renders it intolerable to the young man. To the girl, whom we have presumed to be not yet disillusioned, the prolonged sexual tension still has all its instinctive significance of being preliminary to an emotionally final love-choice, and it is not at all intolerable but on the contrary very agreeable.

Thus we are spectators not of a mere vulgar physical seduction but of a psychic drama. The young man is in the position of knowing about a devalorization of love-choice of which the girl is still happily ignorant. To her the state commonly called virginity is simply the state precedent to the beginning of *a* sexual union in which she instinctively hopes to find a lasting happiness; it is true gold to be spent in making the *right* love-choice.

But to the young man in the light of his knowledge of current economics this precious treasure of preliminary sexual selective power, her virginity, is merely an awkward and inconvenient bundle of post-war paper marks and rubles. 'Oh, hell, spend it! It only amounts to a nickel all told, kid.'

A nickel is still a nickel. If her treasure of selective power has shrunk to these poor dimensions, it can still be exchanged for a momentary amusement. It is in this mood of disillusionment that she begins her early adult sexual career. And it is important to note that she has been 'seduced' not by merely physical means but by an intellectual argument however crudely put; and that this argument, far from being a lie, comes very near to being the plain truth.

It is so near to being the truth that it is no wonder if it has more weight with young adult minds than the anxious warnings of those patriarchal moralists who tell the young woman that by losing her virginity she will necessarily decrease her chances of marriage. She will not necessarily do so; she may actually increase her chances of marriage and of a happy marriage to boot. For the devalorization of love-choice is really not as extreme as it may appear to the disillusioned young woman. Her love-choice can be expended, if not (under these social-economic circumstances) in gaining immediately a lasting happiness in matehood, yet in securing a foothold on the pathway which leads to such matehood. Beginning with its lowest terms, it may and often does secure her the company of young men, one after another, among whom she may find her mate—and from whose company she might be effectively debarred by her fearfulness over losing her status as a virgin. To that extent she may find herself in precisely the situation of the Trobriand young woman, for whom the only opportunities for ultimate marriage lie in the process of having sex-affairs with one young man after another until she finds a mate.

There are, to be sure, some realistic drawbacks to this procedure, which we shall enumerate. But first it must be noted that the contrary procedure, recommended by the Moralists, may not, in these social-economic circumstances, work even as well. Where marriage must be *indefinitely delayed,* the girl who chooses to preserve her virginity can be observed to be, in general and in spite of specific exceptions, losing year by year her powers of attracting men, her ability to get along with them, and her chances of ever marrying. The non-virgin may have paid bitterly and painfully for her increased emotional experience, her understanding of and adaptive powers with regard to men, her continuing sexual charm, and her unwithering feminine good looks; but these are among the means by which matehood is to be, if at all, achieved in later adult life. The young woman who has relied upon her mere physical inexperience in sex finds that, in itself, an increasing disability and liability. The girls on the verge of becoming 'old maids'—'old maids' in looks, in temperament, in habit, and in social awkwardness—who go about trying desperately and even recklessly to get rid of the virginity which has stood them in such ill stead, are painful evidences of the failure of this patriarchal precept. Such women are more convinced of the rightness of the other method than are those who have tried it.

We now come to the drawbacks of the other method, a method which might be described in the words: 'if a girl can't get what she wants, she'd better take what she can.' It is perhaps best adapted to girls who do not know clearly what they want—who are as a matter of fact still not sexually mature in the years assigned to early adulthood. These girls receive with less shock the disappointments of love, because love means less to them. If they are sufficiently infantile they can get a great deal of satisfaction out of their sexual affairs by considering them egotistically in the light of exploits. Nor are we entitled to regard this as neurotic unless it represents so fixed an emotional trait as to interfere with the possibility of later mating and the satisfactions of marriage. At the earlier adult stage when marriage is for social-economic reasons 'out of the question', it is, with reference to current social purposes—such as they are—a more or less socially approved trait (as we have already found it to be in Samoa). If, that is to say, social-economic conditions tend to pass young women of marriageable age from bedfellow to bedfellow for several years, it is just as well that they should get some satisfaction out of it by construing it as a series of triumphs rather than a humiliating situation. And those who can so favorably construe it are likely to be those who though adult in age are not yet fully adult in emotion. Indeed—and this is one of the most truly regrettable features of the whole situation (a really tragic feature) —it is too often the emotionally adult young woman, forbidden by social-economic conditions to marry young and unable to content herself with anything less than real matehood, obliged to reject with instinctive disdain the use of sex-relations as a trivial and irresponsible amusement and able to conquer her primary sexual impulses, who becomes an 'old maid'. Social accidents, such as emigration to colonial countries where women are in great demand, have shown that many 'old maids' make good wives in every respect. They are 'old maids' because they cannot accept the indignities to their instincts offered by irresponsible sexuality. A certain proportion of them thus represent the tragic wastage of social-economic conditions which are hostile to mating.

Perhaps, however, some of the above implications require clearing up. They may seem to smack of the patriarchal notion that to a 'good' girl a succession of lovers is unthinkable. That was not the meaning intended. Up to the time of definite and emotionally 'final' choice, a wide and long series of selective contacts is normally appreciated by anybody, male or female:—there cannot be, in this experimental and adolescent sense, 'too many' lovers. But no one, male or female, likes to be frustrated in an adult or 'final' choice. The young man, however, is accustomed to fall back upon adolescent notions of progress (correct in their place), or upon more infantile notions of egotistic exploit, to make the pain of frustration more endurable and particularly to make socially determined frustration compatible with self-respect. A sense of emotional frustration results from the forbidding of an *open and acknowledged* (or domestic) sexual relationship, and from the enforced avoidances of an appearance of permanence in the relationship—all of which enforced avoidances are symbolic of the fundamental enforced avoidance of having children. The instinctive urge toward the reproductive goal is felt emotionally by lovers as a quality of 'foreverness' in the relationship, and the enforced repudiation of that goal is felt emotionally as a painful defeat of the instincts—unless the sexual defeat can be construed as an egotistic triumph.

There is no real instinctive 'defeat' in the pre-adult period in which one still *has* a choice of mates; it is only when one has *made* a choice of mates that defeat is possible. The English language, by offering us only the same word, 'choice', in these two mutually exclusive and temporally successive meanings distinguishable only by the verbal context, obliges us here in the interests of clearness to call attention to the fact that in the *act of choice* one necessarily *gives up the power of further choosing;* and, though the choice may be actually impermanent, its emotional permanence, its 'foreverness for the time being', is the significant thing about it—which we have here sought to emphasize by speaking of it as an 'emotionally final choice'. Now the adolescent emotions normally welcome a succession of necessarily impermanent love-affairs in which finality (usually symbolized by the sexual act) is avoided and freedom to choose thus maintained. But the fully adult emotions, having renounced the power of further choosing, by an emotionally final act of choice, are outraged by a sexual 'freedom' which is in reality merely a coercive restriction to an adolescent kind of love-making, however it may be given an apparently adult dignity by the use of sex-relations. This enforced childishness is then sought to be justified emotionally, so that it will not be intolerably humiliating; and since the sexual instincts are utterly unable to furnish emotional justification for their own defeat, the egotistic instincts are called upon to reconcile the individual to his (or her) lot.

An amusing and instructive instance of this reinterpretation of sexual defeat as egotistic triumph is furnished by two versions of the same incident in the writings of Theodore Dreiser. In his novel, *The 'Genius'*, we are given—mixed with alien matter derived from observation—some admittedly autobiographical material; in *A Book About Myself* one of these incidents is set forth in a very different light. Let us take first the incident as portrayed in the novel—the self-comforting interpretation. The hero of the novel is an artist; he falls in love with a girl, who returns his love; but (as 'geniuses' do) he moves on to larger fields of life and love, leaving her behind; their letter-writing lapses, but after an interval he hears from her—she indicates that she knows he is through with her. "Won't you return me the notes I have sent you from time to time and my pictures? You won't want them now." And there is a touching postscript:

"I stood by the window last night and looked out on the street. The moon was shining and those dead trees were waving in the wind. I saw the moon on that pool of water over in the field. It looked like silver. Oh, Eugene, I wish I were dead."

It reveals to us the depth and the pathos of her love for him. We pity the poor girl. The situation is hurried past in the novel, but as readers we pause to reflect that it is in the nature of 'geniuses' to climb to success by setting heel upon the bleeding hearts of women. We feel the inevitableness of this girl's heartbreak. Comforting, is it not, to the male ego?—but now let us see the emotional context of the same letter, in its original form, in the writer's actual life. The girl wrote: "I want to know if you won't send me back the letters I wrote you. You won't want them now." And there is the touching postscript:

"I stood by the window last night and looked out on the street. The moon was shining and those dead trees over the way were waving in the wind. I saw the moon on that little pool of water over in the field. It looked like silver. Oh, Theo, I wish I were dead."

In this more candid autobiography it appears that the young man wanted very much to marry the girl; and the only reason he didn't was that he was a dreamer and couldn't earn enough money to support a wife (which both took for granted as necessary); it was in search of a better job that he went away; and still unsuccessful, he lost hope of ever marrying her; it was a frightful wound to his masculine pride when she wrote asking him to send back her letters—and the wound was not a clean sharp wound such as might have been made by her ceasing to love him; it was gangrened with the corroding knowledge that she still did love him. Now it is young Theodore that we are sorry for, even more than the girl. He has been robbed by poverty of his sweetheart. Shall he defy fate and ask her to join him? "Twenty dollars a week was very little for two. * * * I did not see how I was to save much or how I could support a wife. In addition there was the newness of my position here. * * * By nature where things material of [or?] futurial [*sic*] were concerned I was timid, but little inclined to battle for my rights or desires, and consequently not often realizing them. * * * Sympathizing with the pain which Alice was suffering, and alive to my own loss of honor and happiness, still I hesitated to pull down the fine picture of myself which I had so artistically built up, to reveal myself as I was, a man unable to marry on his present salary." He could not decide either to send for her or give her up. "My natural tendency was to drift, to wait and see, suffering untold agonies in the meanwhile."

Here is no 'genius' riding his high horse, but a suffering and ashamed young man. "These mental stresses were always sufficient, however, to throw me into a soulful mood. * * * Indeed my heart was torn by the inextricable problems which life seemed ever to present and I fairly wrung my hands as I looked into the face of the hurrying world. * * * Only silence and the grave ended it all." It must have been soothing to his shame, and healing to his hurt honor, when in some such 'soulful mood' the answer came that it was all right for a 'genius' to leave his sweetheart—there would be for him, as there always are for 'geniuses', other sweethearts. Now he could feel sorry for the girl, but he need not feel sorry for himself. It is rather pleasant to feel sorry for other people; it is being sorry for oneself that hurts. He was relieved of that intolerable pain. We may believe that in such a fantasy-theory, which later had exemplification in a novel, he found, as he tells us he did in poetry-making, "a golden key to a world of beauty and light where sorrow and want could never be".

The general applicability of such consolatory theories to painful individual situations can easily be seen. A secret sexual union which is socially frustrated may instinctively seem tragic until the ego is reassured by some theory of exploit—a consolation, it has already been pointed out, not restricted to men. However, it has been suggested that these consolatory constructions are not so easily put upon sexual defeats by some young women, including, there is reason to believe, those who are most emotionally adult. For extremely repressed young women, who are in their physical adulthood still emotionally tied to a father image, and with a tendency to regress into homosexuality, such a period of exploit may serve the purpose of reassurance (in fictitious terms, it is true) of their heterosexuality; it may keep them out of overt homosexuality during early adulthood and confirm them in their enjoyment of the society of the other sex—not, to be sure, without the possibility of its constituting a habitual neurotic compromise beyond which they will never advance, but with the other possibility of being outgrown in time and normal sexual adulthood ensuing. Just what is the prognosis in an individual case is hard to state but not difficult even for people with no special technology to see: it depends in a given case on whether the pre-adult pattern of sexual exploit is more and more easily accepted as time goes on, or whether it is less and less easily accepted—the latter meaning that the girl is growing up emotionally toward capacity for adult love.

There are, of course, no statistics on the number of young women who, under these circumstances of social frustration, experiment with a succession of secret sexual affairs before arriving or failing to arrive at adult matehood; but observation, the modern novel and drama, and the public reactions to the subject, suggest that they are very numerous. Most readers of this book will be able to call to mind several if not a score of examples. On *a priori* grounds a great many would be expected in the period of rapid break-up of patriarchal conventions with its lingering effects of patriarchal training. The greater opportunity for illicit sexual affairs would not account for them, without a patriarchal background which keeps young people from having strong instinctive mating impulses and on the other hand allows them to be more or less satisfied with secret intrigues.

Back of all these young people stands an army of unhappily married parents, who have not been able to help their children grow up to healthy adult heterosexuality because they were infantile themselves. They—the parents—have not been able to furnish their children the examples of happy and successful manhood and womanhood; nor have they furnished by their own marriages an incentive to achieve adult mating; they have not been able to refrain from exploiting their children emotionally to make up for the absence of normal love in their own lives; and often enough they have not been able even to give their children the fundamental assurance that they are loved.

These young men and young women are thus the products of psychically unstable homes. In lieu of the real stability which only mate-love can give, the parents have desperately held their homes together by mutual coercion or by self-repression. They have sought to give the illusion of the stability of Gibraltar to marriages that were a hollow shell; but the children, who are less impressed by what people say than by how they act, have not been deceived. They are psychically a species of orphans with the orphan-psychology of uncertainty, inferiority, self-pity and fantasy-consolation. If a certain number of them, against such odds and by whatever roundabout route, achieve at last the capacity for mate-love, that is much to their credit.

We have not, however, concluded the tale of the drawbacks to this post-patriarchal psychology. The economic difficulties of mating have at the same time made young men more timid in love and young women more enterprising. The enterprise of the young women, taking the form of willingness to enter into secret sexual unions, is so obviously a way of gambling upon a future marriage that—or so it is reported—the less reckless young men tend to take the traditional feminine attitude of sexual evasiveness, retreat and flight. The reversal of the traditional rôles of the sexes, in so far as it has occurred, is not a happy one. The traditional rôles after all conform to the instinctive sexual pattern of our species. Girls really prefer to be pursued, and men really prefer to do the pursuing.

This, to be sure, is one of those generalizations about 'the difference between men and women' which have recently become discredited. The reasons for that is the fact that such generalizations were almost invariably made from a patriarchal point of view, with the purpose of shoving women back into convenient categories and of ignoring the rich variety of feminine human nature. A sentence beginning 'Women are——' is still naturally suspect; and even if it ends 'beautiful', the presumption is that their alleged beauty is to be used as an excuse for making them sit on a cushion and sew a fine seam and feast upon strawberries, sugar and cream instead of doing something they would rather do. So that we can get no forrader here without making a distinction between instinctive and non-instinctive human activities.

The instinctive purposes of mankind are permanent in a sense in which no cultural purposes can be: the cultural purposes change, the instinctive purposes remain just what they were. We may therefore be prepared for at least some tendency toward fixity in the emotional relations by which the *instinctive* purposes are carried out, though meanwhile the emotional relations by which *cultural* purposes are carried out may keep on changing. We know that sexual organisms have a different attitude toward life than asexual organisms, in being *not self-sufficient but dependent upon the other sex,* so that their activities center not only about food-getting but about sexual union. We know that animals have a different sexual pattern from plants, one in which sexual selection begins to operate through *individual choice.* We know that the animals which care for their young have developed *modes of courtship.* We know that the higher mammalian sexual pattern is definitely one of *competition between males and choice by the female.* We know that in savage life *the male makes the sexual advances and that the female provokes and then accepts or rejects them*—and when she accepts them, at least for the serious purpose of mating, does so only after *delay and retreat.* We know that in patriarchal life, in which the natural courtship pattern was largely abrogated and replaced by social arrangements permitting no individual choice, it nevertheless crept back at every opportunity. We know, moreover, that the emotional tensions of courtship have a definite biological value in securing prolonged parental care for the young. So upon the whole it does not seem rash to speak of *the natural courtship pattern as a permanent tendency in human nature.*

But this courtship pattern involves retreat by the female in order to encourage the male to pursuit. What we are now considering are the psychological results of a state of affairs in which females do not dare flee for fear they will not be pursued—in which they have to do the pursuing and men the fleeing. The psychological fact is, and it can be confirmed by the slightest observation, that men are not at ease in the rôle of hunted creatures. Unless their primary sexual instincts are very weak, they are confused and embarrassed. The pursuit of females is an instinctive male 'duty', and running away from the other sex is instinctively felt to be cowardly and shameful. The human male is geared to chase girls, not to evade them—and he is happiest when, so to speak, he gets a run for his money. Girls, moreover, are confused and awkward in their rôle of overt huntress; they are instinctively geared to make a sexually correct choice only under conditions of male competition for them. Mutual female competition for the same man does not bring all their sexual instincts into play—it brings their egotistic impulses into play instead, with the result that they take incredible pains to capture a man whom they do not sexually want. The situation is one in which their behavior is muddled and stupid.

In natural human courtship the man who makes the advances has made a preliminary selection upon grounds of primary sex attraction; and the girl who has encouraged the advances of several men must make a final selection not only upon these primary grounds but upon ultimate (though perhaps unconscious) considerations of their fitness for permanent matehood (or prolonged parental care). This distribution of selective function permits the man to be normally attracted by all female beauty, and puts upon the girl the tasks, first of discrimination between the kinds of 'strength' offered her for the care of her future children, and second of turning the primary sexual attraction of the chosen male into love by delay and emotional tension. It might be possible to work out a better scheme or a fairer one, but that is how it is arranged in our species; and perhaps there is no unfairness in putting upon the sex that bears children the final responsibility for the selection of the fathers. In any case, they get along best that way.

They do not get along so well when the tasks of selection are reversed. There is perhaps no 'reason' why the other arrangement should not work so well; but the proof of that pudding is in the eating. Women can chase after men on the basis of primary sexual attraction only by regressing to a pre-adult boyishness; and men can exercise the traditional feminine responsibility of sexual discrimination only under peril of regressing into girlishness. If men are to enjoy an instinctive manhood, they need the privilege of following up their primary sexual attractions; but if they are not to waste their time in rather meaningless fornication, their advances must be met by some resistance, which will selectively test the power of these primary attractions and develop the most powerful one of them into love. If girls are to enjoy an instinctive womanhood, they need the privilege of being wooed by a number of men on urgent primary sexual grounds, so that they may choose which man is to be turned into an acceptable lover and mate. By a reversal of rôles they are both cheated of the tension of the love-drama of pursuit by the man and capture of the girl—by which alone they have instinctive assurance of the significance of their sexual union.

So patent has this become that upon practical grounds, and without any understanding of the psychic issues involved, girls are being advised by the wiseacres to go back to the Victorian damsels and learn the art of getting men to pursue them by pretending to an independence they may not feel. "My dear friend, don't be a pharisee!" says Cypria to her shocked friend Saccharissa in *The Technique of the Love Affair.* "I recommend nothing that the chastest women have not practiced from earliest time. * * * They repulsed advances they longed to encourage, and encouraged advances they seemed to repulse", etc. The idea of going back in modern conditions to Victorian artifices need not detain us; but only the spectacle of young women very ill at ease in a rôle they do not enjoy would suggest the need of such advice. The situation is one with which mere feminine artfulness cannot cope. The difficulty is that the young men cannot afford to support a wife, and Victorian artfulness cannot quite simper that off.

But there is, interestingly enough, another field of mating opportunity for young women besides that afforded by timid and ambitious young men. It is perhaps less an opportunity than a desperate gamble, but it is taken insouciantly enough by large numbers of girls; sometimes it results dramatically in disaster, most often perhaps in wastage of emotion and youth, and sometimes in complete success. This field is offered by the large numbers of unhappy marriages already in existence. By breaking up an unhappy marriage an enterprising young woman stands a chance—even if only a 1000-to-1 chance—of getting a mate. The man, having already won his place in the world, is not afraid of a girl in the way that she finds ambitious younger men are. He can surrender himself to her charm and enjoy her society. He can even give her the rare and blessed pleasure of being pursued. Of course he does not intend to marry her; she understands that quite well. He is, in his degree, a pillar of society and he has no intention of doing anything more rash than conduct a discreet sexual intrigue. That is usually the best she can get out of it. But she knows that men do sometimes divorce their wives and marry their sweethearts. She reassures herself against hurt by believing that all she wants is an hour or two now and then out of the world in their 'secret cave'. She does not need to believe otherwise; her sexual instincts will take care of the rest, and if a mating is possible her instincts will find the way to it through whatever wreckage of divorce may be necessary.

This situation has not escaped the notice of the wives in these unhappy marriages, who throughout the middle class are in a state of uneasiness verging upon panic at what appears to them the precariousness of their positions. They are probably inclined to exaggerate the danger; they underestimate the social timidity of their husbands and the mere force of habit. But they are aware, as no one else is, of their own sexual frigidity or of the danger of their husbands' finding themselves not half-impotent in other arms. They know that their Gibraltar is a hollow mockery, and they regard every pretty stenographer as a possible supplanter. They may be right, at that.

A comic or tragic twist, as you please, is sometimes given to the situation by the intrusion of economic motives into such an intrigue—so that it is not love-choice on the girl's part but the desire for security which motivates her; and when the home has been wrecked and a new one set up on its ruins, it is the same home over again—and all the agony has gone to bring about another unhappy marriage.

In these situations, whether or not the second marriage is a real mating, the existence of the children by the first marriage is a complication. Society more and more turns its attention to the attempt to protect by legal means the rights of the children of emotionally bankrupt marriages. That will continue to be an important problem throughout the period of transition from patriarchal marriage. Society must do what it can to give security to children who lack the real security of a father and mother who are emotionally adult and in love with one another. It has practically given up the hope of saving, for the children's sake, marriages which are merely a mutual attempt to conceal sexual failure; it is rapidly giving up the belief that they are, so far as the children are concerned, worth saving. It finds that the only realistic prospect of security for children lies in what would have seemed in patriarchal times—and still seems to patriarchal minds—a fantastic dream: marriages that will endure on a basis of mutual and happy love.

But the census informs us that youthful marriages are in fact increasing. It does not say in what classes, and we are obliged to depend on observation, which reports that the increase is in all classes. For girls who do not expect to do wage-work afterward, early marriage appears to be brought about by an increase in young men's wage-earning power. But in the middle class the increase in early marriage means the mating of young men and young women both of whom expect to continue at their jobs and who are able to delay the advent of children for a few years. It may mean also to some extent a changed parental attitude which permits of subsidies to youthful marriages.

The postponement of children and continuance of the wife at her work is in itself a mode of 'subsidizing' marriage, as we shall see. We will now consider these ways of subsidizing early marriage, taking the parental subsidies first.

CHAPTER XV

THE MODERN MATING PROBLEM

§ 1. Subsidies for Early Marriage

Marriages were necessarily subsidized under the patriarchal régime—the initial subsidy being furnished usually by the bride's family in the form of a dowry. Subsidy was a mode of parental control of marriage-making.

The middle class revolution tended to sweep away all modes of parental control of marriage-making, first by establishing a legal age, usual 18 for girls and 21 for men, at which they had the right to marry without parental consent; and incidentally by abolishing dowries, which were in middle-class idealism regarded (on the whole, correctly) as a means of 'buying' a husband. What this abrogation of the dowry custom really did, however, was to transfer effective control of youthful marriages from the bride's family to the groom's.

Economic adulthood was by the middle class regarded as being, in a man, the capacity for supporting a wife and family; and in a woman, the capacity for performing household duties. According to this standard a girl was marriageable when she had been *trained* to cook, sew, etc.; but a man was only marriageable —if the standard were strictly maintained—when he had achieved an *actual* earning capacity adequate to supporting a wife and realistic prospects of being able to support children as they came along. This meant that practically all girls were marriageable at 18; but that a man might not be marriageable till 30 or 35 years of age.

Marrying between 30 and 40 represented, indeed, the most sober and cautious middle-class male practice. John Ruskin's father, for example, at the age of 24 asked his cousin if she would marry him when he had 'an independence' to offer her; she waited; nine years later, when James Ruskin's business was flourishing and he had paid off his father's debts, he 'claimed her hand'. But young men were not always as sober and cautious as that; and middle-class society has somewhat grudgingly accepted the obligation of helping youthful marriages—partly by an increase in salary, partly by such family help as could be offered, including sometimes the sharing of one of the parental homes with the young couple, and also by wedding presents. But the middle class has in general had a shamefaced attitude toward giving such assistance, as though it were a reflection upon the young bridegroom. He is supposed not to need practical assistance, even though it is well known that he does; even the wedding presents must have the air of luxuries, not of necessities. Everyone knows that a young man just out of college has ordinarily no chance of maintaining a wife, let alone a family, without assistance; but in the background, however consciously repudiated, there lurks the cold-blooded middle-class tradition of waiting until the man is 35 or 40 and has 'established' himself.

Proposals have been made—which of course apply only to the more prosperous part of the middle-class—that young lovers should be enabled to marry by parental subsidies: even, for example, while in college. But the question which has to be asked is: Does this mean a parental subsidy to *any* love-choice the young man or the young woman may make? or a subsidy to a match approved by the parents? It would in practice so obviously be the latter that this turns out to be only another way of letting papa and mama pick the young people's mates. Modern parents desirous of emancipating their children would object to accepting such control.

Higher education used to be in prosperous middle-class families a concession offered or yielded as a special favor by the parents, as it still often is to daughters. It was, so far as the sons were concerned, a kind of temporary reprieve from the harsh battlefield of life. More recently a college education has come to be increasingly taken for granted, especially for sons but frequently also for daughters. It is not regarded as a special parental favor but as a right to which they are entitled; and, while it still represents in many ways a prolongation of adolescence, it is also conversely an escape from parental domination and a beginning of adult life. This higher education is—and we bring in the fact for further illustrative purposes—sometimes partly guaranteed to a child by 'endowment' insurance kept up from infancy by the parents and maturing at college age. Such insurance could also be used to endow early marriages of sons and daughters. This, or some such impersonal mode of subsidy customarily practised, and of a kind not calculated to give the parents responsibility for their children's marriages, would presumably not be repugnant to the fundamental tendencies of middle-class culture. It would throw upon the young people themselves the responsibility for the use of the endowment. It would give a social seriousness to youthful love-choice which is now lacking. And as sons and daughters commenced a work career, they could invest their savings in this fund, making it more their own.

In order for anything like this to happen, of course, the middle class would first have to make up its mind about early marriage —whether it is desirable. If our interpretation is correct, the middle class does desire early marriage, but not on terms of parental control. It is offended at the idea of people marrying before they are able to look out for themselves economically. It regards marriage as an adult institution. In all these respects it represents a break with patriarchal tradition. Even its preposterous long engagements, so characteristic of Victorian times, were its tribute to the ideal of a marriage independent of parental control. Those Victorian males were going to be in a position to make their own marriages if they had to wait till they were 50 years of age!

Such a mode of marriage-endowment, moreover, is not necessarily limited to the middle class. If our civilization should discover that it desires early marriage, then marriage-endowment could take its place along with accident insurance as a form of social insurance, regulated by law and contributed to by all parties concerned. It is not the business of such a book as this to work out such plans, but only to show that if the wish to solve the problem exists it can be solved in terms acceptable to our culture and conforming to our historical tendencies.

The greater problem of poverty in general would not thereby be solved, but a special problem of poverty would be solved. For *the desperate sexual compromises of youth spring from poverty*—not from the poverty of a class but *the poverty of youth in all classes.* The son of well-to-do parents, during early adult life—from 18 until he has finished college, got a job, found out if it is the right job, and secured several raises in salary—is poor; he is dependent on the bounty of his parents; he is in the position of a beggar—and though he may have a lot of spending money, he is none the less a beggar with a beggar's psychology. He can, it is true, stop going to school and get a job; but if the theory is that society needs young men with some education, then it seems only reasonable that society should regard education as a preliminary apprenticeship to a job and be prepared to pay for it as such. The medieval apprentice got paid for learning his trade; not very much, but it was paid as a lump sum at the end of his apprenticeship, so that he had something to begin adult life upon.

The same considerations apply to girls. But before the whole situation can be dealt with, our civilization will have to realize that work is not the instinctive center of our human lives and that love is; that work gains its chief emotional and practical importance as a means, not of *self*-support, but of *mutual* support of those who are joined together in mate-love and family-love.

When industry was a family matter, that was quite clear. The man's work and the woman's work—and, as they grew up, the children's work—served chiefly the maintenance of that union. The situation became obscured when society dispensed with love as a basis of that union and introduced authority instead. In a family originating in mate-love, the children learn, not from compulsion but by example and in emulation, the lessons which will make them, when they come to mate, mutually able with their mates to support a similar union. In a culture in which women's work is different from men's, these will be different tasks; but as it is discovered that these distinctions are wasteful, they will tend to be in many respects the same tasks.

Let us consider some of these tasks. We may take the simple tasks of washing clothes and of killing game for food. In earlier stages of culture the first tends to be the woman's and the second the man's task; but neither of them suppose that in washing clothes or killing game they are 'expressing themselves'. If a girl does not know how to wash clothes she will not be able to take her share of the work necessary to maintain a mating and she will never get a husband; if a young man does not know how to kill game he will never get a wife. But times change and the washing of clothes and the killing of game are both done outside the home; moreover, it is the young man who has a job in the laundry, and the girl who as stenographer in a meat-packing plant is assisting (though indirectly) in the killing of food-animals. Of the young man we can still say that if he doesn't know how to perform *some* task by which he can undertake his share of the support of a sexual union, he will never get a wife. But the girl's economic situation is vaguer. It will, however, become more clear when we consider the young man's situation more carefully.

The young man has, let us say, contributed some of his money to the support of his parental family; but, not to complicate the situation, we will suppose him not to be in the tragic situation of having them really and permanently dependent upon him. What does he do with his wages? He spends them partly for clothes. To what end? That he may not freeze, of course. But that is not all. He dresses as well as he can. Why? Because it gains him approval, both from his own and the other sex. It is, indeed, of the approval of the other sex that he is increasingly aware. He is, in fact, dressing to attract the attention and admiration of girls. He is advertising himself as a young man who has a good enough job so that he *can* dress well. He is advertising himself as a possible mate.

We will not prolong this inquiry indefinitely, but we must take up his amusements. He spends some of his money in going to the movies. Why? Surely this is a purely self-regarding action, taken without any unconscious view to matehood! Besides, he may go with another young man. What do they see? They see their crude unconscious fantasies of sexual mating in politely censored form on the screen: they see their dreams come true, and they are encouraged. Why does our young man go with another fellow and not with a girl? Because they don't like girls? No, because they are both somewhat afraid of girls, and they gain courage by hunting in pairs. Girls, it seems, also hunt in pairs. And so our young laundryman becomes acquainted with our stenographer. Next week they go to the movies together. His work is a means of bringing about the possibility of sexual union, as surely as his savage ancestor's ability to kill game was. His work takes its meaning, not from the fact that it keeps *him* from starving to death, but from the fact that it brings him into the society of girls, gains him the exclusive company of one of them, and enables him in the end to help support their children. Work is for him, as it is for most of male mankind, a means of bringing about and helping to maintain a sexual and family union.

But what about the girl? Let us suppose her similarly free to spend her money, or some of it, as she chooses. What does she spend it for? Clothes, chiefly, with which to gain the approval or envy of her own sex and the attention and admiration of the other. But her clothes do not suggest to the young man that she is a capable stenographer who can draw down a good wage; they say for her: 'Look, I am beautiful, I am a girl, don't you want me?' They are an advertisement of her as a potentially delightful sweetheart, and they call the attention of his instincts to her as a possible mother of his children; though his conscious mind is far from the thought of helping to support her babies, that is what it will come to in the end. Wage-work is to her a means of bringing about—though not as yet of maintaining—a sexual union. She expects to do her share of maintaining that union in their home; she expects to quit her job.

But if she should quit her job, what would she do? Have babies? Her laundryman husband cannot afford to support her and a baby yet. That is why he does not say anything—in spite of the opportunities she gives him—about their getting married.

Several things may happen. Of them all we will briefly outline three possibilities. (1) She may, because of their poverty, give up the idea of marriage and (a) drop him, or (b) enter into a sexual relationship with him; in the latter event *her work will be a thing separate from her love-life.* (2) She may recklessly marry him, have the babies they cannot afford, and be inclined to look back upon her office work as a lost paradise in which she had money for pretty clothes—and if she dreams of going to work it will be as an escape from domesticity. Again *work (outside the home) will be a thing alien to her harassed love-life.* (3) She may marry him, and manage not to have babies, but nevertheless quit her job; she will not have enough to do, or enough that is interesting to do, and his wages will so poorly support them both that she will look back to or forward to office work; but she will feel that going to work is a reflection upon his masculinity, and so will he. Again, *her work (outside the home) will be a thing alien to and hostile to her love-life.*

There remains one more possibility to discuss; but we may pause to note that the other possibilities thus briefly sketched, stupid as they may seem, are the logical developments of the situation in our period of transition from patriarchal society and under the influence of patriarchal idealism. The connection of man's work with love remains plain; but it bears a double burden of responsibility, because *the taking of woman's work from the home into office or factory has severed its apparent relation to her love-life.* It is true that her work in office or factory can, though inconveniently, subserve her love-life quite as surely as if she were washing his shirts and cooking his meals. But for either of them to perceive this requires either extraordinary intelligence such as can compass a break with tradition, or *an education which will unmistakably point it out.* We will suppose them to be capable of working it out for themselves, assisted perhaps by example. So (4) they get married, postpone babies for a few years, meanwhile both keep their jobs, and save and build toward the future. *Here, at last, her work outside the home is not alien to her love-life; it helps maintain their sexual union and helps provide for the children who will later be born of it.*

This elaborate exposition is intended to show the emotional complication that has been introduced into both men's and women's love-lives by the taking of work for women so largely out of the home. It is a situation hard to adjust to; hard not only in psychology but in plain geographical fact. However clumsily, women's work was once attended to all under one and the same roof. But to cut a woman's work-life in two, and put some miles of street-car track in between, and ask her to keep running back and forth and do justice to both halves, is asking a great deal. Nor has the exaggerated emphasis of the middle-class feminist movement on the importance of work for women, and its disdain for or indifference to her very real and inescapable problems of adjustment to the home as wife and mother, been a salutary influence. If the situation is to remain as it is for women, they need an education which will enable them to relate their work outside the home to their love-lives in ways both realistically useful and emotionally stimulating.

We have, however, arrived in our discussion at the mode of *subsidizing early marriage by the economic contributions of the wife during a period of voluntary abstention from childbearing.* We have seen that it is not only an economic but also an educational problem. And we will now transpose it into that realm and see how it looks from that point of view. The environmental setting this time will be one which takes young people to college instead of to work at the age of 18.

§ 2. Young Love and Economics

First we will consider (1) the ordinary way of young love; and then (2) another way.

(1) The conditions of characteristically modern life are such that young John and young Jane are permitted to grow up from childhood through adolescence in comparatively free companionship with others of the opposite sex and of their own age-class. Since girls tend to mature earlier than boys, Jane at 18, 19 or 20 will be making an instinctive love-choice among young men of 21 to 24 or thereabouts. John and Jane have played with each other and with other girls and boys. They have had a variety of adolescent romances and a variety of experimental physical contacts of a conventional sort in dancing, romping and 'petting'; and they have had a variety of experimental companionships—by virtue of all of which they have arrived at what would be, except for social conditions, a psychosexual adulthood. If social-economic conditions permitted them to marry, they would be ready to do so.

They would, that is to say, be ready to make a serious and responsible choice of a permanent mate. John and Jane would take each other as husband and wife.

But John and Jane can not easily do that. John must finish college and get a job. Perhaps the profession he has chosen is not for him the right one; he must take some years to make sure. If he should marry now, as he sees it, he must give up the right to experiment with his career; worse than that, he may have to cut short a long educational preparation for a chosen career and take the first job he can get—since a young man who gets married is supposed not to be a child any longer and is not regarded as entitled to further educational subsidies from his parents. His ambitions are thus in immediate conflict with his mating-wish. Moreover, long engagements are out of fashion, for good reasons. The result is that at precisely the point where, under different social-economic conditions, John and Jane would marry each other, John and Jane avoid one another.

They are in fact abruptly barred from one another. The bars are not of iron but they are just as strong as iron. These invisible bars are their recognition of the impossibility of immediate mating. They are not fools. And they do not want to get their hearts broken. They do not want to surrender emotionally to a mutual love that hasn't a chance of social ratification. So they try to accept the verdict of society, try to believe that their mutual love is all nonsense. Reluctantly, and not without backward glances, they turn their backs upon one another. They see each other recede gradually into the limbo of the might-have-been.

They live, we observe, under conditions in which nobody can prevent them from having overt sexual relations with one another if they choose; but they generally choose not to. They choose not to, because that would make it harder for them to part, that would bring them too dangerously near to a marriage which would be impossibly rash; and they are sensible young people. But the reason which bids them not have sexual relations with each other does not apply to others with whom they are *not in love.* Nobody can prevent them there, either. John almost certainly, in the period of years before his marriage, has such sexual relations; that may be taken for granted, and we will devote our attention to Jane.

Jane has played with the boys of her own age-group (meaning a group a few years older than herself); she has 'petted' with them, 'kept company' (in the useful older phrase) with them, and gone through the whole process of sexually-selective courtship with them, up to the final act of mating; but not only John, who would have been her final love-choice, but her whole age group of young men, is barred from her *so far as marriage is concerned.* It will be years before they can marry; and when they are able to do so, there will be a new crop of girls for them to choose from. John cannot marry Jane now; and when he is ready to marry, and looks back for his lost sweetheart, he will find her imaged to him in, say, Jane's younger sister—now a gawky adolescent and not of the slightest erotic interest to him, but some years later a young woman in youthful bloom. John and all John's friends will not marry any of the girls they have 'petted' and 'gone with'; they will marry those girls' kid sisters.

The kid sisters will have been playing with, 'petting' with, and 'going with' boys of their own age-group; but they will have to turn from those boys, who still have their ambitions to pursue, to John's age-group, which by that time will have established itself in the world and be ready for marriage.

And Jane is now under precisely the same social compulsion. If she is to find a husband, she must turn away from John and his age-group to an older age-group of men who are in a position to marry. She will marry the man whom *her* older sister had to give up some years ago.

She will make herself attractive to this older group of marriageable men; she will get herself a husband from among them, if she can. But there will be a preliminary reluctance in going about the business of getting married in so artificial and cold-blooded a fashion. She will, secretly at least, be rebellious against her fate. She will want to have her fling before she settles down.

Meanwhile, there is her own age-group of young men—all of them unmarriageable at present, but all of them attractive to her. She has played with them, petted with them, gone with them; and since she is not in love with them there is no reason why she should not have a romantic sexual 'affair' with one or more of them before her marriage.

Thus John almost certainly and Jane with increasing probability have sexual affairs within their own age-group—but not with each other. The practical result of this scheme of marriage is that young men and young women may have sexual relations within their own age-group with anybody except those with whom they are seriously in love; that, at least, is the way it is observed to work out. They may go through a courtship with those whom they may not marry; and they must marry those with whom they have never gone through a normal courtship period.

This means, in effect, that the whole courtship period tends to be robbed of its instinctive seriousness, and to be understood as a period of irresponsible sexual amusement.

Its psychological likeness to the patriarchal marriage scheme is obvious. The chief difference is that whereas under the patriarchal scheme no self-respecting young man would consent to settle down in marriage without first sowing his wild oats, this now tends to be true also of young women.

But this whole procedure involves a surrender to lingering patriarchal ideas and to lingering remnants of patriarchalism in our social-economic structure.

(2) The other way of young love throws the patriarchal ideas overboard, and struggles toward more modern social-economic arrangements.

The patriarchal ideas which it throws overboard are (a) the notion that a man must support his wife when she is not incapacitated for wage-earning by motherhood; and (b) the notion that household services are all that a wife may perform in behalf of a marriage. These imply the successful use of birth-control methods, and the ability of wives to earn money in work outside the home before and after the childbearing and nursing period. The recognition of women's work outside the home, and of educational preparation for such work, as *being a part of the marriage system,* and not something alien and hostile to it, would modernize our social-economic system at this point. Women's work outside the home is still regarded as a stopgap before marriage or a refuge from unsuccessful marriage, or as a humiliating necessity due to male economic inadequacy—as, in short, an alternative to wifehood. This is true not merely in the realm of ideas but in the realm of practical fact. Satisfactorily married women are still supposed not to work for wages. It is as though railroads or automobiles were regarded as *emergency* methods of getting some place, to be used only by lame people! When we can transform our conception of the relation of women's work to wifehood and motherhood so that wives and mothers will be expected to do for wages outside the home the share of the world's work which they once did inside the home, then we will be able to make more convenient terms for them in wage-labor. As it is now, wage-labor puts up hurdles against wives and mothers, and almost compels them to choose between being fully female and being wage-workers. The feminist movement, after achieving votes for women, has lost practically all its influence among modern women who wish to be both wives-and-mothers *and* workers, by taking a reactionary stand and accepting the patriarchal and masculine standards of wage work as something which women must adapt themselves to—instead of asking industry to adapt itself to women as wives and mothers.

The efforts of modern wives to use their wage-work as a means of subsidizing their mating and family life runs into serious practical difficulties, particularly after children are born. The stringent demands of industry—adjusted so far only to the non-childbearing half of our species—make some neglect of children and home by wage-working wives and mothers almost inevitable. This, we may believe, is a temporary situation which can be remedied when we have realized that mothers belong in industry and that they need not be asked to behave as if wage-work were more important than their children when they take a job. The full acceptance of this idea will also change the relations of men to their work; we shall no longer have to accept the preposterous pretence that work is an end in itself—we will be able to see it as being what it normally is for almost all mankind, a means to other ends and chiefly the end of mate-love and family life.

But even as things are, the subsidizing of marriage by the wife's work outside the home *before* maternity, can be successfully effected, and does serve to lift from young men the intolerably heavy burden of responsibility which would otherwise require them to postpone marriage and repudiate the seriousness of young love. It enables them to marry young and to marry the girls they love, instead of dutifully having meaningless sexual affairs with a long series of girls whom they don't love.

Judge Lindsey has adopted for such matings the term 'companionate marriage'. In his discussion, informed and generous and essentially valuable though it is, he makes concessions to patriarchal prejudices which we in these pages are unwilling to make and which oblige us to reject the term 'companionate marriage' as descriptive of what we are talking about. Patriarchal skepticisms as to romantic love, and as to the wisdom of youthful love-choice are met in his argument with the suggestion that divorce without alimony (so long as there are no children) would serve to end these companionate unions if they proved to be lacking in the possibility of permanence. Divorce without alimony when there are no children is fully defensible for other reasons. But its intrusion into the argument at this point suggests that these companionate marriages may be regarded by a patriarchal-minded public as convenient stop-gaps before a real marriage. Indeed, the discussions of companionate marriage, whether favorable or unfavorable, have usually tended to assume that the proposed arrangement would give legal protection to the illicit and impermanent sexual affairs now going on among young people—relieving them of the necessity for secrecy and hypocrisy and protecting their self-respect. These purposes are not unworthy ones; but from the point of view taken in our present discussion, they are merely adaptations to a patriarchal psychology and to the lingering remnants of the patriarchal social-economic order. Legal marriage is not necessary for young people to conduct pre-marital sex-affairs with self-respect, as many of Judge Lindsey's illustrations show; and on the other hand the whole tenor of our culture seems to require that marriage, however experimental in fact, should psychologically represent the public ratification of a love-choice which is regarded by the parties themselves as final. The idea of giving the name of marriage to pre-adult sexual experiments runs counter to what seem to be fundamental tendencies of our non-patriarchal civilization.

At all events, and whether we are right or not, we shall proceed according to the view that marriage is an adult arrangement, intended as permanent; and that the opportunities for liquidating mistakes should be offered to wives and husbands by society rather than incorporated in the marital pledge by the lovers themselves as possible loopholes of escape. It can be psychologically adult only when it represents a serious and final choice; and (generally speaking, and usually in the educated class) it can represent a serious and final choice in early manhood and womanhood only when its economic responsibilities are shared by a wage-earning wife and a wage-earning husband, rather than piled upon the shoulders of the man alone. For the general use by young men and young women of this mode of marriage, knowledge of efficient methods of birth-control is necessary; and the increasing spread of such knowledge, despite present legal impediments, may be taken for granted. But in order for these temporarily childless marriages to be emotionally complete matings, their temporary childlessness has to be construed *not as a loophole still left open for escape* but as a period of nest-building, as it were, in preparation for the children that are to come: temporary childlessness not for the sake of 'freedom' but for the sake of children later, who will confirm the permanence of the marriage.

The biological demand is for parents sufficiently in love with each other to remain together for a period long enough to bring up their children. The prolonged care of a child required by civilization extends this period—for a single child—to something like sixteen years; if there are more children, the requisite length of love between the parents is accordingly longer; if the children are spaced out with due consideration for the health and well-being of the mother, the necessary love-period becomes still longer; and if there is a period of years before the children are born, that must be added. It makes an interesting sum in arithmetic. A girl, let us say, marries at 20; has her first child at 25; has two other children, two years apart; and she and her husband expect to remain in love with one another until the youngest child is 16:—that means 25 years altogether and brings her to the age of 45, or past any reasonable opportunities for making a new love-choice. What it comes down to in effect is 'till death us do part'. There is every reason why society should offer to relieve them of that obligation if they are manifestly incapable of bearing it; but there is no sense in pretending that this is not the obligation which they take upon themselves when they marry. If this is—as some think—too much to expect of human nature, if it is an absurd and impossible demand, then society must either reinstitute its social coercions to keep them together whether they are still in love with each other or not; or else it must undertake to let them go their ways and take care of the children in State nurseries and schools. And if it appears that it is not good for children to be brought up by parents who don't love each other, and not any better to be brought up in institutions, then we must either throw up our hands in despair, or else turn to 'living happily ever after' as the only practical solution of the problem.

§ 3. Education for Matehood

To young lovers the idea of living happily ever after does not seem at all absurd or impracticable. They believe that, no matter how it may be with others, they will keep on loving forever. But their sexual instincts, which have brought them to this vision of the future, cannot ensure its coming true. Against that possibility there are a thousand kinds of childishness waiting to vitiate and defeat their love. It may take a great deal of painful experience before they will have grown up enough emotionally to be capable of an enduring love; and even so, they will probably have to struggle daily with the infantilities that remain in their nature. They may never be able to achieve anything better than a habitual working compromise between their childishness and their love. It is not to be expected that we should know much about the art of growing up, after all these centuries in which nobody was allowed to grow up. It is not to be expected that we should know very well how to love freely and fully, after all these centuries in which love was feared and curbed. Some instinctive knowledge we do have; but we do not know how to use it. Jealousy, for example—we do not know how to take the alarm which warns us of possible impending loss, and we may either grow helplessly sick with it or we may fatuously try to reason ourselves out of any respect for it. We do not know very well how to share each other's inner lives—we veer between being clumsy intruders and polite strangers. Passion can for a while heal the hurts we deal each other; but unless we can learn more of love in the meantime, passion will hardly serve as a medicinal balm forever. So uncertain are we still of the importance of love, that science yet hardly ranks it as a subject for investigation on a par with the meanest bacterium. It is true that psychology, having begun to take education seriously, and having found out the way to deal with children, now suddenly realizes that these laws of education apply also to the childishness of adults. *It is true that we now know that the way to get along with a lover in the permanence of marriage is to continue one's own emotional education and become a little more grown up all the time; and that the way to wreck the most promising marriage is to lapse a little more all the time into childishness. The art of staying in love is no longer an utter mystery.* But the education for life, which will be also an education for love, still remains what the airplane and the wireless were until a short time ago, unworked-out possibilities. Considering our historic situation, we may take for granted that most marriages will be bungled in practice, that some will be tragic and some comic failures. That there are so many marriages which blunder toward success instead of toward failure is all to the credit of our instincts.

It is toward a reorganization of education that this view tends most of all. For what are we educated? For being gentlemen? or being wage-workers? or being happy? If for being happy, then we must recognize that our happiness is bound up with success in love more than anything else. It is perhaps impossible to state our rights as sexual beings without seeming to exaggerate them at the expense of our humanness. But our humanness will not suffer from a recognition of our sexual rights. And our sexual rights have long enough been made subservient, not even to broad human considerations, but to property fears.

Education for marriage may suggest an emphasis upon the specific technique of the sexual act. That is not here intended. Indeed, once the traditional repressions of heterosexuality are removed and the goal of matehood left clearly in sight at the end of the path of adolescent education, it is probable that these specific technical aspects of sexuality will appear so simple and obvious as to require no special attention. The proper technique of physical love-making is hard to learn only for those whom repression has made partly impotent or partly frigid—a state of affairs which patriarchal education has, it seems, made all but universal, but which need not be regarded as a permanent condition of human nature. It does not take years of experience or wide variety of experience to learn the art of love in its physical aspects; indeed, years of experience and a wide variety of experience may and frequently do only confirm people in their sexual infantilisms and incompetencies. On the other hand, the freeing of the mind from patriarchal sex-inhibitions can and does bring about adult capacity for physical love-making without further practice or experiment. Some good people regard previous sexual experience by one of the two parties to a marriage as necessary for its success. No amount of actual sex experience by either or both parties to a marriage will in the least degree assure its success. The failure of youthful marriages is to be ascribed not to lack of previous sex experience but to psychic ungrownupness, which may in turn be largely due to insufficiency of courtship experience. An adolescent courtship period which is an emotional education is tremendously important. But there is no magic in the sexual act to transform an emotionally half-grown person into a fully adult one.

The education here suggested is thus not one devoted to the preposterous inventions of those Oriental books which undertook to minister to male impotence by sexual oddities; and still less to a study of sexual perversions. Such an education would, of course, restore physical sex to its place in the physiology courses and would include some practical and non-alarmist and very early instruction on the subject of venereal disease along with similar instruction about other diseases. As Professor Isabel Davenport says: "Children should no more be able to recall when they first heard of or began to learn about the dangers, sources of infection and prevention of gonorrhea and syphilis than they could in regard to tuberculosis."

The same writer has outlined for girls such an education as is here suggested, when she speaks of "the training of girls for their legitimate inheritance of marriage and motherhood, and their responsibilities and rights in connection with all that these imply * * *. It comprehends not merely a pubertal and adolescent training aimed toward making girls physically and mentally fit for maternity and wifehood, but it strikes at the very roots of the girl child's treatment and the social attitude toward her, from the day she is born. It comprehends not only the training of adolescent girls (and boys) into a favorable attitude toward marriage, but the whole broad subject of the conventions and practical relations between the sexes in everyday life—in home and education, in work and play, from infancy on. It comprehends not merely training girls and boys to save a marriage fund, and to work out the problem of the maintenance of a home and the support of children together, but it involves the working out of a new type of home life and child care, suitable to a new industrial and economic age."

To recapitulate the argument: the patriarchal standard which requires the husband to be the sole wage-working supporter of a wife and family requires the postponement of marriage and the frustration of early adult love, and tends to turn the adolescent period of courtship from one of emotional education and responsible selection into one of purposeless sexual pleasure-seeking. But the adolescent courtship period can be made a responsible one and early marriage can be made generally possible, through an economic cooperation of husband and wife in wage-work during at least the early years of marriage, in preparation for children. This requires not only knowledge of birth-control methods but an education in general for matehood.

If marriage is thus a goal for young men and women, not too hard to be attained, always clearly in sight, and one which they approach with their intelligence as well as with their instincts, successful progress in formal education can be accepted by the instincts as a part of the competitive sexual selective process. One of the difficulties of mating is that none of the means of 'showing-off' by which young men and young women attract each other is very revelatory of the qualities of mind and spirit which make for success or failure in marriage. Education is too divorced from life to make its tests worth much in the sexual realm. An education for life, with matehood as its immediate goal, would provide tests which would have some significance for marriage.

The alternatives need not be described again in detail, but they amount to an encouragement of one or another form of sexual infantilism, irresponsibility and promiscuity; and if marriage is made too difficult or the delay is too prolonged, it means an encouragement of both unconscious and overt homosexuality. The question is: do we want to train young people for—we need not hesitate to use the phrase—living happily ever after in hetero-sexual matehood, or for living tormented and frustrated lives of homosexuality, impotence, frigidity and purposeless promiscuity. We have our choice

CHAPTER XVI

ART, ANXIETY AND MANNERS

§ 1. Anxiety and Symbolic Relief

It has been suggested from time to time in these pages that art has a peculiar relation to life: that its business is not to inculcate duty, not even the biological duty of growing up; that its function is rather to fulfill immediately in a symbolic way a variety of impulses which for one reason or another would be socially unacceptable if expressed directly in realistic action—and it might be added here that its most important function is to give symbolic fulfillment to impulses that cannot be expressed in realistic action at all. Some remarks on that score have been scattered through these pages at points where they seemed apposite and were needed to correct an impression of dogmatic narrowness in this view of behavior. But something remains to be said in explanation of the fundamental relation of art to anxiety and of the differences between ritual, art and neurosis. It is a highly technical subject and people who are fairly open minded on the subject of behavior are likely to be touchy about art, which is indeed a kind of religion; so that anyone whose prejudices have not been offended or whose pieties have not been outraged by the previous pages is likely to be disgusted by our intrusion into this field. People who hold nothing else sacred, still hold art sacred; and to them what follows will be mere blasphemy. Nevertheless, in fulfillment of our promise, we proceed.

But to such readers an important concession may be made at the outset. This view of the function of art does not pretend to be a definition of it nor to exhaust its significance. Indeed, there is something so emotionally derogatory of the importance of art in this 'explanation' of its function that this alone should warn us not to take it as a *final* explanation. As when science, having resolved certain physical phenomena into electrons or what-not, still leaves the beauty of a sunset after all unexplained, so this view of art as a symbolic relief of anxiety doubtless leaves it exactly what it was before. Nevertheless, inadequate as this explanation is, it does help us to understand some of the relations of art to life, and may be taken—not as explaining art out of existence and not as affording us any deeper emotional appreciation of art—but for just as much as it may be worth to us in *thinking* about art.

We must begin, however, with anxiety, which in this view is the parent of ritual, art and neurosis. We will deal first with anxiety and savage ritual.

The primitive ritual sex-orgy has been referred to more than once in these pages. Here we may point out the situation under which it arises. The animal organism is adjusted to respond by appropriate action to stimulus. In the lower animals these responses are fixed species-habits, instinctive modes of behavior, correlated with organic structure and unchanging except as the organic structure changes by evolution or mutation into a new species. In mankind there is a high development of the brain-power into the realm of judgment or choice of responses. This means a delay between stimulus and response. Now stimulus brings about in the nervous organism a kind of irritation which increases into a vague suffering until it is relieved by responsive action. It happens, however, that situations may arise in which we cannot find *any* appropriate realistic response to stimulus—because outward circumstances seem to provide none. Here we may illustrate, without going back into savage life.

A young man, parted from his sweetheart, is going eagerly to meet her; but the journey, say by railway train, is long, and the stimulus of imagining their meeting cannot find expression in caresses, simply because she is not there to caress. Under these circumstances the anxiety (as we call this vague nervous suffering from stimulus unresponded to in action) increases until it demands relief; and realistic response being impossible, symbolic response takes its place. The law of nervous organisms is that action of some sort in response to stimulus is more important than the 'right' responsive action. So we see the young man take out a photograph of his sweetheart and (when nobody is looking) kiss it. Having done so, he feels better. It is doubtless realistically absurd to kiss a piece of pasteboard when one wishes to kiss a girl; but the symbolism, which makes the picture stand for the girl, gives him the opportunity to discharge his anxiety in action.

Situations may also arise in which there is an obvious realistic response to stimulus which is forbidden by some social rule. Thus, in an earlier stage of his acquaintance with the girl, the young man may have wanted to kiss her but dared not; romantic literature provides us with examples, which are perhaps still to be found in these more realistic days, of symbolic substitutes for the forbidden action—the young man carries away a glove, a handkerchief, a flower, or something associated with her person which could symbolize her, and kisses that.

Now these symbolic actions are ritual in their nature; they are certainly not art, and they are not in the least neurosis, but they represent the roots of both. We will now consider savage ritual.

The savage, wanting food, takes realistic means to get it; he kills food-animals, hunting them with marvellous skill and patience. But in this situation there are things beyond his control; some years there are not enough food animals—the children die, the women starve, the men grow desperate. As the hunting season approaches, the stimulus is terrific, the anxiety unendurable. It requires symbolic relief. In many savage tribes there is at this juncture a hunting dance; some take the part of the hunted animals, others the part of the hunters, there is a mimic slaying on a grand scale—and everybody feels better. The relief of these anxieties by symbolic action is felt to be an assurance of good hunting in reality—indeed, the symbolic performance is taken as constituting control over reality. This is magic. In the same way, the reproduction of food animals may be controlled, according to primitive belief, by a symbolic sex ritual in which human beings act the part of the mating animals. And there you have your savage ritual sex-orgy. It is a product of desperate anxiety, and it is a symbolic action performed in lieu of a realistic action, there being no realistic action to perform. Symbolic rites of rolling together in the fields were performed in recent times in

Europe by peasant husbands and wives to encourage the growth of crops, Frazer tells us.

What we have to note is that anxiety produces the rite, and that the rite produces the belief in its magical effectiveness. The belief in magic then gives social protection and encouragement to the ritual. The ritual, in addition to being realistically silly, may be cruel and is frequently a great deal of trouble. Ritual touch-avoidance, for example, an offshoot of savage food-anxieties, puts savages to an infinite deal of trouble; the hunters may not touch women at certain times lest they be infected with womanly weakness; the king-priest in whom the magic powers over Nature are concentrated may not be touched by an ordinary man or may not touch the earth lest he blight it, etc., etc. But these elaborate avoidances and compulsions have social sanction and are a part of primitive religion and government.

Amid all the sillinesses and cruelties of primitive magic, there are other things to be noted. So long as the whole tribe is getting relief from food anxiety in a hunting dance, it is ritual, being merely self-expression. But when part of the tribe—the women and children and the old men past hunting age—sit and look on, something new has happened. The dancers are then expressing not merely their own wishes, but those of the audience as well. The ritual (as Jane Harrison has pointed out) becomes art when it has an audience whose emotional need it fulfills.

Out of the primitive ritual dance, it appears, have come all our arts. Painting and sculpture record its symbolic incidents, poetry is the verbal part of its enchantments or spells, the drama is its traditional repetitive form. Magic at once encourages and restrains the arts. The cave men drew and carved animals wonderfully well, because magic sanctioned it; but they appear to have been afraid to draw or carve human faces, because (as anthropologists are inclined to conclude) they might be accused of making these images for purposes of death-magic. When they drew or carved women, they left them (with one feeble exception so far discovered) invariably faceless and almost armless and legless, but they exaggerated in what is to us a grotesque way their loins, rumps, breasts and sexual parts generally, because (or so we infer) these were of magical importance to the tribe. Indeed, the savage concentration upon impersonal sexuality in female imagery is one reason for the ban placed upon female nudity in art by later patriarchal religions (Christianity in chief), and by some religions (Jewish, Mohammedan) upon imagery of any kind—it smelled to them of cruel and obscene witchcraft, idol-worship, human sacrifice and sex-orgies; and the nostrils of our censors are still so full of that primitive stench that they still cannot look at a painted 'nude' without trying to save the world from a pestilence that has been banished these many centuries! We need not suppose that the paleolithic artist was moved by magical considerations in his paintings any more than Michelangelo was moved by strictly Christian motives in his religious paintings, or, for that matter, Rockwell Kent or Albert Steichen by strictly commercial motives in their advertisement-art. Artists may correctly be presumed to have purposes of their own broader than any of the social sanctions under which they operate.

The change from a hunting to an agricultural régime, by giving a more realistic assurance of food, diminished food-anxieties and knocked the foundation from under primitive magic. When the plough came in, magic began to go out. It went out slowly, for the security afforded by the agricultural régime was itself precarious. But the better the agricultural methods, the fewer the ritual sex-orgies. War, which was increased by agriculture—or by the existence of harvests tempting to nomads and pirates—tended to bring in human sacrifice on a grand scale as a new tribal ritual; but the more peaceful the era, the scarcer was the smoke of sacrifice. The machine is creating still greater economic security—and though this again is threatened by wars which bring back the old anxieties and the old magic in all but its crudest forms, yet where the machine goes the old gods must depart. And such private anxieties as cannot find relief in art or in harmless ritual without magical assumptions, but use forms of symbolic relief which are hostile to our culture, are accounted neuroses or psychoses. We have seen what a frightful social nuisance Miss R's touch-avoidance neurosis was; and when we catch people performing murder to relieve themselves of their anxieties, we usually lock them up in insane asylums.

Private ritual, if not part of a compulsive system, may be harmless; and public or customary ritual behavior of a harmless sort ranks as good manners. Examples of this will be given later. And art, divorced from its ancient magical pretensions, far from threatening our civilized life, adorns it. Yet both manners and art, on the one hand, and the neuroses on the other, springing from the same psychic root of anxiety and being kinds of symbolic relief, are akin to the old magic rites in interesting and instructive ways.

We may illustrate this likeness and these differences by a homely example. A savage youth in love may take a part of a girl's clothing to use in a love-charm; that is magic. A Victorian youth, in the early stages of a courtship, might have stolen his beloved's glove; and because that tender theft was recognized as a part of a courtship which would presumably lead to matrimony, it would have been accounted a piece of gallantry or good manners. But if on a second visit he stole another glove and subsequently a third and a fourth, he would have been considered 'queer'; and if it were reported that in his room he had a collection of several dozen ladies' gloves, he would have been forbidden the house. Such a person would be, as we say now, neurotic; some inward barrier blocks the path to love-making; possession of the girl's glove is not for him a step toward possession of her hand and heart—it remains permanently symbolic of woman to him, and is all he can ever venture to possess. A lover may beg a lock of his mistress's hair, and that is gallantry; but the man who carries a scissors in his pocket and snips off the curls of young girls in street-cars is a wretched neurotic.

But let us ask why the following quatrain has been regarded as especially beautiful:

> "I sometimes think that never blows so red
> The Rose as where some buried Caesar bled;
> That every Hyacinth the Garden wears
> Dropt in her Lap from some once lovely Head."

We may call to mind the ancient barbaric practice of murdering people to make gardens grow. Fitzgerald and Omar may never have heard of it. But they had heard that 'the blood of the martyrs is the seed of the Church' and similar phrases in which the old savage idea is embodied metaphorically. The barbarian, in his anxiety about food, carried out the practice literally; the civilized poet, in the anxiety of frustrated love which we call grief, comforts himself with the primitive fancy that the lost friend lives again in the rose. And perhaps it is beautiful *because* it is so primitive—because it is a thing that science would never say.

Consider, moreover, the last two lines of the quatrain. If it does not seem too offensive, remember the primitive use of the sex-orgy to make gardens grow. Perhaps Omar or Fitzgerald did not intend to suggest that the hyacinth dropped from the lovely head in the midst of a kiss, but it seems to convey that suggestion in a shadowy way. The idea that kisses make gardens grow would not have been offensive to Omar or Fitzgerald; and it is only a more refined and civilized version of the idea which was taken literally by savages. The savages were worried about food; the civilized poet is sad about wasted kisses and is comforted by the primitive fancy that at least their sweetness lives again in the hyacinth. And perhaps it is because the idea is so primitive that it appeals to us.

Guano, we know as a matter of scientific fact, will produce better crops than any amount of blood and kisses. Yet there is a non-realistic part of our minds, a childish and fanciful part which we have in common with the savage, that makes us understand his logic even while we shrink from it or laugh at it. In mere verbal poetry with the physical aspect of the idea refined to the most shadowy and romantic allusion, there is nothing at which the most delicate-minded civilized reader need smile, nothing from which he need shrink; and as such it seems beautiful. *Art, then (for both its creators and its appreciators), affords a dignified refuge for primitive symbolism, and is a socially approved kind of symbolic behavior for the relief of anxiety.*

If Fitzgerald had killed somebody in his back yard to make his roses grow, he would have been locked up in an insane asylum. But for expressing this delightfully primitive idea (among others less primitive) in rhythmically satisfying words, he is rewarded with world-wide fame.

It may perhaps seem uncalled-for to trace the idea back to its primitive roots; but the contrast with science is at least instructive. The poet does not characteristically undertake to teach realistic agricultural methods; we prefer to take our scientific directions for the use of guano from prose writers. We feel that scientific description of Nature is not the function of the Poet; he delights us precisely when he imports into his description some touch of childish fantasy, which always as a matter of fact harks back to savage magical beliefs. Thus we should not tolerate from a scientific prose-writer the sentimentality of suggesting that a tree knows or cares whom its leaves may shade, or of otherwise making a tree the symbol of the human wishes of the writer; yet we—or at least our Victorian grandparents—regarded this poetic description of an English cedar as especially beautiful:

"O, art thou sighing for Lebanon,
In the long breeze that streams from thy delicious East,
Sighing for Lebanon,
Dark cedar, though thy limbs have here increased
Upon a pastoral slope as fair,
And looking to the South, and fed
With honey'd rain and delicate air,
And haunted by the starry head
Of her * * *
* * * * *
And over whom thy darkness must have spread
With such delight as theirs of old, thy great
Forefathers of the thornless garden, there
Shadowing the snow-limb'd Eve from whom she came."

In the same way, it is not a scientifically useful description of birds and beasts or of Nature in general than we require from the poet, but preferably statements of another sort which may be realistically absurd and untrue:

"Hail to thee, blithe Spirit!
Bird thou never wert,
That from Heaven, or near it,
Pourest thy full heart
In profuse strains of unpremeditated art."

"Thou wast not born for death, immortal Bird!
No hungry generations tread thee down".

"Tiger! Tiger! burning bright
In the forests of the night,
What immortal hand or eye
Could frame thy fearful symmetry?"

"O wild West Wind, thou breath of Autumn's being,
* * * *
Make me thy lyre, even as the forest is".

The anxieties here ministered to in symbolic identifications of Mankind with Nature—the baulked love-wishes thus symbolically fulfilled in Tennyson's poem, the painful ambitions thus allayed in Shelley's poem, the fears of death thus calmed in Keats's poem, the terrors of a strange universe thus harmonized with concepts of order in Blake's poem—are among the emotional needs of mankind which the conquest of machine power has not removed and which it may be no future conquests of power over Nature can ever remove: for such art there would thus appear to be a permanent function of solace; and such emotional reconciliations of man with a hostile universe, such efforts to 'justify the ways of God to man' or to justify man in his quarrel with human fate, will doubtless continue to be ranked among the noblest of human endeavors. That is to say, in the realms in which man is still powerless he still needs the consolations of the helpless child and the helpless savage—though he is too intelligent to attribute to these emotional consolations any magical usefulness in altering outward realities. Their usefulness is strictly emotional: they make us feel good—and that is usefulness enough for art.

In divesting art of its illusory function of technical usefulness, men have attempted to make clear to themselves the important distinction between the realm in which symbolic action can legitimately operate (the realm of the emotions), and the realm in which realistic action is required (the realm of outer reality). The Trobriand Island savage chants speed-magic as he builds his boat. We do not chant speed-magic as we build our ships; and if we break a bottle of champagne against the bows when we launch them, it is because it is a pretty and 'poetic' ceremony of which we have forgotten the meaning—which possibly harks back to some barbaric rite of bathing the prow with the blood of a human sacrifice in order to make it go faster. But we rely upon engines to achieve speed, not on symbols. The Trobriand Island ship-builder, so Malinowski tells us, chanted:

"I shall take hold of an adze,
I shall strike.
I shall enter my canoe,
I shall make thee fly, O canoe [calling it by its name],
I shall make thee jump!
We shall fly like butterflies,
Like wind.

We shall disappear in a mist,
We shall vanish.
You will pierce the straits of Kidimwatu,
You will break the promontory of Saramwa,
Pierce the passage of Loma,
Die away in the distance,
Die away with the wind,
Fade away with the mist,
Vanish away.
Break through the sea-weeds [on landing].
Put on your wreath [of sea-weeds],
Make your bed in the sand.
I turn round [look back],
I see the Vakuta men,
The Kitava men [our rivals],
Behind me;
My sea,
The sea of Pilolu;
To-day the Kudayuri men will burn their fires [of welcome].
Bind your grass-skirts together [like a flying-witch],
O canoe,
Fly!"

This was a magic spell. To-day the poet of the machine, Kipling, writes a "Hymn of the Triumphant Airman". It is archaic in style, extravagant in assertion, and harks back to the magic speed-spells of old; but it is not a magic spell, it is a poem:

"Oh, long had we paltered
With bridle and girth
Ere those horses were haltered
That gave us the Earth—

"Ere the Flame and the Fountain,
The Spark and the Wheel,
Sank Ocean and Mountain
Alike neath our keel."

The Sun God alone could go faster than we, says the poem; so we challenge him with our airships. Starting westward at dawn, we bid him overtake us if he can!

It is, naturally, not in the fields of effort where science has given us new powers to rely upon, but in the realm of personal relations where we are still comparatively at the mercy of malign accident, that anxieties are most easily aroused and most in need of art to allay them. Poetry, in lieu of other art forms, will be most convenient here for illustration. Love and death are especially the situations which put us in need of poetic ministrations. So identical in emotional origin are poetry and magic that a great deal of funeral poetry consists of quasi-magical incantations, sometimes deliberately and sometimes reluctantly archaic and more or less rationalized—and as true to modern emotions as they are false to the modern realistic ideas of death which are entertained in the same mind at the same time:

"Be to her, Persephone,
All the things I might not be,
Take her head upon your knee."

"Flow gently, sweet Afton! among thy green braes,
Flow gently, I'll sing thee a song in thy praise;
My Mary's asleep by thy murmuring stream,
Flow gently, sweet Afton, disturb not her dream."

Love-poetry also frequently takes the form of quasi-magical incantations asserting power over hostile realities. Malinowski has furnished us examples of magic love-spells from the Trobriand Islands. The *sulumwoya* spell is guaranteed to give "a full and undivided sway over the loved one's heart". It is chanted over a mint-plant boiled in coco-nut oil; the lover then seeks to enter the girl's hut by night, and spill some of it below her nostrils, so that she may dream of the magic-maker. Less certain methods are smearing the oil over her hands, or dipping a nosegay in the oil and flicking it under her nose. Her knowledge that love-magic is being used may realistically help to bring about the desired results; but these results are attributed to the magic, even when it is accompanied by exceedingly realistic methods of attracting her attention and declaring his feelings, such as are usually sufficient in civilized life to bring success in love. The *solumwoya* spell is so frank and detailed in its statement of the lover's wishes that only its beginning and end can be quoted here. It begins in sheer wish-fulfillment:

"O, her sensual excitement!
O, her erotic swoon!
O, desire, O feminine swoon!
My clasping, thy clasping, kindle our erotic swooning
My embraces, thy embraces, kindle our erotic swooning!"

The spell goes on to specify exactly every detail of his love-wishes, and concludes:

> "Thou goest my way, crying for me,
> Thou enterest my house, smiling at me.
> My house is shaken with joy, as thou treadest my floor.
> Tease and tear out my hair, [[there is a good measure
>   of erotic cruelty in Trobriand Island love-making]]
> Drink my blood,
> So that my feelings are glad."

The wholesale assurances of conquest in this spell should serve to allay erotic anxieties and transform the most timid lover into an enterprising one. Erotic poetry has notoriously served the same quasi-magical purposes for youth, offering to young men the picture of feminine surrender and generating the confidence in ultimate success, so necessary in courtship to compensate against the sense of helplessness and unworthiness or inferiority. Poetry, however, merely as read to himself by an anxious lover, lacks the element of action which is the essential and here the practical part of ritual. Poetry accordingly becomes love-ritual when it is written to, or read to, the beloved. Thus the poets have been, as Dante pointed out with regard to Paolo and Francesca, the go-betweens in many a love-affair. Yet, though actually much made use of ritualistically by youth in the preliminary stages of love, poetry has no great standing as an art in that capacity, where after all it can be and often is dispensed with. Art disdains to be what willy-nilly it generally is, a means to other human ends; it demands that it, or its creation-and-appreciation, be an end in itself. It in a sense achieves that height when it symbolically fulfills wishes not realistically to be fulfilled:

> "Come to me in the silence of the night;
>   Come in the speaking silence of a dream;
> Come with soft rounded cheeks and eyes as bright
>   As sunlight on a stream;
>   Come back in tears,
> O memory, hope, love of finished years."

Here it is Time that is the realistically overwhelming hostile force of Nature, which can be triumphed over by Love only symbolically, in dreams and in the poetry of dreaming. Again Love would triumph over its enemy Death in dreams:

"The breaths of kissing night and day
Were mingled in the Eastern Heaven:
Throbbing with unheard melody
Shook Lyra all her star-chord seven:
When the dusk shrunk cold, and light trod shy,
And dawn's grey eyes were troubled grey;
And souls went palely up the sky,
And mine to Lucidé.

"There was no change in her sweet eyes
Since last I saw those sweet eyes shine;
There was no change in her deep heart
Since last that deep heart knocked at mine.
* * * *
I joyed for me, I joyed for her,
Who with the Past meet girt about:
Where our last kiss still warms the air,
Nor can her eyes go out."

But lesser hostile forces of Nature, involving only temporary delays, may yet arouse anxieties in the lover which can be allayed only by quasi-magical incantations or appeals, desperately earnest or half-playful:

"Swiftly walk o'er the Western wave,
Spirit of Night!
Out of the misty eastern cave,—
Where, all the long and lone daylight,
Thou wovest dreams of joy and fear
Which make thee terrible and dear,—
Swift be thy flight!"

"O Night, O jealous Night, repugnant to my measures!
O Night so long desired, yet cross to my content!
There's none but only thou that can perform my pleasures,
Yet none but only thou that hindereth my intent.
* * *
"Sweet Night, withhold thy beams, withhold them till to-morrow!
Whose joy's in lack so long, a hell of torment breeds.
Sweet Night, sweet gentle Night, do not prolong my sorrow:
Desire is guide to me, and Love no lodestar needs.
* * *

"And when my will is wrought, then, Cynthia, shine, good lady,
All other days and nights in honor of that night,
That happy, heavenly night, that night so dark and shady,
Wherein my Love had eyes that lighted my delight."

All these examples have been chosen by way of illustration of a mode of symbolic action indubitably primitive yet socially acceptable, many of them ranking as great poetic achievements; and, because socially acceptable, not constituting neurotic behavior. It might be objected by one familiar with the concept of 'repression' that these examples do not involve such repression—their original motivation being wholly conscious. On the contrary, it is doubtful if this ever really occurs in art; repression appears to be there involved as truly as in the neuroses. At all events, examples can easily be furnished of art which does involve repression—that is, in which there is good evidence that the artist himself and his public in general are not wholly if at all consciously aware of the nature of the forbidden impulse which is thus finding expression in symbolic action—yet which is none the less, and sometimes even more, socially approved.

"A savage place! as holy and enchanted
As ever beneath a waning moon was haunted
By woman wailing for her demon-lover!"

"For your sake I have braved the glen
And had to do with goblin merchant men."

"Deep in the earth I rested now;
Cool is its hand upon the brow
And soft its breast beneath the head
Of one who is so gladly dead."

"I fled Him, down the nights and down the days;
I fled Him, down the arches of the years."

The artist takes, even though unwittingly, the great privilege claimed by Walt Whitman:

"Through me forbidden voices,
Voices of sexes and lusts, voices veil'd and I remove the veil,
Voices indecent by me clarified and transfigured."

The poet Wordsworth has written—thinking, to be sure, as did his readers, that he was writing about something else—a glorious paean to the narcissism that is the core of art:

"O joy! that in our embers
Is something that doth live,
That nature yet remembers
What was so fugitive!
The thought of those past years in me doth breed
Perpetual benediction: not indeed
For that which is most worthy to be blest;
Delight and liberty, the simple creed
Of Childhood, whether busy or at rest,
With new-fledged hope still fluttering in his breast:—"

Not, that is to say, the realistic process of growing up, of becoming adult—

"Not for these I raise
The song of thanks and praise;
But for those obstinate questionings
Of sense and outward things,
Fallings from us, vanishings;
Blank misgivings of a Creature
Moving about in worlds not realized,
High instincts before which our mortal Nature
Did tremble like a guilty Thing surprised:
But for those first affections,
Those shadowy recollections,
Which, be they what they may,
Are yet the fountain-light of all our day,
Are yet a master-light of all our seeing;
Uphold us, cherish, and have power to make
Our noisy years seem moments in the being
Of the eternal silence: truths that wake
To perish never:
Which neither listlessness, nor mad endeavour,
Nor Man nor Boy,
Nor all that is at enmity with joy,
Can utterly abolish or destroy!
Hence in a season of calm weather,
Though inland far we be,
Our Souls have sight of that immortal sea
Which brought us hither,
Can in a moment travel thither,
And see the Children sport upon the shore,
And hear the mighty waters rolling evermore."

It is not, then, the psychological mechanisms involved which make the difference between neurosis and art (or other sublimations of forbidden impulses), but the practical test of social conditions—which are able to welcome one set of symbolic activities while being obliged to reject another set. Art is socially acceptable (as touch-avoidance, for example, is not) in civilized life because it fits in, interferes with no essential social discipline, but tends to make other people 'feel good' and constitutes one of the bonds by which people are united in civilized life.

For socially forbidden impulses there is thus in civilized life a socially permitted kind of symbolic expression in art; and those who are unable to use this, but must fall back upon socially unacceptable forms of symbolic expression for such impulses, are the neurotics. Both the neurosis and the art which we have thus far discussed are modes of dealing with anxieties which arise from a baulking of human impulses by the hostile forces of Nature—by Fate or Fortune, as it were. Yet there is reason to believe that these situations are not the primary ones with which art is fundamentally concerned at all: that these situations in adult life could be satisfactorily met without the solace of art, except that they revive the unconscious memory of still earlier and specifically infantile hurts and griefs and become the surrogates of these—that they are laden with the burden of 'forgotten' infantile wishes too ridiculous to be consciously entertained by an adult: and that the primitive or savage or childish elements in art are the symbols of wishes more childish still. What these may be will presently be suggested.

In the meantime we know that the art works which relieve our deepest-hidden, most unconscious anxieties, are the ones which constitute our most valued aesthetic achievements; that the world values *Hamlet* and *Oedipus Rex* without ever succeeding in explaining on aesthetic grounds in just what consists their superiority to simpler, more obvious and more superficial works of art.

But let us turn to the artist's audience, to ourselves, and see what are or appear to be the satisfactions which we get from art.

Our individual share of human nature is wider far than our individual lives of action can ever be—infinitely wider than the paths of useful habit along which we come to walk. There remain many impulses which have expressed themselves only in a partial way, in a broken-off way; and about these broken little actions, leading in this way and that away from the well-trodden paths of habit, there are clustered a multitude of impulses which have scarcely been expressed in action at all. Beneath the comparatively neat and orderly surface of daily action there is this chaos of disjoined action and frustrated impulse. Perhaps in some unimaginable kind of life we could live out all these impulses, follow all these actions through to their ends; and perhaps if that were done, these actions would have some wild and grand pattern of their own. As it is they are merely chaos. And this chaos aches with vague anxiety for some kind of fulfillment and order.

Along comes the artist. He too has his private chaos; and being more sensitive than the rest of us and more hurt by this chaos, he has put it into order experimentally, given its impulses fulfillment—not in the world of action, for frequently he is far more incapable than the rest of us of achieving any order there, but symbolically in the fantasy world of art.

It may happen that in bringing order out of his private chaos he is dealing with frustrated impulses so unlike our own, or fulfilling them in so unrecognizable a set of emotional symbols, that his music, or poetry, or painting or fiction is meaningless to us. In that event, though he may be a great artist to others, he is of no value to us. It may be that he must wait for some future generation to understand and value his work. It may be that no one will ever understand and value it.

But if his art work—his poem, for example—does deal with our chaos in an emotionally recognizable set of symbols, then it gives fulfillment in fantasy to those unfulfilled impulses of ours, it gives order to those meaningless broken bits of forgotten action that led nowhere in reality. We do not know that this is what it is doing for us, nor is it important that we should know. It is enough to know that we are happy in the enjoyment of this work of art and that we live for the moment in a greater and fairer world than the narrow one of action. We seem to be in touch with eternal things.

The suggestion of 'eternal things' brings us close to religion. But we may remember that Art was once a part of Religion, and that great poets (such as Shelley) have assigned to Art a religious function in the modern world. If Art has such a religious function, it is one which it is freer—oddly enough—to exercise than the Church itself is. For Art has freed itself from magical pretensions, which the Church has been very reluctant to do. When poetry grants us the privilege of communion with absent loved ones, it does not get into any unprofitable arguments with Science as to the 'reality' of these proceedings. Hamlet can take upon himself the burden of our unconscious guilt without our having to quarrel with historians as to whether there ever 'really' was any Hamlet. Art has finally had the sense to recognize that it operates in a realm apart from fact and that it owes no responsibility to fact—it knows that it is enough of a miracle that it should make wishes come true within its own realm without falling into the savage error of supposing that these wishes magically operate to control the forces of Nature. Art will never have to burn people at the stake for the heresy of asserting that it was not, as a matter of fact, "stout Cortez" but a man named Balboa who from a peak in Darien "stared at the Pacific". For the credit of Art, not being bound up with its statements of fact, does not in the least depend upon whether its Apostle Keats was right or wrong in his history. Nor will the priests of art ever have the awkward job of trying to explain what, in plain *fact,* is meant by such passages as these:

> "The pulse of war and passion of wonder,
> The heavens that murmur, the sounds that shine,
> The stars that sing and the loves that thunder,
> And music burning at heart like wine".

And as the credit of Religion, thus bound up by the Church with magical pretensions to having a meaning in the realm of facts, does inevitably decline among rational people, its religious functions have to be performed for them, if at all, by Art. This should prepare us for the recognition of the service that Art performs in absolving us of our sense of guilt.

A vague sense of guilt is a kind of morbid anxiety. The Church—in spite of evidence to the contrary in the experience of every priest or pastor with his flock—assumes that people know what they are 'guilty' of; but the truth is that they don't. They merely try to attach their sense of guilt to some 'crime' or 'sin',—

and sometimes they commit crimes or sins in order to have something that they may rightly feel 'guilty' about, as every psychotherapeutist knows. People usually feel guilty about crimes they *want* to commit—the unsatisfied anxiety is the sense of guilt. But people do not feel at all guilty about having committed crimes or sins which they really wished to commit; in that case they are notoriously shameless, and have the best consciences in the world. It is when the crime or sin is committed in the endeavor to fulfill an unconscious wish, and turns out not to be a satisfactory fulfillment of the wish, that the extreme and baffled sense of disappointment takes the form of remorse. The reason why some people have to commit one crime or sin after another is that they cannot find the crime or sin which they really want to commit; and they may be driven further and further into sexual perversion or sadistic brutality in the search for it. Indeed, the crime or sin they want to commit can never be committed, because it lies back in the past, in infancy. And there it is not really a crime or sin at all, it is a set of instinctive emotional attitudes of love and hate toward the parents which have been rejected from consciousness and replaced there by affection and duty. Religions have always offered more or less satisfactory resolutions of these lingering infantile anxieties of repressed infantile love and hate toward parents, in ritual and belief and poetic myths of the gods. But as the Church loses its usefulness because of its mistaking of its field and its silly quarrels with Science, the function of resolving or granting absolution to these infantile anxieties devolves more and more upon Art. The Church in its prime of social usefulness was marked by magnificent outbursts of poetic myth-making and aesthetic creativeness in general. Now the Church is notoriously sterile in these respects, it is Art that effloresces into religious myth-making and offers the consolations of emotional absolution in a magnificent variety of forms. Every good novelist is taking part in the making of our modern Bible, every good artist helps adorn our Temple. Among our artists few except Bernard Shaw have realized that they are performing a religious function which the Church has bungled and practically failed at; nor is it important that they should realize it. If the authors of the despairingly cynical maxims of *Ecclesiastes* and the robustly sensual *Song of Songs* had realized that they were collaborating upon a 'religious' work, it might have cramped their style—as it would doubtless cramp the style to-day of such prophets as H. L. Mencken and such myth-makers as Ernest Hemingway, in whose consolations so many troubled spirits find appeasement.

But to return to the fundamental core of Art—under its outward wrappings of imitation of Nature, of instruction in politics and love and civilized living, what do we find? We need not look if such things are too offensive; or we may deny that such things are there—it is all the same. But if we choose to look and not to deny what we see, we find symbolic overleapings of the incest barrier we find infantile fantasies of reunion with the mother and of father-slaying; we find symbolic resolutions of narcissistic self-worship and of homosexuality. These are the unfulfilled childish impulses which linger throughout life as a vague anxiety and demand relief—in Religion, in Art, or in Neurosis. Religion has built magnificent structures, fane upon fane of myth and symbol, to give these infantile anxieties absolution. Art has inherited that task and builds its noble architecture into the skies for the same purpose. And for those who cannot find peace in one or the other of these temples, there are the dangerous, jerry-built, insecure structures of alcoholic fantasy, drug-fantasy, neurotic fantasy, which too often fall down and overwhelm their dwellers in ruin. The structures of Religion pretend to be magically somehow both in and out of the real world, and they may be very disappointing to people who take their contradictory pretensions too literally. Those of neurosis pretend to be in the real world, but are alien to it and hostile to it—they interfere with real life and make it more or less unlivable. Those of art are out of reality, but in the happiest relations to reality. Religion aside, we may say that Art offers us a socially acceptable alternative to the neuroses and psychoses which are the socially unacceptable ways of finding relief from lingering infantile anxieties.

We cannot, indeed, all of us be artists; that is, we cannot all expect to produce symbolic forms which will be valuable to others for anxiety relief. It will be enough for psychic health that we 'appreciate' the symbolic forms of other artists—the ones which have served generation after generation of audiences in music, painting, sculpture, and imaginative literature, together with the new ones which may happen to suit us better still:—and, in addition to these, that we create for ourselves such tunes, or pictures, or verses as may fall short of Art, being comparatively useless to others, but which give us satisfaction. All this means that we will be in psychically better health if we dance, sing, play some instrument, improvise music of our own; go to plays, and indulge in amateur theatricals or charades; read novels and poetry, write a little, look at pictures (movies not by any means excluded), draw a little or paint a little—and so on, according to our tastes; and that these efforts at appreciation and creation of art will by no means be wasted if we do not become professional critics or professional artists, since they will make us happier and freer human beings, better citizens and lovers.

Another practical conclusion is very obvious; it is that as our civilization becomes more stringent in its demands for adulthood, there is all the more need for the utmost *liberty for art.* It may be *our* business to grow up, but art—if it is to be of any use to us—must have the privilege of being primitive or childish. No doubt it will often successfully disguise its primitiveness, its childishness—it may pretend to be preaching to us or instructing us—but unless it is permitted to speak to our unconscious minds, to sublimate our unconscious wishes in its rhythms and forms and verbal images, it might as well shut up shop. It is hard enough to be adult in our behavior; it is impossible to be wholly adult in our unconscious minds; and it will be easier for us to be successfully adult in behavior if our unconscious childishnesses can be given disciplined release in the beauty of art.

Does it seem implausible that the glorious structures of art should have been erected to give peace to such ridiculously petty and absurd infantile anxieties? We have at least the analogy of the pearl to give our skepticism pause. Around that grain of irritation the organism throws film after film of nacreous smoothness; and what would be the occasion for the pearl at all but the grain of dirt? The analogy must serve us here in place of more cogent proof. But we may adduce, by way of illustration, one of the noblest utterances in all the world of poetry, with some comments:

"Let me not to the marriage of true minds
Admit impediments. Love is not love
Which alters when it alteration finds,
Or bends with the remover to remove:
O, no! it is an ever-fixéd mark
Which looks on tempests and is never shaken;"—

Does it matter that in the realm of actual human experience this is *not true?*—that it is as absurdly false as the story of the whale that swallowed Jonah? And should it matter, further, that it was, as a matter of fact, written by one man to another man out of the pain and despair of homosexual folly, as a defiance of the hateful truth of the situation? Its value is not in the least impaired for us by that fact; the translucent beauty of the pearl has covered up the grain of silly infantile sexuality which is its core. And perhaps only the victim of such tragic infantilism could in his agony have so transcended reality into the realm of pure and serene wish-fulfillment which is our Eternity:

> "Love's not Time's fool, though rosy lips and cheeks
> Within his bending sickle's compass come;
> Love alters not with his brief hours and weeks,
> But bears it out even to the edge of doom.
> If this be error and upon me proved,
> I never writ, nor no man ever loved."

That trumpet note cries out triumphantly through the night of our failures and follies in love, through our trials and errors, our blunderings and defeats, and it speaks a poetic truth which seems truer to us than the facts can ever be.

§ 2. Manners

Manners have, or may have, much the same relation to anxiety that art has; manners are, indeed, a kind of ritual, which has relief of anxiety as its function. We have been so accustomed to think of manners as something dead that we forget that the deadest manners were once alive. We will not concern ourselves here with dead manners, however, but will deal with living manners.

Manners are a kind of formal play. Formal play differs from informal play in being traditional and fixed in form; but the fixed form is such as expresses a wide variety of impulses. A good work of art is one of which the emotional meaning cannot be exhausted in any explanation; and the same is true of a good game. The satisfactions of chess or tennis cannot be exhausted by any description, any more than the emotional satisfactions of *Hamlet* can be. The same thing is true of those kinds of formal play which come within the realm of manners. The satisfactions of giving and attending dinner parties would be inexhaustible even to catalogue. The revivalist who denounces dancing as an incitement of sexual interest, the psychologist who commends it as a socially commendable mode of symbolic satisfaction of sexual interest, the aesthete who praises it in terms of its rhythmic satisfactions, the physical culturist who praises it as good muscular exercise, the matron who uses it as a means conducive to her purpose of marrying off her daughter, the shy girl to whom it is a fearful ordeal and a test of her feminine attractiveness, the popular girl who goes to the ball-room glowing with expectations of tribute to be rendered to her charms, the wife who wonders why her husband doesn't enjoy dancing with her as much as he used to before they were married, the fiddler who looks on, detached and philosophic and perhaps cynical—all these have seen some of the emotional aspects of this formal play, but not all of them together have seen all its aspects. It is, then, not as a final explanation, but as a selection of the aspects of certain kinds of formal play which are within the scope of our inquiry, that we point out this: formal play gives socially harmless or useful expression to impulses of vanity and cruelty—or what would be vanity and cruelty if otherwise expressed. This is no more than has already been said of art. Play is an even more universal mode of expressing narcissistic impulses; and formal modes of play are those which have been found to be particularly successful in expressing them.

We will speak particularly of dancing, with reference to a special transition situation in which it occupies a significant psychic rôle.

The transition situation is this. Women no longer in modern society occupy the subordinate place which they had in the patriarchal era. But women in love relations with men still occupy, by the instinctive preference of both sexes, a place which though not subordinate might seem so: they are selectively responsive to men, and they enjoy stimulating men to erotic aggression. Now in the patriarchal era the desired sexual aggressiveness of the male could be symbolized in their actual social and economic relations; the man's 'masterfulness' was the more easily accepted by the woman since it could be construed as a loverlike quality.

In our time, however, the social and economic relations of men and women are beginning to be so different, they tend so clearly toward equality, that the young man who tries to be 'masterful' in his social and economic relations with women often only succeeds in making a fool of himself and of offending the girl he wishes to impress. The fact is, or may be, that she knows as much as he does, and has as much or perhaps even more immediate earning power; she desires to be consulted about any *practical* matter which concerns them both and does not wish to have her consent taken for granted in such matters. The young man is, or may be, intelligent enough to realize that. But he is engaged in wooing her. His instincts bid him take the aggressive not only in directly sexual ways but in symbolic actions concerning her; here the tradition of patriarchal 'masterfulness' comes in as a ready resource, and he finds himself bossing her around and doing her thinking for her.

Usually, unless she has some neurotic protest against her own femaleness, she will be pleased at these 'masterful' airs in the youth so long as they concern trivial matters; she will not mind being treated as if she were helpless and brainless, she will rather enjoy it, unless it is a matter of practical importance—and then she will be indignant at his presumption. The fact is that he needs some socially harmless and agreeable ways of demonstrating his male aggressiveness; and she needs similar ways of expressing her female responsiveness. If they try to use their actual social and economic relations as a symbol of their instinctive sexual relation, they will get into trouble. He will find himself demanding that she quit her job and be a doll, while he tries in vain to earn the money to support the kind of establishment that 'masculine' pride dictates. He will find himself making wrong decisions about money, from which her sensible advice could have saved him.

But they can find, apart from social and economic realities, in the field of formal play and manners, the symbolic 'male' and 'female' relation which they desire. They can find it, for example, in dancing together. There he can make all the decisions without asking her whether to turn to the right or left, whether to do this or that; and it is her business to respond automatically to these decisions. In the dance, as in Milton's Paradise, "he for God only, she for God in him"—he responds to the music only, she to the music as it is expressed through him. And there is no doubt that among all the other emotional satisfactions of all kinds in dancing, this traditional 'maleness' and 'femaleness' is one satisfaction. It is not a duty but a pleasure. And it does not imply anything as to the world of economic reality. She can be Milton's Eve on the dance-floor without giving up her rights as a sensible and economically capable human being outside.

Formal play, then, can become the refuge of emotional attitudes which cannot without harm express themselves in realistic action. Sexual aggression, to be sure, belongs to the realm of overt sexual behavior, and can find agreeable realistic expression there—though even there (or perhaps especially there) it can be offensive if exaggerated, as it sometimes is by males who need to dramatize their masculinity because they are unsure of it. Sexual aggression in any event does not any longer belong in the practical realm of social and economic life. It belongs to the play world. If a man buys a girl flowers, she will be pleased even if they are not the kind of flowers she prefers; she may enjoy being relieved of the decision as to where they will have dinner, what wine they will have with it, what play they will see afterward, on the theory that he is using his judgment as to what she would like best;—but if he announces that he has bought a house for them to live in without consulting her, she will be outraged. To be sure, the illustration is not a very apt one, since patriarchal tradition, by recognizing the home as her peculiar sphere, gives her the right to be consulted there. But patriarchal tradition is not a safe guide for him. He may be fully within his traditional patriarchal rights and still behaving like a fool in our modern world. The only realms in which he may safely display masculine masterfulness for purposes of erotic effect and get the results which he expects, are in the play world—and not in all parts of that, for part of that has become as sexually democratized as social and economic life in general. In the games which men and women play together, for example, 'chivalry' is out of place. These games are devoted to the expression of other impulses not less important.

It would be interesting if we could go on to discuss the modern manners in which infantile attitudes are being harmlessly and agreeably expressed. But these modern manners are still in formation and any illustrations which might be found would not be very generally recognized.

Thus there is certainly a tendency to express narcissism in the rather primitive but socially agreeable form of an increasing physical nakedness, which when done under the aegis of physical culture is very useful in promoting bodily health; but it is not yet general enough, perhaps, to rank as manners. The use of the telling and hearing of so-called 'dirty stories' by adolescents and grown people in groups where both sexes are present is also an interesting sublimation of a variety of infantile impulses; but, this too is perhaps open to the objection of not being sufficiently general to be called anything but 'bad manners'. Perhaps all that can be said is that the need for new manners is more obvious than are the usages which definitely meet such a need.

But our play life is the field in which we have infinite opportunity for the satisfactory expression of certain instinctive attitudes, certain realistically outworn patriarchal attitudes, and above all of our infantile vanity and cruelty. Is it too much to hope that the development of this play field, through the extension and democratization of leisure by modern machinery, will make us eventually less susceptible to the vicarious expression of our infantile impulses in the Pied Piper 'leadership' that now tends to lead us helplessly toward destruction?

§ 3. Heroism

A hero—in the sense in which we are here using the word—is someone in history, legend or the world of imagination with whom we can identify ourselves on the grounds of our common faults and weaknesses but who, by his elevation into some kind of extraordinary success—or into some nobility of failure which (like martyrdom) can rank as a success—gives us self-respect, hope and courage. He may be a wholly imaginary person like Hamlet; a half-legendary person like Cleopatra (for we will defy grammar and call the women 'heroes' too); or a real person like François Villon or Isadora Duncan. The medieval saints were usually heroes in this sense, having their full quota of human faults and weaknesses; and one who dared not in his prayers approach the awful and alien goodness of God could always find a saint with a sufficiently disreputable past, who could understand a poor sinner and to whom one need not be afraid to pray.

The modern zest for raking up forgotten scandals in the lives of the great has been much misunderstood; it is really done in the desire to save them for us. People who are merely good or merely successful are of no great psychological use as heroes—they are too alien from us. Thus the poet Stevenson's life was prettified out of common humanity; and it was his true friends who tried to tell us some of the less refined aspects of his career. The hero's weaknesses, so necessary in order to enable us to identify ourselves with him, may be in the nature of a physical defeat or peculiarity; they may be like the short stature of Napoleon, who appears to be (secretly) the hero of almost every short man; or like Cyrano's long nose, which has comforted many an adolescent lad who is sensitive about the size of his nose or his ears or his feet. The prime heroic weakness is very frequently a simple inability to live up to the approved social or moral code in sexual conduct. He may be afraid of women, or impotent; or, on the other hand, his weakness may be to find every woman irresistible. Often enough the sexual divagations of the hero (male or female) are exaggerated by the worshippers. In particular, because of their own misgivings and bad consciences about their own sexual divagations, they like to impute to the hero a carefree attitude in his (or her) love-affairs. They are disappointed when they learn that even he (or she) is trying to be virtuous and has feelings of remorse or shame about what seems to the worshippers a godlike (or goddess-like) career of happy wantonness.

Thus the hero, when a real person, is simply a living art-work fulfilling by his behavior the infantile wishes of his public. For our aesthetic need is not necessarily restricted in its satisfaction to what are ordinarily termed works of art. The aesthetic hunger can and does nourish itself directly upon living realities and upon the memory and report of them. We wish people to have been—and still to be, occasionally—in life as well as in art, free from the social restrictions which we ourselves obey. We feel that such persons are superior; and we are the more able to justify our admiration when we can point to the cultural benefits which they may have bestowed upon mankind. So it comes about that artists of all kinds are among our heroes. It often takes all of an artist's energies to create his art, to bring symbolic order out of his emotional chaos; and his external life in frequently all the more disorderly. We not only forgive him that, but rejoice in his failure. François Villon need not know how to live without picking pockets—well, we want somebody to be above the law. Shelley need not know how to make a success of his marriages; to us they are failures more glorious than any domestic success could have been. We may lay the tasks of common honesty and of domestic adjustment upon ourselves; but we do not lay them upon Villon and Shelley. They may be still children in their financial and erotic lives; they have gained rank among the seraphim by their poetry.

To be sure, Villon may have been just as desirous of being honest, Shelley just as anxious to be happy in marriage, as the humblest citizen among us. Shelley was agonized with the memory that the outcome of his theory of free love was that Harriet had gone to the dogs and drowned herself; he knew he had meant Utopianly well, but the results were plain to see. The problem was never absent from his mind for a day and hardly for an hour, and still he could never decide whether "his branded and ensanguined brow" was "like Cain's or Christ's". He did not find it as easy to forgive himself for his failures in love as the admirers of his poetry find it to forgive him; never for a moment did he believe them to be glorious. And if his poetry puts him for us among our seraphim, he still might say: 'How like damnation is this Paradise!'

It is clear, however, that these heroes are selected more or less accidentally by the world in accordance with its spiritual needs; heroism is not an office for which anybody can deliberately prepare. The best anyone can do is break the social rules on the strong probability that he will be regarded as one of the common crowd of vulgar law-breakers, but with an off-chance of about one in ten million of being made a hero after he is dead. Perhaps, too, we are losing our need for such heroes. I know a man who has all the makings of a modern hero; at least, he has something which may be called crude genius in him and he has broken every written and unwritten law of honesty and common decency. He is admired by those whom he exploits, but is generally regarded as a poisonous nuisance; yet many a hero was a nuisance when alive and we may yet see ponderous and admiring tomes written about his life:—but I doubt it!

There is, however, one common ingredient in the make-up of heroes which can be cultivated with a fair certainty of getting at least some of the rewards of hero-worship. It is infantile self-love or narcissism. We have all, as infants, gone through that stage as a normal part of our development; we have given it up—usually rather reluctantly—as we grew older. But our unconscious minds have never ceased to regret that lost Paradise. And when we come upon the narcissist, though we may consciously despise him we unconsciously envy him. This unconscious envy may emerge into consciousness in the form of hate: if we have had to give up being babies, by Heaven this fellow shan't be allowed to get away with it! Or we may find in some real or alleged intellectual or artistic trait an excuse for his (or her) infantilism, and express our envy as hero-worship.

Thus every artist, and to perhaps a less degree every intellectual, is given some social encouragement in being infantile; it is traditionally regarded as a part of the artistic temperament. Poets, painters and actors in particular are permitted to be babies, and their cruelties, selfishnesses, and irresponsibilities tend to be admired rather than reprobated. Their talent, or the talent imputed to them (for it often scarcely exists in fact), is the excuse for their atrocities of behavior. Women by reason of extreme beauty are often given the same privilege of never growing up, encouraged to be narcissistic exploiters of other people. Those, however, whom the narcissist exploits most cruelly seem to be his (or her) destined victims; if they were not being exploited by this one, they would be exploited by another and perhaps a worse one. They have to be exploited by somebody. They are afflicted with a longing to be narcissistic themselves, and at the same time have been so trained to inhibit these impulses that they can enjoy their narcissism only vicariously; they are doomed to be the host to some parasite.

Other people, not so grievously afflicted, let themselves be exploited for a time by the narcissist and then suddenly rebel, declining—often very rudely—to be exploited any longer. The narcissist thus tends to live in a shifting social world, being obliged ever and anon to move on to green fields and pastures new. Besides, the competition between narcissists is frightful; each needs a clear field all to himself. Nobody after all hates a narcissist like another narcissist; they are deadly rivals. The permission and encouragement to narcissism, moreover, may be partly dependent upon youth and beauty, especially in default of more substantial excuses of an artistic or intellectual sort. The great artist who after all produces nothing worth mentioning is eventually recognized as a mere narcissistic parasite. And there is always a crop of younger and more beautiful and hence more effective parasites being produced; so that the aging narcissist has a hard time of it. Babied all his life, he cannot turn to ordinary usefulness or ordinary social adjustments; and unless he is very famous indeed or has found some particularly helpless and long-suffering victim with considerable economic power, he is in a desperate case.

These remarks may seem ungenerous in view of the fact that the narcissist does give us some of the same enjoyment as a work of art; he (or she) does liberate our spirits, does make us unreasonably happy, does give us a glimpse of a Paradise beyond our social bondage, does invigoratingly reveal the breadth of human nature so unwillingly renounced by us in growing up. But a work of art does these same things; and it can be thrown aside till it is wanted again. The sad truth is that the only socially tolerable narcissist is a dead narcissist; Casanova in a book does not cheat you at cards, Cleopatra in a play does not make you spend your money buying her pretty things and your valuable time waiting around for her. If our most admired narcissistic heroes and heroines of fiction could by some magic spell be made to come alive and give us the delights of their company, most of us would soon enough grow sick of them and would hasten to pronounce the magic spell which would pack them back again between the covers of the books from which they so dazzingly emerged. The narcissist, then, is a work of art who happens to be alive and breathing; and only a few such paragons can be either tolerated or supported by any society at the same time. Aristocratic society, indeed, supported a good many. The poor lived vicariously through their princes and did not begrudge them their splendors or their lawless liberties. But in democracies where everybody hopes to live and enjoy life on his own account, the social need of these symbolic figures is accordingly less. And to the extent that we manage to find socially suitable ways of expressing our own infantile impulses instead of having to repress them, we find that our tolerance of narcissists is accordingly diminished. A few eminent dead narcissists can amply fulfill our demands.

It would not be true to say that modern life does not tolerate narcissists at all, and it would be a most improbable prophecy to predict their complete disappearance in any future Society. But it seems correct to say that the young narcissist of to-day is not likely to be encouraged; he (or she) is more than likely to be told by kind friends: 'You ought to go and be psychoanalyzed.' The fact is that the narcissist is an expensive luxury which is being more conveniently supplanted by Art. The artist nowadays is likely to try very hard to be personally a grown-up person, proud of the extent that he is such and ashamed of any childishness that may still linger in his actual conduct.

There remains still another kind of heroism, narcissistic at base but quasi-parental in form and thoroughly disguised as political, military, religious or other social activities *for our benefit*. It is clear that the modern world still finds uses for this kind of heroism. It is not essentially different in the pulpit, in the Cabinet or in G. H. Q., from what it is in the studio, the green-room or the boudoir; but whereas a few people are exploited by artistic and erotic narcissists, vast multitudes are exploited by the others, and whole nations may be sacrificed to their infantile egotism and quasi-parental bossism. People will be led to wallow in superstition and set back the clock of scientific progress by the narcissistic charm and quasi-parental authority of an eloquent revivalist; nations will be led into imperial adventures that will end in slaughter and famine, by the infantile egotistic charm and quasi-parental prestige of a dictator; armies will go cheerfully to useless and horrible deaths under the spell of a narcissistic and absolutely powerful military leader: nor will history deny their greatness, since this is what historic greatness is. And in smaller fields, these political, military and religious narcissists will achieve their infantile satisfactions in 'leadership' at our expense and indeed to the satisfaction of most of us. Presumably this will continue to be the case until we achieve socially harmless self-expression of these infantile impulses, when we will no longer need or tolerate the vicarious 'greatness' which is now to be had through our Tamerlanes and Ghengis Khans. In the meantime these reflections should make us more tolerant of the egotism of movie actors, who have never harmed anybody to speak of, and of our Casanovas, who are comparatively unselfish, generous and decent fellows when measured beside the pious herdsmen who lead us into the slaughter-house of war.

There remains, to be sure, the possibility—the emotionally logical possibility, at least—of a leader who will really lead us for our benefit and not for his own; and perhaps a few 'great' political, military and other social leaders have answered to this description. Every parent who brings up his children to be able to dispense with his authority and care is such a leader on a small scale; every teacher who uses his opportunities for the real education, the real freeing of the young people in his charge, is such a leader on a wider scale; every scientist who helps to give mankind the knowledge which frees them from the need of authority is such a leader upon a grand scale. But the patriarchal régime has emphasized the other aspects of parentage, its coercive and hypnotic aspects; and our conceptions of leadership follow still in the main the patriarchal pattern of the parent who keeps his children from growing up. The heroes who are most respected are not the Promethean fire-bringers but the father-gods who kill us for their sport and make us think it is all for the best. Yet our modern civilization does tend, through painful experience, to begin to distrust its father-god heroes, does tend to respect more and more its Promethean teachers. The genuineness of these latter can be roughly gauged by whether they are trying to enable their pupils to dispense with their authority. Science alone has formulated such a discipline. The doctor who is interested chiefly in using *his* power to relieve suffering begins to smack of the medieval priest and the savage magician; while the doctor who is interested in helping to bring about a state of affairs in which his services can be largely dispensed with, through educating the public in sanitation, preventive medicine and health, is recognized as modern. In the psychoanalystic branch of psychotherapeutics, invented and developed by Freud, the great step which made it a modern science was the step from the hypnotic cures of Charcot to the method of re-education of the individual; the emotional relationship of 'parent' and 'child' is utilized because it is found necessary, but the treatment is not complete until this emotional relationship (the so-called 'transference') is dissolved and the patient set on his own feet. In this discipline, the analyst who for his own glorification or convenience or any other reason does not 'dissolve the transference' but keeps the patient in emotional child-like subjection to himself as a quasi-parent permanently, is regarded as a fool or a scoundrel. How far politics and military 'science' and ethics are from this modern notion is obvious. Can political leaders ever be expected to train their constituencies to get along without them? Can generals train their armies to dispense with commands? Can religious and ethical teachers train their followers to decide questions of behavior for themselves? If not, then this is a confession that politics, war and ethics all belong to an infantile stage of our human development; and however long we may remain in this stage, nothing is clearer than that the institutions which such kinds of leadership represent will have no place in the affairs of a socially adult and self-determining humanity.

CHAPTER XVII

DO WE NEED A PHILOSOPHY OF LIFE?

§ 1. Philosophies of Life

We have almost finished the inquiry announced at the outset. We have found out what is meant by the modern concept of psychic health. It has been shown that psychic health means full emotional adulthood, the capacity for heterosexual love and for responsible work. It has been seen what relation art has to this struggle. It has been seen that the chief difficulties which we encounter in growing up are inherited from the patriarchal family system and its property anxieties, and that our assurance of gaining general freedom from these lies in our new machine powers of production.

In the first chapter it was said that a part of the growing-up process is the task of achieving a philosophy ot life—gaining a view of things, however implicit, which will serve to explain to boy and girl their place in the human scheme and reconcile them to the destiny of struggle. The philosophy of life is built in childhood; and the more successfully it is built, the more implicit, the more taken for granted, it is. Let us consider what are the elements of this ethological education, what its purposes are, and how far it can be dispensed with in the modern world.

After early infancy, in early childhood, there normally begins, with increasing physical independence, the process of emancipation from parental care. We learn to dress ourselves and how to get along without parental assistance in various ways. We learn also to get along with other children. What we are really learning is, very gradually, to give up our babyhood. When we learn not to cry over every little hurt and to eat our vegetables because they are good for us, we are being prepared for adult life. Habit is the basis of this education, but it is re-enforced by parental approval and disapproval. It may easily come to depend too much on parental sanctions, and our modern effort is to keep it as much as possible on a habit basis; but parental approval and disapproval are important in effecting the transition from the crude self-love and spontaneously reflexive life of infancy to the habit-trained control of reflexes in later life.

So far, then, education in what one 'ought' to do is forward-looking, preparatory to ultimate personal independence.

But in later childhood, beginning usually with the first school years, or less effectually before that, there comes ordinarily in all societies a kind of teaching which is designed to replace direct parental approval with self-ratified social standards, making possible our ultimate freedom from personal guidance by our parents. It continues up to adult life, and in our civilization is largely a preparation for the control of sexual reflexes which will be demanded of us in adolescence and later. It is an attempt to give an emotional meaning or justification to all the parental controls or repressions which have been inflicted upon us as children every day of our lives—an attempt to make us accept this discipline willingly instead of reluctantly, and ultimately inflict this discipline upon ourselves. Thus, though it prepares us for adult freedom by making us our own jailors, with conscience speaking always on behalf of papa and mama, it aims to extend parental sanctions throughout life.

According to what behavior it applies to and at what age it is applied and under what social auspices, this inculcation of parental sanctions is called by such various names as good manners, religion, loyalty, duty, conscience, decency, pride, ethics, good sportsmanship, common sense, ideals, good citizenship, enlightened self-interest and philosophy. All these furnish emotional and intellectual reasons for behaving as papa and mama want us to behave. They impute emotional value to non-instinctive or anti-instinctive behavoir by giving us what amounts to parental approval—the approval of society, or God, or conscience or one's 'higher' self.

This kind of teaching has been notably successful in securing people's loyal and self-sacrificing adherence to large social purposes, whether we regard these purposes as good or bad. It enables us to fast when hungry, to go toward danger, to refrain from love-making when sexually attracted.

This teaching, however, presupposes a conflict between social purposes and instinctive wishes. All this rigamarole is not necessary to enable us to control our reflexes and delay the fulfillment of our instinctive wishes. There are indeed some fundamental places at which necessary social purposes lack instinctive backing, which has to be replaced by social controls. We probably no longer need to teach disgust with regard to the urinary and defecatory processes, but we still need to maintain the habitual social control of sexuality represented by the incest-barrier in family life. However, beyond this necessary human minimum of non-instinctive control, the huge elaborations in savage and in patriarchal life of avoidances, fears, repressions, codes of honor, sets of moral and ethical principles, standards of gentlemanliness and ladylikeness, notions of sin and virtue, and the fantastic artifices of good manners, merely point to the difficulty of trying to follow social purposes which lead in an opposite direction from our instinctive wishes. The social purposes pull us one way, our instincts pull us in the other, and between them we are pulled to pieces. This age-old effort has never been successful and the results were most of all unhappy when the social purposes did prevail over human instincts.

At all events, such a struggle is increasingly unnecessary in modern life, since our modern social purposes are increasingly in accord with our instincts. We should thus expect to find in modern life less and less use for artificial codes, morals and ethological philosophies of life.

But these have been only the formal half of our education in conduct. Along with it has always gone a kind of informal education in play with one's own age-group. In patriarchal life this supplied a necessary corrective to the insistent and interminable inculcation of parental 'oughts' and 'ought nots'; and it did so by going to the other extreme. In association with our peers in the free activities of play without any parental or quasi-parental 'leadership' of an ethical sort, we had the opportunity for the exercise of our instinctive impulses as well as for fairly uninhibited reflex activity. Age-group social sanctions were thus provided for all that was natural in us. In play we threw off the constraining parental harness, we were noisy, silly, giggling, romping, unmannerly, rude, belligerent, cruel, curious, obscene—the whole bag of natural propensities was let loose for a holiday. Relief was thus afforded from what otnerwise might have been the intolerable emotional tension of trying to live up to (or failing to live up to) the expectations of our parents and elders. Out of sight of critical parental and elderly eyes, in the company of our own age-group, we could be our natural and unedified selves. In this social milieu of our own we could attend to some of the positive aspects of growing up. For the parental codes were in essence negative, they involved in every instance the suppression or restraint of instinctive and reflexive responses to stimulus. But life, we felt, must have positive instinctive and reflexive values if it was to be worth living. Our instincts and reflexes needed freedom and exercise. All duty and no play—being just nice children and remembering to say 'thank you' under the approving-disapproving parental gaze, with no free outlet to our impulses—would not only make us dull boys and girls, but would hinder our ever growing up to any degree of healthy manhood and womanhood. We had to learn how to grow up in spite of our parents, in such play-time as we had; and though we did not succeed, perhaps, any too well, we did our best.

For adult life, in providing the social circumstances under which the inhibitions of childhood—whether in the realm of sex or of aggression—could be lifted, meant in effect the breaking of most of the rules so carefully learned in earlier life. These rules were to be broken, it was true, only under approved institutional or customary circumstances; but broken they must be if we were ever to function as adults. In adult life, if it were to be successful, our whole instinctive and emotional equipment had to be available for use as needed. Life, we somehow knew, could not be learned by being merely polite, eating our vegetables and keeping our clothes clean. We had to want to break anti-instinctive rules, we had to have at least some actual experimental practice in stretching them, or we would be helpless when we grew up and were told abruptly that we must now do (as it indeed seemed to some of us) precisely those things which we had always been solemnly assured were 'wrong'! When we were handsomely presented with adult freedom, we would not know what to do with it if we had never strained at the parental leash during all the years before. And in tragic fact, those boys and girls who remained too closely tied to the parental apron-string, who never got out to play with the rest of us, did quite preposterously continue to obey the childish rules even when they were supposed to be grown up.

Only free play, then with those of our own age-group, could sufficiently protect our childish minds from parental ethological education to permit us to remain on anything like friendly terms with our instinctive natures. This positive encouragement of our instinctive nature was able to counteract to some extent the deadly effects of parental repressions. So that if we were not watched too carefully we managed to grow up after a fashion. But this dual system of education tended in itself to create a dualism in our natures, a 'higher' and a 'lower' self, and laid the basis for future neurotic conflicts.

Moreover, as the parental ethological education went to extremes of refinement, so did the age-group education go to extremes of crudeness and brutality by way of redressing the balance. And, as in conventional British school life, this crudeness and brutality might be a frightful ordeal for sensitive natures. What passes as 'play' might be, for many others besides young Shelley at Eton, a horrible barbaric tyranny.

But play need not be so crude and brutal, if parental ethological education is not too damnably refined. And our modern ideal of education throws overboard the whole dualistic arrangement at the outset. The need of age-group education is taken account of, its natural teachings are encouraged. There are things that parents cannot do for children and playfellows can. Adjustment to one's own age-group in play is now accounted a part of education, not a thing alien to it or something that happens only by accident. The preaching rôle of the parent is accordingly minimized to as near nothing at all as parental anxieties will permit. We realize that the reason why duty and manners and loyalty and what-not bulked so large in patriarchal education is that the instinctive play and sexual instincts could not be used for patriarchal life-purposes, as they can for ours, and had to be replaced with an enormous mass of filial devotion. If young people were to be content to marry and work without exercising any choice of their own in either field, if the instinctive impulsions of sex and play were not available for marriage and work, then filial 'duty' had to be magnified to cover the whole of life. But to the extent that our lives are really modern we do not need the concept of duty.

We are, doubtless, not yet free enough from the effects of patriarchal repressions to be able to produce many triumphant illustrations of lives in which the concept of duty is not needed or used at all over long stretches of time—though everyone knows of happy aspects of his or her life to which such a concept would be ridiculously inapplicable. These aspects of life, momentary and fragmentary though they may be and however intermixed with failure, are the prophecies of a kind of life possible to a generation free from patriarchal repressions and able to become really grown-up.

Wholly adult lives lived from such almost wholly instinctive motives are, of course, not possible in a world still cluttered up in the realms of work and love with remnants of patriarchal tyranny. In the field of work, the population at large has little free choice of tasks and little opportunity to exercise the normal play instincts in the performance of these tasks. The patriarchal Father, having been cast out from other fields, remains enthroned in economics in the form of the presumably all-wise and certainly all-powerful private owner of industry, and the workers are still supposed to content themselves with the rôle of obedient and loyal children. Their frequent inability when opportunity offers to take a more adult and responsible attitude toward their work is used as an argument for the necessity of maintaining the old patriarchalism in ownership and control. But the banishment of patriarchalism from industry will be required to complete the modernization of the world. The value of our new machine powers of production in freeing us from anxieties will not be fully realized until these powers are taken out of patriarchalistic class-control and put at the service of humanity. In the realm of love, too, there are vested interests of an institutional sort to delay progress. But we may look forward to a generation free to make its choices in love and able as adults to assume and enjoy the responsibilities which these choices bring.

But if the parental rôle of preaching duty to children may be expected to disappear, that will still leave parents with plenty to do for their children. Aside from the immense service of not lying to them, of answering truthfully and simply and without emotional attitudes the simple questions that children ask, there is a fundamental service which parents can perform for children: they can be healthily in love with one another. They will thus have no morbid need to exploit their children's love; and they will—without having to try—furnish their children examples of adult man-and-woman happiness. Their normal love for their children will be the natural encouragement to the children's progress in the task of growing up. And all this means that they, the parents, have to be really adult. That is what children need—parents who are emotionally adult: not parental preaching.

Such young people, not lied to by their parents or emotionally exploited by them but encouraged to grow up, will hardly need, it would seem, much of any explicit 'philosophy of life' to help them through adolescence, to explain to them their place in the human scheme and reconcile them to the destiny of struggle.

For the young people of to-day, less fortunately situated, an explicit philosophy of life of one sort or another is doubtless needed. In place of healthy instincts operating in a healthy social-economic world, we have partly-crippled instincts operating in a partly-sick world where privilege preys upon poverty and where property-anxieties still too generally paralyze the love-emotions. The young people of to-day do need encouragement in order to face bravely the tasks of adult life, work and mating.

They have a right to know that it is not altogether their fault if life seems difficult to them; they have a right to know how things got this way and what prospects there are of their getting better, before they are asked to adjust themselves as best they can to things as they are. A serviceable philosophy of life for adolescent youth is one which offers them the hope of ultimate health in society at large as well as in their individual lives. Such a philosophy will explain the fears of young people as due not merely to their individual shortcomings in adaptation but to our general social-economic backwardness. And in giving young people the knowledge upon which to bring themselves nearer to psychic adulthood, it will give them also the knowledge upon which they can base their endeavors to help bring the contemporary world a little nearer to social-economic health.

This means that the task of promoting mental hygiene must be courageously correlated with the task of promoting social-economic hygiene—not, Mrs. Partington-like, merely try to sweep back, wave by wave, the individual neuroses which are but the spume of the great social-economic tides of anxiety and despair which sweep from the past across our world.

§ 2. The Mental Hygiene Movement

Some twenty-two million young people in the United States sit looking at the pictorial supplement of the Sunday newspapers. At least it is the one thing we can imagine them all doing of a Sunday morning.

They look at the pictures, which are mostly of athletes and actresses and people at play. These are the heroes and heroines of youth. They are national possessions—these young human bodies full of grace and power. Twenty-two million young people look at what might be a fifth-century Greek athlete by Myron, kneeling at the starting block. Twenty-two million young people look at a girl dancer, standing on bare tiptoes, head flung back, slim young arms lifted high, body poised and serene.

To these twenty-two millions of young people the athlete and the dancer are partly a memory and partly a wish. Some have been there—they have played games at school, or in the alley, and theirs is the taut body kneeling at the starting block; they have danced, in restaurants, to the phonograph, to the radio, and theirs is the serene poised body on tiptoe. To others this is less a memory than a wish. The 1920 census reports over a million children of 10 to 15 years engaged in 'gainful occupations'—one-twelfth of the total number of all children of that age in the country. Looking at pictures such as these, buying an evening paper on the way home from work to see whether the Yanks or the Giants have won a baseball game, may be their only mode of participating in our national cult of play. Their bodies may be worn out, poisoned, deformed and disabled while still in youth by industrial tasks. This glimpse of others at play is not much for a proud civilization to give these of its children. But it is something. It is a seed that our civilization casts everywhere. It is a certain cultural attitude toward the body. And it is a prophecy that year by year these experiences will be less vicarious. For these girl dancers and boy athletes are the poetry of what may be called our modern physical health campaign.

The great modern psychic health campaign, just beginning,

has its poetry, too. In the conclusion of one of his latest books, Freud permits himself to express what might seem an extravagant hope. After remarking upon the pressure of modern civilization upon its populations, and the need for 'corrective measures', he goes on to ask: "Does it seem too fantastic to expect that psychoanalysis, in spite of the many difficulties it encounters, should be called upon to furnish this corrective agent? Maybe some American millionaire will one day donate enough money for the psychoanalytical training of the social workers of his country, thus creating an emergency corps, to fight neurotic conditions brought about by present-day life." At this point, Freud brings in an imaginary reader who inquires incredulously:

" 'You mean some sort of a new Salvation Army?' "

And Freud answers boldly: "Why not?"

Freud's dream of a psychoanalytic Salvation Army has not quite literally come true. But something not less dramatic has happened in America.

The name of Clifford Beers has in it a poetic thrill for those who know the story. He—as it is related in his autobiography, *A Mind That Found Itself*—was a business man who became mentally sick and was shut up in one after another of the half-medieval 'insane-asylums' which we then maintained. There, without any such assistance as he might have received from modern psychotherapeutic science, he heroically fought his way back to mental health. That is not a unique case, thus far; it has happened before. But Clifford Beers did not then simply go back into business and conceal as best he could this painful episode in his life. He had seen the barbarity and folly of our institutional treatment of the mentally sick and he determined to spend the rest of his life fighting for scientific treatment for mentally sick people. He realized, moreover, that the causes of mental sickness extend far back into early life, and that a little wise guidance in childhood or adolescence would save many an individual to a life of usefulness and happiness—would spare them years of neurotic torment and the possibility of psychotic breakdown. He realized, too, the relations of mental sickness to the problems of crime. He founded the National Committee for Mental Hygiene, in which educators, physicians, psychotherapists of all sorts, judges, social workers and all others interested in preserving and restoring psychic health are now joined together in one of the most gigantic and romantic efforts in human history. Within a brief time the Mental Hygiene movement has seen hundreds of child-guidance clinics established. It has seen its work of investigation and guidance extend down to day-nurseries and kindergartens, up through grade-schools and high schools into colleges—wherever young people can be helped out of neurotic struggle and into the ways of psychic health. It sees the beginnings of similar work in large business and industrial establishments. It has made psychiatric surveys of prison populations and is formulating legislative programs for the proper treatment of delinquents. "Such work", it declares in its statement of its purposes, "is not only for the mentally disordered and those suffering from mental defect, but for all those who, through mental causes, are unable so to adjust themselves to their environment as to live *happy and efficient lives.*" And the movement has now become international in its scope.

From the work of the Mental Hygiene movement the impetus to this present essay, as well as many of its materials, have been derived. That movement should not be held responsible for any errors in interpretation or emphasis which may have been unwittingly committed in these pages, but it is as a tribute to its purposes and an effort toward their furtherance through public education that this essay on how to grow up into usefulness and happiness in our modern world is submitted to its readers.

THE END

BIBLIOGRAPHY

ADLER, ALFRED. *The Case of Miss R.: The Interpretation of a Life Story.* New York (Greenberg), 1929.

ANDERSON, V. V. *Psychiatry in Industry.* New York (Harper), 1929.

[Ed.] *Mental Disease and Delinquency: A Report of a Special Committee of the New York State Commission of Prisons.* New York (NCMH*), 1919.

ALDRICH, C. A. "The Prevention of Poor Appetite in Children". NCMH pamphlet reprint from *Mental Hygiene,* Oct., 1926.

ALVERDES, FR. *Social Life in the Animal World.* New York (Harcourt), 1927.

ARISTOPHANES. *Ecclesiazusae.* Rogers' transl. London (Bohn).

Lysistrata. The Seldes transl. of Smolin's transl. for the Moscow Art Theatre. New York (Brentano), 1925.

ARISTOTLE. *Politics.* Jowett's transl. Oxford.

Constitution of the Athenians. Botsford's transl., i-iv, in Botsford and Sihler's *Hellenic Civilization,* pp. 137–41.

AUGUSTINE, ST. *Confessions.* Watts' transl. & Latin text. (Loeb).

BARKER, LEWELLYS. "How to Avoid Spoiling the Child". NCMH pamphlet reprint from *Mental Hygiene,* April, 1919.

BEERS, CLIFFORD. *A Mind That Found Itself.* New York (Doubleday), 1908.

BINGHAM, ANNE T. "What Can Be Done for the Maladjusted?" NCMH pamphlet reprint from *Mental Hygiene,* April, 1920.

"The Application of Psychiatry to High-School Problems". NCMH pamphlet reprint from *Mental Hygiene,* Jan., 1925.

BIRD, GRACE E. "The Value of Mental Hygiene in the Secondary School". NCMH pamphlet reprint from *Mental Hygiene,* April, 1927.

BLAKE, WILLIAM. *The Marriage of Heaven and Hell.* In *Poetical Works.* Oxford.

BLANCHARD, PHYLLIS. *The Adolescent Girl.* New York (Dodd-Mead), 1926.

"Sex in the Adolescent Girl". In *Sex in Civilization,* pp. 538–61.

"The Family Situation and Personality Development". NCMH pamphlet reprint from *Mental Hygiene,* Jan., 1927.

BLUMGART, LEONARD. "Observations on Maladjusted Children". NCMH reprint from *Mental Hygiene,* April, 1921.

BOSANQUET, HELEN. *The Family.* New York (Macmillan), 1923.

BOTSFORD, G. W., and SIHLER, S. G. *Hellenic Civilization.* New York (Columbia U.), 1929.

BRIFFAULT, ROBERT. *The Mothers: a Study of the Origins of Sentiments and Institutions.* New York (Macmillan), 1927.

BRUUN, LAURIDS. *Van Zanten's Happy Days: A Love Story from Pelli Island.* New York (Knopf), 1922.

* National Committee for Mental Hygiene.

BURNHAM, WILLIAM H. "Success and Failure as Conditions of Mental Health". NCMH pamphlet reprint from *Mental Hygiene,* July, 1919.

BURNS, ROBERT. *Poems and Songs.* (Everyman).

BURTON, ROBERT. *The Anatomy of Melancholy.* All-English text, ed. by Floyd Dell and Paul Jordan-Smith. New York (Farrar), 1929.

CAMPBELL, C. MACFIE. "Mental Hygiene in Industry". NCMH pamphlet reprint from *Mental Hygiene,* July, 1921.

"Education and Mental Hygiene". NCMH pamphlet reprint from *Mental Hygiene,* July, 1919.

CATULLUS. Marris's transl. & Latin text. Oxford, 1924.

CHESTERTON, MRS. CECIL. *In Darkest London.* New York (Macmillan).

CHESTERTON, G. K. *Robert Browning.* (English Men of Letters.)

Child, the Clinic and the Court (The): a Group of Papers by Jane Addams, A. L. Jacoby [& 25 others]. New York (New Republic). 1925.

CHURCHILL, WINSTON. *The World-Crisis, 1916–1918.* New York (Scribner), 1927.

COBB, STANLEY. "Applications of Psychiatry to Industrial Hygiene". NCMH pamphlet reprint from *Journal of Industrial Hygiene,* Nov., 1919.

COLCORD, JOANNA C. *Broken Homes: a Study of Family Desertion and its Social Treatment.* New York (Russell Sage), 1919.

Concerning Parents: a Symposium on Present Day Parenthood. New York (New Republic), 1926.

CONYBEARE, F. C. *Myth, Magic, and Morals: A Study of Christian Origins.* Boston (Beacon), 1925.

COOPER, JAMES F. *Technique of Contraception.* New York (Day-Nichols), 1928.

CORSON, HAROLD F. "Factors in the Development of Psychoses in College Men: A Study of Twenty-five Cases". NCMH pamphlet reprint from *Mental Hygiene,* July, 1927.

Critic and Guide, The Medical. Ed. by Dr. W. J. Robinson. New York.

DAVENPORT, ISABEL. *Salvaging of American Girlhood: A Substitution of Normal Psychology for Superstition and Mysticism in the Education of Girls.* New York (Dutton), 1924.

DAVIS, KATHERINE BEMENT. *Factors in the Sex Life of Twenty-two Hundred Women.* Publications of the Bureau of Social Hygiene. New York (Harpers), 1929.

DELL, FLOYD. *Janet March: A Novel.* Revised ed. New York (Doran), 1927.

DOOLEY, LUCILE. "Analysis of a Case of Manic-Depressive Psychosis Showing Well-Marked Regressive Stages". *Psychoanalytic Review,* Jan., 1918; qtd. in Blanchard, *The Adolescent Girl,* pp. 164–167.

DAWSON, ERNEST. "Non sum qualis eram bonae sub regno Cynarae". *The Home Book of Verse,* p. 918.

DREISER, THEODORE. *The "Genius".* New York, 1915.

A Book About Myself. New York (Liveright), 1922.

ELLIS, HAVELOCK. *Man and Woman.* 6th ed. London (Black), 1926.

Sexual Inversion (vol. ii of the *Studies in the Psychology of Sex*). Philadelphia (Davis), 1923.

Sex in Relation to Society (vol. vi of the *Studies*). Philadelphia (Davis), 1923.

Affirmations. Boston (Houghton), 1926.

EMERSON, RALPH WALDO. *Poems.*
EMERY, E. VAN NORMAN. "Revising Our Attitude Toward Sex". NCMH pamphlet reprint from *Mental Hygiene,* April, 1927.
Encyclopedia Britannica. 11th ed. & 13th ed.
EURIPIDES. *Medea.* Murray's transl. New York (Oxford U.).
Bacchae. Murray's transl. London (Unwin).
FEIGENBAUM, DORIAN. "Psychological Problems of Childhood and Youth and Their Relation to Education". Pamphlet reprint from *Proceedings of the Second Biennial Conference of the World Federation of Education Associations,* 1927.
FERENCZI, S. *Contributions to Psychoanalysis.* Boston (Badger), 1916.
FIELDING, MICHAEL [pseud.]. *Parenthood: Design or Accident?* A Manual of Birth Control. Introd. by H. G. Wells. London (Labor), 1929.
FIELDING, WILLIAM J. *Sex and the Love Life.* New York (Dodd-Mead), 1927.
FISHER, BOYD. "Has Mental Hygiene a Practical Use in Industry?" NCMH reprint from *Mental Hygiene,* July, 1921.
FRAZER, SIR JAMES GEORGE. *The Golden Bough.* Abridged ed. New York (Macmillan), 1928.
Folk-Lore in the Old Testament. Abridged ed. New York (Macmillan), 1927.
FREUD, SIGMUND. *Three Contributions to the Theory of Sex.* Nervous and Mental Disease Monograph Series. New York & Washington, 1918.
Introduction to Psychoanalysis. New York (Liveright), 1920.
The Problem of Lay Analysis. New York (Brentano), 1927.
GEDDES, PATRICK, and THOMSON, J. ARTHUR. *Sex.* (Home U.)
GIBBON, EDWARD. *The Decline and Fall of the Roman Empire.*
GLUECK, BERNARD. "Types of Delinquent Careers". NCMH pamphlet reprint from *Mental Hygiene,* April, 1917.
"Psychiatric Aims in the Field of Criminology". NCMH pamphlet reprint from *Mental Hygiene,* Oct., 1918.
"Psychiatric Treatment and Probation". NCMH pamphlet reprint from *Mental Hygiene,* Oct., 1924.
"Report on the Ninth International Prison Congress". NCMH pamphlet reprint from *Mental Hygiene,* Jan., 1926.
GLUECK, SHELDON. "State Legislation Providing for the Mental Examination of Persons Accused of Crime". NCMH pamphlet reprint from *Mental Hygiene,* Jan., 1924.
"Psychiatric Examination of Persons Accused of Crime". NCMH pamphlet reprint from *Mental Hygiene,* April, 1927.
Greek Anthology, The. Paton's transl. (Loeb).
The Girdle of Aphrodite: The Complete Love-Poems of the Palatine Anthology. Transl. by F. A. Wright. (Broadway Translations.)
The Poets of the Greek Anthology. Transl. by F. A. Wright. (Broadway Translations.)
GREENE, ELIZABETH. "Results of Five Years' Psychiatric Work in New York City High Schools". NCMH pamphlet reprint from *Mental Hygiene,* July, 1927.
GRIMM, THE BROTHERS. *Household Tales.* (Everyman.)
GROVES, E. R., and OGBURN, W. F. *American Marriage and Family Relationships.* New York (Holt), 1928.
Habit Training for Children. Pamphlet. New York (NCMH), 1924.

HAIRE, NORMAN ED. *Some More Medical Views on Birth Control.* New York (Dutton), 1908.
HAMILTON, G. V. *A Research in Marriage.* New York (Boni), 1929.
HAMILTON, G. V., and MAGGOWAN, KENNETH. *What Is Wrong With Marriage?* New York (Boni), 1929.
HAMILTON, MARGARET. "Mental Hygiene and the Parasite". NCMH pamphlet reprint from *Mental Hygiene,* Jan., 1921.
HARRISON, JANE ELLEN. *Ancient Art and Ritual.* (Home U.)
HART, BERNARD. *The Psychology of Insanity.* (Cambridge Manuals), 1929.
HAVILAND, C. FLOYD. "Mental Hygiene Needs Arising Subsequent to School Life". NCMH pamphlet reprint from *Mental Hygiene,* Oct., 1922.
HEALY, WILLIAM, and BRONNER, AUGUSTA F. "Medico-Psychological Study of Delinquents". NCMH reprint from *Mental Hygiene,* July, 1919.
HERODOTUS. Rawlinson's transl. (Everyman.)
HERRICK, ROBERT. *Poetical Works.* Oxford.
HESIOD. Mair's transl. Oxford, 1908.
HINGSTON, R. W. G. *Instinct and Intelligence.* New York, 1929.
HOHMAN, LESLIE B. "The Formation of Life Patterns". NCMH pamphlet reprint from *Mental Hygiene,* Jan., 1927.
HOLLINGWORTH, LETA S. *The Psychology of the Adolescent.* New York (Appleton), 1928.
Home Book of Verse, The. Ed. by Burton Egbert Stevenson. New York (Holt), 1922.
HOUSMAN, A. E. *A Shropshire Lad.*
Last Poems. New York (Holt), 1922.
IBRAHIM, PROF. (A digest by 'F. K.' of an address by Ibrahim on 'hospitalism' and its cure by individual nursing appears in *Kosmos,* No. 6, 1918; qtd. from in Feigenbaum, *q.v.*)
IBSEN, HENRIK. *The Wild Duck.*
JACOBY, A. L. "'When a Feller Needs a Friend': The Adolescent Delinquent", in *The Child, the Clinic and the Court.*
JARRETT, MARY C. "The Psychopathic Employee: a Problem of Industry". NCMH pamphlet reprint from *Medicine and Surgery,* Sept., 1917.
"The Mental Hygiene of Industry". NCMH pamphlet reprint from *Mental Hygiene,* Oct., 1920.
"The Practical Value of Mental Hygiene in Industry". NCMH pamphlet reprint from *Mental Hygiene,* May, 1921.
JONES, ERNEST. *Papers on Psychoanalysis.* New York (Wood), 1918.
JOYCE, JAMES. *Portrait of the Artist as a Young Man.* New York (Huebsch), 1916.
Judge Baker Foundation Case Studies: Series 1. Case Studies 1 to 20. Boston (Judge Baker Foundation), 1922–23.
JUVENAL. Evans's transl. (Bohn).
KAMMERER, PERCY GAMBLE. *The Unmarried Mother: A Study of Five Hundred Cases.* Criminal Science Monograph. Boston (Little-Brown), 1926.
KEATS, JOHN. *Poetical Works.*
KEITH, ARTHUR. *Man: A History of the Human Body.* (Home U.)
KENWORTHY, MARION E. "The Mental Hygiene Aspects of Illegitimacy". NCMH pamphlet reprint from *Mental Hygiene,* July, 1921.

KIPLING, RUDYARD. *Collected Verse.* New York (Doubleday), 1912.
"Hymn of the Triumphant Airman". New York *World,* Sept. 6, 1929.

KÖHLER, WOLFGANG. *The Mentality of Apes.* 2d ed. New York (Harcourt), 1927.

KOLB, LAWRENCE. "Drug Addiction in Its Relation to Crime". NCMH pamphlet reprint from *Mental Hygiene,* Jan., 1925.
"Types and Characteristics of Drug Addicts". NCMH pamphlet reprint from *Mental Hygiene,* April, 1925.
"Pleasure and Deterioration from Narcotic Addiction". NCMH pamphlet reprint from *Mental Hygiene,* Oct., 1925.

Kosmos: Handweiser für Naturfreunde. Stuttgart.

LANE, E. W. *The Manners and Customs of the Modern Egyptians.* (Everyman.)

LEPLAY, P. G. M. *Les Ouvriers Européens;* qtd. in Bosanquet, *The Family,* pp. 76–82.

LINDSEY, BEN B., and EVANS, WAINWRIGHT. *The Revolt of Modern Youth.* New York (Liveright), 1925.
The Companionate Marriage. New York (Liveright), 1927.

LONDON, JACK. *John Barleycorn.* New York (Century), 1913.

LUCIAN. *Dialogues of the Hetaerae.* In *The Works of Lucian of Samosata,* transl. by H. W. & F. G. Fowler, vol. iv. Oxford, 1905.

LUCRETIUS. *On the Nature of Things.* Munro's transl. (Bohn).

LUDOVICI, ANTHONY. *The Night Hoers.* London (Jenkins), 1928; reviewed in *Critic and Guide,* Feb., 1929.

LUNDBERG, EMMA O. *Children of Illegitimate Birth and Measures for Their Protection.* Children's Bureau, Dept. of Labor. Washington, 1926.

MACCURDY, GEORGE GRANT. *Human Origins: A Manual of Prehistory.* New York (Appleton), 1924.

MALINOWSKI, BRONISLAW. *Argonauts of the Western Pacific.* New York (Dutton), 1922.
Crime and Custom in Savage Society. New York (Harcourt), 1926.
The Father in Primitive Psychology. New York (Norton), 1927.
Sex and Repression in Savage Society. New York (Harcourt), 1927.
The Sexual Life of Savages. New York (Liveright), 1929.

Marriage Laws of Soviet Russia. Russian Soviet Govt. Bureau. New York, 1921.

MEAD, CHARLES W. *Old Civilizations of Inca Land.* Handbook, American Museum of Natural History. New York, 1926.

MEAD, MARGARET. *Coming of Age in Samoa: A Psychological Study of Primitive Youth for Western Civilization.* New York (Morrow), 1928.

MENNINGER, KARL A. "Adaptation Difficulties in College Students". NCMH pamphlet reprint from *Mental Hygiene,* June, 1927.

Mental Hygiene: Quarterly Magazine of the National Committee for Mental Hygiene. New York.

Mental Hygiene Surveys of New York County Jails and Penitentiaries, With Recommendations (Report of a). New York (NCMH), 1924.

MEREDITH, FLORENCE. "The Administration of Mental Hygiene in Colleges". NCMH pamphlet reprint from *Mental Hygiene,* April, 1927.

METCHNIKOFF, ELIE. *The Nature of Man.* New York (Putnam), 1903.

MEYER, ADOLF. "The Right to Marry: What Can a Democratic Civilization Do About Heredity and Child Welfare?" NCMH pamphlet reprint from *Mental Hygiene*, Jan., 1910.

MILLAY, EDNA. *Renascence and Other Poems*. New York, 1917.

Second April. New York, 1921.

MILLER, NATHAN. *The Child in Primitive Society*. New York (Brentano), 1928.

MOFFATT, JAMES. *The New Testament: A New Translation*. New York (Doran), 1922.

MOWRER, ERNEST R. *Domestic Discord: Its Analysis and Treatment*. (U. of Chicago), 1908.

MURRAY, MARGARET ALICE. *The Witch-Cult in Western Europe*. Oxford, 1921.

OVERHOLSER, WINIFRED. "Psychiatry and the Treatment of Offenders". NCMH pamphlet reprint from *Mental Hygiene*, April, 1927.

PFISTER, OSKAR. *Love in Children and Its Aberrations*. New York (Dodd-Mead), 1924.

PLATO. *The Republic*. Spens's transl. (Everyman).

Protagoras. Wright's transl. In *Socratic Discourses by Plato and Xenophon*. (Everyman.)

Symposium. Shelley's transl. In *Five Dialogues of Plato on Poetic Inspiration*. (Everyman.)

Laws. Bury's transl. (Loeb), 1926.

PLUTARCH. *Parallel Lives*. Perrin's transl. (Loeb). Stewart & Long's transl. (Bohn).

POPENOE, PAUL. *Modern Marriage: a Handbook*. New York (Macmillan), 1925.

PRATT, GEORGE K. "The Problem of the Mental Misfit in Industry". NCMH pamphlet reprint from *Mental Hygiene*, July, 1922.

PRUETTE, LORINE, and FRYER, DOUGLAS. "Affective Factors in Vocational Maladjustment". NCMH pamphlet reprint from *Mental Hygiene*, Jan., 1923.

Psychiatric Clinic in Collaboration with Sing Sing Prison, First Annual Report of. New York (NCMH), 1917.

"Psychiatric Examination of a Child". NCMH pamphlet reprint from *Mental Hygiene*, April, 1926.

QUEEN, STUART ALFRED, and MANN, DELBERT MARTIN. *Social Pathology*. New York (Crowell), 1925.

RICHARDS, ESTHER LORING. "Practical Aspects of Parental Love". NCMH pamphlet reprint from *Mental Hygiene*, April, 1926.

RICHMOND, MARY E., and HALL, FRED S. *Child Marriages*. New York (Russell Sage), 1925.

Marriage and the State. New York (Russell Sage), 1929.

ROBERTS, MARJORIE. "Italian Girls on American Soil". *Mental Hygiene*, Oct., 1929.

ROBINSON, WILLIAM J. *Woman: Her Sex and Love Life*. New York (Critic and Guide), 1924.

A Doctor's Views on Life. London (Unwin), 1927.

ROSSETTI, CHRISTINA. *Poems*.

ROSWITHA, *The Plays of*. Transl. by C. St. John. London (Chatto), 1923.

RUGGLES, ARTHUR H. "College Mental-Hygiene Problems". NCMH pamphlet reprint from *Mental Hygiene*, April, 1925.

SAVILLE, W. J. V. *In Unknown New Guinea.* Philadelphia (Lippincott), 1926.

SCOTT, AUGUSTA. "Neuropsychiatric Work in Industry". NCMH pamphlet reprint from *Mental Hygiene,* July, 1923.

Sex in Civilization. Ed. by V. F. Calverton and S. D. Schmalhausen. New York (Macaulay), 1929.

SHAKESPEARE. *Sonnets.*

Romeo and Juliet.

SHAW, BERNARD. *Man and Superman.*

Androcles and the Lion.

SHELLEY, PERCY BYSSHE. *Collected Poems.*

SINGER, CHARLES. *A Short History of Medicine.* New York (Oxford U.), 1928.

SMITH, JESSICA. *Woman in Soviet Russia.* New York (Vanguard), 1928.

SOLLAS, W. J. *Ancient Hunters and Their Modern Representatives.* 3d ed., revised. New York (Macmillan), 1924.

STENDHAL (HENRI BEYLE). *Red and Black.* E. P. Robins's transl. New York (Richmond), 1898.

STEPNIAK, S. *The Russian Peasantry*; qtd. in Bosanquet, *The Family.*

STEVENSON, R. L. *Poems.*

SWINBURNE, A. C. *Poems and Ballads: First Series.*

SYMANS, ARTHUR. Ed.: *A Pageant of Elizabethan Poetry.* London (Blackie).

TAFT, JESSIE. "Some Problems of Delinquency"; qtd. in Thomas, *The Unadjusted Girl,* pp. 200–209.

"Mental Hygiene Problems of Normal Adolescence". NCMH pamphlet reprint from *Mental Hygiene,* Oct., 1921.

"The Relation of the School to the Mental Health of the Average Child". NCMH pamphlet reprint from *Mental Hygiene,* Oct., 1923.

TARKINGTON, BOOTH. *Seventeen.*

TAYLOR, MARIANNA. "The Child and the Home: An Extract from a Survey of Mental Health Conditions in a Metropolitan District". NCMH pamphlet reprint from *Mental Hygiene,* Oct., 1922.

Technique of the Love Affair, The. By a Gentlewoman. New York (Simon), 1928.

THOMAS, W. I. *Sex and Society: Studies in the Social Psychology of Sex.* (U. of Chicago), 1913.

The Unadjusted Girl. Boston (Little-Brown), 1928.

THOMPSON, C. MILDRED. "The Value of Mental Hygiene in College". NCMH pamphlet reprint from *Mental Hygiene,* April, 1927.

THOMPSON, FRANCIS. *Poems.*

THOMPSON, R. LOWE. *The History of the Devil: The Horned God of Western Europe.* New York (Harcourt), 1929.

TROLLOPE, MRS. *Domestic Manners of the Americans.*

VANWATERS, MIRIAM. "Youth in Conflict". In *The Child, the Clinic and the Court.*

"Juvenile Court Procedure as a Factor in Diagnosis"; qtd. in Thomas, *The Unadjusted Girl,* pp. 195–9.

VERRILL, A. HYATT. *Old Civilizations of the New World.* Indianapolis, 1929.

WATSON, JOHN B., and LASHLEY, K. S. *A Consensus of Medical Opinion Upon Questions Relating to Sex Education and Venereal Disease Campaigns.* New York (NCMH), 1920.

WATSON, JOHN B. *Psychological Care of Infant and Child.* New York (Norton), 1928.

WELLS, H. G. *The World of William Clissold: A Novel.* New York (Doubleday), 1926.

WHITE, WILLIAM A. "Underlying Concepts in Mental Hygiene". NCMH pamphlet reprint from *Mental Hygiene,* Jan., 1917.

WHITMAN, WALT. *Leaves of Grass.*

Democratic Vistas.

WILLIAMS, ALBERT RHYS. *The Russian Land.* New York (New Republic), 1927.

WILLIAMS, FRANKWOOD E. "The Relation of Alcohol and Syphilis to Mental Hygiene". NCMH pamphlet reprint from *Mental Hygiene,* Dec., 1916.

"Anxiety and Fear". NCMH pamphlet reprint from *Mental Hygiene,* Jan., 1920.

"Community Responsibility in Mental Hygiene". NCMH pamphlet reprint from *American Review,* Jan., 1913.

"Confronting the World—The Adjustments of Later Adolescence". In *Concerning Parents.*

"Can Youth Be Coerced?" NCMH pamphlet. New York, 1927.

"Mental Hygiene and the College Student". NCMH pamphlet reprint from *Mental Hygiene,* April, 1921, and April, 1925.

WILLIAMS, GERTRUDE MARVIN. *Understanding India.* New York (Coward-McCann), 1928.

WILLIAMS-ELLIS, AMABEL. *The Exquisite Tragedy: An Intimate Life of John Ruskin.* New York (Doubleday), 1929.

WOOLLEY, HELEN T. "Enuresis as a Psychological Problem". NCMH pamphlet reprint from *Mental Hygiene,* Jan., 1926.

WRIGHT, F. A. See *Greek Anthology.*

XENOPHON. *Constitution of the Lacedaemonians;* selections, in Botsford and Sihler, *Hellenic Civilization,* pp. 131–6.

Economicus; selections, in Botsford and Sihler, pp. 494–508.

NOTES AND REFERENCES

Page

8. Sex as Magic: Murray, *The Witch-Cult in Western Europe;* Thompson, R. L., *The History of the Devil: The Horned God of Western Europe;* Frazer, *The Golden Bough.*
13. Infancy: Freud, "The Infantile Psychology," *Three Contributions to the Theory of Sex; The Problem of Lay Analysis,* p. 250.
14. Puberty: Freud, "The Transformation of Puberty," *Three Contributions,* page 73.
15. The feminine rôle: Ibid, pp. 80-81.
16. Aurignacian period: Sollas, *Ancient Hunters,* chap. viii; MacCurdy, *Human Origins,* vol. i, chap. vii, vol. ii, pp. 169-174.
17. Quasi-matriarchal institutions: Briffault, *The Mothers,* chap. viii.
18. Inheritance by the youngest son, and by the youngest daughter: Frazer, *Folk-Lore in the Old Testament,* chap. ii.
23. Sparta: Plutarch, "Life of Lycurgus" and "Comparison of Lycurgus and Numa": Xenophon, *Constitution of the Lacedaemonians;* Aristotle, *Politics.* Cp. Thebes: Plutarch, "Life of Pelopidas," xviii.
24. Athens: Aristotle, *Constitution of the Athenians;* Xenophon, *Economicus;* Aristophanes, *Ecclesiazusae* and *Lysistrata;* Euripides, *Medea;* Plato, *Republic, Protagoras, Symposium* and *Laws;* the *Greek Anthology.* Marriage Age in Greece: Plutarch, "Lycurgus"; Xenophon, Economicus, vii:5; Aristotle, *Politics,* vii:16; Hesiod, *Works and Days,* 698; Plato, Laws, vi:787.
34. Roman marriage: the plebeian form, *Ency. Brit.,* 11th ed., art. "Roman Law," 23:537; the aristocratic adoption of the plebeian form, Wright, *Ovid: The Lover's Handbook,* introd., pp. 74-76, and Briffault, *The Mothers,* vol. ii, pp. 243-250.
35. St. Augustine, *Confessions,* lv:2; vi:15.
36. Lucian, *Dialogues of the Hetaerae,* viii. Five drachmas, about a dollar; the later Attic talent was about a thousand dollars, the Roman talent about $363.
37. Lesbia: Catullus, lviii.
42. Emerson, "Brahma."
44. Gibbon, *Decline and Fall of the Roman Empire,* chap. lxxi.
45. LePlay, *Les Ouvriers Européens;* qtd. in Bosanquet, *The Family,* p. 76. Stepniak, *The Russian Peasantry;* qtd. in Bosanquet, *The Family,* p. 83.
46. Williams, G., *Understanding India,* p. 256.
57. Demosthenes, *Contra Neaeream.* Catullus, lxi.
59. Bundling: Calhoun, *Social History of the American Family,* vol. i, p. 130.
63. Juvenal, *Satires,* vi:82-110.
66. Freud, *Introduction to Psychoanalysis,* p. 396.
69. "This 20-year old youth": Jacoby, "'When a Feller Needs a Friend': The Adolescent Delinquent," in *The Child, the Clinic and the Court.*

Page

74. Wells, *The World of William Clissold*, vol. ii, pp. 463-465.
81. "medieval heretical sect": Ellis, *Sexual Inversion*, pp. 3-4.
86. Sanitation among the anthropoids: Alverdes, *Social Life in the Animal World*, p. 51. Köhler, *The Mentality of Apes*, pp. 297-298.
91. Aldrich, "The Prevention of Poor Appetite in Children," Mental Hygiene, Oct., 1926.
94. Plato, *Protagoras*.
96. LePlay, *Les Ouvriers Européens;* qtd. in Bosanquet, *The Family*, p. 79. Herodotus, i:31; Plutarch, "Life of Solon," xxvii. Hollingworth, The Psychology of the Adolescent, p. 49.
100. Thompson, C. M., "The Value of Mental Hygiene in College," *Mental Hygiene*, April, 1927.
102. Chesterton, Mrs. Cecil, *In Darkest London*, p. 86.
103. Richards, "Practical Aspects of Parental Love," *Mental Hygiene*, April, 1926.
104. Hingston, *Instinct and Intelligence*, chap. iv.
105. Obstetrical forceps: art. "Obstetrics," *Ency. Brit.*, 111th ed., 19:964.
106. Singer, *A Short History of Medicine*, p. 164.
107. Hollingworth, *The Psychology of the Adolescent*, p. 113.
108. Menninger, "Adaptation Difficulties in College Students," *Mental Hygiene*, June, 1927. Ruggles, "College Mental Hygiene Problems," *Mental Hygiene*, April, 1925.
115. Mead, M., *Coming of Age in Samoa*, p. 246.
119. Aristotle, *Politics*, ii:3:7.
120. Queen and Mann, *Social Pathology*, p. 39. Abbott, art. "Child Labour and Child Welfare," *Ency. Brit.*, 13th ed., 1:609.
122. Smith, *Woman in Soviet Russia*, chap. x.
125. Instinct: The view of instinct here adopted is intended to follow Malinowski's use of the term in *Sex and Repression Savage Society;* Malinowski's conception of instinct is based on that of Lloyd Morgan (see Morgan's art. "Instinct" and "Intelligence of Animals," 11th ed. *Ency. Brit.*) and the views of A. F. Shand (see Shand's art. "Character," 13th ed. *Ency. Brit.*).
127. Mowrer, *Domestic Discord*, pp. 133, 149.
128. Colcord, *Broken Homes*, p. 53. Healy, in Kammerer, *The Unmarried Mother*, introd., p. xii.
129. Malinowski, *The Father in Primitive Psychology*, p. 70; *The Sexual Life of Savages*, vol. ii, p. 194.
130. Spencer and Gillen, qtd. in Thomas, *Sex and Society*, p. 179.
131. Aristotle, *Politics*, i:5:7; i:13:7; vii:16:9.
133. Watson, *Psychological Care of Infant and Child;* anti-mothering, pp. 82, 83, 84, 81, 69, 80; routine, 121-122; dress, 110, 93-94, 106-107; sex-education, chap. vi. Feigenbaum, *Psycholological Problems of Childhood and Youth and Their Relation to Education*, pp. 4-5. Ibrahim: *Kosmos*, No. 6, 1918.
144. Illegitimacy laws: Lundberg, *Children of Illegitimate Birth and Measures for their Protection*, pp. 16, 17, 19, 20; art. "Norway," *Ency. Brit.*, 13th ed., 2:1087; *Marriage Laws of Soviet Russia*, p. 55; Kammerer, *The Unmarried Mother*, pp. 277-283, 330-334.
145. Ellis, *Sex in Relation to Society*, pp. 380-387.

Page

146. Calhoun, *Social History of the American Family*, vol. i, pp. 130-133.
147. Hamilton and MacGowan, *What Is Wrong With Marriage*, pp. 231, 246.
148. Illegitimacy and delinquency: Kenworthy, "The Mental Hygiene Aspects of Illegitimacy," *Mental Hygiene*, July, 1921; Lundberg, *Children of Illegitimate Birth and Measures for Their Protection*, pp. 10, 13, 14, 15.
149. Lindsey and Evans, *The Revolt of Modern Youth*, p. 257.
150. Shaw, *Man and Superman*, act i.
151. U. S. marriage statistics: Groves and Ogburn, *American Marriage and Family Relationships*, pp. 151, 153-154.
157. Saville, *In Unknown New Guinea*, p. 228. Malinowski, *The Sexual Life of Savages*, vol. ii, p. 341-342; vol. i, p. 77.
158. Bruun, *Van Zanten's Happy Days*, pp. 90-95.
160. Mead, M., Coming of Age in Samoa, pp. 155-156, 160, 175-178.
166. Blanchard, "Sex in the Adolescent Girl," *Sex in Civilization*, p. 547, 549.
174. Birth-control as requiring "energy, self-control and persistence": Reise, Dr. Bertha, "Present Trends in Birth-Control—Germany," *Birth-Control Review*, Nov., 1929. Cp. Cooper, "Technique of Contraception." (H. G. Wells, introd. to) Fielding, in *Parenthood: Design or Accident? A Manual of Birth-Control*, pp. 71-73.
175. Robinson, editorial, *Critic and Guide*, Feb., 1929. Lindsey and Evans, *The Revolt of Modern Youth*, pp. 80, 81.
180. Ellis, *Affirmations*, p. 113.
181. Whitman, "Ventures on an Old Theme," *Democratic Vistas*, p. 149.
183. St. Augustine, *Confessions*, viii:7.
184. St. Paul, *I Corinthians*, vii, St. James' version. "Spiritual brides": Conybeare, *Myth, Magic, and Morals*, pp. 212-224. Moffatt, *The New Testament: A New Translation*, p. 255.
186. "Sacrament," *Ency. Brit.*, 11th ed., 23:997.
187. Plutarch, "Life of Lycurgus." Aristotle, *Politics*, vii:16:15. Frazer, *Folk-Lore in the Old Testament*, p. 269. Ludovici, *The Hight Hoers*, p. 242; qtd. in review by Dr. C. P. Blacker, *Critic and Guide*, Feb., 1929.
188. Shaw, *Androcles and the Lion*, act i.
192. Plato, *Republic*, v. Malinowski, *The Father in Primitive Psychology*, p 77. Saville, *In Unknown New Guinea*, pp. 77-78.
193. Saville, ibid., p. 76. For abortion among savages, see Miller, *The Child in Primitive Society*, pp. 31-36, and bibliography; Metchnikoff, *The Nature of Man*, pp. 102-103.
194. Singer, *A Short History of Medicine*, p. 2.
195. Art. "Infanticide," *Ency. Brit.*, 11th ed., 14:516.
199. Ferrero, G. *Les Lois Psychologique du Symbolisme*, qtd. in Kammerer, *The Unmarried Mother*, op. title p.
202. Prof. X. and Dr. Y. The naïve and uncritical acceptance of current property institutions may be illustrated by the following excerpts: Prof. P. remarks that "the community has its rebels against the civil and social codes in its psychopaths and irreconcilables, while industry finds it necessary to contend with its

Page

radicals and agitators." Dr. S. solemnly evokes the ghost of Hippocrates, with his four 'humours,' and finds that the "revolutionary trade unionist" has a "choleric" temperament. Prof. P. mourns over the ability of a "psychopathic employee" to "destroy in a week the entire morale of a plant which it required years of patient effort to build"; he does not inquire what kind of 'morale' it is that can be destroyed in a week by a single individual, nor does he mention wages or hours. Dr. S. helpfully compares "tendencies to violence in the insane with like tendencies shown in industry"—meaning tendencies shown by workingmen, not employers. Their colleague, Dr. B., however, insists that "it could not be concluded from this or any other examination that all strikers, whether agitators or not, are psychopaths!"

203. Frazer, *Folk-Lore in the Old Testament,* p. 169.

204. Ancient Yucatan: "At the festival of the spring florescence, virgins were cast into the sacred well at Chichen-Itza as a sacrifice to the rain-god Chac-Mool. * * * Although to our civilized and modern minds the thought of hurling living maidens to a terrible death in a yawning black pit savors of unspeakable savagery and cold-blooded cruelty, it was not so regarded by the Mayas. No doubt the girls destined for the sacrifice felt immensely proud of being chosen by the priests for the purpose. It was the highest honor that could be bestowed upon a virgin, and the girls' faith, and their firm belief that they were winning eternal happiness and that their spirits would become brides of the deity, made them willing martyrs. No doubt they vied with one another for the honor * * *."—Verrill, *Old Civilizations of the New World,* p. 139.

205. Shell-shock: Williams, F. E., "Anxiety and Fear," *Mental Hygiene,* Jan., 1920. Churchill, *The World-Crisis,* 1916-1918, vol. ii, p. 208.

206. Van Waters, "Youth in Conflict," *The Child, the Clinic and the Court,* p. 19. Williams, F. E., "Can Youth Be Coerced?" (pamphlet), pp. 3-6.

210. Lucretius, iv, Bohn, 157-161. Euripides, *Medea,* Murray's transl., p. 35. *Judge Baker Foundation Case Studies, Series* 1.

222. Plutarch, "Life of Lycurgus."

225. Van Waters, qtd. in Thomas, *The Unadjusted Girl,* p. 199; pp. 223-224.

227. Thomas, *The Unadjusted Girl,* p. 109.

228. *Greek Anthology,* vi:280. This version is from Botsford and Sihler, *Hellenic Civilization,* p. 705. Rome, dolls given to Venus: *Ency. Brit.,* 11th ed., art. "Puberty," 22:626.

229. Herrick, "To the Virgins, to Make Much of Time," in *Hesperides.*

232. Chicago Vice Commission's report: qtd. in Kammerer, *The Unmarried Mother,* p. 69. Young Puritans at Play: Dell, *Janet March,* pp. 143-144.

234. Kammerer, *The Unmarried Mother,* Case 21—p. 136; Case 27—p. 152. Davenport, *The Salvaging of American Girlhood,* pp. 69, 175-176, 185, 188. Some of the questions asked by prospective school-teachers are: "Does washing or destroying the napkins while a girl is menstruating increase the flow or make the period

Page

longer?" "If a man uses a cover when intercoursing with a woman will he get consumption?" "Why do boys have to have sex intercourse after they are 14 so they get consumption if they don't?" "How is the disease called siflis caught by two perfectly clean people kissing? i. e., by 'contraction'?" "Is siflis caught by sex intercourse during menstruation?" "If a man gets a certain disease is it true that he can transfer it to his wife?" "Why does a girl feel so ashamed because she menstruates?" "Is there any decent way of looking upon this matter of bearing a child?"

235. Watson-Lashley questionnaire: *A Consensus of Medical Opinion Upon Questions Relating to Sex Education and Venereal Disease Campaigns*, pp. 52-53.

236. Hamilton, *A Research in Marriage*, p. 389. Van Waters, qtd. in Thomas, *The Unadjusted Girl*, p. 199. The immediate reference is to sexual exploitation in the moving-picture industry.

237. Segregation of the sexes; in patriarchal immigrant groups: Roberts, "Italian Girls on American Soil," Mental Hygiene, Oct., 1929; below the leisured classes, etc., Davenport, *Salvaging of American Girlhood*, pp. 191-271; in schools, Hollingworth, *Psychology of the Adolescent*, pp. 132-136; and homosexuality, Davis, *Factors in the Sex Life of Twenty-two Hundred Women*, chaps. x, xi.

239. Blanchard, *The Adolescent Girl*, p. 169, footnote. Taft, "Some Problems of Delinquency," qtd. in Thomas, *The Unadjusted Girl*, p. 206.

240. The White Logic: London, *John Barleycorn*, p. 308. Jack London mistook the effect for the cause. Williams, F. E., "The Relation of Alcohol and Syphilis to Mental Hygiene," *Mental Hygiene*, Dec., 1916.

242. "Oh, I have been to Ludlow Fair": Housman, *A Shropshire Lad*, lxii. Kolb, "Drug Addiction in its Relation to Crime," *Mental Hygiene*, Jan., 1925; "Types and Characteristics of Drug Addicts," *Mental Hygiene*, April, 1925; "Pleasure and Deterioration from Narcotic Addiction," *Mental Hygiene*, Oct., 1925.

246. Housman, *Last Poems*, xii.

252. Hart, *The Psychology of Insanity*, pp. 122-125.

253. Adler, *The Case of Miss R.*, pp. 200-217.

255. Ibid., p. 290, 305.

257. Williams, F. E., "Community Responsibility in Mental Hygiene," American Review, Jan., 1923.

259. Dooley, qtd. in Blanchard, *The Adolescent Girl*, pp. 164-167.

260. Elgin State Hospital: *Annual Report of the Illinois State Charities Commission*, 1912; qtd. in Robinson, *A Doctor's Views on Life*, pp. 263-264.

261. Ferenczi, *Contributions to Psychoanalysis*, p. 40.

263. Jones, *Papers on Psychoanalysis*, pp. 326-328.

264. Anderson, *Psychiatry in Industry*, pp. 9-10.

265. Jarrett, "The Mental Hygiene of Industry," *Mental Hygiene*, Oct., 1920. Cp. Jarrett, "The Psychopathic Employee: A Problem of Industry," *Medicine and Surgery*, Sept., 1917; Jarrett, "The Practical Value of Mental Hygiene in Industry," *Mental Hygiene*, May, 1921; Campbell, "Mental Hygiene in Industry," *Mental*

Page

Hygiene, July, 1921; Fisher, "Has Mental Hygiene a Practical Use in Industry?", *Mental Hygiene,* July, 1921; Scott, "Neuro-psychiatric Work in Industry," *Mental Hygiene,* July, 1923; Pratt, "The Problem of the Mental Misfit in Industry," *Mental Hygiene,* July, 1922; Pruette and Fryer, "Affective Factors in Vocational Maladjustment," *Mental Hygiene,* Jan., 1923; Cobb, "Applications of Psychiatry to Industrial Hygiene," *Journal of Industrial Hygiene,* Nov., 1919.

266. Dowson, "Non sum qualis eram bonae sub regno Cynarae." *The Home Book of Verse,* p. 918.
268. Williams, F. E., "Community Responsibility in Mental Hygiene," *American Review,* Jan., 1923.
270. "Psychiatric Examination of a Child," *Mental Hygiene,* April, 1926.
275. Williams, A. R., *The Russian Land,* chap. iv. Lane, *The Modern Egyptians,* chap. xi.
276. Grimm, the Brothers, *Household Tales.*
287. Stevenson, *Underwoods,* i:4.
289. Mead, M., *Coming of Age in Samoa,* p. 87.
290. ———. *Ibid.,* p. 88. Herrick, "An Epithalamie to Sir Thomas Southwell and his Ladie," *Hesperides;* cp. "A Nuptiall Song, or Epithalamie, on Sir Clipseby Crww and his Lady," *Hesperides.*
291. Commenge, qtd. in Ellis, *Sex and Relation to Society,* p. 276.
292. Stendhal, *The Red and the Black,* chap. xlvi. Malinowski, *The Sexual Life of Savages,* p. 345.
296. ———. *Ibid.,* p. 63.
297. ———. *Ibid.,* p. 75.
302. Chesterton, G. K., Robert Browning, p. 21.
303. Roswitha's plays: *Callimachus; Abraham; Paphnutius.* Joyce, *Portrait of the Artist as a Young Man,* p. 164.
307. Hollingsworth, *The Psychology of the Adolescent,* pp. 136-137.
308. Pfister, *Love in Children and Its Aberrations,* p. 484.
309. Williams, F. E., "Confronting the World: The Adjustments of Later Adolescence," in *Concerning Parents,* pp. 138, 149-159.
312. Elizabeth Barrett's father: Chesterton, *Robert Browning,* chap. iii.
316. Malinowski, *The Sexual Life of Savages,* pp. 67, 81. Mead, M., *Coming of Age in Samoa,* pp. 157, 153.
317. Calhoun, *Social History of the American Family,* vol. ii, pp. 13, 15. Aristotle, *Politics,* vii:16:6.
318. Calhoun, *Social History of the American Family,* vol. ii, p. 14. Trollope, *Domestic Manners of the Americans,* chap. v.
319. Early maternity: Metchnikoff, *The Nature of Man,* pp. 92-94.
320. Groves and Ogburn, *American Marriage and Family Relationships,* pp. 157, 221. Richmond and Hall, *Marriage and the State,* p. 123; *Child Marriages.*
321. Age-definitions of adulthood or the end of adolescence: at 25 in man, 21 in woman—*Century Dict.;* at 22, when the eruption of the permanent teeth is complete—Keith, *Man,* p. 34; practically at 20 or more in men, 18 or 19 in girls—Geddes and Thomson, *Sex,* p. 119; at 18 for both sexes—Watson, *Psychological Care of Infant and Child,* p. 173; at 18 for both sexes—Robinson, *Woman,* p. 69; at 22 for both sexes—Fielding, *Sex and the Love-Life,* p.

Page

287; at the end of the 'teens for both sexes—Hollingworth, *Psychology of the Adolescent,* p. 1; in men at later than 20, full growth apparently not reached till 35, at 20 in woman—Ellis, *Man and Woman,* p. 45. Thus adolescence ends or adult life begins, or the growth process is completed, at 18, 19, 20, 21 or 22 in girls, and at 18, 20, 22, 25 or later in men: take your choice.

322. Colcord, *Broken Homes,* p. 26. Viracocha: Garcilasso, qtd. in Mead, C. W., *Old Civilizations of Inca Land,* p. 107.

330. Popenoe, *Modern Marriage,* p. 113.

337. Dreiser, *The Genius,* p. 104.

343. *The Technique of the Love Affair,* p. 5.

347. John Ruskin's father: Ellis-Williams, *The Exquisite Tragedy: An Intimate Life of John Ruskin,* p. 10-11.

358. Lindsey, *The Companionate Marriage,* p. 172, etc. Judge Lindsey's own view of the companionate marriage, however, is that it is "entered into with the expectation on the part of society, and of the persons marrying, that it will be permanent, and that it will probably change over to the procreative or Family Marriage later, as most of them coming under my observation," he adds, "have done" (p. 195).

363. Davenport, *Salvaging of American Girlhood,* pp. 247, 257-258.

368. Frazer, *The Golden Bough,* p. 137. Harrison, *Ancient Art and Ritual.*

370. Fitzgerald, *Rubáiyát of Omar Khayyám,* 4th ed., xix.

372. Tennyson, *Maud,* xviii. Shelley, "To a Skylark." Keats, "Ode to a Nightingale." Blake, "The Tiger." Shelley, "Ode to the West Wind."

373. Malinowski, *Argonauts of the Western Pacific,* p. 132. Printed there as prose, here arranged in free-verse form.

374. Kipling, "Hymn of the Triumphant Airman," New York *World,* Sept. 6, 1929.

375. Millay, "Prayer to Persephone," *Second April.* Burns, "Sweet Afton." Malinowski, *The Sexual Life of Savages,* vol. ii, p. 371.

376. Rossetti, C., "Echo."

377. Thompson, F., "Dream-Tryst." Shelley, "Night." "O Night, O Jealous Night": anon., no. 269 in Symons, *A Pageant of Elizabethan Poetry.*

378. Coleridge, "Kubla Khan." Rossetti, c. "Goblin Market." Millay, "Renascence." Thompson, F., "The Hound of Heaven." Whitman, "Song of Myself," 24.

379. Wordsworth, "Ode: Intimations of Immortality from Recollections of Early Childhood."

382. Keats, "On First Looking Into Chapman's Homer." Swinburne, "The Triumph of Time."

385. Shakespeare, *Sonnets,* cxvi.

392. Shelley, *Adonais,* xxxiv.

393. Narcissistic parisitism: Hamilton, M. J., "Mental Hygiene and the Parasite," *Mental Hygiene,* Jan., 1921.

406. Freud, *The Problem of Lay Analyses,* p. 185.

INDEX